NEW

AMERICANISTS

A Series Edited by

Donald E. Pease

LOOSE ENDS

Closure and Crisis in the American Social Text

Russell Reising

Duke University Press   *Durham and London 1996*

© 1996 Duke University Press
All rights reserved
Printed in the United States of America on acid-free paper ∞
Typeset in Berkeley Medium by Tseng Information Systems, Inc.
Library of Congress Cataloging-in-Publication Data
appear on the last printed page of this book.

CONTENTS

Loose Ends is a sequel of sorts to *The Unusable Past: Theory and the Study of American Literature* (Routledge, 1986). My primary objective in *The Unusable Past* was to organize and analyze the major critical and theoretical accounts of American literary production, and to trace the double repression characteristic of theories of American literature; that is, repression in terms both of what is excluded from study *and* of the order imposed on the field so as to make it visible and comprehensible. *Loose Ends* will be much more directed at the analysis of specific literary and cultural works. The six central chapters pursue the socio-ideological issues that infuse and disrupt the works of their respective creators—Charles Brockden Brown, Phillis Wheatley, Herman Melville, Emily Dickinson, Henry James, the Disney Studio. In this way, these readings respond to my claims that the most influential "theories of American literature" tend to suppress the social and political tensions within American literary culture in favor of demonstrating some vision of an "end of ideology" consensus, albeit sometimes in the form of the jeremiad (as elaborated by Sacvan Bercovitch). My primary goal in these interventions is to resuscitate precisely those unresolved (perhaps irresolvable) tensions that, though strategically and often brilliantly elided by a generation increasingly referred to as the "old Americanists," can be resituated at the constitutive core of each work's cultural life.

While not explicitly concerned with canon issues, *Loose Ends* does respond to my analysis of the homogeneity of the American canon by including works by variously positioned creators, works of varying degrees of marginality (even my readings of canonical authors deal with relatively minor texts—*Israel Potter,* for instance, is still Melville's least appreciated and analyzed narrative), and works from a variety of genres (one chapter on Wheatley's poetry, one on a Melville novel, one on a Dickinson poem, one on a James short story, and one on a Disney animated film). I have intentionally chosen works from a broad historical range (late eighteenth century through mid–twentieth century) and have included a broad spectrum of works (the "high-culture" work of Henry James through the pop-culture work of the Disney Studio). By so doing, I have selected works with significant critical histories, and I hope to have suggested the pervasiveness (though not the representativeness or "Americanness") of the issues I address.

My focus will be on how these narratives of intense subjective interest and interpersonal drama resonate with the conflicts and tensions of American society. They are never merely aesthetic, never merely personal, familial, or private. It is at present virtually a cultural studies truism that no cultural text can be read in isolation from the social and political tensions adjacent to those works and that aesthetic moments of thematic significance always also embody socio-ideological pressures and issues. The readings that comprise *Loose Ends* proceed according to these assumptions and contextualize their primary texts with respect to various pertinent "extraliterary" discourses. For example, the introductory discussion of Brown's *Wieland* argues that the novel needs to be read with constant reference to both the rhetorical and physical forms of violence characteristic of the colonization of New England by the settlers usually grouped together under the term "Puritans." The chapter on Phillis Wheatley's revolutionary poetics reads a number of her works through various historical and political commentaries on slavery and racism, usually within the geopolitical venue of "Christian" Boston. *Israel Potter,* I argue, can be read as Melville's critique of the rhetorical and ideological economy driving the production of historical and literary-historical discourses from Revolutionary times to Melville's authorial present. In my chapter on Emily Dickinson, I approach her "I started Early – Took my Dog –" as a rejoinder to the colonizing tendencies of male authors of the so-called American Renaissance, and as a critique of sexual violence against women. When I turn to James's "The Jolly Corner," I focus on the ways in which that text represents James's highly problematic and contradictory articulation of turn-of-the-century issues of gender and politics. And my analysis of *Dumbo* argues that Disney's 1941 film stages a variety of social tensions (racism, labor unrest, America gearing up for World War II) within the generic constraints of the animated children's feature. Each of these analytical projects synthesizes a version of New Historicism's interest in the mutually constitutive nature of any sociohistorical era's multiplicity of discourses with a postdeconstructive attention to the ways in which apparently marginal narrative moments can, when pursued, not only reveal and unravel the contradictions that are often elided within that narrative's generative thematics but also reverse traditional hierarchical relationships within any discursive field.

I introduce the entire book with a discussion of the ways in which the concluding moments (loose ends) in these texts not only fail to resolve or conclude important narrative issues, but exacerbate, problematize, and sometimes explode exactly the issues which generate the narratives and which, according to many theories of closure, are precisely those narrative energies that conclusions exist to domesticate. The problem is that those issues (domestic and sexual violence in Wheatley; class and economic antagonisms in Melville; violence against women in Dickinson; both the regressive male response to explosive social and economic change symptomatic of the consolidation of capitalism in the United States and progressive feminist politics in James; and issues of social, racial, and economic oppression in Disney) often remain veiled in these texts until and unless we notice the ruptures that trouble their closing moments. These attempts at closure and resolution recast the entireties of these fractured texts, whose major themes are themselves stressed and contested. Failed endings signal the reality that these issues have not been and will not be concluded. The formal imperative of concluding these works, thus, clashes with the impossibility of actually resolving the ideological tensions within them. Each of my discussions suggests that literary and cultural analysis properly recognizes and integrates the concerns of several historical eras—that of the work's ostensible setting, that of its construction, and that of our moment of interpretation.

I should at this point clarify just what I am claiming about the readings I perform in this study. Each reading takes as its inspiration, or, perhaps, as its rhetorical occasion, various tensions, incoherences, elisions, even struggles that cluster within the concluding lines, pages, or moments of these works. I try to trace the implications of what we might call intrusions or eruptions of the ordinary within the aesthetic field of each cultural text. More than the ordinary, however, these eruptions also thrust into our consideration of the narrative's dominant thematics various social antagonisms which both the narratives themselves and their processing within the dominant Americanist paradigms have labored to tame or suppress, largely by harnessing critical activity within a strictly aesthetic field. To be sure, these are occasions of my own making or exploitation, but they are also stresses lurking and sometimes tugging at the margins of these texts. Peter Rabinowitz might include the moments I pursue as examples of what he calls "rules of rupture" (65–68). Arresting our attention in special ways, Rabinowitz suggests, intratextual elements such as breaks in continuity, blatantly irrelevant and inappropriate details, shifts in plot direction or style carry the potential of radically refocusing our perceptions of those elements ruptured by the appearance of such interruptives. Even more to my purpose is Rabinowitz's notion of extratextual "real-world" norms that, when brought to the aesthetic experience by any particular subject, provide unpredictable and unaccountable angles of vision capable of disrupting a creator's and a culture's sense of narrative coherence and closure. As Rabinowitz puts it, "such reading against the grain . . . depends on authorial reading for its political force; it is valuable not because it points out certain features, but because it points out certain features that the author did not intend to be particularly noticeable" (70). From the spectacles provided by the coverage of domestic tragedies in the popular media, to my classroom experiences, my love of dogs, and my own children's disappointment with circuses, my provocations function as rhetorical levers into these endings (and, hence, into these entire narrative fabrics), but also as those intersections of the ordinary with the aesthetic that *Loose Ends* pursues. It might be even more precise to cast these generative encounters as the events that make possible the critical articulations that these readings advance, as the specifically personal and situated lenses that bring into focus, that provide the interest in, and language for, a particular critical practice.

The clearest expression of the dynamic I am advancing and practicing in *Loose Ends* is found in Heidegger: "philosophy will never seek to deny its 'presuppositions,' but neither may it simply admit them. It conceives them, and it unfolds with more and more penetration both the presuppositions themselves and that for which they are presuppositions" (358). Applied without too much violence to the original context, Heidegger's remarks clarify what is probably an undeniable assumption of any act of interpretation, literary or otherwise. It is almost necessary for all critics or theorists to foreground the extent to which their own constructed and situated positions (variously contextualized)—that is, their ideological presuppositions and predispositions—inspire, shape, maybe even determine their reading practices. Our own trainings and interestedness intersect with an object of inquiry, producing an unfolding of significances, both the anticipated *and* the surprising, in an evolutionary spiral that might well render futile any attempt to demarcate our presuppositions, conscious and otherwise, from the various fields of meaning staged within the object of our inquiry. Only its entry into a social realm can determine the success, the plausibility, the persuasiveness, and the resonance of the analytical act.

I would like to thank various friends, students, and colleagues who have contributed their time, interest, and expertise to this project. Tim William Machan of Marquette University has improved this entire manuscript in numerous ways with his shrewd observations and finely tuned editorial eye. I would like to take this opportunity to thank him for many years of friendship, support, Viking revels, and road trips. In addition to figuring as an exemplary colleague during our Milwaukee years, Claudia Johnson of Princeton University has read and improved my discussions of Emily Dickinson and Henry James with insightful interventions and timely bibliographic recommendations. Ronald Schleifer of the University of Oklahoma helped me focus an early version of my Phillis Wheatley chapter and has, through his friendship, example, and sheer chutzpah, been a regular source of energy and ideas. Special thanks to my colleagues at the University of Toledo and to Jeff Gears and my other teachers and fellow students at Jeff Gears Martial Arts America.
Donald Pease of Dartmouth College and editor of the Duke Univer-

sity Press New Americanists series has provided extraordinary support and encouragement throughout the final stages of the writing and preparation of this book. His own work has inspired and provoked me into any number of my own current engagements. At Duke University Press, Reynolds Smith and Sharon Parks have facilitated the project with their advice and cooperation.

Jim LeBlanc and Sarah Ross occupy places in my heart and imagination too intense to be precisely located. Their influences on my thinking are many and deep. I also thank Barbara Foley, Gerald Graff, Greg Meyerson, and Jill Koloske—enduring influences and inspirations—for their friendship and encouragement.

Finally, I would like to thank my family. My wife, Alma A. Mac-Dougall, has performed her editorial rites over the entire manuscript, redeeming many of its excesses. *The Unusable Past* was written while my daughter Maggie (now fourteen) was an infant and toddler; this one has grown, along with my twins, James and Natasha, over the past ten years. My children have gotten me through many a crisis in confidence; this book is dedicated to them and to their futures.

LOOSE ENDS: AESTHETIC CLOSURE

AND SOCIAL CRISIS

While the countless tribes of common novels laboriously spin vails of mystery, only to complacently clear them up at last; and while the countless tribe of common dramas do but repeat the same; yet the profounder emanations of the human mind, intended to illustrate all that can be humanly known of human life; these never unravel their own intricacies, and have no proper endings; but in imperfect, unanticipated, and disappointing sequels (as mutilated stumps), hurry to abrupt intermergings with the eternal tides of time and fate.—Herman Melville, *Pierre; or, The Ambiguities*

When Mark Twain stops *Adventures of Huckleberry Finn* by having Huck decide to "light out for the Territory" rather than return to "sivilization," he "concludes" his work only nominally. The abruptness of the novel's stopping is only slightly less jarring than that cessation Mark Twain must have felt when, after having a riverboat smash Huck and Jim's raft, he earlier stopped work on the novel, putting it aside for about three years, from 1876 to 1879. This second stoppage provides no satisfactory conclusion to the narrative's generative thematics, no clarification, no tense ambiguity, no protomodernist frustration of easy solutions, no liberating (or puzzling) openness: it simply ends. *Adventures of Huckleberry Finn* shapes a fictional narrative world and navigates its various communities and stresses without completing its imaginative work. Given the ignorance, stupidity, brutality, hypocrisy, fraud, heartlessness, and exploitation that Mark Twain's narrative posits as definitive of the antebellum U.S. South as well as of his own Reconstruction era, Huck's choice of running farther west is indicative not only of his own desire to escape the world he has laid bare, but also of Mark Twain's unwillingness, perhaps inability, fully to resolve the very issues his picaresque narrative has conjured. While it might itself function as an emblem of the westward mania that has driven isolatoes, idealists, and malcontents into newly occupied territories at least since the time Eric the Red decided that Greenland was too crowded for his tastes and voyaged to Vinland, Huck's and Mark Twain's "lighting out," their refusal to address or to impose any effective resolution onto the social world the novel constructs, can equally be read as a failure. The arbitrariness and abruptness of Huck's decision *not* to struggle to right the wrongs he has experienced suggests Mark Twain's cynicism, perhaps, but it could equally suggest his honesty. *Adventures of Huckleberry Finn* stops without in any way ameliorating the moral, economic, cultural, juridical, racial, and political evils it has so pointedly represented; no changes of heart, of law, of ethics intervene into the sickness of the novel's world. The death of Pap Finn, the tarring and feathering of the King and the Duke, the clarification of Jim's actual status as a free man following his manumission by the widow on her deathbed, and Tom and Huck's safe return to their homes provide no catharsis, no metaphorical or conceptual counterforce to the systemic brutality of life under slavery. Buck Grangerford's murder, the emergence of other con men to replace the King and the Duke, and the narrative's exposing of the inhumanity and racism underwriting the consciousnesses of all but one or two of the novel's "good and kind" characters serve at least to neutralize the impact of any putatively "happy" implications of the work's more upbeat moments.

There are obviously various ways of accounting for Mark Twain's choices. His own deepening cynicism and misanthropy could surely produce a novel content to expose the absurdity of life in late-nineteenth-century United States. Exhaustion and/or some writerly crisis of confidence could again have proven too oppressive for him to work more rigorously through the issues he raises. We might even speculate that Mark Twain's failure to "resolve" the loose ends of his narrative constitutes his triumph as a realist who refuses to impose utopian closure onto his recalcitrant subject matter. Or we might pursue the possibility that no novel, no social text, can resolve in its imaginative work the crises, tensions, and vexations that characterize the social and cultural world of its genesis, that any appearance of having done so is tantamount to political, moral, and rhetorical bad faith. It is this possibility and some of its related issues that I examine in *Loose Ends: Closure and Crisis in the American Social Text*. I will be reading works as diverse as Phillis Wheatley's poetry, Charles Brockden Brown's *Wieland*, Herman Melville's underread and underrated *Israel Potter: His Fifty Years of Exile*, an Emily Dickinson poem, Henry James's late fiction, and the Disney Studio's animated classic *Dumbo*, works that span nearly the entire history of the United States of America, paying special attention to the ways in which these and other works struggle to cordon off their narrative worlds, and to how the moments of stoppage with which they conclude paradoxically function to exacerbate, to reopen, the very tensions they are meant (or are to appear to mean) to "conclude."

I hope I am not falling prey to some naive expectations about just how cultural works are supposed to conclude. I am certainly not advocating some neat, thorough, premature, or totalitarian imposition of an ending that clarifies the entirety of a narrative world. I am not proposing any prescriptive utopian agenda. As Frank Kermode cautions early in his still provocative *The Sense of an Ending,*

> we cannot . . . be denied an end; it is one of the great charms of books that they have to end. But unless we are extremely naïve, as some apocalyptic sects still are, we do not ask that they progress towards that end precisely as we have been given to believe. In fact, we should expect only the most trivial work to conform to pre-existent types. (24)

Loose Ends will instead examine moments of closure in works that are anything but trivial with an eye toward reading the significance of what I will call a particular kind of anti-closure. I am concerned, in other words, not with proposing that Phillis Wheatley should have written differently, but with what it means that she can stop a poem celebrating the rising of the morning sun with an image of herself blinded and violated by the appearance of that sun, the very moment her ode exists to represent.

No approach to closure in American literature has yet accounted for such conundrums. In fact, two recent considerations of closure in American literature concentrate on different issues entirely. Joyce A. Rowe, for example, attempts to define the essential difference between literature produced in the United States from "that produced by comparable writers abroad" by relating what she calls "equivocal endings" to the ostensibly visionary ambitions of literary production in the United States. According to Rowe, the endings of American works

> are equivocal in a special thematic sense, as they simultaneously promote and deny a visionary ambition already defeated in the body of the work. . . . Yet these endings all adhere to a similar convention: they redeem or rehabilitate the ideal by recasting it in alternative terms. However equivocally it is stated, the protagonist refuses either to reconsider or to abandon visionary hope. (1, 2)

The endings Rowe characterizes as "equivocal" are, as these remarks suggest, closely and coherently related to the thematics of the works they conclude. I would also add that the conventional approach governing both Rowe's identification of an "essentially" American theme and also her choice of texts (all mainstream, canonical works by white, male authors—*The Scarlet Letter, Adventures of Huckleberry Finn, The Ambassadors, The Great Gatsby,* and, briefly, *Moby-Dick*) seems not a little anachronistic. In another consideration of "the politics of openness and closure in American literature," Milton Stern has thematized openness as utopian and closure as "a pulling in, tight control and gravitational centralization, compacted time and space," associating, even in 1991, such qualities with the cold war demons of totalitarian grayness: "conservative control and limitation" (4–6). Reminiscent of R. W. B. Lewis's alternatives of "the party of hope" and "the party of irony," Stern's model deals largely with the thematic binary opposition central to approaches to American literature popularized by D. H. Lawrence, William Carlos Williams, George Santayana, Van Wyck Brooks, and other early-twentieth-century thinkers, many of whom pitted some image of openness to possibilities of existence in a "new world" and the United States against "Puritanical" forces of resistance and denial. Interested as they are in advancing thematic definitions of American literature, neither of these studies concerns itself with the structural problems posed by what I am calling anticlosure and the "loose ends" associated with it.

Closure, whether poetic, narrative, cinematic, or other, can surely take many vexingly ambiguous and frustrating forms. Not only are we suspicious of a conclusion that appears to tie together most of a work's vagrant energies into some neat bundle, but effective and provocative conclusions often frustrate readerly expectations for the reconciliation or resolution of major tensions that have driven their narratives. The gigantic and enigmatic white presence at the conclusion of Edgar Allan Poe's *The Narrative of Arthur Gordon Pym* brings that work to an abrupt and puzzling halt, but its enigmatic appearance conjures up horrors more or less consistent with those of the entire narrative. Similarly, Melville's warning that "something more may follow of [the] masquerade" of *The Confidence-Man* projects that novel into an unknown, dystopian future of cynicism and hopelessness, but one largely anticipated and prepared for by the twists and turns of the entire work. Hester Prynne's return from Europe to counsel women against utopian desire and revolutionary praxis at the end of *The Scarlet Letter* may crush many readers' desires for Hester to emerge as a feminist heroine, but it merely consolidates the misogyny driving much of Nathaniel Hawthorne's fictional project, just as Miles Coverdale's "shocking" announcement that he loved Priscilla closes out *The Blithedale Romance* in an anticlimactic, almost hackneyed, exposé of his own horror before the feminine. Henry James strands Isabel Archer, who cannot but return on "the very straight path" to Gilbert Osmond at the end of *The Portrait of a Lady,* in what is not only an oppressive but also a problematic (but thematically consistent) conclusion to that novel. Carrie Meeber-Wheeler-Maddenda's rocking near the end of *Sister Carrie* posits a future of unfulfilled desire, though this lack of final fulfillment in no way challenges the logics of Dreiser's first novel. Nor does the unspoken word at the conclusion of Edith Wharton's *The House of Mirth* force us back into the novel to revisit some moment we aren't even aware of having missed or misread. Nick Carroway's rhapsodic conclusion to *The Great Gatsby* or Jake Barnes's cryptic "isn't it pretty to think so" at the end of *The Sun Also Rises* are both metaphorically and dramatically related to their respective novels, even though they interpose different types of ambiguity. Flannery O'Connor's story always ends with some superficially cryptic but ultimately coherent, violent epiphany consolidating her rigidly conservative religious beliefs. When he has Oedipa Maas await the "crying of lot 49" at the conclusion of his second novel, Thomas Pynchon strands the reader amidst wildly diverse speculations, but we can hypothesize either some clarifying climax or, more likely, an anticlimax consistent with the novel's own plays on paranoia, entropy, or some covert and totalizing alternative postal regime. The fact that we don't know what lot 49 (or, for that matter, what V) is, while tantalizingly frustrating, is fully consistent with Pynchon's thematics. Bob Dylan's concluding stanza to "All Along the Watchtower"—

> Outside in the cold distance
> A wildcat did growl.
> Two riders were approaching,
> The wind began to howl

—resonates with apocalyptic mystery, though its ambiguity is fully consistent, not only within the song and with the rest of Dylan's work in *John Wesley Harding,* but with the Western apocalyptic tradition at least from the time of Revelations.[1] We might not know where we are or what impending doom we face, but we've been there before. These works all pulse toward these final moments, which, however ambiguous or ironic, nonetheless crystallize many of their narratives' primary concerns. In all these cases, the openness and ambiguity of the conclusions are themselves versions of closural coherence, even when the coherence functions to conclude narratives without obvious or stable teleological end points.

Even such closural moments as these confirm standard theories of closure. Barbara Herrnstein Smith clarifies a still dominant structure of beliefs in *Poetic Closure:*

> The writer also wishes, however, that we have no further expectations at the end of the play, novel, or poem, no "loose ends" to be accounted for, no promises that go begging. The novelist or playwright is likely to end his work at a point when either nothing could follow (as when the hero dies) or everything that could follow is predictable (as when the hero and heroine get married). The poet ends his work at some comparable point of stability, but unless (as sometimes happens) the poem follows a temporal sequence, this point will not be something we could

call "the end of the story." It will, however, be a point of stability that is either determined by or accommodates the poem's formal and thematic principles of structure.

Closure occurs when the concluding portion of a poem creates in the reader a sense of appropriate cessation. It announces and justifies the absence of further development; it reinforces the feeling of finality, completion, and composure which we value in all works of art; and it gives ultimate unity and coherence to the reader's experience of the poem by providing a point from which all the preceding elements may be viewed comprehensively and their relations grasped as part of a significant design. (35–36)

Thus, even when the final passage of a work, Pynchon's *The Crying of Lot 49*, for example, projects the reader into a completely unarticulated narrative space, that space and the relationship it opens between the reader and the preceding narrative is densely rooted in and prepared for by the narrative itself. Whether the conclusion finalizes its narrative by confirming an excessively teleological structure or by adumbrating the vaguest, most projective openness, and whether the narrative has propelled us to its concluding moments with or without sufficient textual data to render its ending immediately coherent, even the most experimental conclusions (Don DeLillo's, for example) most commonly confirm, extend, complicate, qualify, or at least resonate significantly with the rest of the works they conclude. It might even be problematic to attempt so thorough a demarcation between work and conclusion. Final passages must function in a conclusive structural sense, but they are often thematically inseparable from everything preceding them in any particular work. While *Moby-Dick*'s (or any work's) epilogue stands in an obviously "concluding" relationship with the bulk of Melville's narrative, even T. S. Eliot's "Till human voices wake us / And we drown," which concludes "The Love Song of J. Alfred Prufrock," emerges as the revealing culmination of the entire poem, both thematically and, almost coincidentally, structurally. To return to Barbara Herrnstein Smith, "closure . . . may be regarded as a modification of structure that makes *stasis*, or the absence of further continuation, the most probable succeeding event. Closure allows the reader to be satisfied by the failure of continuation, or, put another way, it creates in the reader the expectation of nothing" (34). Of course "the expectation of nothing" does not eliminate the common necessity for readers to pursue their thinking beyond the final moment of reading or viewing; the narratives have already provided the necessary components for that postexperiential interpretive work.

D. A. Miller has offered a powerful reading of closure in the nineteenth-century European novel which counters Smith's study of the various logics of poetic closural coherence, at least relative to traditional fictional narrative. Critical of the teleological compulsion common to traditional studies of closure, Miller suggests the definitive theoretical flaw driving prior investigations:

> once the ending is enshrined in an all-encompassing cause in which the elements of a narrative find their ultimate justification, it is difficult for analysis to assert anything short of total coherence. One is barred even from suspecting possible discontinuities between closure and narrative movement preceding it, not to mention possible contradictions and ambiguities from within closure itself. (xiii)

By thus reifying closural moments, traditional narrative theory has unnecessarily constructed endings as the embedded and fully coherent essence of the narrative act, which, given the numerous energies and agendas driving toward some perfectly revelatory, demystifying closural epiphany, can only be imagined as fully sufficient as both origin and telos of narrativity. Miller, in fact, pushes the opposite extreme by arguing that no closure can fully and coherently extinguish the various energies driving the narratable, by which he means the very possibilities and conditions of narrative; that is, those "instances of disequilibrium, suspense, and general insufficiency from which a given narrative appears to rise" (ix). While granting the crucial differences of novelistic subject matter as well as the historical specificity of novelistic structure, Miller nonetheless locates the "failure" of novelistic closure in two "primary determinations," the psychoanalytic "drift of desire" and the linguistic "drift of the sign," both of which drive narrative away from "a full and settled meaning." As Miller sums it up, "the narratable *inherently lacks finality*. It may be suspended by a moral or ideological expediency, but *it can never be properly brought to term*" (xi; my emphasis).

Miller's readings of Austen, George Eliot, and Stendhal are subtle and often brilliant; I will refer to only one of them to suggest how his theory works when deployed in specific analytical acts. George Eliot cannot successfully close *Middlemarch* because, as Miller puts it,

> it is as if the novelist could not help seeing the persistence of the narratable even in its closure. As a consequence, closure appears to take place only through a strategic misreading of the data— a misreading that is at once shown to be expedient (expressing a moral command), efficacious (settling the final living arrangements of characters), and erroneous (deconstructed as a repetition of what is supposed to overcome). The resulting ambiguity, of course, is bound to make conclusion less conclusive. (188–89)

I would like to affirm Miller's demonstrations while still creating a space for both theory and practice at a different level of specificity. Miller may be quite correct in his demonstration of the mutually reinforcing erotic and semiotic restlessness of narrative praxis; perhaps no narrative (poetic, novelistic, cinematic, or oral) can ever finally and perfectly close. However, I will be examining a dimension other than the essentialist, totalizing perspective he brings to bear on traditional nineteenth-century fiction. Austen's, George Eliot's, and Stendhal's failures to bring their narratives to appropriate (or even acceptable) moments of quiescence are, according to Miller, essential, inevitable even, to the very act of narrative. That is, narrative as we know it is unimaginable without the very originary energies and deeply embedded ideological assumptions that both elicit the narrative act from a prenarrative silence and render futile any attempt effectively to conclude in the ways valorized by traditional narrative (and poetic) theory.

I will be pursuing an array of absences, excesses, and final passages which function very differently relative *both* to the thematic and structural dimensions of the works they conclude *and* to the extra-narrative worlds with which these works have their most plausible relationships. Unlike Miller, I will argue that the works I discuss in *Loose Ends* collapse into anti-closure because of historically specific concerns and narrative agendas, not due to an essentialist given of narrativity as such. Perhaps it is possible to demonstrate alternative anti-closural moments within the same works by refocusing on either (or both) the psychoanalytic or semiotic drifts definitive, as Miller would have it, of all narrative praxis. But in *Loose Ends* I will be paying more attention to the ways in which these works construct narrative worlds and evoke narrative themes with historically determined parameters that, as aesthetic constructs, these works cannot bring to successful conclusions. The issue I am interested in is the ideology of cultural productivity as embodied within these works. My own perspective, then, will at least in part account for just how I perceive the conclusions of these works as anti-closural as well as how and why I pursue these texts' situatedness within particular social and historical contexts.

I also differ from both Smith and Miller with reference to the relationship of these works to the extranarrative contexts of their genesis and production. According to Smith, "one of the most significant ways in which form contributes to our sense of the integrity of a poem is by, in effect, drawing an enclosing line around it, distinctly and continuously separating it from less highly structured and nonmimetic discourse" (25). She further elaborates: "one of the functions or effects of poetic form is to 'frame' the poetic utterance: to maintain its identity as distinct from that of ordinary discourse, to draw an enclosing line, in other words, that marks the boundary between 'art' and 'reality'" (238). Miller incorporates an awareness of the nonnarrative, referential realm within his own theory of the impossibility of closure:

> The otherness of closure suggests one of the unwelcome implications of the narratable—that it can never generate the terms for its own arrest. These must be imported from elsewhere, from a world untouched by the conditions of narratability. Yet as soon as such a world is invoked in the novels—its appearance is necessarily brief—its authority is put into doubt by the system of narrative itself. . . . In essence, closure is an act of "make-believe," a postulation that closure is possible. (266–67)

For both Smith and Miller the "world" beyond the parameters of the autonomous work of art oppose, almost threaten, the imaginary inviolability of the cultural product. The "enclosing line" for which Smith argues must remain utterly stable for poetic discourse to be perceived as poetic, that is, for it to be distinguished from what she calls "less highly structured and nonmimetic" or "ordinary" discourses. Given the rigidity of these generic-discursive police lines, closure must function as a liminal moment, a threshold subdiscourse which simultaneously provides closure to the poetic utterance and initiatory openness to the postpoetic world. For all the differences between Miller's work on the futility of closure and Smith's on the varieties of closure, both agree on the nature of the pre-, post-, or transnarrative. Miller assumes that narrative would, of its own inertia, be ceaseless were it not for the forceful imposition of imported conditions "from a world untouched by the conditions of narratability." In other words, both Smith and Miller draw equally rigid lines between the internal and external worlds of the work and its environs (we assume historical, social, political, economic, cultural). Whereas for Smith that "other world" must be kept at bay in order for the poetic utterance to evolve and conclude coherently, for Miller both the emergence of narrative and its impulsion throughout narrative space function to keep the nonnarrative world forever beyond the possibility of narrative imagining. For Smith, poetry must stop. For Miller, narrative cannot stop. But for both, that stoppage is parasitically dependent on the aesthetic negation of the nonaesthetic.

I will be reading works whose relationship with the "other world" of the nonnarrative is essential to the very construction of their inner, intratextual worlds. The poems, short stories, novels, and films addressed in *Loose Ends* (perhaps all representational praxis with a linear or temporal dimension) can't close, precisely because their embeddedness within the sociohistorical worlds of their genesis is so complex and conflicted. These are works that admit of no "enclosing lines," works that repeatedly problematize the very possibility of such lines. The loose ends which characterize the concluding moments of these works function largely as provocations for the reader to reproblematize the very assumptions brought to the aesthetic experience and to reimagine the entire world of the work of art, especially those gestures beyond the works that often disappear as quickly as they catch our attention. They force us to return to the beginnings of the works we've just completed, but they do so only by (and after) indirectly revealing shadow narratives that have been lying latent within the dominant thematics of the works from which they emerge. These works conclude either by eliciting, via their final passages, counterreadings to the narratives, or by eliding the very tensions that need to be addressed for the works satisfactorily to "conclude." Once the primary narrative themes of the works I will examine stray into the realm of the social world otherwise elided by their narrative drives, that social world and the tensions elicited by these works' referential gestures infiltrate and recast nearly every dimension of their intratextual environments. The dynamics established by such necessary interconnections between textual zone and interdiscursive contexts circulate within the works even as they open the works to the influx of issues and struggles beyond their particular borders.

I will refer to these recoverable counternarratives as "shadow narratives," and by them I mean something akin to Fredric Jameson's notion of the political unconscious. In these cases, however, I suggest that the shadow narratives configure a massive residue of sociohistorical reference, usually generated by the sociohistorical pressures on the cultural moment of a text's genesis and encoded within these narratives by elaborate systems of transtextual gesturing. In Phillis Wheatley, references to the economics of slavery (however unobtrusive they appear) disrupt the superficially accommodationist gestures of her poems. In *Israel Potter: His Fifty Years of Exile*, Melville's complicated attack on the popular visions of the American past frustrates (to the point of self-sabotage) his attempt to recover a popular readership by offering them "nothing of any sort to shock the fastidious." As when he refers to *Pierre; or, The Ambiguities* as "a rural bowl of milk," Melville surely protests too much when he adds, "there will be very little reflective writing in it; nothing weighty" (*Israel Potter* 182). In Henry James's "The Jolly Corner," the density with which James represents turn-of-the-century New York's worlds of social, economic, and gender instability inhabits his text so thoroughly as to refigure the overt claims of his protagonists to exist beyond such crypto-naturalist determinations, recontextualizing them to reveal precisely the opposite of their expressed meanings. Similarly, in *Dumbo,* the superfluity of sociohistorical referents (including child abuse, labor unrest, vicious class rivalry, racism, and World War II) represented within the narrative of the little elephant with the huge ears explodes any possibility this film has of successfully containing the volatility of its social issues within its explicit genre, that of children's feature.

In one sense, such details are tangential to the dominant narrative of each text, but in another sense, cultural production is virtually impossible without them. As Peter Rabinowitz remarks,

> no matter how fantastic a novel's premises, no matter how unrealistic the setting, the authorial audience and the narrative audience must share some beliefs about reality in order for the situations and actions to have the consequences they do and for the plot to get from point A to point B. That's because every fictional world, like every real world, requires a history, sociology, biology, mathematics, aesthetics and ethics. (100–101)

What is true, say, in Kafka, Borges, García Márquez, Kobo Abe, Pynchon, or Haruki Murakami holds equally for the more superficially conventional works I address in *Loose Ends.* The structuring of their narratives requires a scaffolding within the recognizable world of material things, social issues and tensions, and historical recollections: these simply constitute the frame of any narrative, but, in the cases of the works I will examine, these frames refuse to remain marginal and, instead, infuse the works with the stresses inherent within their narratives. By scaffolding I mean something similar to traditional notions of "setting" or "background" or "environment," but I mean to suggest that we can pursue them even farther into a denser field of material referents which constitute the sociohistorical basis for narratives of all sorts, however tangential they may seem to the social world of their eras (or, for that matter, of ours). Of course, some elements of a narrative world's "setting" serve symbolic or allegorical functions, like the temple turned summer house in *Wieland,* the forests and prairies in Cooper's works, "the prison door" and rose bush at the beginning of *The Scarlet Letter,* the sailors' and ship's equipage and the whale's penis in *Moby-Dick* or Wall Street in "Bartleby the Scrivener," Walden Pond, the house Silas Lapham tries to build in Boston's Back Bay, Gilbert

Osmond's bibelots in *The Portrait of a Lady* or Paris in both *The Princess Casamassima* and *The Ambassadors*, the tiny "pigeon house" into which Edna Pontellier moves in Chopin's *The Awakening*, the cash register at the conclusion of Crane's "The Blue Hotel," the Chicago fire in Dreiser's *The Financier*, bullfighting in *The Sun Also Rises*, the bear in Faulkner, the valley of ashes and billboard in *The Great Gatsby*, or the mass Unification Church wedding that opens DeLillo's *Mao II*.

Perhaps all narrative constituents carry figurative residue, but those narrative elements I will be focusing on are, in many ways, profoundly demetaphorized. Yet they are not neutral, not excess material baggage, not dead weight. Neither (strictly speaking) symbolic, nor neutral, these elements take on narrative significance by virtue of being charged with the social issues which they are instrumental in representing and which, as a result of their status in these narratives, exert transformative energies within each work. Charles Brockden Brown's references to the religious affiliation of the elder Wieland wouldn't necessarily have the weight I attribute to them unless *Wieland* dwelled obsessively on problematics of subjectivity attributable to early American Protestantism. Phillis Wheatley's mentions of Christianity and her utilization of conventional light and dark imagery cease being conventional and, in fact, assume dangerous volatility once Wheatley attempts to articulate the status of African American slaves living in "Christian" Boston. Melville's concluding throwaway remark about Israel Potter's original personal narrative going out of print might be merely innocuous were it not for his novel pursuing the interconnections between the reputations of the "founding fathers" and their manipulation of the economics and technologies of the emerging print culture. The scenes of the roustabouts working facelessly and shrouded in darkness and of the clowns deciding to lobby for better pay would merely be filler in Disney's *Dumbo* were it not for the fact that *Dumbo* was made during a bitter animators' strike at the Disney Studio. Similarly, the notion that Dumbo's flying results in the development of a prototype for "Dumbombers for Defense" might merely be another example of animated whimsy if *Dumbo* hadn't been released in the early years of World War II. However, by being the representational vehicles for such volatile energies within the narratives we will examine, these otherwise marginal scenes and allusions become charged with the tensions, authorial animus, and ruptures in the social fabric that they import into their narrative worlds.

As a virtual requisite for any representational scheme, these elements I refer to as scaffolding comprise the entire range of social, economic, historical, political, psychological, even architectural assumptions and moments without which narrative theme or plot would be impossible, hopelessly abstract. But while they provide the structuring and complexity of details that fatten up any narrative and make coherence possible, these elements also have the potential to take on a counternarrative life of their own and, paradoxically, to make coherence impossible. Once these texts open up channels outside of themselves via such necessary social gesturing, their intranarrative structures and logics are themselves opened up to possibilities probably impossible to foresee, and certainly impossible to contain. The discourses, events, objects, technologies, and histories to which they allude circulate within and among themselves, accruing a self-reproducing inertia which, by virtue of its proliferation, not only consolidates the presence of these discourses, but also has the potential to recast the dominant narrative, its issues and themes. Once textual borders are ruptured by such conduits, there is no justification and no way again to arrest the mutually constitutive trafficking between intra- and extratextual realms. In other words, the "enclosing lines" which both Smith and Miller accept as constitutive of "literary" discourse can't really exist, unless we as consumers consent to the arbitrary (and theoretically impossible) demarcations they impose.

When Spencer Brydon in "The Jolly Corner," for example, articulates his own discomfort over the transformation of New York's material being by architectural and technological innovations, he merges his being with rather than distinguishes it from those very historically specific fractures. When Melville closes *Israel Potter* with a reference to books going out of print, the technologies and economies of both history and literature are smuggled into a work concerned with precisely those issues, but in a way that remains obscure until the actual evocation of such economic concerns in the novel's penultimate sentence. For these writers, the sensitivity of the issues they address (sensitive both within each creator's oeuvre but also within their social moments) heightens the disruptive potential of such social referents until they assume what amounts to a life of their own by the concluding moments of their works. The shadow narratives they conjure have, in almost every case, been suspended or suppressed by the drift of the dominant narrative, but they have never been totally effaced. We may not even remember that Emily Dickinson begins her poem "I started Early – Took my Dog –" with a structurally significant reference to a dog, since the dog simply disappears after the first line. But, by poem's end, the stresses and ambiguities of Dickinson's poem require us to revisit its every unit, and the disappeared dog suddenly reemerges with new importance. Such moments have existed parasitically (perhaps symbiotically is a better term, suggesting as it does the mutually constitutive dynamic I am pursuing between dominant and shadow narratives) throughout their texts, but have remained submerged, in some cases as a result of oversight or conscious subordination, but more commonly by virtue of the thoroughness with which they violate the ideological conventions which their host narratives struggle to adhere to. They restage, in other words, a different drama, a return of the repressed counterhegemonic residue that the dominant narratives haven't quite erased.

The relationship between these dominant and shadow narratives is even more conflicted than this formulation suggests, however. I am also suggesting that this shadow narrative constitutes not only an alternative narrative to its host, but one which, paradoxically, often carries an alternative intentionality of the work itself. The works we will examine tend to be narratives of struggle, works of highly volatile ideological significance, most of which oppose some dimension of the dominant culture's hegemony but which also struggle to speak in a language compatible with that culture's ideological preeminence. The dilemma these works often confront is how to speak in a language that will simultaneously reinforce *and* dismantle a particular facet of the status quo of their cultures. In the case of Phillis Wheatley, I suggest that her conventional odes "signify"; that is, according to African American literary theory and practice, they speak from within while simultaneously reconfiguring the terms of the dominant culture's discourses. As I will consequently demonstrate, when she begins her best-known poem, " 'Twas mercy brought me from my Pagan land," she is actually struggling to characterize the barbarity of the slave trade and the hypocrisy of the Christian culture that could countenance trafficking in human beings. Similarly, the apparent naïveté of Dickinson's speaker belies her poem's negotiation of issues of intense volatility, including sexual violence and the oppression of women.

Perhaps what I am offering throughout *Loose Ends* is an analysis of what oppositional discourses look like and how they function prior to their recognition and formalization within the dominant discourse of a culture. In Raymond Williams's familiar tripartite model of the "dominant," "residual," and "emergent" forces and structures inhabiting any sociohistorical epoch, these shadow narratives and the discourses from which they are constructed smuggle into these works the "emergent" implications of the tensions and representational struggles of their eras. The particular discourses I will investigate tend, not surprisingly, to constellate around issues pertaining to race, class, and gender, although it may well be that virtually any oppositional discourse (gay or lesbian, for example) initially struggles to occupy some similarly secretly coded, liminal space on the margins of the dominant culture. These cultural artifacts all carry shadow plots, some of which are smuggled in by their creators, some of which emerge by virtue of the fullness of their respective text's referential schemes, at times in violent opposition to their creator's likely plans. In other words, I am interested not only in how oppositional energies are consciously deployed by politically engaged artists but also in how they can erupt, seemingly of their own inertia, from within various narratives. To paraphrase a recurring theme from Steven Spielberg's *Jurassic Park*, the notion that "nature finds a way" to protect and advance itself in spite of the most careful attempts of civilization and science to control it, in these narratives I will argue that "resistance finds a way."

That these shadow narratives often remain invisible or are simply ignored as unimportant until the host narrative's desperate attempt at aesthetic closure is, very likely, no surprise. Marianna Torgovnick makes an appropriate point: "It is difficult to recall all of a work after a completed reading, but climactic moments, dramatic scenes, and beginnings and endings remain in the memory and decisively shape our sense of a novel as a whole" (3–4). In his extraordinary anatomy of narrative structures, Rabinowitz concurs with Torgovnick when he suggests that "last sentences . . . cannot serve to focus a reading experience (at least not an initial reading experience). But they do often serve to scaffold our retrospective interpretation of the book" (62). The function of conclusions is often precisely to provide that end point which enables us finally to configure the narrative strands that may have remained frayed or unresolved prior to the text's final moment. In fact, we often only "see" the narrative from the perspective of its finale. Again, Rabinowitz offers a systematic reading of such functions. Focusing on various "rules of notice," those textual features which call our attention to any work's heightened moments, he notes that "the stressed features in a text serve as a basic structure on which to build an interpretation" (53). Not surprisingly, Rabinowitz includes in his catalog of such "privileged positions" "titles, beginnings and endings (not only of whole texts, but of subsections as well—volumes, chapters, episodes), epigraphs, and descriptive subtitles" (58). I would like to build on Rabinowitz's classificatory system by conflating his remarks on "privileged positions," especially endings, with his idea of "rules of rupture." While "we tend to skim over the even and the unbroken," he admits,

> disruptions attract our notice. This explains why we notice the pyramid rising above the desert, and also why we notice certain details in literary works. Specifically, textual features stand out both when they disrupt the continuity of the works in which they occur and when they deviate from the extratextual norms against which they are read. (65)

The conclusions that I will examine in Loose Ends literally conflate these two notions: the very concluding moments upon which we quite naturally focus simultaneously disrupt the expectations we bring to them. To be sure, the "loose ends" we will encounter "disrupt the continuity of the works in which they occur," but they do so not by violating "the extratextual norms against which they are read" but, paradoxically according to Rabinowitz's calculus, by taking those norms seriously and by invading the narrative (aesthetic) logic with the pressures that the very extratextual norms intrude upon the text in question. These works reinscribe what had appeared to function merely as conventional, referential scaffolding for their major thematics as themselves alternative, disruptive, and, quite remarkably, dominant themes.

Of course, my own priorities and commitments partially determine which narrative moments I focus on and which contextual discourses I import within my own analyses, but I have cast these readings broadly enough to be responsive to the fullness of the particular narratives I address. I am suggesting a more aggressive intertextuality, or perhaps merely a more literal and referential account of intertextual work than usually characterizes what we now call the "New Historicism." To be sure, I identify with many of this school's methods and assumptions, but differ, I believe, in a fundamental way. Orthodox New Historicist work commonly posits a noncausal, nonintentional matrix, and constructs a macrodiscursive space within which all discourses of a particular era or social formation circulate and inevitably colonize any semiotic act with the traces of an underlying ideological-discursive system. In *Loose Ends* I want to pursue not only the mutually constitutive discursive life of all textuality, but the specific system of cultural and historical reference that the elisions, silences, gaps, and closural anomalies I call "loose ends" direct us to. Rather than following any causal model of influence or pressure, I regard historical and contextual discourses as an elaborate cultural archive that constitutes something like a cultural unconscious within which and out of which cultural production occurs. In so doing, I admit to privileging, or at least provisionally isolating, the particular texts I address. My readings will focus on specific works, and, although I do not grant them any essential primacy or hierarchical superiority, I see these works (as, indeed, I see all works) as semiotic nodes into and out of which the discursive worlds of their cultures flow. Perhaps in "old historicist" manner, I pursue the irreducibly referential dimension of these cultural products—again, not to argue for a causal linkage among the various constituents of these textual relays, but rather to investigate their absorption and compression of a massive array of discourses, agendas, and energies which their own echoic systems engage.

I offer the discussion of Charles Brockden Brown's first novel, *Wieland; or, The Transformation: An American Tale,* in chapter 1 in two spirits, as an outline for a reading of that work and as a methodological introduction to the strategy of reading that will be practiced (with some variations) throughout *Loose Ends.* As the prompt for a historicized return to Brown's narrative, the discussion will necessarily be partial, focusing on one particular ensemble of textual and narrative logics — specifically, those pertaining to Brown's negotiation of early New England Puritanism as a persistent ideological subtext for early Republican United States — while merely suggesting a fuller application of the method I employ. As methodological overture, the discussion is not meant to suggest that I believe in any causal connection between *Wieland* and the other works I examine. Rather, I am interested in particular discursive practices deployed under certain creative pressures, pressures to some extent intentionally chosen by the artists and to some extent determined by the socio-ideological milieus within which these particular works are constructed. Brown's *Wieland* happens to be a novel I have been thinking of for a number of years in many contexts and happens to illustrate quite well a number of the interrelated narrative practices I am interested in.

That many "theories" of American literature (as well as less ambitious critical projects) begin with *Wieland* either as a prototypical ur-text for some tradition in literary production in the United States or as a coincidentally (chronologically) initial text in their systems prompts me to clarify more carefully than I otherwise might just what my intentions are relative to this particular work of literature. Each of the works I examine in *Loose Ends* will, I hope, be able to stand alone, or at least outside of some intraliterary, historical lineage. Wheatley's practice in her conventional odes in no way "influences" Brown's work, which, also, doesn't affect Melville's work in *Israel Potter,* and perhaps I don't even need to argue that Henry James's "The Jolly Corner" neither responds to Emily Dickinson's "I started Early – Took my Dog –" nor prefigures the Disney Studio's animated classic *Dumbo.* While I will occasionally situate one or more of these works within some context that includes others does not obscure the fact that each of these cultural products was constructed under remarkably different personal, historical, and economic circumstances by creators (or, as in the case of *Dumbo,* groups of creators) working within decidedly different (and usually completely unrelated) genres and oeuvres.

The relationships among these works aren't, in any conventional sense, relationships of content or theme, but rather of practice and structure, of the intersections between cultural text and sociohistorical context. I believe these works not only are discussable together but also constitute a core set of works from which further theorizing can be pursued, primarily as a result of my perception that they were created within and in partial response to social and historical crises and that these fractures in the fabric of post-Revolutionary U. S. society have exerted powerful and, very likely, irresistible pressures on the cultural products themselves. I will, in other words, pursue one set of aesthetic practices that emerges from the complicated intersection of cultural production and sociohistorical situatedness. Both of these sectors are incomplete: that is, neither the cultural works nor the social stresses to which they refer and which are inscribed within their fractured aesthetic frames have been resolved. These open narratives, one might argue, can even be perceived as open and fragmentary *because* life in late-twentieth-century United States remains fragmented by the social crises embedded within these works. That we respond to the aesthetic signals is a function of our living within the stressed contexts of a society still in the grips of racial, gendered, and economic struggle.

In this respect, *Wieland* is paradigmatic and symptomatic of a particular site of cultural struggle rather than itself an influence on prior and subsequent works created within different sites of different struggles. I will address Brown's text to demonstrate several components of the reading program to which the "loose ends" of my title refer. First, these include conclusions that not only fail to "conclude" the generative thematic and ideological issues of their works' primary origins and concerns but actually exacerbate those very issues that traditional (and, for that matter, many experimental) closural strategies and practices either respond to or resolve. These closural failures tend to be functions of unresolved narrative themes reexerting pressures that are both revealed by and constitutive of the failures of these works' endings to address their central thematics in any way commensurate with the social and historical issues they invoke. In other words, the issues that these endings neither resolve nor render coherent are strangely elicited rather than repressed by the works' final moments. In referring to these rampant moments as "loose ends," I mean to take the metaphor seriously and to suggest that the presence of these strands at work's end opens the possibilities (or, as some might have it, poses the dangers) of unraveling at least one entire (and apparently dominant) agenda of the narrative fabric. Second, these narratives tend to include a variety of deictic gestures that virtually require us to supplement their narrative worlds with the discourses and concerns derived from many sectors of social and cultural practice to which these works allude and from which they draw. These moments occur throughout most of the works I examine, but commonly emerge with a high degree of counternarrative visibility as a result of the narratives' closural failures. We recognize, that is, the internal conflicts and referential instabilities of these works when, by virtue of their endings, they emerge as an alternative and supplementary referential grid capable of displacing what had been established by various generic and conventional practices as the works' dominant thematics.

Since each chapter will take up the varied, though often related, historical and social issues implicated within its work's narratives, much of the theoretical agenda elaborated above will be more thoroughly fleshed out in individual discussions. Quite maddeningly, work of this sort requires almost complete retooling for each new work under consideration. For example, the historical research that opens up so much of Phillis Wheatley's odes plays little or no role in my discussion of Brown's *Wieland*, even though those works both emerge in late-eighteenth-century colonial and early Republican America. Similarly, while my discussions of Melville's *Israel Potter* and Emily Dickinson's "I started Early – Took my Dog –" both engage, among other things, the writings and cultural capital amassed by Ralph Waldo Emerson, they approach Emerson's work and field of force very differently, especially with reference to questions of gender and class. Needless to say, my research on Disney's *Dumbo* has little relationship to anything that precedes it in *Loose Ends*. While I attempt to develop a coherent project of both theory and practice, I would not pretend that the readings I offer are in any way complete, and they are certainly not comprehensive, although a fifty-page discussion of a short poem by Emily Dickinson might be mistaken for either of these options. I would contend that no reading of these works can aspire to "completeness" or, more certainly, to "finality," precisely because the social stresses and crises that fragment these works' closing moments still paralyze much social thought and political action in the United States. Contemporary Western culture is still too explosive a theater for the wars over class, race, and gender being fought on the streets of the United States for any literary or cinematic representation adequately to comprehend, let alone resolve, the political crises signaled within these works. Finally, a theoretical and ideological clarification: While I oppose the disposition in contemporary literary and cultural studies which views all forms of closure (and, in some cases, narrative as such) as "totalitarian" or "oppressive," I nonetheless believe that these *are* works which restlessly stage unresolved social dramas, and, as such, they are works whose own ruptures and conflicts are bound to remain problematic. There is an important difference between arguing that closure *cannot* or *should not* occur and demonstrating that, in certain cases, it *has not,* and then pursuing the implications of those loose ends.

Oh God said to Abraham, "Kill me a son."
Abe said, "Man, you must be puttin' me on."
God said, "No."
Abe said, "What?"
God said, "You can do what you want, Abe, but
The next time you see me coming, you better run."
Abe said, "Where do you want this killing done?"
God said, "On Highway 61."
—Bob Dylan, "Highway 61 Revisited"

On Monday evening, January 19, 1987, two days before I first taught Charles Brockden Brown's *Wieland; or, The Transformation: An American Tale* in Milwaukee, Wisconsin, Keith R. Kolata, a resident of Milwaukee's South Side, murdered his wife, Debra, and his two children, Constance (age four) and Jacob (age two), with a butcher knife. The first newspaper accounts hinted that a domestic squabble was behind the slaughter. Later reports eventually revealed that, soon after butchering his family, Kolata called the home of his brother-in-law and asked him to come over immediately, claiming that the "devil had taken over the weak part of him." During his discussions with police, Kolata claimed that he murdered his family because "he loved God," and, more troublingly, "because God told him that he had to do it, and that he [Kolata] loved God, and that he loved everybody." Before the police had even arrived at the crime scene, Kolata had taken a brief walk with his horrified brother-in-law, telling him that at the time of the murders he was "happy and sad at the same time."[1]

This ghastly case, one of the more spectacular instances in the gruesome history of murder in Milwaukee and Wisconsin (the state

notorious for Jeffrey Dahmer's horrifying binge of murder and cannibalism and for providing the real-life models for the mass and serial
killers represented in *Psycho* and *The Silence of the Lambs*), parallels
remarkably that upon which Brown draws for his own representation
of family mayhem in *Wieland*, his first published novel. In one highly
reported and commonly acknowledged source to which Brown refers
in the early pages of *Wieland*, upstate New Yorker James Yates threw
his Bible into his evening fire and then slaughtered his wife and children with a butcher knife, supposedly at the urging of the voice of
God.[2] Shirley Samuels has also called our attention to another case
which, due to its high visibility in the last years of the eighteenth
century, could equally have been on Brown's mind. William Beadle,
who committed suicide after murdering his wife and four children,
left letters in which he declared "himself a deist," expressed his devout belief that "the deity would not willingly punish one who was
impatient to visit his God and learn his will from his own mouth face
to face," and confessed his belief "that it is God himself who prompts
and directs me" (Samuels 20, 21, 31).[3]

I juxtapose this contemporary case of Kolata's divinely inspired
murder with both Brown's fictional murders and their likely historical antecedents, paradoxically, to domesticate the lurid but consistent
example of domestic violence that generates *Wieland*'s narrative and
to suggest that the bizarreness of Brown's tale cannot be marginalized
as some isolated example of "mere" religious fanaticism. The violence
and murder at the heart of *Wieland* cannot remain some grotesque act
that we imagine possible to be perpetrated only by some backwoods
isolato from the distant past. To some extent, the meaning of *Wieland*,
or at least the meanings of the most violent moments in that work,
continues to evolve amidst contemporary American urban existence.
"What happens in *Wieland*," to quote the title of Jane Tompkins's important reading, cannot be nicely cordoned off by some historical or
discursive police line—it is still happening. Indeed, the social conflicts inscribed within and, to some extent, generative of all the works
discussed in *Loose Ends* still remain unresolved and, perhaps, emerge
as compelling narrative themes precisely because we confront them
in many facets of our daily lives.

Indeed, legal records in the United States over the past two centuries reveal that in fact thousands of cases have been tried in which the murderers claimed to have killed their victims—usually family members—while under direct orders from God. The first such recorded incident that I have found is in John Winthrop's *History of New England*, where he reports that on December 6, 1638,

> Dorothy Talbye was hanged at Boston for murdering her own daughter, a child of three years old. . . . falling at differences with her husband, through melancholy or spiritual delusions, she sometimes attempted to kill him, and her children, and herself, by refusing meat, saying it was so revealed to her, etc. . . . she was so possessed with Satan, that he persuaded her (by his delusions, which she listened to as revelations from God) to break the neck of her own child, that she might free it from future misery. (282–83)

A number of recent spectacular murder cases conform to the model. Joseph Kallinger reported to Flora Rheta Schreiber (author of the bestseller *Sybil*) that in 1974 he had murdered his fourteen-year-old son and a ten-year-old boy from their neighborhood because "he was acting under the influence of voices from God and that the two killings were preparations for his larger mission of killing all human beings on earth." Also in 1974, Albert Korb "testified that the 'voice of God' told him his wife was a witch and should be destroyed." Korb admitted to sawing his wife into pieces, burying her in a Pittsburgh park, and later retrieving portions of her body, which he ate in spaghetti sauce. Etna Huberty, widow of James Oliver Huberty, reported that, just prior to the rampage in which he murdered twenty-one and wounded another nineteen people in a San Ysidro McDonald's in 1984, her husband had been talking to God, who, according to Huberty, was "two feet high and had a long beard." Also in 1984, Grace Rebecca Bray claimed that "voices from God told her to kill her two young children" by slitting their throats. In 1985, Albert Houston strangled Anastasia Burgess to death with an electrical cord and cut the throat of her cat with a knife, claiming that "God told him Burgess was a threat and had to be killed. He said God also told him the cat was evil and had to be destroyed." In another 1985 incident, Sylvester Townes told police that he had stabbed his mother more than twenty times while she lay helpless in her bed because "the voice of God told [him] to kill her." Perhaps most notoriously, when Mark David Chapman pleaded guilty to the murder of John Lennon, he insisted that he had chosen "to follow the instructions of God" and that he "believe[d] he was doing God's will." An Associated Press release (undated) indicates that God may even order his ministers on earth to do his murderous bidding, for it reports that "a 'voice' told a Baptist deacon [in Plymouth, Massachusetts] to abduct, rape and murder his 13-year-old neighbor." So common are such cases in recent history that some murderers actually fabricate narratives of God ordering them to kill their families, believing that the "God made me do it" plea is likely to result in an acquittal. In 1986, James Curtright eventually admitted to fabricating exactly such a lie in his trial for murdering his mother and sister. Curtright told a psychiatrist that "he made up the story about hearing the voice of God to avoid being punished for his crime. He said he got the idea after reading about an abortion clinic bombing in which the suspects claimed they heard a voice of God" ordering them to kill clinic doctors and patients.[4]

Through the nineteenth century the American legal system was itself structured to account for such murders, a fact that surely testifies to their not infrequent occurrence. According to David Brion Davis, "in 1844 Chief Justice Lemuel Shaw [Herman Melville's father-in-law] of Massachusetts ruled that a murder was excusable if the killer acted under the delusive but sincere belief that he was obeying a command of God, which would supersede all human and natural laws" (93). Furthermore, in John Neal's 1822 novel *Logan: A Family History*, one character proposes that a well-intentioned man would be acquitted in God's eyes: "if he *meant* rightly, God will hold him guiltless, as he would the maniack who should dip his hands in the blood of his own mother!" (2: 228). To be sure, some of these murderers and thousands of others have been cleared after being declared mentally incompetent due to insanity. But the sheer numbers of murders committed by humans who believe they have been told by God to murder their wives and children (cases of women murdering their husbands under orders from God are rare) suggest something at least to some degree communal, whether as a communal hallucination or as a mass lunatic projection of some psycho-ideological frenzy. Of course, the biblical God *did* order Abraham to murder Isaac, adding plausibility to these killers' claims in the minds of the faithful. In fact, one of the complaints that John Winthrop's Assembly had with Anne Hutchinson was her contention that "Abraham was not in a saving estate till he offered Isack and so savinge the firmnes of Gods Election he might have perished eternally for any Worke of Grace that was in him" (Hall, *Antinomian Controversy* 352).

We never find out exactly who or what told Theodore Wieland to murder his wife, children, housekeeper, sister, and best friend, but every indication in the narrative is that he, too, believed he was acting under God's urgings. The horrifying connections between Charles Brockden Brown's fictional reworking of an actual case in New York State and the proliferation of similar murder cases throughout the colonies and the United States press us to seek beyond *Wieland's* discursive boundaries for possible explanations of crimes almost too heinous to recount.

To argue that *Wieland's* meanings cannot be contained within the narrative parameters of Brown's text will surely not surprise many readers sensitized to the New Historicist dynamics of reading and to Derrida's now virtually canonical manifesto: "Il n'y a pas de hors texte," a reminder that nothing exists outside of textuality. Rather than functioning as a caution to those who would prematurely demarcate text from context and cultural work from social world, however, the spirit of Derrida's remark has frequently been deployed to wall off texts from contexts, to refetishize textual boundaries and to return aggressively to the formalist-inspired explications of isolated literary works. In this reading of *Wieland,* I would like to challenge such formalist and literary-autonomist residue (which, in fact, runs contrary to Derrida's own explicit clarifications of his method and agenda) by arguing that, in the case of *Wieland* (as in the cases of other works I discuss in *Loose Ends*), many narrative moments, citations, footnotes, appendixes, symbiotically related works ("Memoirs of Carwin the Biloquist," and perhaps even *Alcuin*) exist as complex deictic gestures to a realm beyond any putative narrative boundary. Such gestures repudiate the possibility of any such boundaries and redirect our hermeneutic activity to the apprehension of the narrative world in at least as full and various a context as its many markers elicit. To offer a revision of Derrida's remark (actually a revision that is fully consistent with what I take to be the spirit of Derrida's work in general), I would counter il n'y a pas de dedans du texte—that there is nothing *within* the text, that any literary meaning is, strictly speaking, impossible without recourse to a transliterary world of ordinary language and ordinary experience. Therefore, any interpretive procedure by which we construct meanings for a cultural artifact always situates that text in a densely social and historical world.[5] It is, perhaps, this tremendous ordinariness of literature—its congruence with our world of lived experience—that is the greatest scandal to traditional (at least academic) literary criticism and that has driven the evolution of literary criticism for much of the twentieth century.

ii

That there may be nothing within Charles Brockden Brown's text, or at least nothing that we need in order to decode the narrative of Brown's titular Wieland family, is a likelihood that problematizes our response to that work from its earliest pages. In fact, setting aside the commands of God for a moment, the novel more or less requires us to consult extratextual sources in order to comprehend its own numerous and, frequently, generative conundrums—*Wieland* repeatedly asks questions that cannot be answered, at least not without recourse to sources, discourses, entire archives alluded to but absent from Brown's narrative world. We learn in the novel's earliest pages that Theodore Wieland Sr. embarked on his religio-fanatical hegira after happening upon the words "Seek and ye shall find" when he casually opened up and glanced at a Bible. We never find out whether Wieland ever knew exactly what he was seeking, though we are fairly certain he never found it. The narrative provides no conclusive evidence upon which to base even a reasonable hypothesis about the object of his search. It and its characters suggest numerous possibilities, to be sure, but none of them even merits sustained narrative consideration, let alone consensus among those characters with vested interests in finding a solution to the enigma of Wieland's religious fanaticism and bizarre death. Clara, for one, pursues this futile line of questioning:

Was this the penalty of disobedience? this the stroke of a vindictive and invisible hand? Is it a fresh proof that the Divine Ruler interferes in human affairs, meditates an end, selects and commissions his agents, and enforces, by unequivocal sanctions, submission to his will? Or, was it merely the irregular expansion of the fluid that imparts warmth to our heart and our blood, caused by the fatigue of the preceding day, or flowing, by established laws, from the condition of his thoughts. (19)

Later, as she agonizes over her brother's murderous rampage, Clara reaches another speculative impasse: "Presently, I considered, that whether Wieland was a maniac, a faithful servant of his God, the victim of hellish illusions, or the dupe of human imposture, was by no means certain" (187). In *Wieland,* as in many Hawthorne tales, unresolved suggestions, possibilities, and theories proliferate. Hawthorne commonly layers numerous similarly categorized alternative explanations (from the mysterious to the perceptual to the scientific) for narrative conundrums such as Hooper's black veil, Young Goodman Brown's forest experience, or what (if anything) Dimmesdale exposes on his chest near the conclusion of *The Scarlet Letter,* in order to suggest the relativity, situatedness, and interestedness of human perceptions. The multiple suggestions littering much of *Wieland,* however, amount to nothing, even though they are offered in the spirit of explanation. They suggest neither perspectival relativism nor character bias (although most characters advance theories consistent with their general outlooks). They are all merely dead ends, possibilities which may or may not be true, but which either can't or won't be tested out within the narrative frame. The difficulties ensuing from this experience for Wieland Sr., for his relatives, his children, and their associates, and for us as the narrative's readers are immense.

Nor is Wieland's original inspiration following his epiphanic reading of "Seek and ye shall find" an isolated moment in Brown's text. Clara's narrative returns compulsively, especially early on, to similar moments of thwarted, futile, or abortive quests for answers to problems that range from the mysterious to the hopelessly banal. Clara, in fact, affirms the centrality of a flawed and partial pursuit of truth and stability to her own narrative project:

My narrative may be invaded by inaccuracy and confusion; but if I live no longer, I will, at least, live to complete it. What but ambiguities, abruptness, and dark transitions, can be expected from the historian who is, at the same time, the sufferer of these disasters? (147)

While her narrative may appear to possess a quantitative complete-ness, Clara grants the inevitability of her "history" being riven by incompleteness, the "dark transitions" that must fracture her text in some of its most crucial junctures. Even prior to any of the grue-some events that both befall the younger Wieland generation and retrospectively traumatize Clara's narrative capacity, Clara refers to this phenomenon while also foreshadowing the eventual orgy of de-struction. Her brother, she tells us, is enthusiastically pursuing a re-search project "of collecting and investigating the facts which relate to that mysterious personage, the Dæmon of Socrates," and, while her "brother's skill in Greek and Roman learning was exceeded by that of few, and no doubt the world would have accepted a treatise upon this subject from his hand with avidity, . . . this and every other scheme of felicity and honor were doomed to sudden blast and hopeless exter-mination" (48). Most such moments occur in the narrative present. For example, Clara recounts her doubts regarding the claims of an itinerant sculptor who sells Theodore Wieland a bust of Cicero that he "professed to have copied . . . from an antique dug up with his own hands in the environs of Modena." Apropos of nothing in particular that should have aroused suspicion, Clara adds, "Of the truth of his assertions we were not qualified to judge" (23–24). Shortly after this admission of the impossibility of determining the validity of a truth-claim, Pleyel interrupts a debate he is engaged in with Wieland by accusing Wieland of misquoting a Latin term:

> Pleyel accused his companion of saying "*polliciatur*" when he should have said "*polliceretur.*" Nothing would decide the con-test, but an appeal to the volume. My brother was returning to the house for this purpose, when a servant met him with a let-ter from Major Stuart. He immediately returned to read it in our company. (30)

As a result of this postal delivery and the onset of a rainstorm, the heated debate over the proper subjunctive form of the Latin verb for "to make an offer, to promise," is never resolved; in fact, it is never again mentioned.

The group of intimates retires to the Wieland house only to get embroiled in another debate concerning some particular mentioned by Major Stuart in the letter that had just interrupted the attempt to adjudicate the proper Latin verb form. According to Clara, the truth of some description in the major's letter "was questionable," and

> to settle the dispute which thence arose, it was proposed to have recourse to the letter. My brother searched for it in his pocket. It was no where to be found. At length, he remembered to have left it in the temple, and he determined to go in search for it. His wife, Pleyel, Louisa, and myself, remained where we were. (31)

Wieland returns from his attempt to recover the letter, but sits silently, "absorbed in meditation." The group "thought that he only waited for a pause in the discourse, to produce the letter. The pause was uninterrupted by him. At length Pleyel said, 'Well, I suppose you have found the letter'" (31). However, while mounting the hill to the temple Wieland is so perplexed by having heard the first of Carwin's ventriloquistic projections that he never locates the letter, instead, when he returns, initiating another mysterious topic (the unknown voices that punctuate the action for much of the remainder of the narrative). The letter is never recovered, and the debate regarding the truth of Major Stuart's claims about the cataract on the Monongahela River is never decided. It is never even mentioned again as a mystery that remains to be solved—it simply drops out of the narrative.

Henry Pleyel recounts to Clara another similar experience, one which also bears foreboding resemblance to the elder Wieland's chance happening across the biblical passage "Seek and ye shall find." Inexplicably stopping in to call on a Mrs. Baynton, Pleyel inadvertently picks up a newspaper and, in an act which "was rather mechanical than voluntary," reads of Carwin's supposed guilt for one murder and one robbery. Flying into a passion, Pleyel decides to inform all the others when he realizes that,

though the information [he] possessed was, in one sense, sufficient, yet if more could be obtained, more was desirable. This
passage was copied from a British paper; part of it only, perhaps,
was transcribed. The printer was in possession of the original.
 Toward his house I immediately turned my horse's head. He
produced the paper, but I found nothing more than had already
been seen. (129–30)

All Pleyel succeeds in finding is a greater mystery concerning why
Mr. Hallet was so intent on having the story published in the United
States after he received it from Ludloe (who sent him the story from
England). We, of course, learn in "Memoirs of Carwin the Biloquist"
that Ludloe's own version of Carwin's guilt is highly suspect, and we,
like Pleyel, are left with nothing concrete, or even remotely reliable,
upon which to base our conjectures. In each of these cases, the characters seeking some factual confirmation, some material emblem, or
some irrefragable source of truth all either have their quests suddenly
interrupted and aborted or are stymied by the vertiginous swirl of
contradictory or unreliable documentation.

 The same dynamic informs many other attempts to clarify or consolidate information throughout Clara's narrative, especially in matters involving human motivation. When the group at Mettingen
speculates about the possible motivation for Louisa Stuart's mother's
disappearance, Clara narrates their perplexity in great detail:

> This tale was a copious theme of speculation. *A thousand ques-*
> *tions were started and discussed in our domestic circle,* respecting
> the motives that influenced Mrs. Stuart to abandon her country.
> It did not appear that her proceeding was involuntary. *We re-*
> *called and reviewed every particular that had fallen under our own*
> *observation.* By none of these were we furnished with a clue. Her
> conduct, after the most rigorous scrutiny, *still remained an im-*
> *penetrable secret.* (29; my emphasis)

Clara regularly punctuates such passages with equally careful language to indicate the lengths to which she and her friends have gone
in their attempts to discover answers. She is especially thorough in
recounting her attempts to comprehend both the mysterious voices

which seem so benevolent at first and Carwin's enigmatic presence. After Clara is terrified by voices plotting her murder in a closet near her bed, she and her companions struggle in vain to illuminate the mystery: "I will not enumerate the various inquiries and conjectures which these incidents occasioned. After all our efforts, we came no nearer to dispelling the mist in which they were involved; and time, instead of facilitating a solution, only accumulated our doubts" (61). Similarly, soon after meeting Carwin formally, Clara remains "wholly uncertain, whether he were an object to be dreaded or adored, and whether his powers had been exerted to evil or good" (71). Clara's growing familiarity with Carwin results in no greater understanding:

> His visits were frequently repeated. Each day introduced us to a more intimate acquaintance with his sentiments, but left us wholly in the dark, concerning that about which we were most inquisitive. He studiously avoided all mention of his past or present situation. Even the place of his abode in the city he concealed from us.
>
> Our sphere, in this respect, being somewhat limited, and the intellectual endowments of this man being indisputably great, his deportment was more diligently marked, and copiously commented on by us, than you, perhaps, will think the circumstances warranted. Not a gesture, or glance, or accent, that was not, in our private assemblies, discussed, and inferences deduced from it. It may well be thought that he modelled his behaviour by an uncommon standard, when, with all our opportunities and accuracy of observation, we were able, for a long time, to gather no satisfactory information. He afforded us no ground on which to build even a plausible conjecture. (71–72)

Even in one of her final audiences with Carwin, Clara returns to the basic structure of these protracted musings. As Wieland enters the deserted house in which Carwin is attempting to convince Clara of his innocence, Carwin exits quickly, leaving Clara to the following speculation: "I had drunk in, with the most vehement attention, every word that he had uttered. I had no breath to interrupt this tale by interrogations or comments. The power that he spoke of was hitherto unknown to me: its existence was incredible; it was susceptible of

no direct proof" (216). This speech is made doubly significant by the
fact that Carwin's explanation of his incomprehensible ventriloquistic
powers is doubled for the reader by virtue of the novel, *Wieland,* apparently being the first in the language in which the word "biloquist"
appears (as Edwin Fussell notes, "Brown had 'biloquist' a decade before the *OED*" [173]). As a result, the reader (or at least Brown's
contemporary reader) shares Clara's confusion; both Carwin's vocal
skill and Brown's narrative deployment of ventriloquism as a new
component in gothic narrative flummox their respective audiences.
In these cases, as in so many others throughout *Wieland,* the seeking of knowledge rarely, if ever, results in finding. But the care with
which Clara elucidates her group's efforts suggests the centrality to
her narrative of these futile quests. Carwin provokes numerous such
passages of frustrated ratiocination, and an equal number in which
Clara represents her confusion as emotional chaos.

There is a certain discursive consistency, then, when Clara includes
in her narrative the courtroom transcript of Theodore Wieland himself recounting his own "seek and ye shall find" story. Early in his
calm version of the recent events at Mettingen, Wieland soliloquizes:

> My days have been spent in searching for the revelation of that
> will; but my days have been mournful, because my search failed.
> I solicited direction: I turned on every side where glimmerings
> of light could be discovered. I have not been wholly uninformed;
> but my knowledge has always stopped short of certainty. Dissat-
> isfaction has insinuated itself into all my thoughts. (165)

Of course, we never discover the original source of the voices Wieland believes ordered him to butcher his family. Clara's premature
certainty is that Carwin, since he had already admitted uttering the
other "mysterious" voices in the narrative, must also have issued the
orders to kill. But Carwin's own denials of his complicity in Wieland's
bloody rampage are thoroughly credible. Nothing in the narrative
contradicts his protestations of innocence. As he puts it, after con-
fessing to every act of ventriloquism we as readers have heard about,

> I have uttered the truth. This is the extent of my offences. You
> tell me an horrid tale of Wieland being led to the destruction of

his wife and children, by some mysterious agent. You charge me with the guilt of this agency; but I repeat that the amount of my guilt has been truly stated. The perpetrator of Catharine's death was unknown to me till now; nay, it is still unknown to me. (216)

Given the thoroughness of his preceding confession, Carwin's surprise and denials here ring plausible. Despite Clara's rash conclusion that "his tale is a lie, and his nature devilish. As he deceived me, he likewise deceived my brother, and now do I behold the author of all our calamities!" (216), there is no evidence that anyone has any idea who or what ordered Wieland to murder his family. Clara's later admission that "whether Wieland was a maniac, a faithful servant of his God, the victim of hellish illusions, or the dupe of human imposture, was by no means certain" (187), is as close as she or we ever get. For all the seeking that goes on in *Wieland,* nothing of importance is ever found.

Wieland even advances crucial narrative mysteries that, while recognized and commented upon by various characters, are neither pursued as mysteries nor resolved. For example, not only do we never discover the locus from which the voice or voices ordering Wieland to slaughter his family emanate, but his entire descent into hallucinatory madness and homicidal frenzy occurs beyond narration. Theodore more or less disappears, returning indirectly to the narrative only when Clara reads the transcript of his courtroom testimony and again when he returns to Mettingen intent on following subsequent directions to murder Clara. In rendering the etiology of his madness (or his commitment) obscure and essentially indeterminate, *Wieland* fails even to speculate about its course in transforming Wieland from loving husband, father, brother, and friend into demented (or righteous) slasher. Equally absent, but more bizarrely so, is any attempt to take seriously or to investigate the elder Wieland's claim (and the physical evidence) that he received a powerful blow on his arm just prior to being scorched. The point is made three times in rapid succession. First, when Clara recounts their initial view of her father after his experience, she notes that "he was naked, his skin throughout the greater part of his body was scorched and bruised. His right arm exhibited marks as of having been struck by some heavy body." As the father's condition deteriorates, Clara again calls attention to this wound when she notes that "a mortification speedily shewed itself in the arm, which had been most hurt. Soon after, the other wounded parts exhibited the like appearance." Finally, Clara's father himself offers the only firsthand testimony possible, reporting that "he was in the act of turning to examine the visitant, when his right arm received a blow from a heavy club" (18). Of course, the likelihood that Wieland was, in fact, attacked by a human assailant receives no attention, as nearly every one of the surviving relatives flies into metaphysical speculations and forever mystifies the tragedy, although Clara's skeptical uncle withholds judgment, suspecting that "half the truth had been suppressed" (18). Bernard Rosenthal has commented on this and two other anomalies in Clara's narration, suggesting that they "are symptomatic of the ambiguity that suffuses Brown's novel; that they fit his pattern of showing how untrustworthy the senses are" (108). Ambiguous to be sure, but, whereas Rosenthal's intention is to construct Brown as an important precursor to writers like Poe, Hawthorne, and Melville for whom "the theme of illusion and reality [is] so central" (121), I rather argue that these narrative absences function more as intentional structural fissures and deictic prompts than as thematic nodes.

Amplifying this pervasive textual dynamic, Clara pauses to comment on two males of her family whose lives revolve around the rigorous pursuit of stable truths. Even the historical Christoph Martin Wieland, whom Clara's narrative specifies as her fictional family's most illustrious relative, was, according to John McCarthy, engaged in a "continual struggle for certitude, for the right answers" (9), in his Neoplatonic philosophical investigations. Configuring a complex interplay between the fictional and historical dimensions of Brown's narrative, the historical Wieland's passion is replicated in Theodore Wieland, Clara's brother. Both Theodore and Henry Pleyel, of course, are rigidly dedicated to the pursuit of truth via their respective and mutually exclusive worldviews. In addition, however, Wieland is himself dedicated to the project of "restoring the purity of the text" of Cicero, the "chief object of his veneration," an undertaking that consumes his scholarly time. As Clara points out, her brother pursued all possible avenues to insure the success of his occupation, especially that of textual comparison and collation: "he collected all the editions and commentaries that could be procured, and employed months of severe study in exploring and comparing them" (24). Of course, he never completes his project.

That neither Wieland attains his object poses several problems for any reading of *Wieland*. First, it establishes a generational dynamic that complicates any attempt to comprehend the male Wielands and the ghastly acts and fates of the father and son whose deaths and murders stymie any final analysis. By so doing, it problematizes the narrative's construction of subjectivity, introducing generational, genetic, historical, and even geographical variables into the narrative's attempt to come to grips with either character's beliefs and actions. Second, and more pertinent to my own project, the erasing of boundaries between the life of the historical C. M. Wieland and Brown's fictional constructions of the lives of the Wieland father and son suggests a significant narrative contestation of the viability of any such barriers, a contestation further bolstered by the narrative's embedding of several references to actual historical events and personages within its own gothic frame. In other words, I take the failures of any of the searches that occur throughout *Wieland*, which function on many levels, as themselves an integral component in Brown's representational scheme. By staging so many failed attempts to discover answers, the narrative is alerting its audience to the likelihood that its many enigmas are ultimately irresolvable, or, more precisely, that these mysteries are unsolvable if we remain confined within the novel's textual boundaries. What I propose is that so systematic an impasse within the narrative requires us to range far outside the novel's own borders into the discourses of history, science, politics, religion, and gender.

Brown himself triggers such a complex relationship between *Wieland* and its intertextual environment in his "Advertisement," in which he both reminds his readers that they might "recollect an authentic case, remarkably similar to that of Wieland" and in which he situates his tale historically "between the conclusion of the French and the beginning of the revolutionary war" (3). The narrative proper, furthermore, is occasionally interrupted and supplemented by Brown's footnotes, which clarify historically significant (and thematically crucial) details. For example, in order to substantiate the plausibility of the elder Wieland's death by spontaneous combustion, Brown provides the following footnote:

> A case, in its symptoms exactly parallel to this, is published in one of the Journals of Florence. See, likewise, similar cases reported by Messrs. Merrille and Muraire, in the "Journal de Medicine" for February and May, 1783. The researches of Maffei and Fontana have thrown some light upon this subject. (19)

As if to underscore the importance of the pursuit of textual purity, he also glosses his characters' perusing "the Della Crusca dictionary" by noting that the "Accademia della Crusca was founded in Florence in 1582 with the primary object of purifying the Italian language" and that "in 1612 it issued the famous dictionary *Vocabulario della Crusca*" (42). Finally, and again to convince his readers both of the plausibility of narrative improbabilities and of the necessity of ranging widely outside his own text for resources central to its reading, Brown explains the physiological and acoustical details of biloquism or ventriloquism, complete with references to two contemporary specialists in the field. This note meshes with the narrative's numerous returns to frustrated searches for certainty when it admits that, despite some significant research into the phenomenon, "this power is difficult to explain" (198). Brown's own supplementary footnotes, then, erode the very credibility they are meant to establish and reinsert the vexed relationship between "seeking" and "finding" that the narrative offers as an ur-theme for its own emergence.

iii

What kind of reading strategies do such frustrated and contradictory moments of textual searching make possible or require? Can we view *Wieland*'s densely and thoroughly thematized trope of "seek and ye shall find" as an allegory of our own reading process? Are we prisoners in the closed textual world of the novel *Wieland; or, The Transformation: An American Tale* in a manner commensurate with Clara's enclosure in the claustrophobic world of Mettingen? Are we, like Clara, doomed to ricochet from one dead-end narrative search to another, often forgetting that the search in which we are currently engaged is itself a doubly or triply removed digression from earlier thwarted attempts to verify some prior narrative detail? Is *Wieland* some impossibly prototypical modernist text whose repeated moments of abandoned and frustrated desire for certainty image a modern, relativistic world devoid of epistemological stability? Is it a text whose most obvious themes and superficial narrative texture embody the truisms of poststructuralism's lessons regarding the impossibility, at least at deeper levels of textual meaning, of unambiguous linguistic signification?

Another way to pose these questions is to ask whether or not *Wieland* (or any cultural work, with or without *Wieland*'s obvious provocations) can still be regarded as an autonomous and closed narrative world whose borders are closely guarded from extratextual incursions and correspondences. While the moments we have been considering certainly call into doubt the reliability of sense perception (as Bernard Rosenthal and numerous other critics argue) and signal what Roland Hagenbüchle in his title calls "the nineteenth-century crisis in epistemology," I am more interested in pursuing how Brown himself works in *Wieland* to defetishize the notion of the autonomous text. Hence, some issues which we can characterize as "ambiguous" so long as we have recourse only to the data contained within the narrative need to be reconstructed as prompts that problematize the textual grid within which traditional formalist hermeneutics operate. Readers could, of course, affirm any combination of these possibilities (whether specifically with reference to *Wieland* or to literary signification in general), and the critical history of Brown's novel resonates with many such interpretive possibilities. I would like to follow a different route with respect to *Wieland*'s proliferating loose ends and argue that we can pursue them beyond the textual borders of Brown's work to examine their intertextual linkages with the much more capacious and flexible discursive world of the late-eighteenth-century United States. The novel, in fact, invites and, in some cases, requires us to violate its own borders. Consistent with the other readings I will offer in *Loose Ends,* Clara's attempt to close off the narrative of her traumatic family history by so egregiously violating important elements of the narrative world she has created itself forces us to deny her assertions. In other words, her own conclusion, which most critics of the novel have belittled as tacked-on, blindly moralistic, and ineffective, not only fails to resolve the central questions that drive her narrative (and all of the subsidiary ones we have considered), but actually fails to reconcile her audience to the very claims she advances by way of sealing off her tale from further analysis.

In one obvious sense, "Memoirs of Carwin the Biloquist," itself not identical with Clara's narrative in *Wieland,* supplements the highly charged but "imperfect" (to use a term Clara relies on throughout her narrative to remind us of the tentative and incomplete state of her recollections) vision of her work. Brown was working on the "Memoirs" at the time *Wieland* was sent to press in September of 1798, but it was "forgotten and thrown aside until November, 1803, when [Brown] needed material for his new *Literary Magazine*" (Pattee xliii-xliv). Originally conceived as an extension of *Wieland,* the fragmentary "Memoirs" soon exceeded Brown's original plan to merge them into his novel. As a result, the "Memoirs" were not published until five years after the original appearance of *Wieland* and were not then incorporated within that work. This creates bizarrely incoherent and anomalous moments within *Wieland* proper. Just after Wieland's suicide, Clara acknowledges that her uncle knows the details of Carwin's life:

> Talk not to me, O my revered friend! of Carwin. He has told thee his tale, and thou exculpatest him from all direct concern in the fate of Wieland. This scene of havock was produced by an illusion of the senses. Be it so: I care not from what source these disasters have flowed; it suffices that they have swallowed up our hopes and our existence. (233)

The problem is that Carwin, while clearly referred to in *Wieland* as one whose whole story is capable of vindicating him, is almost completely inexplicable to the reader (let alone Clara) without recourse to the supplementary text of his memoirs, a literary project of which he had already informed Clara during their final meeting:

> I purposed to seek some retreat in the wilderness, inaccessible to your inquiry and to the malice of my foe, where I might

henceforth employ myself in composing a faithful narrative of my actions. I designed it as my vindication from the aspersions that had rested on my character, and as a lesson to mankind on the evils of credulity on the one hand, and of imposture on the other. (212)

Even this revelation is prepared for well in advance, however. Brown concludes the "Advertisement" to his novel with the following gesture to this potential text: "the memoirs of Carwin, alluded to at the conclusion of the work, will be published or suppressed according to the reception which is given to the present attempt" (3). Brown clearly imagined the "Memoirs" as a supplementary document, one which would clarify Carwin's conduct within Wieland while also accounting for his character and history more densely than the novel could, either because of narrative constraints or the thematic necessity of surrounding Carwin with an aura of mystery. Of course, there is also a prayer of sorts embedded within Brown's remark in his "Advertisement": since the appearance of Carwin's memoirs is explicitly linked to the success of Wieland, its existence is already parasitical on the consumption and reception of Brown's dominant narrative. The symbiosis between these two texts, however, is not only remarkable, but paradigmatic of the other numerous intertexts to which we must have recourse in reading Wieland. In other words, while the answers to the questions posed within Wieland are not offered explicitly within the novel, they do exist elsewhere, either embedded in Brown's related work or within the macrodiscursive space of Brown's cultural moment.

There is nothing peculiar about Brown's representational strategies; surely the evolution of most narratives, especially in the case of mystery writing, mandates either delaying or suppressing significant information in order to create the suspense necessary for the convincing representation of characterological or narratological mystery. Carwin needs to be underdetermined. Brown must underrepresent his background and motives. The narrative or thematic logic, then, coincides with the narrative economy which prohibits the inclusion of significant data within Wieland proper. Wieland's difference is that neither the specifics of Carwin's motivation nor the details of either the elder or younger Wieland's manias and deaths are ever revealed in the narrative per se. Within *Wieland* none of the primary areas of uncertainty, doubt, and mystery is ever narrated, let alone clarified, and yet Clara's conclusion requires us simply either to forget them or to buy into her patently inadequate strategy of closing her narrative. By so doing, *Wieland* ends in a way that exacerbates virtually every one of its generative tensions and every one of its gothically brutal deaths. Not only is *Wieland's* end a conclusion in which nothing is concluded, but Clara's attempt to close her narrative with the clarification (and rectification) of the novel's remaining domestic issues and with the pat moral of her final paragraph merely returns us to the narrative more acutely aware of her failure to account for major moments in her narrative either plausibly or convincingly. We are, in a sense, back to the beginning, still disturbed by the deaths, murders, and voices that fill so much of *Wieland's* narrative world. We may seek, but we can't find the very things we are looking for.

iv

In what follows I will suggest that the gaps within *Wieland* and its anti-closural final chapter (loose ends of the two varieties we will be studying) function as oblique solicitations inviting the importation of contextual discourses usually assumed to exist either outside of or merely parallel to any cultural text. I plan to pursue some of the ways in which *Wieland* resonates with social and historical data and to indicate Brown's status as a fictional historian of early American culture. I agree with Myra Jehlen's dictum that "the dominant literary forms of each historical epoch are those which are not only ethically but aesthetically linked to contemporary issues. . . . the predominant genre (or genres) speaks politically whatever it says" (133). Brown's *Wieland* can be understood in generic terms as a historical allegory. That is, it resembles Cotton Mather's *Magnalia Christi Americana*, which fuses the identities of its many paragons of Puritan devotion with their Old Testament figural antecedents, with an ideological essence, and with a sense of American locale and destiny in order to construct exemplary biographies.[6] It also anticipates Hawthorne's meditations on early American history, which brood on the failures, not the triumphs, both individual and communal, of various kinds of American dogmatism and historical bad faith, offering those historical sketches as negative portraits of American exceptionalism. I would even go so far as to suggest that Brown is pivotal in American literary history, linking Mather's representational strategies, which blur history into fiction, and Hawthorne's, which blur fiction into history. Brown completes, as it were, Mather's project and develops the prototype for what we understand (with the help of Michael Colacurcio's *The Province of Piety*) to be the Hawthornian historical genre in ways which we have not yet fully grasped, largely as a result of the ways in which critical and historical thought continue to read the relationship of cultural text and sociohistorical context.

Brown himself called attention to the political nature of his narrative in a letter he sent along with a copy of his novel to Thomas Jefferson. There the novelist stresses the social significance of his fictional narrative by comparing it to "social and intellectual theory . . . the history of fact in the processes of nature and the operations of government" (quoted in Fussell 177). Surely he had more in mind for his work than the bizarre tale of religious frenzy and ventriloquism that most early critics of *Wieland* perceived.[7] Brown also situates his text in a national, if not immediately historical, context as early as his title page: *Wieland; or, The Transformation: An American Tale.* But in what sense is *Wieland* "an American tale"? There is little critical consensus concerning the "Americanness" of Brown's work, although various speculations have generated many of its most interesting readings.

Michael Davitt Bell and others have argued that the novel registers early America's distrust or fear of art, a plausible notion partly substantiated by early sentimental novels such as *The Power of Sympathy* and *The Coquette*, both of which provide melodramatic and morbid illustrations of fiction's impact on delicate sensibilities. Designating *Wieland* as "conceivably the major literary landmark between the Declaration of Independence and the appearance of *The Pioneers* by James Fenimore Cooper in 1823" (185), Edwin Fussell traces Brown's subtitle to his engagement in the creation of a distinctly American literature, in "his need to define and embody the typifying communal experience of that new polity, to write the nation into an existence more deeply and genuinely constitutional than the merely assertive and legalistic, to give it a character, a personality and a soul" (171–72). Fussell identifies Clara Wieland as the American protonovelist struggling to consolidate in narrative form the energies of a new culture. In other words, *Wieland* is an American tale, for Bell, Fussell, and others, in that it is by an American author and embodies the traumas of fictionists in the early Republic. Alan Axelrod offers a compatible perspective when he argues that the "American tale" subtitle appended both to *Wieland* and to *Sky-Walk* seems "unambiguously to proclaim their author's intellectual and aesthetic independence from the Old World" (3). Other critics have worked within this general frame of reference but cast Brown's work more negatively, not as a celebration of independence from Europe but as an anxious meditation on the "empty" (Ridgely) or "orphaned" (Tompkins) state of colonial existence. Roland Hagenbüchle focuses on the "profound cognitive anxiety" at the heart of the crisis of epistemology represented in Brown's work and in nineteenth-century American fiction in general (123). Shirley Samuels argues that the Americanness of Brown's tale resides in its generic resonance with the tutelary tract, in this case functioning

> to prepare the way for the notion that institutions are a necessary supplement to the family. Without the formal institutions of education, religion, "benevolent societies," orphanages, or prisons, the new republic would be susceptible to the chaos unleashed within the Wieland family. (53)

And in Emily Miller Budick's view, "*Wieland* is the first of many American tales to record the story of the new American Eden and the fall that took place there," a fall Budick attributes to an Enlightenment belief that America can be freed from the burden of history (26).

There is yet another critical approach to Brown's "American tale," one which situates *Wieland* with specific reference to two earlier ideological formations: American Puritanism and Enlightenment rationality. Beginning with Larzer Ziff's still influential "A Reading of *Wieland*," some of *Wieland*'s best critics have returned to that novel's tense meditation on specific periods of the American cultural past and have argued that it criticizes either religious fanaticism or Enlightenment optimism, usually designating one of these loosely defined belief systems as a positive force capable of highlighting the inadequacies of the other. Thus Ziff argues that Brown "penetrates beneath the principles of the optimistic psychology of his day, and recognizes the claims which Calvinism makes on the American character" (51). Michael T. Gilmore similarly bases his reading on his assumption that

> Brown's subtitle "An American Tale" suggests that he saw in his central foursome a microcosm of the bourgeois American society that by 1798 stood in defiant opposition to the Puritan past. . . . The God-charged universe of Cotton Mather and Jonathan Edwards has narrowed to a common sense world that would have gladdened the heart of Benjamin Franklin. (110)

To Gilmore's way of thinking, the central failure of characters in *Wieland* is their fall into simplistic Enlightenment optimism via their failure to accept the Calvinist doctrine of original sin and predestination.

While numerous readers of Brown's work have flirted with its sociohistorical status, many such readings have balked at what must seem too strict a socially and historically referential analysis. William Hedges is representative when he insists that "Brown gives [his tale] no plausible social context, indeed does his best to isolate both Wieland and his almost equally fanatical father from any contact with American Protestantism" (120). Hedges's objection stems from a reductive assumption that fictional narratives represent historical data in direct and obvious ways, an expectation that has, in fact, hampered cultural criticism in the United States at least since Lionel Trilling's influential diagnosis-become-dictum that American literature has only a tangential relationship to American social reality. David Brion Davis articulates another prevalent strategy when he advances, and then immediately retracts, the skeleton of a historicized approach. After suggesting that *Wieland*'s early accounts of the family's European past, its tale of the elder Wieland's persecution and emigration to the colonies, and the suggestively Calvinist and Enlightenment ideologies represented by Theodore Wieland and Henry Pleyel are "almost an allegory of American colonial history," Davis immediately cautions that "such a drama of historical allegory cannot be pushed too far" (89), though he provides neither a sense of limits nor any rationale for this barrier.

Norman Grabo formulates a compatible devaluation of *Wieland*'s historical reference, providing an aesthetic rationale. According to Grabo,

> to say that Wieland is about the evils of religious fanaticism, or about the inadequacy of the human senses, or about a young girl's fear of hysterical madness may be correct, but only coarsely approximates what the story is doing. We come much closer to the enigma of this book when we say it is about the growing consciousness of the desire for power, the desire to be God. This force is powerful, deadly, and strangely erotic, and marrying it finally to some kind of rationality (as Clara finally marries Pleyel) is not achieved without trauma. (179)

Grabo here replaces whatever historical frame he implies through terms such as "religious fanaticism" and "the inadequacy of the human senses" (roughly the Calvinist and Enlightenment frames of reference I am interested in) with the psychodrama of an individual will to power. Readings which would posit more specific and historically conditioned readings can, in Grabo's view, "only coarsely" approach the narrative's real core. Grabo fills out his interpretive scheme with a timeless, universalist bias characteristic more of American "cultural criticism" of the 1950s and 1960s when he adds:

> Brown, however, does not use his fiction primarily to explore abstract ideas or philosophical absolutes. This is the direction Poe would take. Instead Brown rests in human experience, in the confused hints and uncertainties, the sufferings and anxieties that complicate all relationships of property and sex. . . . Brown's fiction is a muddled process, then, by nature enigmatic and paradoxical because the process is constant and universal, and therefore timeless. (185)

Grabo opposes the representation of "abstract ideas" or "philosophical absolutes" with what he valorizes as a patient examination of the particularities of individual human "sufferings and anxieties," a split reminiscent of Lionel Trilling's elevation of the writings of Henry James over those of Theodore Dreiser and virtually the entire naturalist tradition by virtue of James's more "human" and more "intimate" ability to plumb the depths of individual consciousness. Again, I would trace at least part of Davis's hesitancy and Grabo's "aesthetics" to the cultural moment of Davis's own writing—to the dominance of the Trillingesque vision of American fiction and to the difficulty post-McCarthyite America posed to culturally and historically interested critics attempting to formulate critical perspectives on the American past.[8] For them, human pathology, the human condition, or the convenient fallibility of "human nature" were acceptable foci of moral and ethical critique, but systematic institutional corruption or structural inequalities were off-limits.

Even from this perspective, however, there is a contradiction at the heart of Grabo's paradigm. His stress on "the confused hints and uncertainties, the sufferings and anxieties that complicate all relationships of property and sex" is offered as a justification for his subsequent universalization of Brown's thematics. We might challenge Grabo's assumptions on numerous grounds, primary among them the counterargument that it is precisely the particular "relationships of property and sex" that render Brown's narrative historically specific. To claim that such relations, whether of ownership or of sexuality, are universal simply seems untenable in a critical climate increasingly sensitive to the historical, class, racial, and gendered specificity of such social and cultural constructions. For whatever reasons, however, the contours of *Wieland*'s reception history have been determined until recently by a reigning ideology of literary and cultural consumption that devalued or denied certain possibilities for sociohistorical critical practices, even at the cost of incoherence and contradiction in assessments such as Grabo's.

Brown's text establishes its cultural context in several decisive ways, not all of which are coherent or mutually compatible. Immediately, in his prefatory "Advertisement," the novelist situates his tale and his characters in a specific historical milieu: the period between the French and Indian Wars and the Revolution, in other words, in a period of religious, political, and economic ferment. Clara Wieland calls attention to these upheavals early in her narrative:

> The sound of war had been heard, but it was at such a distance as to enhance our enjoyment by affording objects of comparison. . . . Revolutions and battles, however calamitous to those

who occupied the scene, contributed in some sort to our happiness, by agitating our minds with curiosity, and furnishing
causes of patriotic exultation. (26)[9]

Brown situates his narrative within so volatile a historical moment,
yet abstracts his characters and main action to its periphery, in
order, I believe, to test the efficacy of conflicting social theories in a
laboratory-like vacuum. William Hedges argues as much when he asserts that "immediately behind Brown's work lie the tensions of the
1790's, a period of the testing of the new Constitution. These tensions
were strikingly like the ones that Marius Bewley says constituted the
split in American Experience" (113). Hedges, however, fails to pursue
the significance that split assumes in Brown 's text.

The second, perhaps primary, way that *Wieland* mediates a specific
social moment lies in the manner in which Brown contextualizes his
characters with striking historical depth, aligning the Wielands with
a spectrum of American Puritan ideas, Pleyel with cliches of Enlightenment rhetoric, and Carwin the ventriloquist with Catholic (both
upper- and lowercase) liberalism. While Brown's own upbringing as
well as that of his most influential intellectual mentor, Robert Proud,
was Quaker, there is no reason to suggest that his narrative cannot
be read with reference to the culturally and socially more influential
form of religious enthusiasm that we commonly call Puritan. Consistent with this approach, Alan Axelrod goes so far as to suggest that
Proud himself frequently seemed more compatible with the stern-
ness, occasional morbidity, and rhetorical excesses of Puritanism than
with the pacifist leanings of orthodox Quakers (71–74). Furthermore,
Axelrod comments that

> the novelist's religious ambivalence suggests that, while Charles
> Brockden Brown indeed was not Young Goodman Brown the
> Puritan, neither was he, say, John Woolman or William Penn the
> Quaker. We should, in any case, avoid stereotyping Quakerism
> as the mild religion of Woolman and Penn; it could, of course,
> take other forms as well. (70)

I would argue, consistent with Axelrod's own perspective, that
Brown's personal background or affiliations are not adequate, nor are

they consistent or definable enough, to account for, let alone to limit, the frame of reference of his fictional work.

Brown's text begins as many Puritan sermons, poems, and diary entries end (and, for that matter, as Franklin's *Autobiography* begins) —with the "Application": "Make what use of the tale you shall think proper. If it be communicated to the world, it will inculcate the duty of avoiding deceit. It will exemplify the force of early impressions, and show the immeasurable evils that flow from an erroneous or imperfect discipline" (5). Of course the discipline that comes immediately to mind in *Wieland* is Carwin's careless use of his biloquism. He hasn't practiced enough "discipline" in the sense of discretion or care. However, if we read "discipline" in the sense of "a branch of knowledge or of teaching," as in an intellectual discipline, we get a different angle on Brown's moral. In that case, the Calvinism/antinomianism of the Wielands, and of the history of American Protestantism in general, and the Enlightenment rationality of Pleyel emerge as erroneous or imperfect disciplines, imperfect just as Clara's father's account of his bizarre experience in the summerhouse/temple is judged "an imperfect tale" by reason that "half the truth had been suppressed." Furthermore, this emphasis renders as feeble Clara's concluding remarks on the shared responsibility and mutual complicity of Wieland and herself in the disasters that have befallen their family. As Clara concludes her work, she offers this final analysis of their fates:

> the evils of which Carwin and Maxwell were the authors, owed their existence to the errors of the sufferers. . . . If Wieland had framed juster notions of moral duty, and of the divine attributes; or if I had been gifted with ordinary equanimity or foresight, the double-tongued deceiver would have been baffled and repelled. (244)

Clara's admission here is not without its own hazards and subtleties. Among other difficulties is her complete silence with relation to Pleyel's own frenzy of jealousy, generated by his own "imperfect discipline." Both Wieland and Pleyel jump to rash and, as far as we can tell, completely incorrect conclusions as a result of their reliance on limited auditory impressions. And in both cases, those impressions are deeply associated with their expressed ideological beliefs and agendas. In other words, the theoretical rigor of these still vital colonial ideologies produces a one-dimensional and hence, for Brown, dogmatic vision that deconstructs, through its rigid systematization, its own inner coherence.

Brown situates the Wielands (father and son) within a Calvinistic lineage through significant textual data, the narrative presences that establish the framework within which the various absences are constructed. The elder Wieland, like numerous Puritan converts (Quakers as well), becomes converted by an accidental insight into Scripture. He glances at an open text of the Cammisards (a French antinomian sect, especially significant considering the "antinomian" extremism of Theodore Wieland) and his eyes light on the words "Seek and ye shall find." This reading experience transforms the elder Wieland's life, and he devotes himself to biblical study. For the elder Wieland, we learn that the Bible "was the fountain beyond which it was unnecessary to trace the stream of religious truth; but it was his duty to trace it thus far" (9). Thus begins his Puritan-like devotion to textual purification. Like the Puritans, Wieland's residence in England becomes "almost impossible, on account of his religious tenets," and he emigrates to America. Brown adds more density to Wieland by connecting him with Puritan codes of behavior, dress, and style:

> The empire of religious duty extended itself to his looks, gestures, and phrases. All levities of speech, and negligences of behaviour, were proscribed. His air was mournful and contemplative. He laboured to keep alive a sentiment of fear, and a belief of the awe-creating presence of the Deity. Ideas foreign to this were sedulously excluded. To suffer their intrusion was a crime against Divine Majesty inexpiable but by days and weeks of the keenest agonies. (9)

Once successful in his quest for religious freedom, Wieland also embarks on the missionary quest among the "unbelieving nations," here the North American Indians:

> In addition to these motives for seeking a new habitation, there was another of the most imperious and irresistible necessity. He had imbibed an opinion that it was his duty to disseminate the

truths of the gospel among the unbelieving nations. . . . The belief, after every new conflict with his passions, acquired new strength; and, at length, he formed a resolution of complying with what he deemed the will of heaven. (10)

Brown adds a deviant turn to Wieland's regimen. Wieland

was frugal, regular, and strict in the performance of domestic duties. He allied himself with no sect, because he perfectly agreed with none. Social worship is that by which they are all distinguished; but this article found no place in his creed. He rigidly interpreted the precept which enjoins us, when we worship, to retire into solitude, and shut out every species of society. According to him devotion was not only a silent office, but must be performed alone. (11)

The son, Theodore Wieland, is consistent with his father in many respects, suggesting Brown's bizarre collapsing of genetic determinism and divine predestination into a terrifying design of fatalistic doom. The similarities between her brother and father arouse Clara's fears that she, by virtue of being of the Wieland blood, may be doomed, singled out and fattened up for some awful visitation of divine wrath. Theodore Wieland's deportment, as Clara narrates, was grave, and his mind was "enriched by science, and embellished with literature" (23); he pursues a life dedicated to "settling and restoring the purity of the text" (24). Clara defines her brother precisely thus: "Moral necessity, and calvinistic inspiration, were the props on which my brother thought proper to repose" (25). What Brown embeds in his construction of the Wieland males is a catalog of attributes spanning the history of the radical Protestant settlement in North America, including a condensation of the general history of immigration due to persecution, the missionary zeal among the Indians of a John Eliot, the anxiety both feel over the state of souls, an abundance of self-mortification and discipline, and the purging of foreign elements in their thinking, reminiscent of the rigidity and brutality commonly ascribed to John Endicott. Clara also characterizes her father and her brother in terms reminiscent of the Puritan aesthetic of the "plaine stile" and characteristic simplicity of demeanor, both of which eschewed all ornamentation and carriage not specifically rooted in Scripture and not functionally necessary. She notes that her father's religious duties extended to his "looks, gestures, and phrases," and she returns to the idea elsewhere in her narrative. Her father's temple, for example, "was without seat, table, or ornament of any kind," and, when she begins reading her father's manuscript later in the novel, she mentions that "the narrative was by no means recommended by its eloquence; but neither did all its value flow from my relationship to the author. Its stile had an unaffected and picturesque simplicity" (12, 83).

Wieland's specific constellation of religious duties does not correspond to any particular, traditional practice common to the Puritans who settled in New England. It does, however, resonate with both historical and literary significance. As Darrett Rutman, T. H. Breen, and others have demonstrated, Puritanism as a socioreligious construct fragmented into scores of splintered and often irreconcilable beliefs and practices depending, theoretically, on differing interpretations of Scripture, but also very practically on both regional differences in immigrants' English backgrounds and the dates of their migrations.[10] As Rutman argues, the differences between congregations were so fundamental that the only viable definition he can offer of American Puritanism is the specific relationship between a minister and his congregation. He cautions precisely those who would hold up some monolithic idea of "actual" or "authentic" Puritanism against various bastardized forms by reminding us that "Puritanism as a historian's concept is an artificial construct, a formulation of reality rather than a reality itself, a part of the framework by which the historian orders his data" (x). David D. Hall's recent study of "popular religious beliefs in early New England" also documents a religious culture which, while loosely united according to some practices and beliefs, was wildly fragmented, incoherent even, at the level of popular belief and worship, especially in the range of superstitious and apocalyptic beliefs adhered to by many early settlers. The problem is that many literary critics intent on ruling out an approach to Brown's text which focuses on its "Puritan" aspect lag far behind the notion of Puritan New England currently subscribed to by the community of American colonial historians. Brown's representation anticipates, in its extremes of solipsism and antisocial behavior, those very traits which Hawthorne would later draw on to construct his "Puritans," including Young Goodman Brown, Richard Digby (the man of adamant), and the Reverend Mr. Hooper, none of whom bear much likeness to "actual" or "real" Puritans. Brown, accordingly, could be distilling this entire history of fragmentation, splintering, and ecclesiastical infighting into the lonesome, antisocial Wieland, whose purity of belief allows of no sectarian fellowship. Lawrence Buell's *New England Literary Culture: From Revolution through Renaissance* persuasively demonstrates that American writing through the mid–nineteenth century struggled to formulate adequate notions of and representational practices for revisiting early New England culture. Given Buell's findings, that Brown's narrative neither articulates a "pure" Puritanism nor meshes with our current understanding of the complexity of "Puritan" culture is neither remarkable nor damning. In all likelihood, Brown pioneered the representation of "Puritans" in the literature of the United States.[11]

That Theodore Wieland resembles, in his fixation on voices, the subjective extreme within Puritanism often called "antinomianism" is a given in much *Wieland* criticism. As Moses Coit Tyler quaintly characterized the psychological state of many settlers in early New England, "they had overpowering manifestations of spiritual force; they heard awful voices in the air; strange sights glimmered before their eyes on the verge of the forest, or flitted along the sea" (137). More recently and less impressionistically, David D. Hall has deepened our understanding of the preeminence not only of mysterious "voices" but of many other phenomena of great interest to early New England settlers. To Hall,

> the people of seventeenth-century New England lived in an enchanted universe. Theirs was a world of wonders. Ghosts came to people in the night, and trumpets blared, though no one saw the trumpeters. Nor could people see the lines of force that made a "long staff dance up and down in the chimney" of William Morse's house in Newbury. In this enchanted world, the sky on a "clear day" could fill with "many companies of armed men in the air, clothed in light-colored garments, and the commander

in sad [somber]." The townsfolk of New Haven saw a phantom ship sail regally into the harbor. . . . *Voices spoke from heaven and children from their cradles.* (*Worlds of Wonder* 71; my emphasis)

Reminding us that the Bible, with "its narratives of visions, voices, witches, and strange deaths," underwrote much of the Puritans' preternatural sensitivity to such mysteries, and that "St. John in Revelation foresaw the 'voice' of God in thunder, lightning, and earthquakes," Hall demonstrates that "visions, dreams, apparitions, unseen voices—all of these were almost everyday encounters, talked about in private and a matter of experience" in Puritan New England (75, 79, 86). Even John Winthrop, who quickly and violently drew the line at the voices of "immediate revelation" Anne Hutchinson claims to have heard, carefully and credulously recorded many such auditory enigmas in his journal (Hall 92).

What has not been noted, however, is that Wieland expresses virtually the same sentiments that condemn Hutchinson when he recounts the history of his murderous acts in courtroom testimony. In the midst of his premurder ecstasy Wieland exclaims, "O! That I might be admitted to thy presence; that mine were the supreme delight of knowing thy will, and of performing it! The blissful privilege of *direct communication with thee,* and of listening to the audible enunciations of thy pleasure!" (166; my emphasis). It was, of course, Anne Hutchinson's insistence that she enjoyed direct communication with God—that "the person of the Holy Ghost dwells in a justified person" (Winthrop 195)—as she believed all Puritans must, that threatened the authority of both heavenly and earthly law as interpreted by the ministers and magistrates of Massachusetts Bay. The transcripts of Hutchinson's interrogation by officials of the Puritan theocracy return frequently to her assertion of "immediate revelation."[12] Indeed, at one pivotal moment during her hearing, Hutchinson herself questioned the deputy governor Thomas Dudley: "How did Abraham know that it was God that bid him offer his son, being a breach of the sixth commandment?" When given the expected answer, "by an immediate voice," Hutchinson responded, "so to me by an immediate revelation . . . by the voice of his own spirit to my soul" (Hall, *Antinomian*

Controversy 337). And in one of his own summaries, Winthrop encapsulated Hutchinson's position in similar language:

> the ground work of her revelations is the immediate revelation of the spirit and not by the ministry of the word. And that is the means by which she hath very much abused the country that they shall look for revelations and are not bound to the ministry of the word, but God will teach them by immediate revelations and this hath been the ground of all these tumults and troubles. (Hall 341–42)

The magistrates found the antinomian threat so palpable that, following Hutchinson's sentencing, the theocracy ordered "the disfranchising and disarming of her closest adherents, who might at any moment receive an immediate revelation directing them to kill her judges" (Morgan, *Puritan Dilemma* 153). The Puritans, it seems, lived in fear of God once again ordering the faithful to murder, a fear at the core of Brown's narrative. Hutchinson's uncompromising resituation of the individual Christian's personal relationship with God, while defensible from within orthodox Puritan beliefs, simply pushed the individualistic bent of the faith too far and threatened anarchy, religious and social, a theme which Jane Tompkins and other critics have often investigated in their writings on Brown. By having Wieland thus reiterate the very concept at the core of the antinomian crisis, *Wieland* represents not just any such eccentric, individualistic departures from strict theocratic orthodoxy, but the very specific and influential case of Anne Hutchinson.

Clara extends the range of the narrative's referential scope when she borrows from the rhetoric of Jonathan Edwards's famous Enfield sermon in her speculations concerning her father's death. Recall that one of Clara's unresolved lines of questioning regarding her father's demise asked, "Was this the penalty of disobedience? this the stroke of a *vindictive and invisible hand?*" (19; my emphasis). The allusion to Edwards's "Sinners in the Hands of an Angry God" is tempting. Moreover, later in the novel she returns to the annihilatory imagery of that sermon when she recounts her anguished response to seeing the mysterious light associated with her father's death and hearing threatening voices: "I was desirous, but unable, to obey; these gleams were such as preluded the stroke by which he fell; the hour, perhaps, was the same—I shuddered as if I had beheld, *suspended over me, the exterminating sword*" (64; my emphasis). Of course Edwards's sermon is saturated with graphic images not only of God suspending us (as though we were loathsome spiders) over a fire and brandishing his terrible sword, but also of Him crushing us like grapes and sprinkling his white raiment with our blood, of God's anger rising like flood waters, and of God's bow being bent "and the arrow ready on the string," ready at any moment to be "made drunk with your blood" (162, 158, 159). As he generalizes, "the arrows of death fly unseen at noonday; the sharpest sight cannot discern them. God has so many different unsearchable ways of taking wicked men out of the world" (154). This particular passage in *Wieland* echoes one of Edwards's most vivid representations of the obliterating force God wields over human beings, that of the exterminating sword Edwards images God holding over his congregation's heads. As Edwards puts it, "the glittering sword is whet, and held over them, and the pit hath opened its mouth under them" (153).

But Brown's work with Edwards also takes less direct forms. For example, when Clara defines Theodore as someone "who deemed it indispensable to examine the ground of his belief" (23), she imports Edwards's repeated warnings of the flimsiness of the "grounds" upon which we literally stand and upon which we figuratively predicate our beliefs. Edwards uses the metaphor of rotting skin covering the abyss over which we hover and into which we are doomed by our own gravity to plummet should God not choose to save us: "unconverted men walk over the pit of hell on a rotten covering, and there are innumerable places in this covering so weak that they will not bear their weight, and these places are not seen" (154). Clara's reference to "moral necessity, and calvinistic inspiration," as the "props upon which [her] brother thought proper to repose" (25) similarly recalls Edwards's rhetorical deconstruction of the stability of any bracing—architectural, communal, physical, philosophical—short of God upon which any belief can rest.

Several critics have observed other Edwardsian echoes throughout *Wieland*. Shirley Samuels, for instance, notes the ways in which "Wieland's account of his journey to God . . . incongruously echoes several passages in Jonathan Edwards's 'Personal Narrative'" (64). Michael Gilmore argues that Clara's denial of evil as integral to human nature rejects Edwards's thinking in "The Great Christian Doctrine of Original Sin" (115), and Norman Grabo compares Theodore's reasoning to that of Edwards in *The Nature of True Virtue* (188). Finally, suggesting that "the line from Edwards to Franklin, and from Edwards to Emerson and Thoreau, is . . . more direct than we might imagine," Emily Miller Budick argues that

> according to Brown, the logical outcome of Edwards's Great Awakening might just be a Theodore Wieland, elevated to the role of saint, or, indeed, to the role of biblical type or even antitype, by a relocation of the typological moment in a natural universe understood as controlled by eschatological patterns. (33–34)

These many references to and echoes from Edwards's work and reputation further establish Brown's characterizations of the Wieland family (especially the Wieland males) as a revisionist history of American Puritanism, from their shared persecution in Europe through the time of John Winthrop and Anne Hutchinson to that of Jonathan Edwards. That the names of Winthrop, Hutchinson, and Edwards never appear in Brown's text is, I argue, fully consistent with the oblique referential strategy he deploys throughout *Wieland*. To find them, we must seek well beyond the borders of Brown's single text. Furthermore, by virtue of these allusive prompts, Brown narrows the focus of his critique to the violence inhering in the discourses of Puritanism which his narrative will return to in the gory crescendo of its dramatic action and to which we will return shortly.

Viewing *Wieland's* violence merely as religious fanaticism or as insanity (though it clearly partakes of both) obscures the degree to which those acts also resonate with Puritan history and rhetoric. Of course, the actual motives for all of Wieland's murders (not to mention the actual cause of his father's incendiary death) remain absent from the narrative. While various characters harbor conflicting suspicions, all such surmises remain totally without substantiation and, as in the case of Clara's assuming that Carwin is responsible, wildly contradictory and out of synch with numerous narrative details. Of all the examples of sought-for proof and certainty, an irrefragable *source* of the novel's mysteries remains the most inscrutably *un*found. Nevertheless, the excess of historical detail pointing to similarities between the Wieland family history and the history of Puritan settlement of New England establishes the scaffolding for a historicizing of the violence enacted within the narrative by Theodore Wieland. The narrative absence of his particular motives and incitements is so egregious that, coupled with the surfeit of significantly positioned historical detail and psychological characterization, it merges in a narrative calculus which invites the importation of historical data (elicited via the excess of historical signification early in the narrative) to supplement the vexing absences which obscure the psychohistorical significance of the murders committed by Theodore Wieland.

In fact, Brown establishes a complex ensemble of narrative signals that direct us to a particular, though not necessarily deeply specified, dimension of early American history. First, the overdetermined characterization of both Wieland men with reference to American Puritan ideology establishes a critical mass of historical allusions framing the narrative action. Second, the proliferation throughout the text of examples of characters (and readers) seeking for but not finding answers to the novel's many mysteries, gaps, and elisions suggests that the intranarrative dimension of *Wieland* cannot provide the data needed to unravel its many enigmas. Finally, Brown establishes an elaborate system of extratextual referents for some of the narrative's puzzles in footnotes, in the "Advertisement," and in the supplementary narrative of "Memoirs of Carwin the Biloquist," without which many of the novel's details are either incredible or simply unavailable. This system dramatizes (almost itself as a narrative thematic) the necessity of a transtextual hermeneutic capable of ranging freely outside narrative borders in pursuit of significant supplementary data and evidence in the various discourses the narrative solicits via its densely historicized early chapters. I should expand on my initial revisionist, post-Derridian manifesto: "Il n'y a pas de dedans du texte"; that is, there is nothing *inside* the text. While the specific relevant moments which *Wieland*'s system of historical mediation elicits are themselves not *in* Brown's novel per se, both the narrative scaffolding and its thematic core ("seek and ye shall find") establish the necessary textual milieu within which such historicizing can occur.

How, though, does such a practice enable us more fully to pursue a narrative issue which is everywhere dominant but nowhere visible? I suggest that Brown's textualized drama of presence and absence draws into *Wieland* a parallel dynamic from the first century and a half of the Protestant settlement of North America, specifically the reality that Puritan history was, in many respects, a bloody legacy not only of exclusionary violence directed against dissenting sects and peoples but also of an essentially gothic and bloody religious discursive system in which neither the actual nor the discursive violence essential to its consolidation and maintenance was ever publicly recognized as such. Like the murderous rampages of Theodore Wieland, ostensibly carried out with divine blessing, the violence of North American settlement (and the internalized violence of the same religious vision) remained illegible as grotesque and genocidal precisely because of the belief that the purification of the gospel in New England was itself both divinely mandated and carried out under divine surveillance. Brown's work in *Wieland* recapitulates the bloody legacy of North American Puritanism from a full panoply of discursive sites.

v

I would like to return to the Abrahamic moment and the examples of spousal murder and infanticide with which I opened. The most chilling moments in *Wieland*—those which recount Theodore Wieland's murder of his family and Louisa Conway—are most commonly read as quintessentially gothic and definitive of Brown's "founding" of a dark narrative tradition that stands as an affront to American pieties. These same moments, however, can also be resituated as Brown's comprehensive reinscription of the common, though grotesque, specifics of America's cultural past. Wieland recounts the murder of his wife in horrifying detail:

> When she could speak no longer, her gestures, her looks appealed to my compassion. My accursed hand was irresolute and tremulous. I meant thy death to be sudden, thy struggles to be

brief. Alas! my heart was infirm; my resolves mutable. Thrice I
slackened my grasp, and life kept its hold, though in the midst
of pangs. Her eye-balls started from their sockets. Grimness and
distortion took place of all that used to bewitch me into transport, and subdue me into reverence. (172)

After throttling his wife to death, Theodore Wieland remarks, "I was
commissioned to kill thee, but not to torment thee," and then rhap-
sodizes:

This was a moment of triumph. Thus had I successfully subdued
the stubbornness of human passions: the victim which had been
demanded was given: the deed was done past recal.
    I lifted the corpse in my arms and laid it on the bed. I gazed
upon it with delight. Such was the elation of my thoughts, that
I even broke into laughter. I clapped my hands and exclaimed,
"It is done! My sacred duty is fulfilled. To that I have sacrificed,
O my God! thy last and best gift, my wife!" (172)

We also know that Wieland was far more brutal in his destruction
of his other victims. Clara reports that she was denied the right of
kissing Louisa Conway's corpse because "such had been the merciless
blow that destroyed her, that not a *lineament remained*" (157; emphasis in original).

Such hyperbole and gore are, to be sure, mainstays in horror fiction and, as David Reynolds demonstrates, saturate the later fiction of
Edgar Allan Poe and many other gothic writers operating "beneath the
American Renaissance," often without any "redeeming" focus. However, throughout *Wieland* Brown repeatedly anchors the most bizarre
and novel occurrences in some transnarrative world, by virtue of the
footnotes and other explanatory gestures (to recent events—that is,
the Yates murders—and the like). I would offer that Brown deploys
such deictic maneuvers precisely to demystify the incredible, to remind his readers of the strangeness both of the everyday and of the
new nation's colonial past, and to return our attention to the world
referred to by his narrative. Brown thus establishes a working relationship between the narrative *Wieland* and the entire ensemble of
data—theological, popular religious, aesthetic, social, political, legal,

and scientific—within which and from which the narrative generates its own discursive archive.

The Pequot massacre, the Salem witch trials, the persecution of the Quakers, and the antinomian crisis are, of course, only the most explicit and widely recognized horizon within which Wieland's religious violence becomes legible. The Puritan penal code provided a juridical basis for overtly inner-directed (and often sadistic) policing. As Moses Coit Tyler observed, "toward the criminal the judges stood not alone as civil magistrates, punishing him in order to prevent others from becoming like him, but as *ministers of divine wrath giving the wretch in this world a foretaste of the pains of hell*" (115; my emphasis). John Winthrop's *History of New England,* for example, recounts some particularly imaginative cases. We read, thus, of a man being "severely whipped and kept in hold for [mere] suspicion of slander, idleness, and stubbornness," and of another who, "for making a fraudulent bargain with a child, had to stand for two hours with his hands tied up to a bar, and a basket of stones hanged about his neck." For committing "an atrocious act of shame," a man named Fairfield, Winthrop notes, was sentenced to be

> severely whipped at Boston, to be severely whipped again at Salem, then to return to Boston and have one nostril slit and seared, next to go back to Salem and have the other nostril slit and seared, then to be kept on Boston Neck so long as he lived, to wear a halter visibly about his throat during the remainder of his life, to be whipped if he should appear abroad without it, and to die if he repeated the original offence. (quoted in Tyler 115–16)

Fairfield was also fined forty pounds.[13]

Winthrop elsewhere reveals a disturbing self-righteousness upon being told that Anne Hutchinson had given birth to a deformed child and, later, that she had been slaughtered by Indians during her exile, seeing in her death not a tragedy of immense human loss, but a divine confirmation of his and his community's judgment and banishment of Hutchinson. Of her giving birth to "a monstrous" child, Winthrop notes that the event signified "her error in denying inherent righteousness," but quickly adds "but that all was Christ in us, and nothing of ours in our faith, love, etc." (277) to assure himself of his own righteousness. Each of these examples was scrupulously rationalized and prescribed by Puritan religious and legal codes, just as Theodore Wieland's murders were committed with God's sanction.[14] According to Kai T. Erikson in *Wayward Puritans,* "perhaps the most terrifying thing about punishment in Massachusetts Bay, after all, was not its fierceness but its cold righteousness. . . . Little attention was paid to the motives of the offender, the grief of the victim, . . . or any other human emotion. The whole process had a flat, mechanical tone because it dealt with the laws of nature rather than with the decisions of men" (188–89).

These are only the most palpable examples of Puritan violence, most of which are generated by specific events and social crises. There exists, however, an equally disturbing and barely suppressed violence (sometimes bordering on sadism) saturating much Puritan rhetoric, some of which is couched in decidedly positive terms and contexts. We know from Scripture that God could watch while Job was tortured, and we know, from the story of Abraham and Isaac, that God might tell a father to sacrifice his son.[15] The best-known and most influential such document in American culture is Edwards's "Sinners in the Hands of an Angry God." The anger and physical brutality of Edwards's God and the swift and violent engines threatening human subjects generate some of the most graphic annihilatory rhetoric in early American culture. In addition to enumerating the diverse naturalistic means by which humans can meet with their destruction, such as surging floodwaters, rapacious lions, and vertiginously slippery footing, Edwards offers numerous visions of God personally taking an active and instrumental role in destroying human beings. Edwards's God always threatens the total devastation of human life via means capable of obliterating all traces of human identity (after the fashions of Wieland and James Yates, Brown's immediate model). As Thomas J. Steele and Eugene R. Delay argue, this martial imagery, "with choler being associated with Mars, creates [in Edwards's sermon] the Lord God Sabaoth, the army-God, of the Old Testament" (249). David D. Hall has clarified that the images of violence deployed within Edwards's rhetoric were not in any way isolated functions of an individual personality or even of a specific historical moment. Noting the social and theological differences that he posits as characteristic of early New England existence, Hall states that "tension never vanished from this system, and *long-nurtured anger exploded* in the Great Awakening" (*Worlds of Wonder* 12; my emphasis).

Indeed, we find equally intense, if not always equally graphic, examples of religious violence elsewhere, perhaps merely literal extensions of St. Paul's adage that "the letter killeth, but the spirit giveth life" (2 Cor. 3.6). Early in 1637, during the first volleys of the antinomian crisis, John Wheelwright barged into John Cotton's afternoon lecture and, accusing him of abiding by a covenant of works, affirmed that true believers "must lay loade upon them, we must kille them with the worde of the Lorde" (Morgan 143). In the words of the Puritan divine Richard Sibbes, the sanctified Puritan was a literal Christian soldier, displaying "a holy violence in the performing of all duties" (Bremer 24). The prolific Increase Mather praised his father's style of preaching, declaring that "his way of Preaching was plain, aiming to shoot his Arrows not over the peoples heads, but into their Hearts and consciences" (Miller and Johnson 494). Edward Johnson, who, as Moses Coit Tyler characterized him, "handled the pen as he did the sword and broadaxe" (140), casts the Puritans quite frankly as warriors in his history, *Wonder Working Providence of Sions Savior,* provoking Peter Gay to label it "a naive military bulletin reporting Christ's victories against Satan in America" (53). Johnson does, in fact, organize his history with militaristic tropes of looming destruction. He exhorts the colonists, for example, to "let military discipline be had in high esteem among you. Gentlemen, Corporales, and fellow soldiers, keep your weapons [among which he enumerates artillery, swords, rapiers, and all other piercing weapons, including, conceivably, Theodore Wieland's penknife] in continual readiness" (10, 11). It seems clear that Johnson does not restrict his import to the metaphorical "sharp sword of Christ's word" (as implicitly violent as that is), but fully embraces, military man that he was, a vision of the Puritans marching manfully and well armed against Christ's enemies, literal and figurative.

Oddly, the violence of such Puritan rhetoric was not reserved for enemies in any simple sense of the word. Early New England culture anticipated more recent times in its fascination with the languages of violence. According to Hall, both commercial and "godly" publica-

tions in the seventeenth century featured lurid and sensational repre-
sentions of various forms of mayhem, often explicitly fictional:

> Fables, marvels, tales of "preternatural" events—as in Foxe's
> *Book of Martyrs,* so in Increase Mather's *Essay* and cheap forms of
> print, such kinds of writing [obviously fabulous and grotesque
> tales] passed as versions of reality. Fact and fiction intermingled.
> Nor were printers unique in their fascination with the theme
> of violence. Nature was for them a matter of destructive storms
> and "fiery" meteors that verged on being instruments of human
> death—and often were, as in the lightning storm that Trundle
> described in *A Miracle, of Miracles.* Violence was a feature of the
> witchcraft stories, tales of martyrs undergoing torture, and nar-
> ratives of murders. But godly writers followed suit. (*Worlds of
> Wonder* 112)

Indeed, many of the more sensational genres that David Reynolds
posits as a cultural realm can be understood as continuations of such
lurid narratives that constituted a dominant strand in early colonial discourse.[16] We often witness similarly charged terms and scenes
playing decisive roles in Puritan poetry, even those works examining
the most intimate relations among family members. In Edward Taylor's "Upon Wedlock and Death of Children" is an obvious example.
Taylor constructs an elaborate conceit in which horticultural processes represent his marriage and the birth of his children. Into this
garden scheme of "beautious leaves," chirping birds, and blooming
flowers, God's hand enters literally as a grim reaper:

> But oh! a glorious hand from glory came,
>> Guarded with Angells, soon did Crop this flowre,
> Which almost tore the root up of the same,
>> At that unlookt for, Dolesome, darksome houre.

Taylor and his wife later lose another child to the same cropping
hand, with the second death captured in more hideous detail:

> But oh! the torture, Vomit, screechings, groans:
> And six weeks fever would pierce hearts like stones.

Of course, Taylor reprocesses these horrors as proof of God's love and of his eventual salvation, but such salvific reassurances cannot erase the heart-wrenching details of two babies dying. Taylor's God, rather like Edwards's, exacts what surely strikes many as a sadistic super-fluity of physical torture and pain.

It is Michael Wigglesworth's always excessive *The Day of Doom*, however, that comes closest to the specifics of the Wieland case in its representation of violence at the heart of early colonial religious life, especially in his representation of family members dramatizing God's destructive will. We know that Puritan doctrine cautioned against any person loving any earthly thing (including another person—spouse, child, parent, friend) overly much, for an earthly love might over-shadow one's proper love for God.[17] Wigglesworth's account of the final moments of earthly life and time, however, offers us particu-larly hardened examples of individuals taking intense pleasure at the damnation of their loved ones. *The Day of Doom* doesn't leave many familial relations unexamined:

197

One natural brother beholds another
   in this astonied fit,
Yet sorrows not thereat a jot,
   nor pities him a whit.
The godly wife conceives no grief,
   nor can she shed a tear
For the sad state of her dear mate,
   when she his doom doth hear.

198

He that was erst a husband pierced
   with sense of wife's distress,
Whose tender heart did bear a part
   of all her grievances,
Shall mourn no more as heretofore
   because of her ill plight;
Although he see her now to be
   a damned forsaken wight.

199

The tender mother will own no other
   of all her numerous brood,
But such as stand at Christ's right hand
   acquitted through His blood.
The pious father had now much rather
   his graceless son should lie
In hell with devils, for all his evils
   burning eternally.

200

Than God most high should injury,
.   by sparing him sustain;
And doth rejoice to hear Christ's voice
   adjudging him to pain.

In passages such as these, as well as in those depicting Wigglesworth's Christ, we witness, in the language of Brown's novel, transformations in the figure of Christ as well as in the human participants in this ultimate drama—from loving wives, bridegrooms, parents, and saviors into figures of absolute and unbending power and vengeance. Parents, spouses, and siblings would all rather cherish the vision of their loved ones falling into eternal torture than cause God to "sustain injury," however slightly any possible swerving from his plan of salvation and damnation might afflict the almighty.

These transformations carry the full weight of scriptural authority that would resonate with justice in the minds of generations of New Englanders raised on such texts as "I [Christ] also will laugh at your calamity; I will mock when your fear cometh" (Prov. 1.26). The chilling cruelty of parents not only accepting, but actually "rejoicing" in their children's damnation would not have struck a seventeenth- or eighteenth-century audience as barbaric or inhumane. Rather, as Jeffrey A. Hammond suggests,

> Puritan readers would have found it appropriate precisely *because* of its apparent inhumanity. Since the psalmist had affirmed that, like Christ, "The righteous shall rejoice when he seeth the vengeance" (Ps. 58.10), the saints' vindictive glee was for

Wigglesworth's readers a sign that the restored will of the elect had been made entirely consistent with God's. Once human attachments were replaced with divine love, the very categories by which people defined their relationships with one another would be utterly destroyed. (51; emphasis in original)

What has quite likely struck many readers as *Wieland*'s most horrifying, most extreme, and most implausible moment intersects with, and, given Brown's interest in historical writing, is quite possibly constructed out of, a vast range of Puritan texts, social and cultural. The utter transformation of Theodore Wieland in these passages would have rung too recently authentic to be marginalized as the frenzied and unpredictable act of a homicidal madman. Just as many citizens would rather believe that political violence and assassinations are the acts of individual psychopaths rather than the result of carefully managed and orchestrated conspiracies, many readers have preferred attributing Theodore Wieland's murderous rampage to mental disease or gothic convention, anything other than viewing him as a highly compressed critique of the violence inherent in the beliefs and practices of Puritan "founding fathers." Rather than an anomalous quirk in this narrative world, and rather than a rupture pointing out the inadequacy of Enlightenment reason in the abstract, the murders in *Wieland* elicit and resituate the logics and dynamics of specific formations from earlier and contemporary American culture. This reading encourages us to revise the valorization of Brown's apparently sensationalistic strain and to reimagine him more aggressively as a historian of American colonial culture, densely rooted in the specific texts and histories of seventeenth- and eighteenth-century American social and cultural life.

I have focused on the historical density of Brown's representational scheme with particular reference to its commentary on the ideology of early New England Puritanism. Even though their characters are far less clearly determined and motivated than is Theodore Wieland's, the roles of Pleyel as embodiment of Enlightenment rationality and Carwin as ventriloquistic avatar of Catholic liberalism could similarly be situated within dense historical contexts. While we get detailed information concerning Carwin's background and motivations,

we get little of Henry Pleyel's family lineage, surely nothing comparable to the densely social and historical specificity that Clara provides concerning her own family's background. We do not know the
Pleyel family's traits, their psychohistories, their family nightmares,
as we know those of the Wielands. However, despite the differences
between Wieland's reliance on "moral necessity, and calvinistic inspiration," and Pleyel's on "intellectual liberty" and the evidence of his
reason, the two characters are revealed as similarly one-dimensional
in their ideological predispositions. Clara thus positions Pleyel within
specific contemporary ideological contours, even though those contours are not projected as historically determined, not narrated as
causally or teleologically rooted in a prior historical moment. It is
precisely Pleyel's contemporaneity, his apparent dislocation from any
historical burden, wherein lies his sociohistorical status as commentary on Enlightenment rationality.

Carwin's Catholicism, his ideological catholicity, not surprisingly,
figures as a principle of deconstruction or, from a Bakhtinian perspective, of dialogical destabilization within the text. By virtue of his
ventriloquism, his ability to speak as though from various positions,
he exposes the aporias inherent in both Wieland's and Pleyel's ideological stances. Carwin's vocal projections make it impossible to determine the exact origin, intention, and meaning of the novel's many
mysterious "voices" and, as a result, decenter and carnivalize the rigid
systems by which both Wieland and Pleyel structure their lives. We
should recall that both Wieland and Pleyel unquestioningly accept
the truth of the various voices they hear because their respective
worldviews set them up to validate whatever environmental prompts
confirm their belief systems. As Clara defines them, Wieland relies exclusively on "moral necessity, and calvinistic inspiration" and Pleyel
on "intellectual liberty," "reason," and sensory evidence (25). We
should also recall that Carwin's humble origins and Ludloe's duping
and manipulation of him position Carwin as a spokesperson for the
disenfranchised and oppressed. His fragmented vocal performances
articulate something like the language of the marginalized and oppressed. The class-specificity of Carwin's ventriloquism, then, is an
important alternative to the crypto-aristocratic privilege and stability
of the leisured lives enjoyed by the entire Mettingen group. Bringing

a similar perspective to another of Brown's works, Cathy Davidson makes an important point:

It did not . . . take the twentieth century to invent Derrida or Bakhtin. *Arthur Mervyn* . . . might best be seen as an early American version of Bakhtin's "dialogical" text, a carnivalesque performance in which the author resolutely refuses to delimit his intentions while also allowing his characters their own ambiguities and even a spirit of "revolt" against any constraining proprieties the text might threaten to impose. In Bakhtin's view, the dialogical text is particularly subversive since it challenges complacency, forces the reader's active participation in the text, and resolutely refuses to assuage uncertainty with comforting, final solutions. (253)

I would only add that Brown constructs an equally "deconstructive" drama in *Wieland,* embedding the very principles of rhetorical and thematic dismantling in his proletarian character, Carwin.

A fuller treatment of the novel could profitably pursue such historical and theoretical density in both Pleyel and Carwin, situating their beliefs, actions, and rhetorical performances within the appropriate discourses of Enlightenment colonial and early Republican United States. The main point of this discussion, however, has not been to mount a totalizing reading of Brown's first novel, but to rehearse the assumptions and practices that I will pursue throughout *Loose Ends,* albeit in more detail than I will in the following discussions. Like the foregoing discussion of *Wieland,* the readings that follow will characterize the moment or moments that emerge as "loose ends" within their respective narratives and will then pursue the intertextual environments and supplementary discourses that their various allusive schemes elicit. I will consider the critical histories of the works I engage insofar as they press significantly on my own concerns and agenda, usually to demonstrate the inertia that has accrued around formalist-inspired readings of these works, and, in some cases, the outright assault on historicizing interpretive practices. Sometimes the loose ends will be visible only in the concluding moments of these works. As is the case with *Wieland,* sometimes the loose ends are issues that permeate the narratives but remain unaddressed and unaccounted for by the works' conclusions. Such is the case, for example, in my discussion of Emily Dickinson's poem "I started Early – Took my Dog –," in which the dog, which occupies so prominent a position as the final word in the poem's first line, simply drops out of the poem, although its absence, I argue, determines much of that poem's operation. In most cases, however, these narratives unravel in both ways.

I'm not sure that this trade is an evil. I want to be convinced of it. I'm sure it's a favor to these poor creatures to bring them to a Christian land. They are a thousand times better off. Here they can hear the gospel and have some chance of salvation. —Simeon Brown in Harriet Beecher Stowe's *The Minister's Wooing*

It's true. I *am* in love with the whole race. I never saw one of them that didn't have perfectly angelic manners. I think we shall all be black in heaven—that is, black souled. —Isabel March in William Dean Howells's *A Hazard of New Fortunes*

Ishmael begins his meditation on "The Whiteness of the Whale" in *Moby-Dick* by cataloging some of the color white's conventional qualities, such as "a certain royal pre-eminence," "gladness," "innocence," "benignity," "honor," "justice," and "the divine spotlessness of power" (188–89). As we know, however, Ishmael quickly fuses these significations with their opposites, and he concludes his reflections with these chilling thoughts:

> Is it that by its indefiniteness it shadows forth the heartless voids and immensities of the universe, and thus stabs us from behind with the thought of annihilation, when beholding the white depths of the milky way? . . . and when we proceed further, and consider that the mystical cosmetic which produces every one of her hues, the great principle of light, for ever remains white or colorless in itself, and if operating without medium upon matter, would touch all objects, even tulips and roses, with its own blank tinge—pondering all this, the palsied universe lies before us a leper; and like wilful travellers in Lapland, who refuse to wear colored and coloring glasses upon their eyes, so the wretched

infidel gazes himself blind at the monumental white shroud that wraps all the prospect around him. (195)

While it might appear that the horrors of whiteness, the "dumb blankness" and the "colorless, all-color of atheism from which we shrink" (195), supplant Ishmael's more positive associations, they in fact coexist in complex solution—the divinity embodied in the snow-white bull incarnation of Jove is inseparable from the terror of the white bear of the poles, the white shark of the tropics, and the albatross; the "divine spotlessness of power" cannot be imagined apart from the monumental white shroud that blinds whoever would gaze at it without protective glasses. Indeed, what *Moby-Dick* consistently requires readers to confront is the interpenetration of such seeming oppositions without limiting the possible meanings of, for example, the whiteness of the whale, the doubloon, the sea (with its lovely surface concealing the universal cannibalism of its depths), or of Ishmael's entire narrative performance.[1]

Long before Melville (and in similar veins, Poe and Dickinson) framed demanding visions of whiteness, the poetry of Phillis Wheatley offered a meditation on the trafficking between whiteness and blackness, a meditation which has, over the past two hundred years, spilled over into critical and ideological debates between accommodation and resistance. Wheatley's originary position in this discourse on whiteness, however, has been obscured by the tendency of Wheatley criticism to focus exclusively on her relationship to blackness and to African American culture (with regard to her contemporary cultural milieu and to ours). That critical tendency offers a representative case concerning the relationship between aesthetics and racial politics in historical, generic, and rhetorical terms. In this chapter I will explore both the critical responses to Wheatley's poetry and the ways in which Wheatley pursued poetic practice in languages and contexts which were, for eighteenth-century readers, almost impossible to imagine. As will become clear in my discussion of Wheatley's "On Being Brought from Africa to America," I offer "trafficking" as a trope suggesting the fluidity, the instability, and the possibility of danger inhering in Wheatley's rhetorical negotiation of her relationship both to her work and to white culture. I mean, of course, to call attention to the ways in which Wheatley casts her own trafficking in the codes of poetic representation against the trafficking in African American slaves common in her culture. Her poetry, struggling within and against that human trade, problematizes or obscures any easy identification and distinction of origins and destinations, intentions and accidents, laws and violations, conventions and disruptions, and black and white. It marks a point at which the discourses of racialized religion, economics, and politics converge and exist relationally within the poetic discourses of the late eighteenth century—not in a way suggesting any amoral, or apolitical, relativity of the slave trade and slave existence, but rather as a means of giving voice to the impact of a slave culture upon the rhetorical practices of the oppressed others of a slave system.

Wheatley exposes the pervasive oppressiveness of her culture's racial codes most originally and most explosively in her strategies of poetic closure, or rather the modes of anti-closure that I am calling "loose ends." Wheatley's subject matter, especially in her conventional odes, is frequently the virtual obliteration of her (and her contemporary African American slaves') identity by the oppressive workings of dominant racist, slaveholding economic and political forms in the United States. The centrality and sophistication of Wheatley's political thought, however, has tended to remain obscure, even doubtful, because it exists in no particular place within her poetic work; she rarely articulates "protest" or "grievances" explicitly or directly. She rather concludes her poems by staging contradictions so dramatic and strained that they often break apart and call the structural and thematic integrity of her entire poetic enterprise into question. These fractured lyrics, the terms and logics of their apparent deconstruction, are anything but failures of poetic strength, originality, or vision. Instead they construct a site of struggle without any specific locale; Wheatley's challenges to her racist culture's denial of her humanity occupy the vexed rhetorical gaps created when her poetic endings aggressively and strategically violate the very codes which have driven the poems they "end." What we experience when reading Wheatley is a recurrent collapse of poetic theme and coherence, the ruptures of which actually open up possibilities of meaning almost impossible within the conventions and for the ostensible audiences of her time. For Wheatley, then, the construction of a viable oppositional discourse requires the construction of "loose ends" whose unravelings and violations of traditional eighteenth-century poetic practice challenge not only the aesthetic, but also the social and political formations of her era.

Quite paradoxically, literary criticism in the United States has only recently begun to respond to Wheatley's significance after struggling in vain to process her work within some framework capable of combining aesthetic and political values. The major issue dividing Wheatley scholarship for several decades has been the debate over whether Wheatley's poetry is a signal of African American protest against white domination or a symptom of, as Terrence Collins suggests in a representative passage, "the depths to which what has come to be called the slave mentality—or self-hate by African-Americans based on introjection of the dominant culture's estimate of their own worth—. . . penetrates the collective mind of Black America" (147).[2] Wheatley's thinking about blackness, however, cannot be isolated from her thinking about whiteness. What I will suggest is that the racially coded terms of Wheatley's odes and her radical strategies for closing those odes in ways that undermine the generic conventions governing their production (and, implicitly, their consumption) often enact the related struggle to destabilize the aesthetic, theological, and racial discourses of her time. In her more conventional odes, as we shall see, Wheatley's work on whiteness subtly turns her poems against themselves, allowing them to be read as conventional lines on "morning," "evening," "virtue," and so on, while at the same time casting them as fractured meditations on the slave subject's obliteration by dominant white culture. Wheatley is least conventional at the same time that she appears merely conventional, most critical at the same time that she appears most complacent.

ii

The contradictory combination of critique and complacency that informs Wheatley's rhetoric and themes has, in fact, determined the contours of the critical understanding of her achievement. One group of critics perceives the accommodationist strategy in her work as definitive (rather than as dialectically complementary) and as expressive of "self-hatred" even, while another group focuses fully on strategies that suggest radical subversion in her work. While Wheatley's work had traditionally been devalued on aesthetic grounds (if it was addressed at all), an emerging African American literary establishment began rejecting Wheatley on *political* grounds in the late 1960s. Interested in discovering a usable literary past for the Black Studies movement, these critics perceived Wheatley primarily as an obstacle to overcome, an early female example of the Uncle Tomism and accommodationism repudiated by contemporary African American literature and literary criticism. Eleanor Smith articulates a common perspective:

> It is this point of view, the black man's point of view, that a Black teacher must be concerned with in trying to develop young black minds. Information must be presented so as to teach students to think Black and examine the information from a black perspective. It must not be assumed that because a person is Black and is teaching Black Studies that he is necessarily contributing to the development of black thought. Most Blacks have been educated by Whites to think white and to promote white racism. It is up to us to reeducate ourselves to think Black and to move creatively beyond the white syndrome.
>
> This leads us back to Phillis Wheatley, a Black woman who was taught by Whites to think white. Because of the strong development of this white mind and a commitment to this white orientation, Phillis Wheatley was not sensitive enough to the needs of her own people to demonstrate a kinship to Blacks in her life or writings. (403)

While much of Smith's manifesto expresses priorities essential to the emergence of Black Studies and preliminary to the current centrality and sophistication of African American literature and theory, once she turns to Wheatley as an example, we need to note that she rejects Wheatley largely on her perception of the poet's failure (elsewhere she suggests refusal) explicitly to address and to attempt to rectify the status of African American slaves in her poetry. This perspective also informs Smith's criticism that "none of Phillis's poems mention the harsh treatment sometimes endured by Prince [another slave of the Wheatley family] at the hands of the Wheatleys" (406). What Smith fails to account for is the manifest white hegemony in all areas of culture, including, of course, control of publishing houses and literary production. In this respect, Smith attacks Wheatley for not doing what would have been virtually impossible for her to accomplish— the publication of overtly rebellious poetry.[3]

Angelene Jamison takes a pedagogical and political tack similar to Smith's when she argues that Wheatley's poetry "embraces white attitudes and values, and it characterizes Phillis as a typical Euro-American poetess. She was detached from her people and her poetry could never be used as an expression of black thought" (409). While Jamison grants that Wheatley should not be ignored because of her accommodationist stance, she asserts that "teaching Phillis Wheatley from a black perspective shows that she was simply an eighteenth-century poet who supported, praised, and imitated those who enslaved her and her people" (416). Other critics echo these sentiments when they suggest that Wheatley "leaves the reader of her poems only slightly aware of her being a Negro and a slave" (Mason xxv), that her poems "serve as one measure of how far removed from the reality of her blackness Phillis had become" (Collins 149), and that "the Wheatleys had adopted her, but she had adopted their terrific New England conscience" (Redding 9). While progressively more modulated, similar sentiments inform Wheatley criticism of the 1980s. Alice Walker, for example, expresses a blend of compassion for and amazement at the "sickly little black girl," but nonetheless regards her poetry as "stiff, struggling, ambivalent," and "bewildered" (237). In 1986, June Jordan, while sensing the political and ontological ambivalence experienced by Wheatley and while grasping the explicit resistance to tyranny in a number of Wheatley's poems, still assumes that much of what happens in Wheatley's verse can be attributed to "regular kinds of iniquitous nonsense found in white literature, the literature that Phillis Wheatley assimilated, with no choice in the matter" (255). Kenneth Silverman's cultural history of the American Revolution assumes this same trajectory, agreeing that Wheatley's work is a simple paean to white cultural hegemony (217). Even outside the context of overt political and pedagogical debate characteristic of remarks from

the late 1960s, subsequent critics—including those hoping to discover an element of rebellion in Wheatley's verse—have tended to
posit Wheatley as a passive, though precocious, young woman whose
verse can't sustain serious interpretive attention. In so doing, this
criticism has suggested the power and interpretive inertia of those
influential early essays critical of Wheatley's accommodationism. Perhaps as a result of this predilection, commentators have focused only
on words and phrases explicitly dealing with Wheatley's African heritage or criticism of English tyranny. They have assumed, in short,
that Wheatley's poetic discourse is obviously referential rather than
rhetorical, that it transparently mirrors her attitudes, priorities, and
beliefs rather than strategically refracts whatever beliefs and ideas
she may have held. Many have also assumed that Wheatley's political
significance can be unproblematically situated with reference to contemporary African American political and aesthetic thought. Hoping
to find active resistance, these readers discover only passivity and accommodation.

Another strain in Wheatley criticism has moved significantly beyond this monolithic (nearly ahistorical) historicism of condemning
the poet's supposed insouciance toward the racial and political in-
justices of her time and has developed different models for assessing
the political energies in Wheatley's work. Summarizing recent trends
in Wheatley criticism, Henry Louis Gates Jr. argues that "much of
the misreading of Wheatley [which presents her as a poet aloof from
"matters that were in any sense racial or, more correctly, 'positively'
racial"] must certainly arise from a blatant unfamiliarity with the conventions of neoclassical verse as well as with the various forms of the
elegy she used" (75). Other critics have demonstrated that Wheatley
did write poems and letters decidedly critical of slavery and racial
inequality in general. John Shields, for one, calls for a renewed and
serious attention to her poetry and rejects the dominance of "socio-
anthropological arguments" in Wheatley criticism (267). According
to Shields, "so complete was [Wheatley's] absorption in the struggle
for freedom that this endeavor governed her conception of poetry,
causing her to be no more imitative than any other good student and
writer of literature" (231). Shields enumerates four ways in which
Wheatley articulates the theme of freedom: in her political statements

supporting America's quest for freedom from Great Britain, in her use of "what Jung called the mandala archetype" to discover psychic freedom and order amidst chaos, in her contemplative elegies that posit transcendental freedom in the afterlife, and in her poetic contemplation of the imagination and the sublime by which she escapes the "unsatisfactory, temporal world" (231).

The most persuasive of such revisionist readings is Sondra O'Neale's discussion of the ways in which Wheatley mobilized conventional ideas and terms within the religious discourses of late-eighteenth-century New England, recasting them as critiques of the oppression and racism of her time. According to O'Neale, the writings of enslaved authors "resemble the Southern plantation hymns of the nineteenth century, which the slaves sung on one level with intense religious commitment and on another level as a code language to protest slavery and to plan for escape" (145). After elaborating on how many of Wheatley's religious and racial allusions subtly undermine religiously based forms of discrimination while they foreground some of the contradictions inherent in the practice of slavery in a Christian culture, O'Neale concludes that

> Wheatley's effectiveness as an eighteenth-century poet and as a writer in the Black American protest tradition has been largely misunderstood. She was more than just an occasional poet who employed neoclassical images and phraseology to flatter her patrons. Having garnered some of her fame from such works, she used her talents and her success to wage a subtle war against slavery. Her methodology included biblical language and allusions that were much more comprehensible to readers in the eighteenth-century revivalist era than to those in this more secular age. She believed that citizens in her biblically knowledgeable society would recognize the scriptural allusions and symbols she used so well, that they would realize the implications of such references and turn from the practice of slavery. (157)

O'Neale's argument represents one tendency in reading Wheatley's "subtle warfare," especially in the sensitivity of her readings of Wheatley's rhetoric and in her stress on Wheatley's rebellious side.

I will later suggest that O'Neale begs a few questions about the efficacy of Wheatley's opposition to slavery, but I would like first to call attention to some central, though questionable, assumptions in her conclusion. O'Neale's study—like many recuperations of Wheatley's "subtle" oppositionalism—assumes a Wheatley intentionally writing propaganda against slavery. O'Neale also assumes a stable readership (of slaves, masters, and other whites alike) almost impossibly sensitive to the linguistic warfare waged by Wheatley. Least convincingly, O'Neale argues that Wheatley believed that her poems, once read, would result in the enlightenment of her white readership and the subsequent abolishment of slavery, a reading simply not borne out by either the history of American slavery or the reception history of Wheatley's work. As opposed to those critics who define Wheatley as purely imitative and accommodationist, both Shields and O'Neale have redefined Wheatley and discovered ubiquitous resistance to slavery and racism. These two extremes—total accommodation and total resistance—have defined the poles between which Wheatley criticism has vacillated. We need to modulate more carefully our sense of Wheatley's aesthetics and politics in order to account for how her poetic discourse may not have rested in either of these extreme positions and have been political in ways that subsequent readers have been almost uniformly unaware of.

The poems and letters most frequently referred to in support of the rebellious side of Wheatley were all written very shortly after the publication of her *Poems on Various Subjects, Religious and Moral* (1773) and after her manumission early in 1774. In these documents Wheatley does, indeed, speak out explicitly and eloquently against slavery. But can we assume that her progressive thinking about racial issues began at the moment of her freedom, or did it develop gradually during her years as a slave? Does her poetry demonstrate an interest in issues of slavery and freedom only explicitly and only after her freedom, or does it also express such sentiments obliquely and throughout her poetic career? Is it even possible to separate accommodation from resistance with any degree of certainty?

In *Roll, Jordan, Roll*, Eugene Genovese suggests that surreptitious tactics characterized slave discourses and other oppositional strategies and account for the complex interplay between resistance and accommodation (an important analogue for the polarities of response to Wheatley's work by critics). According to Genovese,

> the slaves' response to paternalism and their imaginative creation of a partially autonomous religion provided a record of simultaneous accommodation and resistance to slavery. Accommodation itself breathed a critical spirit and disguised subversive actions and often embraced its apparent opposite—resistance. In fact, accommodation might best be understood as a way of accepting what could not be helped without falling prey to the pressures for dehumanization, emasculation, and self-hatred. (597–98)

The important strategy in Genovese's approach is to situate accommodation and resistance dialectically, reading them rhetorically and tracing the complex and dynamic logics of their interaction. Neither accommodation nor resistance existed purely or self-evidently. Emanating as they did from an oppressed culture, slave discourse and praxis need to be imagined in dialectical relationship to the hegemonic white culture, substantiating particular beliefs within that culture while also tactically responding to it. Following Genovese's example helps us to understand just how opposed critical approaches to Wheatley have been stalled by a monolithic attention to either one side or another of Wheatley's representative strategies. We might also note that the "dehumanization, emasculation, and self-hatred" that Genovese demonstrates were avoided by slave-cultural discourses and practices tend to be those traits attacked by critics who perceive an accommodationist Wheatley.

I would like to agree, in part, with O'Neale and to argue that Wheatley's thinking about crucial racial and political issues begins taking shape in some of her earliest poems, but I would like to suggest that the vocabulary in which Wheatley couched her protests goes well beyond her explicit and intentional deployment of religious terminology. In some of her most apparently conventional (and accommodationist) odes, such as "An Hymn to the Morning," "An Hymn to the Evening," and "On Virtue"—those "occasional" poems that O'Neale seems to grant Wheatley wrote merely to "flatter her patrons" (157)—

Wheatley enacts the drama of the racial, sexual, and political subject existing under the dominance of eighteenth-century New England cultural norms. Wheatley's aesthetic work in these odes is radical and embodies the complex trafficking between resistance and accommodation that Genovese identifies as particular to slave discourses.

In this respect, the present study will corroborate William Robinson's broadside against critics who have for many years condemned Wheatley's poetry as being almost totally derivative, especially of Pope (*Phillis Wheatley* 97). Derivative or not, Wheatley's aesthetic work *is* symptomatic of the political drama encoded within eighteenth-century poetry in traditional images of light and dark, black and white. Wheatley's more or less "derivative" or "conventional" strategies of poetic closure, however, cast these black/white images in a manner powerfully disruptive of the cultural practices of dominant white culture. That is, whereas her elegies do, in fact, close with predictable images of consolation and heavenly solace, her odes that are most conventional in appearance close with images of silence, blindness, or violation, each of which undermines the traditional generic and cultural assumptions encoded within the poems. Wheatley deploys other conventional aesthetic terms not only in their poetic sense but also as critiques of the practice of slavery.

I would argue, then, that both Wheatley's aesthetic *and* her political originality have been unappreciated, to some extent even by those interested in rehabilitating both her poetics and her politics. For Wheatley, as for many poets who followed her, to write poetry is both to adhere to the generic constraints of her time *and* to resist racial and political oppression. Wheatley's verse can thus be viewed as a cultural, aesthetic, and political extension of the religious resistance O'Neale reads in Wheatley's poems and letters. The strategies are similar, but the battleground is broader. It is important to stress, however, that Wheatley's work in these poems is not necessarily as conscious or intentional as O'Neale claims, but implicit and immanent, more a drama of the ontological and political ambivalence experienced by the slave subject under dominance—more a "historical" experience—than an explicit account of "protest." We need not, however, rule out the possibility that Wheatley *is* very much in command in these poems and that in them she articulates an early version of an oppositional discourse that would, by the mid–nineteenth century, represent the political positions not only of African Americans but of American women as well.

Wheatley's status can best be grasped by situating her as an African American woman slave poet operating within the linguistic, aesthetic, and racial conventions of eighteenth-century America. According to Susan Willis, the function of history in African American women's writing "involves reconstructing the development of the character's individual personality in relation to the historical forces that have shaped the migrations of her race, the struggles of her community, and the relationships that have developed within her family" (*Specifying* 3). While I will not investigate each of these relationships in detail, a focus on the aesthetics of whiteness in Wheatley provides a context in which to recognize that Wheatley's relationship to different areas of dominant cultural practice is strained, contradictory, and ambiguous.

iii

> 'Twas mercy brought me from my *Pagan* land,
> Taught my benighted soul to understand
> That there's a God, that there's a *Saviour* too:
> Once I redemption neither sought nor knew.
> Some view our sable race with scornful eye,
> "Their colour is a diabolic die."
> Remember, *Christians*, *Negros,* black as *Cain,*
> May be refin'd, and join th' angelic train.

Wheatley's most famous poem, "On Being Brought from Africa to America,"[4] is the work most frequently cited by those who view Wheatley as capitulating utterly to the dictates and discourses of dominant white culture. In a representative passage the historian Edgar J. McManus argues,

> frequently the leading collaborators under slavery were black Christians who had so assimilated white values that they rationalized their own bondage. "'Twas mercy brought me from my

pagan land," wrote Phillis Wheatley of her devotion to Christianity and the teaching of her masters. (104)

While McManus's remarks have been echoed by numerous literary critics, Wheatley's critics (historians and literary scholars alike) have neither situated such positions within the framework of eighteenth-century New England religious organization nor interrogated Wheatley's poem with much interpretive rigor. Wheatley may well have found in her religion some consolation from the limitations and degradation of slave existence. In this poem she does, after all, claim that becoming refined and joining the "angelic train" offer some hope for the oppressed. However, while a black soul could theoretically be saved, the actual practice of African American Christians in Revolutionary Boston was riddled with problems, humiliation, and inequality. As Leon F. Litwack notes, "discrimination was so intense in Boston that by about 1800 the black leader Prince Hall 'could only advise his brethren to be patient and bear up under the daily insults we meet on the streets of Boston'" (16). Such racism, it seems, was not refined away at the church entrance. When they attended services, Litwack reports,

> Negroes found themselves segregated, either in an "African corner," a "Nigger Pew," seats marked "B.M." (Black Members), or aloft in "Nigger Heaven." The Sabbath schools also provided separate quarters for Negro and white children. Religious bodies which offered the Lord's Supper generally compelled Negroes to wait until the whites had partaken of the bread and wine. (196)

Black members who would not comply with such dictates were often forcibly removed, had tar put on their pews, or were even threatened with physical violence (196–98). The security and serenity of Wheatley's "angelic train" was questionable at best and poses a burden as ambivalent and contradictory as do cultivation and literacy for Wheatley. Religious no less than cultural freedom forced Wheatley into a position that seemed to promise release, if not equality, while denying it on practical and sometimes even on theoretical terms.[5] The remarks of Litwack and others would seem to require Sondra O'Neale to qualify her argument that "Wheatley . . . found the biblical myth, language and symbol to be the most conducive vehicles for making subtle, yet effective, statements against slavery" (145). O'Neale's argument that Wheatley's appropriation of religious discourse provided her with the ammunition to wage "a slave's subtle war" against oppression is still a powerful statement on Wheatley's art. However, her assumption of a stable and coherent Christian community sympathetic to the theological equality of African American Christians against whom Wheatley and other slaves could wage such coherent linguistic warfare seems to ignore the contemporary racism and oppression that might render Wheatley's strategies, even if perceived as such, powerless. Even in Boston, Wheatley's "diabolic die" would render her more an "invisible woman" than a "visible saint."

While reference to certain eighteenth-century religious and historical sources problematizes any easy assumptions of Wheatley's work as obviously or primarily accommodationist, this central poem itself introduces and thematizes some destabilizing concepts that remain operative throughout many other early works. Those who have situated this poem as a simple tribute to white cultural, political, and religious dominance have probably responded to Wheatley's apparent contribution to the Protestant poetic subgenre of the "gracious affliction," though no one actually makes those associations explicit. Like Anne Bradstreet's translation of the literal burning of her house into a spiritual lesson on the vanity of earthly desires and a hymn to God's beauty and justice, and like Edward Taylor's similar transcendence of the death of two of his children by reconceptualizing their deaths as proof of God's love, Wheatley's poem seems to invite the analogous latter-day interpretation that her kidnapping and sale into slavery can be reimagined as a gracious entry into a Christian scheme of salvation. In this respect, the poem enacts a translation from the actual and literal to the potential and figurative. And, according to the tradition of the "gracious affliction," such a translation serves not merely to supplement, but to replace (perhaps obliterate) the literal reference of the poem. Religious salvation *supplants* economic and political bondage.

However, Wheatley's poem, while clearly readable in the Protestant "gracious affliction" tradition, also struggles against that tradition's easy shift from literal to figurative—the trafficking of the literal and the figurative—in a number of ways. Positioned immediately after her overtly political poem "To the King's Most Excellent Majesty," in which she urges King George to "set his subjects free!" and immediately before her elegy "On the Death of the Rev. Dr. Sewell," in which she commemorates a descendant of the author of the first American abolitionist tract, *The Selling of Joseph*, "On Being Brought from Africa to America" is situated in a context likely to foreground its political implications, not its metaphorical transumption of the political and literal.

Wheatley's title, moreover, calls attention to the initial act of her being stolen from her home in Africa and sold into slavery, not to the potential reward of eternity in heaven. Whereas the Puritan tradition works to erase the literal in the spiritual fullness of the figurative representation of Christian salvation, Wheatley joins Africa as the scene of her kidnapping with America as the scene of her hypothetical salvation by focusing on the trafficking in slavery that links those two continents economically and politically. Wheatley's foregrounding the trafficking of slaves disrupts the spiritually validated trafficking between the literal and figurative so common in the Protestant tradition and denies the simple replacement of the literal by the figurative by returning the poem to the scene of the original crime. Structurally, while the first four lines of "On Being Brought from Africa to America" seem to focus on the mercy of Christian redemption, the poem emphasizes the final quatrain's focus on racism and inequality. Wheatley reverses, in this maneuver, the usual dynamic of the "gracious affliction" poem, which tends to begin by dramatizing earthly or material loss only to conclude in spiritual consolation and improvement. Stylistically, Wheatley "steals," as it were, the generic horizons of the "gracious affliction" to represent the theft of African children from their parents and homeland.

In other words, if the physical violence and murder definitive of the slave trade is the repressed Other of the Christianizing of African slaves in colonial Boston, Wheatley dramatizes a "return of the repressed" in "On Being Brought from Africa to America." She does so by superimposing the "traffic" between rhetorical figure and spiritual meaning, the substance and sense of religious poetry, onto the "traffic" of African people to America, where their blackness cannot be "refin'd" in any physical way to spiritual whiteness. Wheatley's penultimate line, "Remember, *Christians, Negros,* black as *Cain,*" contributes to this complication by inserting the specter of *memory* into a poem that would seem to require the erasing of all memories of home, parents, freedom, and physical being in order to maintain the institution of slavery.[6] Wheatley's poem performs the mnemonic function of recovering a forgotten source, a lost moment of freedom prior to her insertion into a Christian culture and its hegemonic practices and beliefs. "On Being Brought from Africa to America" re-joins (re-pairs, using Emerson's term from "The Poet") two moments that need to be grasped in their relational totality. (I would argue that Wheatley's poem "On Recollection" is potentially disruptive as well.) Of course, the poem can be read without recourse to the explicit violence and barely veiled hypocrisy of slave-owning Christians, but, as I will be arguing throughout this chapter, Wheatley's poems often sustain two powerfully related but alternative and almost mutually blinding schemes of reference.

Wheatley's trafficking between the literal and figurative registers of "On Being Brought from Africa to America" informs its operations on many levels. Perhaps the most significant fault line in "On Being Brought from Africa to America" centers on the word "redemption."[7] Here Wheatley embeds within one key term both the religious and the political discourses that pervade the poem. In a religious context, of course, redemption signals that glorious moment of the soul's salvation and the certainty of its spending eternity in heaven, and Wheatley's admission of neither knowing about it nor seeking it prior to her enslavement could indicate her appreciation of the religious culture imposed on her new existence as a slave. However, "redemption" also figures significantly in the poem's negotiation of the politics of racism and slavery. As the term designating the granting of a slave's freedom either by purchase or decree, "redemption" disrupts the religious frame by suggesting Wheatley's longing to be outside the very milieu within which "redemption" as a religious term operates. While Wheatley seems to be capitulating to the hegemony of a Christian culture and its metaphysical stress on spiritual matters and eternity, her poem simultaneously casts itself against the very enslavement that some would argue granted her access to such a Christian scheme. Of course, she "neither sought nor knew" the meaning of "redemption" prior to her theft and enslavement since her freedom in Africa would have reduced such a concept to absurdity. The word "refin'd," while frequently read as admitting impurity and the need of transformation, the purification essential to any African American joining the "angelic train," proves to be another pivotal term and quickly slips into other possibilities. "Refined" is a critical choice here, as it simultaneously suggests not only physical purification (as in refined sugar—with Wheatley's pun on "cane" and "Cain" fully operative—or bleached flour and purified metals), but also the moral purification necessary to reach a higher spiritual plain. Wheatley's deployment of the homonymic significance of "Cain" and "cane" is further strengthened by virtue of her choosing the word "sable" to indicate the darker pigmentation of enslaved African Americans. Assuming that many other words could have functioned just as well to represent darker skin color, I would argue that Wheatley chooses "sable" because the word inserts the word "able" and, hence, the name Abel into a poem that already alludes to Cain. Thus casting African Americans as the innocent Abels to the brutality of European American Cains, Wheatley again reverses traditional associations that would have been commonly deployed to support racial domination and the practices of slavery. The so-called mark of Cain, according to Wheatley's calculus, is revealed in the physical brutality of the slave trade and, therefore, marks those European Americans implicated in its practices.

We need also to read "refined" in the more broadly cultural sense suggestive of literacy or cultivation. The popularity of conduct books in the eighteenth century supports this range of significance. As Richard L. Bushman notes, one of the "three interrelated aspects of the ideal of cultivation as experienced by the American gentry" was "personal refinement, meaning grace of bearing and manner, along with fitting accomplishments: dancing above all but also music, drawing, riding, letter writing, needlework (for women), and knowledge of science, languages and history" (358). So predominant was this ideal of cultivated gentility among eighteenth-century women that "the proper education of planters' and merchants' daughters became a minor industry in colonial cities" (357). Wheatley's poetic productions, then, constitute the visible grounds of her cultural refinement.

These three connotations—the physical, the moral, and the cultural—open up a wide range of possibilities within the poem's negotiation of religious and racial issues. Reading "refined" in its primarily physical sense produces a poem that accepts racial stereotypes, specifically of African American inferiority and European American superiority and privilege. African Americans must be physically transformed before joining whites on the angelic train, must be purged, in other words, of their blackness in order to achieve what whites already have. The "angelic train," if we push this reading a bit too far, may not have much of a religious connotation at all, and may refer, instead, to physical loveliness. The impetus of Protestantism to separate the physical from the spiritual may be the object of sarcasm here, as Wheatley focuses on the materialism of Boston society, its backsliding tendencies toward corporeal pleasures.

Such racially divisive hierarchies more or less disappear, however, if we read "refined" in its moral, spiritual, and Christian sense. In this case, Wheatley's assertion that African Americans may be refined and join the angelic train would hold equally true for all Christians. We may, perhaps, even read the comma in the line "Remember, *Christians, Negros,* black as *Cain,*" as functioning as a connective joining Christians and Negroes as equally black with sin, original or otherwise. This reading remains a plausible interpretive move roughly in line with Wheatley's semantic instability. Such a "moral" focus conflicts with the physical reading of "refined" by erasing all earthly (physical) hierarchies and replacing them with a vision of all earthly life marked by sin (blackness), a vision consistent with orthodox Puritan beliefs (see Edwards's "Sinners in the Hands of an Angry God" as an important intertext). As opposed to the physical reading, the moral reading communicates a radically egalitarian vision, at least in theological terms. In its assertion of the spiritual identity of all humans, regardless of pigmentation, Wheatley's poem maintains its oppositional quality by striking at the heart of racism in "Christian" Boston. The direct quote in the line " 'Their colour is a diabolic die' " would expose, in this reading, the unsound theology of its hypothetical racist speaker by emphasizing the invalid equation of physical appearance and spiritual essence.[8] Wheatley's "Remember," then, stands as a multidimensional warning to her readership. Wheatley castigates her obtuse and racist contemporaries by reminding them that if they actually could "remember" their catechism, if they only understood the essence of Christian charity, they would neither harbor the racist beliefs that they do, nor indulge in such unsound and obviously hypocritical theology.

In other words, even at the level of its Christian significance, Wheatley's poem refuses to countenance the evils she everywhere witnesses in Boston. She recovers something like the potentially democratic essence of early New England Calvinism, which held that no social or material evidence could either signify or earn one's salvation. The poorest dung shoveler had as good a chance at being saved as did the richest merchant or magistrate. Reading "refined" in its cultural register, however, casts Wheatley's poem as more potentially egalitarian in purely earthly terms, those of cultural refinement and literacy. If we can extend Wheatley's work in this direction, "On Being Brought from Africa to America" not only declares the grounds for equality, but enacts the achievement of that equality by virtue of its own performance. The acquisition of literacy, then, supplants both the physical and the moral significance by promising the Republican ideals of freedom in this world to all who attain literacy. On the other hand, Wheatley may also again be highlighting the Arminian heresy that would equate earthly appearances with spiritual attainment, and the direct quote in line 6 would exaggerate the obtuse and illiterate perspective of one capable of making such a remark. The error of Boston, according to this line of interpretation, may be in eroding all religious interiority and replacing the spiritual depths of religiosity with the radically secular standards of literacy and cultural conduct. All three readings—the physical, the moral, and the cultural—level criticisms directed at the complacency, the racism, and the bad theology that would equate appearances with essences, and at least the latter two readings hold out something resembling equality to the aspiring slave poet. None of these readings lends itself to viewing Wheatley as accommodationist, or even as particularly pious.

I would suggest that for Wheatley all three senses of "refined" coalesce and present a biological, a theological, and a cultural complex that functions as an index to her own racialized semiotics. Reading "refined" as expressive of Wheatley's desire for racial and/or moral transformation might well lead one to criticize her for accommodationist desires, as might reading "refined" in the cultural sense. However, Wheatley's use of "refined" in this cultural sense also reveals an ambivalence toward (perhaps even a resistance to) the dictates of European American cultural hegemony. The fluidity of these senses of "refined" is another example of Wheatley's discursive trafficking of the codes of her dominant culture. By erasing the barriers between the sacred and the secular, and by enacting the tenuous situation of the African American slave's relationship to white culture, Wheatley demonstrates the mutually constitutive nature of theological, physical, and cultural realms that Protestant New England culture would have separated.[9]

As Kenneth Silverman notes, Wheatley's "interest in poetry was not unusual. Often the test of missionary work was the converts' ability to perform feats that their genteel, pious foster-families cherished as ultimate marks of civilization, like addressing the 'Great Supreme' in verse" (215). Wheatley's accomplishment and the persistence of her work are, however, unusual, and the doubleness of her life is much more complex than even the conditions of her participation in Boston's literary culture would suggest. Wheatley explicitly predicates joining the "angelic train" on the attainment of sacred refinement, but the attainment of secular "refinement" also marks the moment of Wheatley's self-insertion into the discursive practices of white culture and, consequently, the moment she must perforce deny her blackness. It represents Wheatley's contradictory existence as accomplished woman *and* as ornamental slave.

The assumption that the life and works of any cultural figure can be understood as inscribed within a stable and seamless ideological moment is itself problematic. For Phillis Wheatley, however, who was living within a social formation in the midst of religious, political, economic, and racial upheaval, the assumption is, most likely, untenable. Moreover, scholars who would argue that Wheatley's verse simply "reflects" the cultural ideology of the poetic conventions of Pope and of neoclassical verse or of eighteenth-century white Christian orthodoxy and of the social relations of Revolutionary New England are faced with the immediate problem that those areas of practice were not unified to begin with. As we have seen, the status of African Americans within the Christian and social sectors of eighteenth-century Boston (the areas in which, to her detractors, Wheatley has seemed most plagued by accommodationist desires) was riddled with contradictions, internal struggle, or simple incoherence.

iv

As the foregoing discussion suggests, we need to consider that Wheatley's thinking about blackness is not separable from her troubled relationship with whiteness. The burden of whiteness and the volatility of Wheatley's relationship to the cultural and religious discursive practices of eighteenth-century New England society figure prominently in Wheatley's early odes. Whiteness and other terms associated with it (purity, refinement, and others) in fact frequently exist both in opposition to images of darkness and blackness and in a complex and often contradictory relationship among themselves. Light/dark imagery does tend to carry predictable good/bad or pure/impure connotations in Wheatley's work, though Terrence Collins suggests the applicability of reading racial significance into Wheatley's use of otherwise conventional images of light and dark by drawing both on psychoanalysis and on African American historiography:

> Psychoanalyst Joel Kovel and historian Winthrop Jordan have argued persuasively in, respectively, *White Racism: A Psychohistory* and *White Over Black* that in the American experience it is impossible to dissociate the respective value placed on black and white persons from the traditional associations of black-bad, dirty, dead and white-good, clean, alive. When such equations are reinforced by religious symbolism and by cultural and economic devaluation of black people in the institution of slavery and its heirs, the racial significance of a poetic vocabulary permeated by such equations might be credibly posited. (155)

Collins is correct in arguing for a racial subtext to Wheatley's appropriation of light/dark imagery. What he misses, however, is what I have been calling Wheatley's trafficking in white, the extent to which Wheatley structures her poetic work around such conventional oppositions only before proceeding to deconstruct them. Collins also does not note the possibility that, like Melville, Dickinson, Frost, and Freud after her, Wheatley associates whiteness not simply with purity and benevolence, but also with death and obliteration. In each of the odes discussed below, Wheatley's practice of poetic closure interrupts the apparently simple and derivative performances and reinstates the complexity of her status vis-à-vis the discourses of "culture" and "religion."

Wheatley's work in "On Imagination" is not only paradigmatic of her covert poetic practice, but especially significant as both a statement and a dramatization of her poetic theory. After a disarmingly conventional invocation of the Muses, requesting their assistance and attesting to their benevolent powers, Wheatley proceeds to catalog some of the liberatory energies peculiar to the imaginative faculty, especially its ability to soar above all earthly limitations to the point of leaving "the rolling universe behind" and of both grasping "the mighty whole" of creation and of creating new, amazing worlds. Equally potent is imagination's ability to transform the existing world, turning the harshness and constriction of a wintry landscape into a lush and verdant world of rejuvenated spring, a process whose articulation occupies the entire middle of "On Imagination." However, as in "On Being Brought from Africa to America," the force and originality of Wheatley's poetic accomplishment resides not in her arguably conventional poetic themes, but within the logics and vocabularies within which she casts her meditations, within, in other words, her material work and practice of inscription rather than in the generic parameters within which she performs that practice. Furthermore, it is in "On Imagination" that Wheatley's loose ends emerge as the agents of disruptive, revolutionary practice. As in "On Being Brought from Africa to America," Wheatley's trafficking in the codes of her culture's conventions reveals an oppositional awareness, a deployment of the master's language in order to dismantle the master's house.

"On Imagination" is one of Wheatley's conventional odes, resembling numerous other eighteenth-century paeans to the imaginative and creative powers of the mind. Beginning in a doubly traditional manner, with both a hailing of the "imperial queen," imagination, and an invocation of the Muses, the poem opens by attesting to the virtually limitless powers of imagination, "all attest how potent is thine hand," while also requesting the Muses' aid as Wheatley desires to "tell her [Imagination's] glories with a faithful tongue." Operating within a pre-Coleridgian identification of "fancy" and "imagination," "On Imagination" proceeds to celebrate imagination's potency with specific reference to the relationship between mind and the natural, material world. Specifically, Wheatley stages the imaginative negation of winter and the harshness and limitations of life associated with it:

> Though *Winter* frowns to *Fancy's* raptur'd eyes
> The fields may flourish, and gay scenes arise;
> The frozen deeps may break their iron bands,
> And bid their waters murmur o'er the sands.
> Fair *Flora* may resume her fragrant reign,
> And with her flow'ry riches deck the plain;
> *Sylvanus* may diffuse his honours round,
> And all the forest may with leaves be crown'd:
> Show'rs may descend, and dews their gems disclose,
> And nectar sparkle on the blooming rose.

This triumph of imagination over the elements and over the actual contexts of one's life constitutes the core of Wheatley's poem and is the only such revelation of the powers of the imaginative faculty. The lines framing this passage all attest to the actions of imagination, especially the rapidity with which the imagination drives the mental world to transcend the particularities of lived existence. It is not too extreme to argue that, in Wheatley's view, *escape* and *transcendence* (of space and time) are what imagination is all about.

However, like "On Being Brought from Africa to America," "On Imagination" stages these dynamics not from an abstract or conventionally aesthetic angle, but from within the specific discourses of a slave culture, and from the point of view of the slave subject. Also like "On Being Brought from Africa to America," this poem does so through its covert playing on both the language and form of conventional eighteenth-century verse. That the representation of imaginative transcendence (however abstract and however conventional) within a slave poem might encode the slave poet's desire literally to escape the inhuman confines of an enslaved existence is, by now, a well-analyzed trope in African American literary studies. Wheatley, however, early on anticipates the covert and coded practices made so visible in nineteenth-century African American texts by writers like Frederick Douglass and Frances E. W. Harper. In fact, rather like the domestics in Harper's *Iola Leroy; or, Shadows Uplifted,* who deploy a discourse derived from their specific slave functions (cooks refer to whether the "butter" is fresh or rancid to inquire about and report on the North's success or failure in recent skirmishes), Wheatley commandeers the language of poetic conventions, warping them to her own oppositional purposes.

For example, prior to the passage quoted above, Wheatley dramatizes her entry into a creative state of mind in highly volatile terms:

> Now here, now there, the roving *Fancy* flies,
> Till some lov'd object strikes her wand'ring eyes,
> Whose silken fetters all the senses bind,
> And soft captivity involves the mind.

Not uncharacteristic of such accounts of the moment of poetic creation, Wheatley's lines nonetheless disrupt the standard associations of such a convention by simultaneously rearticulating her specific condition as slave. Her allusion to "silken fetters" "bind[ing]" her in a "soft captivity" requires that we account for this particular poem as the product of a slave, herself bound in captivity, albeit on comparatively unbrutal terms; that is, hers are "silken fetters." In other words, Wheatley's imaginings, especially those about imaginative transcendence, are always articulated from the doubly "fettered" and "captive" perspective of a slave subject. Wheatley's lines on the imagination's ability to negate the harsh particulars of lived existence cannot, then, be read outside her own literal enslavement. This double context accounts for much of the poem's imagery, and also for its bizarre anti-conclusion.

The operative contrast between winter's frozen rigidity and spring's luxuriance anchors three related sets of oppositional associations. In one of these oppositions, winter and harshness figure not only Boston's northern climate but also its lucrative engagement in the slave economy from which many of New England's fortunes were made. Spring, and all the effulgence and flowing richness associated with it, by contrast, construct Africa as the negation of all that is cold, all that is Boston. Second and closely related to the geographical contrast, the same meteorological oppositions represent the opposed cultural and attitudinal poles of closed, icy, and austere Protestant New England and pagan, exotic Africa with its sensuously "gay scenes" of murmuring waters, aromatic blossoms, lush forests, sparkling gems and nectars, and blooming roses. Finally, both in the poem's imaginative world and in Wheatley's existential one the "frowns" of winter figure the present (both poetic and actual) while the imaginatively conjured spring evokes memories of an African past, replete with both the climatic and cultural differences enumerated above. In this poem, in other words, Wheatley collapses time and space, and her imaginative negation of winter doubles as her negation of slave existence in North America. As she says in the poem's early lines,

> *Imagination!* Who can sing thy force?
> Or who describe the swiftness of thy course?
> Soaring through air to find the bright abode,
> Th' empyreal palace of the thund'ring God,
> We on thy pinions can surpass the wind,
> And leave the rolling universe behind:
> From star to star the mental optics rove,
> Measure the skies, and range the realms above.
> There in one view we grasp the mighty whole,
> Or with new worlds amaze th' unbounded soul.

The "unbounded" soul, of course, represents not only the imaginative freedom of an enthralled creative mind, but the literal unbinding of a human being from the bonds of slavery.

It is the "bondage" of slavery and its entire disciplinary apparatus with which this poem is concerned. The early references to "silken fetters" and "soft captivity" binding the senses and mind echo, not only in the passage above, but also in the extended section in which imagination transforms winter into spring. Recall the line "The frozen deeps may break their iron bands." Throughout that extended section, Wheatley's imagery remains fairly transparent—predictable wintry images give way to equally predictable spring- and summer-like scenes. In fact, the entirety of the section documents spring's negation of winter, itself imaged only twice, both times in strangely inappropriate terms. The stanza begins, "Though *Winter* frowns to *Fancy's* raptur'd eyes," but the personification of winter "frowning" is not pursued beyond this initial metaphor. I will argue that at the end of this poem and in the companion odes, "An Hymn to Morning" and "An Hymn to Evening," such personification always introduces her veiled struggle against the oppression of the slave subject by slave owners. For now, however, I would like to turn to the only other line which metaphorizes winter's harshness, "The frozen deeps may break their iron bands." It is striking that Wheatley would choose the metaphor "iron bands" as an appropriate image for frozen water; neither iron nor bands precisely figures the idea of a frozen covering of a body of water. On the other hand, the image introduces into the poem one of slavery's most represented images, the slave's manacle. What this intrusion does, then, is to introduce a fourth opposition to the three we examined above, that of the manacled slavery of Wheatley and millions of enslaved African Americans versus their freedom from such restrictions in their homelands. The luxuriance of her representation of Africa in this poem renders the manacled state of her fellow slaves even more oppressive by virtue of the persistence of its tropical luxuriance in the slaves' memories. Only through imagination (or recollection) can the enslaved subject transport herself outside of the immediate context of her oppression and suffering.

It is in the loose ends of its concluding lines, however, that "On Imagination" registers its most disconcerting challenge to the aesthetic and economic codes of Wheatley's culture. Here, Wheatley's strategy of poetic closure violates the logics of eighteenth-century verse and, more importantly, of the poem itself. By so intentionally fracturing stable poetic meaning, Wheatley smuggles in the alternative possibility of her poem's struggle against the entire sociocultural matrix within which it is produced and consumed. In Wheatley's concluding lines, imagination, which throughout the poem possesses virtually limitless power, suddenly self-destructs, seemingly in the midst of the poem's celebration of its potency:

> The monarch of the day I might behold,
> And all the mountains tipt with radiant gold,
> But I reluctant leave the pleasing views,

Which *Fancy* dresses to delight the *Muse;*
Winter austere forbids me to aspire,
And northern tempests damp the rising fire;
They chill the tides of *Fancy's* flowing sea,
Cease then, my song, cease the unequal lay.

While not Wheatley's strangest ending (see my discussion of "An Hymn to the Morning" below), these lines violate nearly every one of the poem's assertions about imagination. The force capable of transcending the limitations of actual seasonal weather suddenly is rendered impotent by the very forces of wintry cold and repression it had earlier overpowered. Winter, as the poetic embodiment of slaveholding Boston's northern climate and oppressive social regime, returns with a vengeance here, not merely "austere" but tyrannical in its denial of imaginative reconfiguration. It "forbids" Wheatley to continue her meditation, and the powers of its frigid reign reassert their carceral functions by "damp[ing] the rising fire" and "chill[ing] the tides" of imaginative creation. To return to the earlier personification of winter, Wheatley's poem gives us a winter that both "frowns" upon summer's loveliness and "forbids" Wheatley as poet from projecting her imagination farther than a harmlessly conventional consideration of the seasons. In its return, winter—which I take here to represent not only the Wheatleys (who exercised punitive control over Phillis's poetic practice) but also the entirety of slavery as a system—reasserts its preeminence, its dominance of the poet's creative processes. Slaves may imagine freedom as an otherworldly religious utopia only so long as those imaginative projections stop short of the insurrectionary implications of Wheatley's "rising fire." The return of the repressed sociopolitical Other of Wheatley's poem could not figure more ominously or oppressively. Back are the northern winds to nip in the bud all of Wheatley's floral imagery and back are the frigid waters that were earlier imaged as manacles. The fantasy of escape, in other words, is strangled, harnessed-in as powerfully as would be an actual escaped slave, captured and returned to the horrors of slave existence. Perhaps the poem's final phrase sums up its entire logic. Wheatley's "unequal lay" that is quieted by the forceful return of northernness collapses aesthetic and economic linguistic registers. The poet's lay, of course, is her musical lines. However, "lay" also evokes a significant economic alternative, "lay" being that percentage of a profit that was distributed among sailors on a whaling voyage (recall Ishmael's "unequal lay" when he signs aboard the *Pequod*). Wheatley's "unequal lay," then, stands as a decidedly overt protest against the very essence of a slave economy, the theft of the slave's labor. Wheatley's poem thus suggests the likelihood that poetry itself is rendered impotent and fantastical by virtue of the economic arrangements under which poetry (at least a slave's poetry) can be produced. Similarly, it is a poem celebrating the powers of imagination which ends by signaling the incoherence of its own theory and the wholesale negation, not only of its own themes and logics, but of the very conditions of its possibility.

The closural anomalies that drag "On Imagination" to its oppressive cessation surface elsewhere in Wheatley's poetic work, especially in her conventional odes that seem to have no possible political significance and for which Wheatley has been castigated as a racial sellout. Whiteness and various allusions to light, brightness, refinement, and purity pervade much of Wheatley's work (usually in contexts with no overt racial overtones). In "An Hymn to the Evening," for example, white=pure/black=impure polarities of racial signification disrupt an otherwise traditional reflection on the evening. After two stanzas setting the physical scene and offering our human breasts as "living temples" of the God who resides over such "majestic grandeur," Wheatley concludes the poem with two stanzas reminiscent, in tone, in rhetorical complexity, and in their racial implications, of "On Being Brought from Africa to America":

> Fill'd with the praise of him who gives the light;
> And draws the sable curtains of the night,
> Let placid slumbers sooth each weary mind,
> At morn to wake more heav'nly, more refin'd;
> So shall the labours of the day begin
> More pure, more guarded from the snares of sin.
>
> Night's leaden sceptre seals my drowsy eyes,
> Then cease, my song, till fair *Aurora* rise.

Wheatley's relationship with darkness in these lines is complex. Darkness contrasts clearly, in one sense, with light. One praises "him who gives the light" and waits expectantly "till fair *Aurora* rise." Darkness, by implication, is the opposite of light, sealing one off from the desired illumination. However, the relationship between dark and light is not, by any means, one of pure opposition, but rather another example of Wheatley's trafficking between them. The "sable curtains" of night allow "placid slumbers" to "sooth each weary mind," with sleep and darkness signaling a period of renovation and renewal similar to Thoreau's winter. Upon awakening from this slumber one is not only "more heav'nly," "More pure," and "more guarded" from sin, but also, repeating a pivotal term from "On Being Brought from Africa to America," more "refin'd." In other words, darkness and light are dialectically related: the world of darkness and sleep supplements the world of light and consciousness.

This relationship, however, is far from neutral. In the final couplet, as "Night's leaden sceptre seals [her] drowsy eyes," Wheatley's song must cease "till fair *Aurora* rise." In addition to the "leaden" scepter suggesting heaviness and materiality, contrasting sharply with the waking state ("more heav'nly, more refin'd"), night and darkness are associated with silence and inarticulacy. The African American poet's song, even in a hymn to evening, must be inspired and validated by "fair *Aurora*" and the realm of light, not by the poet's own private world of darkness and of her own blackness. As in "On Being Brought from Africa to America," *refinement* carries the dual signification of morality and literacy, of religious as well as cultural purity. The "sable curtains" of night, then, may provide refuge and solace, but they shut the poet out from the linguistic capacities crucial to her poetic identity. Thus, however positive the values associated with "fair *Aurora*," the dictates of light close this poem in a silence that must wait for the sun to rise. In the context of her blackness and her slave status, Wheatley's representation of the sun is ambivalent, negating her own color, as it establishes whiteness as an alien, though desirable, force in moral, racial, and thematic terms.

Perhaps Wheatley's reference to waking up "more heav'nly, more refin'd" and to her daily labors beginning "More pure, more guarded from the snares of sin" is the key to another and compatible range of racial significance of the poem, her appropriation of conventional terms of poetic practice for reflecting on the practice of slavery. Her "labours" can be read as mental and moral exertion (preparation for her joining the "angelic train"), but they also can be read, in the context of her slavery, as the physical *labor* she must perform. The poet waking up "more guarded" from sin might also suggest Wheatley's waking up guarded from darkness, paganism, and her own racial identity. Sleep, then, is where one becomes silent and more acceptable to whites (and where one escapes them briefly). Such a reading is, of course, speculative, but such speculation is at least partially prepared for by reading Wheatley's use of light/dark imagery as straining beyond the parameters of eighteenth-century poetic practice to encompass racial and political implications and by pursuing the trafficking between the literal and figurative deployed in "On Being Brought from Africa to America" throughout the Wheatley canon.

"An Hymn to the Morning," a companion piece for "An Hymn to the Evening," enacts a similar dialectic between white and black. In this poem, however, the drama is more volatile, and the consequences more profound. The poem begins with a conventional invocation of the Muses:

> Attend my lays, ye ever honour'd nine,
> Assist my labours, and my strains refine;

Once again, the poetic voice craves *refinement* and assistance in her labors in terms reinstating the racial and political connotations they carry in "An Hymn to the Evening." Here, though, it is her *strain* that Wheatley desires refined. "Strain" adds yet another racial suggestion to this otherwise utterly conventional invocation, implying as it does, and did in 1773, both poetic line and racial lineage. Whereas the poet's song had to cease until "fair *Aurora*" rose in "Evening," Aurora's function in this poem is altered slightly. Wheatley concludes the first stanza with these lines:

> In smoothest numbers pour the notes along,
> For bright *Aurora* now demands my song.

Fair Aurora has risen as "bright *Aurora*," a transformation to which we shall return. More suggestively, Aurora now *demands* the poet's song. Here Aurora's brightness and coercion again complicate a conventional poetic frame by insinuating a power relationship between the "bright *Aurora*" as a shining white emblem and the African American poet craving refinement. Wheatley's song may press for articulation, but her owners also possess the power to demand her labor, poetic or domestic. Wheatley was, as Robinson suggests,

> made to spend most of her waking either reading or writing her "poetic performances" before curious guests, or close beside her mistress reading and discussing the Bible, or visiting among ladies of Boston's first families, holding forth on "feminine topics." (*Phillis Wheatley* 25)

The potentially oppressive implications of Aurora *demanding* Wheatley's song, when read in the context of the reference in "Evening" to the sable curtains of the night allowing "placid slumbers" to "sooth each weary mind," might also require us to add yet another sense to Wheatley's pivotal term *strain,* that of the strain of physical and mental exertion. Her poetic work, then, can function both as autobiographical gloss on her own ambiguous existence as well as general reflection on the status of domestic African American slaves living under the domination—legal, political, economic, and religious—of white culture.

Wheatley's dialectic of whiteness and blackness grows progressively more complex in "An Hymn to the Morning." After a stanza in praise of morning's beauty, Wheatley returns to the power of "bright *Aurora*":

> Ye shady groves, your verdant gloom display
> To shield your poet from the burning day:
> *Calliope* awake the sacred lyre,
> While thy fair sisters fan the pleasing fire:
> The bow'rs, the gales, the variegated skies
> In all their pleasures in my bosom rise.

In a poem ostensibly written in praise of the morning and of the sun's rising, Wheatley must seek the "verdant gloom" of "shady groves," two images of darkness and retreat from the light, to "shield" her from "the burning day." Wheatley concludes "Morning" with an even more oppressive set of images:

> See in the east th' illustrious king of day!
> His rising radiance drives the shades away—
> But Oh! I feel his fervid beams too strong,
> And scarce begun, concludes th' abortive song.

Whereas other eighteenth-century odes to the morning close with images of pleasant light and warmth, in Wheatley's version the sun burns, and the poet must seek the solace of shade as protection.[10] Not only does the rising of the sun—the subject that inspires and makes possible these lines—drive away the shade that Wheatley had sought as protection, but its "rising radiance" and "fervid beams," again, the putative raison d'être of the ode, are "too strong" and drive the poet into silence and inarticulacy. The "feather'd race" might well resume their "Harmonious lays," but the poet is reduced to enforced, almost stunned, silence.

The Christian tradition from St. Paul to John Donne to the American Puritans Edward Taylor and Jonathan Edwards is, of course, regularly marked by representations of God's/Christ's glory blinding the devout Christian in a sunburst of overwhelming brightness. Wheatley, too, represents the omnipotence of divinity and the love of the Christian in similar terms, but only in poems of an overtly religious nature and in elegies. In these companion meditations on morning and evening, however, Wheatley's focus is largely aesthetic and traditional, not religious. Wheatley's innovation in these two poems is to represent the sun both as the giver of light and language *and* as the force that obliterates the poet, or, more likely, the African American poet who would aspire to linguistic and cultural competence in an environment where she is quite clearly marginalized.

"An Hymn to the Morning" may even incorporate into its workings an allegory of its own reading, a signal of the double labor of Wheatley's poem: its apparent fulfilling of generic expectations *and* its violation of those expectations. First, Wheatley's reference to the Muses as "In smoothest numbers pour[ing] the notes along" can refer to Wheatley's strategic sugarcoating of her poetic resistance. She presents *smoothly* (perhaps innocently or unobtrusively—"subtly" in O'Neale's apt wording) reflections of a potentially disruptive political nature. Second, Wheatley later remarks that the "feather'd race" resuming their harmonious lays also "Dart the bright eye, and shake the painted plume." We might discern in this image a signal of the poet's alertness (a darting of her own bright eyes) to possible dangers. Moreover, we might also discover an image of the instability (the doubleness) of her own poetic labor in "shake the painted plume"— if we see this painted plume as a quill, or painting plume, and the "shaking" as Wheatley's own disruption of the eighteenth century's generic guarantees of innocuousness in a poem entitled "An Hymn to the Morning."[11] "An Hymn to the Morning" may be the clearest single statement of Wheatley's problematic position in relation to the codes of literacy and speech in eighteenth-century New England. Whiteness, emblemized here as the rising sun, enables her (even demands her) to speak, but it also is the force that erases or aborts that utterance by which Wheatley articulates her cultural selfhood.

Wheatley's use of light imagery also carries an intimately autobiographical significance. According to an early memoir, Wheatley remembered only a single detail from her African childhood: that *"her mother poured out water before the sun at its daily rising"* (Odell 12; emphasis in original). This preliterate ritual to a life-giving sun contrasts sharply with Wheatley's use of the sun as a symbol of the literacy that negates her African memories and origins. While John C. Shields argues that Wheatley's many references to the sun tend to invoke this childhood memory and serve "her as a powerful source of consolation" (242), his study does not take into account her images of the sun as blinding or overpowering.

In the gendered flux in the poem—from a feminine Aurora emblematic of the first rays of sunrise to a masculine image of the "illustrious king of day"—may also exist Wheatley's representation of her relationship to her mistress and master. Aurora may be gentler than the fierce and fervid beams of the risen sun, as Susanna was probably the kinder of the two Wheatleys, but even the relatively benevolent image of Aurora *demands* Wheatley's song. In these gendered images may also lurk a more sinister commentary on the status of enslaved African American women, who were all too often forced to feel the "rising radiance" and "fervid beams too strong" of their male owners. The images of violation and abortion concluding this ode, then, may insinuate Wheatley's awareness and condemnation of the rape of women slaves by their male owners.[12]

I have intentionally discussed these two hymns in reverse of the order in which they were first published, in 1773. If we read "Morning" after "Evening," the hope that marks the latter's final line, "Then cease, my song, till fair *Aurora* rise," is directly contradicted by the images of blindness, oppression, and abortion that characterize the actual rising of the sun in "Morning." In one sense, this maneuver is motivated by the anticipated presence of morning in "Evening"— that poem represents night and sleep, we recall, as moments in which the weary mind is soothed after a day's labor and in which the sleeping slave is rendered "more heav'nly, more refin'd," "More pure" and "more guarded from the snares of sin." The period of sleep in "Evening," then, is positioned between moments of labor and exertion as a time both of recovery and of preparation for the "labours of the day" ahead. Thus, the possible opposition between night and day as complementary or supplementary moments (of rest and exertion) is deconstructed, and night and day collapse into a relentless cycle of labor and frustration—any possible rest for the slave poet is erased. Also, the presence of Aurora at the conclusion of "Evening" and at the beginning of "Morning" provides a pivot from one meditation to the other. By placing "Morning" first in her book, however, Wheatley provides a seemingly natural movement from morning to night, but she also deflects the more despairing implications of the poems when arranged differently. By placing "On Being Brought from Africa to America" between two overtly political poems, Wheatley's subtle arranging of the poems in her book responds both to a poem's manifest content and also to its printed milieu. In one case, political disruption is veiled within the poem, but heightened by its position, while in the other, the published order of the two odes deflects the explosive potential of their mutually constitutive political commentary. We can even speculate that Wheatley's editorial practice recasts her strategy of trafficking in her dominant culture's signifying practices within the context of typography and editorial intentions.

"On Virtue," another of Wheatley's seemingly conventional works, continues the racial and political debate that informs the works we have already examined. In this case, Wheatley investigates the issues more philosophically and adds greater density and range to the ideological work of these poems by pursuing the contradictions of her status more insistently. Wheatley apostrophizes virtue as a "bright jewel" enthroned with cherubs "Array'd in *glory*" who reside "in the realms of day." Such associations would seem to privilege light (whether as whiteness, brightness, or purity) while depreciating the implied darkness of Wheatley's own racial status, and would seem to lend credence to those critics who attack Wheatley's apparent capitulation to white culture. They do, in fact, do this, but some troubling racial associations disrupt this simple polarization of light and dark, subjecting those images to the same dynamic trafficking that marks Wheatley's other works. Wheatley's personal relationship to this "bright jewel" of virtue is clearly subordinate and, perhaps, despairing. The first lines of the poem state her dilemma succinctly:

O Thou bright jewel in my aim I strive
To comprehend thee. Thine own words declare
Wisdom is higher than a fool can reach.
I cease to wonder, and no more attempt
Thine height t' explore, or fathom thy profound.
But, O my soul, sink not into despair.
Virtue is near thee, and with gentle hand
Would now embrace thee, hovers o'er thine head.

The poet's initial attempt to achieve *wisdom* seems doomed because wisdom is situated *above* her own station, and the poet seems resolved to abandon this quest. One way to read these lines would, of course, regard wisdom as "higher" in a metaphysical sense, beyond Wheatley's ken rather than beyond her literal, physical reach. Virtue, too, is situated above the speaker, but nearer and more familiarly — prepared to embrace her "with gentle hand." So, while both wisdom and virtue are above the speaker, the former remains both too distant and too abstract, while the latter promises potential attainment. Whereas in "On Being Brought from Africa to America" the abstract ideal of Christian salvation ostensibly supplants the material condition of economic and physical slavery, in "On Virtue" the poles are reversed. The abstract and intellectual quality of wisdom is situated absolutely beyond the speaker, while the ideals of ethical and moral standards of conduct are attainable.

The key to this apparent discrepancy still lies, I suggest, in Wheatley's subordinate position relative to either wisdom or virtue as defined within the parameters of white cultural ideals. Both are above her. Near the end of the poem, Wheatley resolves to rename virtue "*Greatness, or Goodness, . . .* To give an higher appellation still," and she closes with the familiar associations of

> Teach me a better strain, a nobler lay,
> O Thou, enthron'd with Cherubs in the realms of day!

Throughout "On Virtue" Wheatley situates herself beneath wisdom and virtue. Furthermore, the poet casts herself in the role of passive lover (virtue might *embrace* her) or as a student whom virtue would teach a proper form of conduct.

These final two lines of "On Virtue" also recall the racial suggestions that tend to characterize these poems. One of the things that virtue might teach the poet is "a better strain," a phrase resonant with plausible racial connotations. Just as Wheatley may awake "more heav'nly, more refin'd" in "Evening," and just as she invokes the Muses to "Assist my labours, and my strains refine" in "Morning," the "better strain" in "On Virtue" carries the possible signification of Wheatley's racial "strain," which may be improved, at least in the conceptual terms of Wheatley's poetic canon, by becoming more white, or more like that of whites. The final line places the source of this "better strain," however, again beyond the poet, "enthron'd with Cherubs in the realms of day!" These concluding lines further problematize two important lines of thought in the poem. Virtue was at first regarded as nearer, and therefore more attainable, than wisdom. But in the poem's final lines, virtue is beyond human grasp, in some angelic retreat significantly beyond the reach of human existence. Furthermore, this transcendent locale is the realm of *day*—of whiteness and brightness—and carries all the associations of the dominant white culture to which Wheatley is subordinated by virtue of her racial, sexual, and economic status.

Embedded in these conventional sounding lines on virtue, as in the poems discussed above, is a representation of the poet's role as the African American slave of the white Wheatleys. While Wheatley's literacy is extraordinary, her owners would clearly have preferred to have her virtuous than wise, more a pious Uncle Tom (whose literacy functions exclusively in his reading of the Bible) than a rebellious Frederick Douglass (whose reading and writing are integral to his liberatory praxis). Good behavior was essential to her role as house servant, while wisdom, as Frederick Douglass's and other slave narratives make clear, was defined as off-limits. Interestingly, the poet can be taught the "better strain" or the "nobler lay" of virtue, but not wisdom, a concept as plausibly within the purview of education as virtue. In addition to these representations of a social hierarchy, the racial suggestions of "On Virtue" are enhanced by significant examples of personification. Virtue is near the poet and "with gentle hand / Would now embrace [her]." Just as Wheatley translates economic bondage into religious liberation in "On Being Brought from Africa to America," she imagines virtue as a "gentle hand," a possible allusion to the less brutal terms of her servitude under Susanna Wheatley. Such an orientation in "On Virtue" accounts for the poet's sense of personal subjection to higher values and helps place Wheatley's poetics in the context of her specific social status as a slave woman. Her owners may have used "gentle hands" (they were known, however, to beat Prince), but they were, nonetheless, above and beyond her in absolute social and economic terms.

Our sense of Wheatley's troubled existence within the Wheatley household is corroborated, in part, by Eugene Genovese's findings on the general condition of house slaves. While Genovese's focus is on southern plantations, his remarks can shed light on the existence of the northern slaves as well, and, potentially, on Wheatley's lived ambivalence. Genovese stresses, above all, the inadequacy of the assumptions often brought to the study of lower classes by social historians and formulates a way "of avoiding the twin elitist notions that these classes [slaves included] are generally either passive or on the brink of insurrection" ("American Slaves" 295). As we have seen, Genovese's cautions are quite to the point for Wheatley scholarship, which has tended to cast Wheatley in one of these polarized roles, but his perspective is equally useful for biographical analysis. Comment-

ing on the many letters and diaries of planters who were shocked by
the "defection of their favorite slaves," Genovese suggests that whites
who fancied themselves the intimates of their house slaves had to face
the fact "that they had been deceiving themselves, that they had been
living intimately with people they did not know at all" (309). The corrective Genovese offers stresses neither passivity nor rebelliousness
as the "nature" of slaves, but the inherent ambiguity of all master-
slave relations. "The master-slave relationship," he argues, "especially
when it occurred in the intimacies of the Big House, was always profoundly ambivalent" (310). Granting that the day-to-day contact between whites and their house slaves did have a profound impact on
the identity of the slaves, Genovese nonetheless resists the suggestion
that physical intimacy generated acceptance on the part of the slaves:

> The house slaves were indeed close to the whites, and of all the
> black groups they exhibit the most direct adherence to certain
> white cultural standards. . . . But this kind of cultural accom-
> modation was by no means the same thing as docility, as Uncle
> Tomism. Even a relatively assimilated house slave could and nor-
> mally did strike back, assert independence, and resist arbitrari-
> ness and oppression. (315)

The overall portrait Genovese draws of master-slave relations on
southern plantations is one of ambivalence and ambiguity, not at all
one that can adequately be characterized as simple or stable. As he
argues, "it is impossible to think of people, black and white, slave
and master, thrown together in the intimacy of the Big House without realizing that they had to emerge loving and hating each other"
(311). Aside from the possible objections that one may raise to suggesting rough equivalence between southern plantations and the New
England household, the appropriateness of Genovese's remarks for
Phillis Wheatley's relations with the Wheatley family is clear. What
literary historians and scholars have accepted as the kindness of the
Wheatleys, the emotional intimacy between Susanna Wheatley and
"her Phillis," and Wheatley's own apparent capitulation to the values
of her white owners and endorsement of their religious translation
of slave owning into missionary generosity need not be accepted

at face value. They need to be examined more critically within the emotional, physical, and political parameters of master-slave relations.

Phillis's general condition under the Wheatleys seems to have been mild, almost pampered; some evidence suggests she was nearly suffocated socially and emotionally. For instance, M. A. Richmond comments that in the Wheatley household,

> hers was a place in which she could not mingle with other black slaves as equals, nor could she encounter whites on terms of equality. She inhabited a strange, ambiguous twilight zone between black society and white society, cut off from any normal human contact with either, denied the sustenance of group identity, doomed to a loneliness that, being particular and peculiar, was more tragic than the existentialist generalizations about the human condition. (20–21)

Furthermore, Wheatley could not have entered the Wheatley household unaffected by the ordeal of her enslavement and voyage to the colonies. As William Robinson speculates,

> during these months, Phillis and the gradually swelling number of other slaves were made to understand that they lived under constant threat of being punished, whipped, or even killed if they did not obey often confusing orders from strange, white-skinned crew members, some of them no more than teenagers. . . . Phillis found that she had, somehow, to absorb and assimilate the threats and the cultural shock of living daily among these people. (*Phillis Wheatley* 7–8)

Robinson offers corroboration for Richmond's position and further suggests the problematic nature of Wheatley's existence when he recounts Susanna Wheatley's becoming furious with Prince, another Wheatley slave, for having had the audacity to sit in the same carriage seat with Phillis while bringing her home. According to Robinson, Mrs. Wheatley's concern for her pet slave often bordered on the oppressive. "Often thinking of Phillis as something of an actual daughter," Robinson notes, "Mrs. Wheatley would try, in vain, to keep her from familiarity with other blacks, even other Wheatley household servants" (24).

Rather than socialize with her contemporaries, Wheatley was expected to be on hand more as a performer than as an actual daughter. As Lorenzo Greene notes, New England slaves were often exhibited in ways that can be regarded as early displays of what Thorstein Veblen was later to term "conspicuous consumption." In a yearly spectacle called "lection day," "the slaves were fitted out in their best clothing and, since the dress of the slave was held to reflect the opulence of his master, owners are said to have vied with one another to see whose slave would be the best attired" (250). While the existing biographical evidence suggests that Phillis was almost certainly spared the humiliation of existing as an emblem of her owners' economic potency, she *did* serve a similar function as a living testament to her owners' high culture. We might recall that she was *expected* to perform poetically to impress guests at the Wheatley home.

One final biographical note indicates possibly even more conflict within the Wheatley household. Phillis was freed by John Wheatley early in 1774, apparently in response to his wife's deathbed wish (Ackers 399–400). However, even this act is surrounded by unsettling inconsistencies. According to Robinson, "she had not been freed merely by the belatedly spontaneous beneficence of her master and mistress," but in response to pressures from friends in England (*Phillis Wheatley* 47). Furthermore, there is no mention whatsoever of Phillis in John Wheatley's will, a strange omission for a master whose slave brought him such celebrity. The circumstances of Wheatley's manumission as well as her neglect in the will of John Wheatley indicate at least some strain within the Wheatley family regarding the importance and status of their slave Phillis.

While these incidents individually might not generate much revision of our sense of the favored status of Phillis Wheatley and of her genial and intimate relationship with the Wheatleys, together they suggest an atmosphere of control, domination, and possible dissension in the Wheatley household that could hardly have left Phillis unaffected or merely complacent. Again, her relationship to dominant white culture is strained and ambiguous. Her achievements at once guarantee her a comparatively easy daily existence, while they also render her little more than the Wheatleys' most prized material possession. From this perspective, we may begin to understand Wheatley's metaphors and tropes of blindness, violation, and oppression not as merely conventional, but as coded representations of the slave's subjection within white culture and of the anguish, pain, and humiliation of even so apparently "easy" a life as Phillis Wheatley had. What is crucial is that we cease processing her rhetoric as transparent and self-evident and that we begin to read her rhetoric as rhetoric—strategic, subtle, and veiled.

v

For Wheatley, as for subsequent African American authors, the confrontation with whiteness is more precarious than are such confrontations in the narratives of Melville, Hawthorne, or Poe. Wheatley's rhetoric, in fact, anticipates a major thematic of later African American literary production, from Frederick Douglass's first illuminating (nearly blinding) vision of Sophia Auld to Invisible Man's waking in a white hospital room (after the explosion at the paint factory) and being surrounded by white doctors in white hospital gowns who insist that he forget his name and his heritage before being released with a clean bill of health. Instead of an ontological and philosophical void capable of accommodating diverse associations, for them trafficking with whiteness is an arena of political and psychological struggle. It can light up the road to freedom, but it can also implicate African American narratives in a cultural discourse that guarantees their domestication. Wheatley's negotiation of the dominant culture's racial and political codes braves the hazards of those terrains and formulates a language capable of being read within the aesthetic, political, and religious discourses of her time, while also capable of representing the drama of the African American subject under the dominance of white discursive practices.

It is important to question the extent to which Wheatley is in control of what I have described as her oppositional poetics and whether such "control" is even necessary and compatible with understanding the social and historical moment in which poetic (and other) discourse arises. The ambivalence and the contradictions embedded in her deployment of racially encoded imagery and in her strategies of poetic closure may, of course, suggest the *mere* problematics of Wheatley's status in colonial Boston rather than a coherent and politically aware arsenal of tactics. Confusion, ambivalence, and contradiction do not necessarily constitute opposition. Nor can we assume that Wheatley's discourse is inherently oppositional simply by virtue of her status as a African American woman slave. To view her in this way would be to ignore the fact that women, African Americans, and African American women *have* frequently internalized sexism and racism to the extent that they could express the interests of those oppressing them. We need to situate particular discourses historically— as thoroughly and as specifically as possible—in order not to simplify and codify power relations by finding power and the resistance to power omnipresent in any discursive formation.

What is crucial, however, and what may well have enabled Wheatley's poetry to be received and processed so smoothly (the only debates surrounding the publication of her works concerned the ability of any African American to write poetry as acceptably literate as hers) is that the disruptions enacted in Wheatley's poetic closures would quite easily and naturally be missed by her readership. Readers' blindness to so potentially explosive a set of propositions would not simply have been a function of repression or of racially biased reading practices. Readers quite likely missed the play of Wheatley's racial and ontological ambiguities due to the absence of any preexisting generic codes for a poetic practice such as Wheatley's. Wheatley wrote, of course, before the establishment and consolidation of "African American" or "women's" literature. It is possible that Wheatley's innovative practice even before manumission boldly, almost prophetically, anticipates the discursive strategies of subsequent African American writers, of women writers, perhaps even of any person attempting to register oppositional language in the midst of a dominant culture hostile to such formulations and at a moment prior to the formalization of generic conventions for such oppositional discourse. Wheatley was, so to speak, writing a form of oppositional verse that was virtually unreadable for a public with certain racial, political, theological, and cultural assumptions. Her poems *were* eminently readable, however, within the discursive practices of her culture in a way that guaranteed their popularity as well as their domestication, simultaneously their transparency as well as their opacity. The "angelic train" Wheatley describes in her poetry, then, can be (and has been) read as a one-way trip to oblivion and racial accommodation, but it might also be read as a prophetic anticipation of the Underground Railroad.

Before addressing the loose ends that evoke the ideological work of Herman Melville's *Israel Potter: His Fifty Years of Exile,* I would like to recount two separate incidents from my experience teaching Melville's 1855 novel. Occurring during the Reagan administration, at the University of Oklahoma (1985) and at Marquette University (1988), these incidents suggest to me not only the historically specific pervasiveness of what was then called Reaganomics (extending in many Reaganological particulars through the Bush era) but also a persistent strain within the history of Melville criticism. While discussing *Israel Potter* with a small group of advanced English majors at Oklahoma, I noticed one woman scowling every time I advanced a sympathetic reading of Melville's protagonist, the loosely historical Israel Potter. I finally asked what the grimaces were all about. This particular student was extremely hostile to Potter because, as she put it, he was far too passive, too weak, too dependent on the narrative's more affluent, powerful, and politically well situated characters, including Benjamin Franklin, John Paul Jones, and Squire Woodcock. Potter didn't try nearly hard enough to better his condition through the hard work and dedication to self-improvement Americans know to be the hallmarks of successful individuality and citizenship. Potter was, she said quite bluntly, too much like contemporary welfare lazes; like them, Potter lived on the dole and contented himself with whatever handouts he could mooch. To punctuate her remarks, she proudly and deftly quoted some appropriate passages regarding individuality and autonomy from Emerson's "Self-Reliance" and "The American Scholar."

Several years later, I encountered a subtly nuanced version of this attitude from a student in a sophomore survey of American literature at Marquette University in Milwaukee, Wisconsin. Having learned from my experience in Oklahoma that students were wont to perceive this novel and its titular hero differently than I ever had, I opened our discussion by asking students to give their general impressions of the Melville character. One young man boldly volunteered his perspective: Potter was a weak, puny character who simply didn't embody valuable "American" traits such as patriotism, hard work, and stick-to-itiveness. Not altogether unprepared, I asked for some specific examples of behavior that motivated this indictment. Without missing a beat (and, as I saw it, somewhat shocked that I had missed the obvious), he responded with an air of scorn and triumph: "Well, he did marry some foreign girl, didn't he?" Israel Potter, in this student's estimation, was a traitor, the eighteenth-century avatar of the sort of villain who, today, would buy a Toyota and help starve the children of unemployed American autoworkers.

These were both very intelligent young adults; both worked hard and, as far as I could tell, were enthusiastic about their work; both volunteered valuable comments in class on an almost daily basis; and both received A's for their final grades. Neither had previously struck me as ideologically rigid or even politically informed; yet both articulated and defended with admirable rigor and enthusiasm perspectives commonly perceived as the hallmarks of Reagan's America, the cowboy-like rugged pull-yourself-up-by-your-own-bootstraps individualism and the "Buy American" (or at least, marry American) nationalism always popular with American industry, even as it relocates its factories to South Korea, Malaysia, Mexico, or some other haven of low wages at the same time it tightens border restrictions for *people* trying to improve their lives. Nor were these students exceptions—similar sentiments (though not always so memorable) have been advanced by numerous other students in my classes (graduate and undergraduate) on *Israel Potter.* In fact, no other work of literature I've ever taught has elicited responses so indicative of what is now commonly called "the politics of reading."[1] These perspectives had simply percolated into their worldviews and taken on the obviousness and solidity of common sense. I have, of course, considered the likelihood that my own ideological commitment, perhaps more obvious in my discussions of *Israel Potter* than of other narratives, draws such attitudes out. Nevertheless, I regularly teach texts of intense political interest from a self-advertised oppositional point of view, and rarely have my remarks on John Winthrop's "A Model of Christian Charity," Wheatley's poetry, Paine's *The Age of Reason*, Cooper's *The Prairie*, Douglass's *Narrative*, Thoreau's *Walden*, Stowe's *Uncle Tom's Cabin*, James's *The Bostonians*, Harper's *Iola Leroy*, Chopin's *The Awakening*, and Wright's *Uncle Tom's Children*, to mention only the most obviously volatile and potentially challenging to various classroom constituencies, aroused attitudes so difficult for me to process.

In their own ways, however, these remarks by undergraduates mirror one of the most influential trajectories of professional *Israel Potter* criticism. Melville criticism has focused inordinately on the characterological dimensions of *Israel Potter,* especially on its most colorful personages, Franklin, Jones, and Potter himself. In fact, the critical community has viewed Melville's Revolutionary beggar quite variously, suggesting a character whose range and ambiguity approaches that of Captain Ahab in its resonance and profound ambivalence. F. O. Matthiessen set the stage for such discussions in *American Renaissance,* when he declared *Israel Potter* (along with *The Confidence-Man*) "to have been produced by a man not at all able to write the kind of books he wanted to, but under a miserable compulsion" (491), and suggested that the novel's only strength lay in the biographical sketches, which demonstrated "how much Melville had reflected on the American character" (493). Richard Chase tacitly accepts Matthiessen's focus. For Chase, Israel, with his "lank and flaxen hair," "is the very essence of the hero-peddler, kin to Brother Jonathan, Major Jack Downing, and Sam Slick" (*Herman Melville* 177). This focus on character often yields disparaging conclusions about Melville's hero. In *Herman Melville* (1950), Newton Arvin argues that, contrary to Melville's earlier characters, especially those filled with adventurous, seafaring moxie, Israel becomes "an almost featureless *recipient* of experience" (246). Charles Feidelson Jr. basically echoes Arvin in *Symbolism and American Literature* (1953), complaining (in the course of a largely negative summary of the novel) that Israel is "an unwilling exile . . . not a seeker, and he lives in a state of passive wonder" (182). In *Melville: The Ironic Diagram* (1970), John Seelye laments that Israel "becomes many things without becoming anybody"; his "many identities add up to no identity at all" (3).

William Dillingham continues along these lines when he reformulates this critical premise with new vigor: "The raving and rebelling hero is gone; profundity becomes effectively camouflaged behind an illusion of vapidity" (244). Focusing on Potter's encounters with the more famous historical characters who people the novel, Dillingham indicts Melville's beggar in even harsher terms:

> Time and again Melville departs from his source and invents such episodes in order to show Israel repeatedly failing the test of self-knowledge and, consequently, moving toward that terrible state of death-in-life that results from a lack of personal identity. (288)

Almost begrudgingly, Dillingham concludes that "Israel does live a long life, but it is an existence devoid of that power and plentitude that accompany genuine inner probing and hard-won self-knowledge and self-love" (293).[2] The power and endurance of critical inertia within the Melvillian "interpretive community" are remarkable. Nearly fifty years after Matthiessen's reading, George Dekker remarks that, "with the end of the War of Independence, Israel's need to hide in the urban wilderness also ends, but by this time he has become, like Bartleby in New York, a spiritual prisoner of his environment and incapable of self-liberation" (195). Such interpretations are strongly biased toward abstract individualism, and the individualizing imperatives of such interpretations constitute the inadequacy of these readings. One of the advances of Melville's work in *Israel Potter* is, in fact, his exploration of the possibilities for a deindividualized protagonist: not one of infinite flexibility and slipperiness as in *The Confidence-Man*, but one which anticipates the notion of the fragile (if not decentered) subjectivity more fully developed in the writings of American naturalism and more recently theorized from various poststructuralist critical perspectives. From this protonaturalist perspective, the very characteristics criticized by many scholars emerge as environmental constituents, not moralistic failures of Melvillian subjectivity.

The longevity of this interpretive paradigm, as well as the ensemble of influential critics formulating and operating within its parameters, requires us to take its claims seriously. This view of Potter as passive antihero, furthermore, gains viability when we situate it as an extension within the once dominant paradigm of Melvillian protagonist as hero/quester/adventurer, which critics generated to account for characters such as Captain Ahab and Bulkington in *Moby-Dick*, Babbalanja in *Mardi*, and, to a lesser extent, the more plausibly autobiographical characters from the early South Seas narratives. The heroics of the characters from these works, the Melville critical community tended to agree, hinged on the potency and inviolability of their autonomous selves and on the massiveness of the odds against which they pitted themselves, often in Shakespearean tragic grandeur. However valid this cluster of ideas may be for Melville's earlier narratives, its explanatory power is severely diminished and/or qualified by the time of *Pierre* (1852), which dismantles any stable environment within which to launch heroic action and discredits most, if not all, individual positions as hopelessly biased, blind, and impotent.

The specifics of *Israel Potter's* representational scheme expose the inadequacy of these critical claims in two significant ways. First, by the time he wrote the novel, Melville had already shed his earlier adherence to a unified (though always conflicted) subject and embarked on an exploration of various alternative selves, ranging from the highly volatile Pierre, the decentered Confidence Man, the static and enigmatic Bartleby, and others. As early as Ishmael's post-Pequodian doubts about the efficacy of Ahab's quenchless feud, and certainly by the time of Pierre's mock-heroics, Melville had abandoned the ideal of a titanically willful Self confidently projecting and fulfilling his desires in an exotic, oceanic wilderness. Almost as if he is following Thoreau's injunction to "be rather the Mungo Park, the Lewis and Clarke and Frobisher, of your own streams and oceans" (369), Melville turned frequently in his post–*Moby-Dick* works to venues of explicit geographical, national, and psychological interiority and, at times, claustrophobia. This is not, of course, to imply that *Moby-Dick* and earlier narratives fail to investigate ontological dimensions of selfhood, only that in *Israel Potter*, "The Piazza," "Bartleby the Scrivener," "I and My Chimney," *Billy Budd*, and others, Melville frequently examines selves and venues not obviously "heroic," and in fact commonly represents characters and locales of nearly paralyzing stasis. Furthermore, the proliferation of post-Revolutionary narratives such as Potter's (most of which advanced comparable claims to pensions) suggests that Melville was already working at the generic level with a postindividualistic discourse. As Walter Bezanson points out, "Potter's sad tale was among the last to appear of the more than two hundred veterans' narratives of the American Revolution which Richard Dorson found to be in print following the War of 1812" (185). To complicate matters even more, Hennig Cohen has discovered that the Rhode Island Veterans Affairs Office and the Rhode Island State Archives have documentation indicating that there were, in fact, *four* different Israel Potters who fought in the Revolutionary War, and that it is a matter of some dispute whether the Israel Potter in question received a pension ("Real Israel Potter" 7). These statistics and the ambiguities they present would seem to suggest that by Melville's time and perhaps for Melville the designation "Israel Potter" lacks any individualization and may well suggest a mid-nineteenth-century Everyman.

A second way in which *Israel Potter* frustrates the claims of the Melvillian interpretive community emerges from the very character of Israel Potter. Even if Melville's focus on the active, adventurous self were still operative, Israel Potter would conform much more to the Melvillian ideal than the critical assumptions of Chase, Seelye, Feidelson, Dryden, Dillingham, and others enable them to recognize. While their approaches may appropriately read the primarily subjective, ontological instability of Ahab, Pierre, and the Confidence Man, they are largely misleading when applied to the historical density of Melville's work in *Israel Potter*. It seems dubious, indeed, to classify Israel Potter as a "featureless *recipient* of experience": he sets out to earn his own fortune against parental wishes and historical odds; he explores the New England and Canadian wilderness; he fights bravely at Bunker Hill; he repeatedly outwits and escapes his British captors; he risks his life as a courier between a secret English underground and Benjamin Franklin in Paris; his ingenuity, principles, and patience enable him to successfully encounter King George III and to escape from Squire Woodcock's chimney; he single-handedly captures the crew of a small boat; he fights, thinks, and acts bravely in the service of John Paul Jones; and he labors diligently to support a wife and family in depressed, postwar London.

This chapter will challenge the characterological bases underwriting much *Israel Potter* criticism, not simply by discarding the assumptions concerning character that motivate their assaults on Israel Potter, but by arguing that, in *Israel Potter,* Melville deploys notions of character and of history and historical analysis from a decidedly oppositional stance. In fact, by situating essentialist questions regarding human character and historical truth within a matrix of economic imperatives, Melville questions not only the possibility of the kind of "American character" that enables so many Melville scholars to devalue Israel Potter and *Israel Potter,* but the validity of a notion of American history intimately bound up with the valorization of this putative "American Self." Melville's own strategies of titling his narratives throughout the 1850s invites such an approach. Stories such as *Moby-Dick, The Confidence-Man,* "Bartleby the Scrivener," and "Benito Cereno" all designate their eponymous characters as profound enigmas to be decoded rather than as necessarily central characters or protagonists. Indeed, narrative point of view in each of these works encourages us to try out, rather than simply accept, the validity or plausibility of the narrator's reading of the enigmatic focus. *Moby-Dick,* for instance, requires us to adjudicate between Ahab's and Ishmael's interpretations of Moby Dick, and complicates that readerly imperative by including numerous other, usually minor, characters to offer their own conflicting analyses; the captain and crew of *The Bachelor,* for example, refuse even to believe in the whale, while the captain of the *Samuel Enderby* knows to avoid the white peril at all costs. When Melville turns to the unreliable narrators in "Bartleby" and "Benito Cereno," on the other hand, much of our interpretive activity centers on reading their flawed and, at times, wildly inhuman understandings of their respective title characters.

Israel Potter's narrator is of a different variety, claiming something like objective and unbiased lucidity. Yet the challenge to the reader remains remarkably similar. Just as the lawyer in "Bartleby" brings certain economically and politically determined prejudices to bear on his experience, and just as Captain Amasa Delano views the events in "Benito Cereno" through the lens of a committed Enlightenment racism, *Israel Potter's* reader comes to that narrative replete with a largely consensual, internalized version of American history. Neither the lawyer nor Captain Delano alters his paralyzing assumptions as a result of the mysteries he witnesses and participates in, and our readings take their deficiencies as a primary narrative concern. Our success as readers of *Israel Potter,* I would suggest, hinges on our ability to shed our preconceived and predetermined understanding of the American Revolution and of the claims of American historiography in general and to allow our experience of the story of Israel Potter to shock, if not to correct, our sense of the American past. To play on Sacvan Bercovitch's influential phrase, in *Israel Potter,* Melville deconstructs the "Revolutionary origins of the American self," but, quite remarkably, he elicits such critical engagement via the loose ends exposed in his novel's highly compressed penultimate chapter, "Forty-five Years," as well as in its final, brief paragraph.

ii

The final passage of *Israel Potter: His Fifty Years of Exile* offers a tenuous and evocative closure for Melville's retelling of Henry Trumbull's original *Life and Remarkable Adventures of Israel R. Potter* (1824):

> He was repulsed in efforts, after a pension, by certain caprices of law. His scars proved his only medals. He dictated a little book, the record of his fortunes. But long ago it faded out of print— himself out of being—his name out of memory. He died the same day that the oldest oak on his native hills was blown down. (169)

Meant ostensibly to close Melville's "Revolutionary narrative of the beggar," this busy paragraph accomplishes many things, including the powerful equation of the ontological, the historical, and the economic implications of Potter's book fading out of print. One's book, one's life, and the endurance of one's name are all literally erased by the economic workings of the literary marketplace, here represented by the naturalistic trope "fading." Literary works, according to this logic, fall prey to the entropic workings of natural process; like bodies, shorelines, and colors, they break down and, ultimately, disappear gradually and imperceptibly with time. The coincidence of Potter dying "the same day that the oldest oak on his native hills was blown down" closes this paragraph, consolidating the naturalistic logic of the entire work. By "naturalizing" the agency of the oak tree being "blown down" by the wind, the narrative not only underscores but also contradicts its deletion of any specific agency in its image of Potter's text *fading* out of print. Far from providing any stable closure for Melville's narrative of the American past, this final paragraph rather unravels virtually every strand of *Israel Potter.*

How are we to process a final passage that intrudes the fact of literary economics—the disappearance of a source from circulation—in a novel by an author whose own literary fortunes had been steadily declining since his earliest successes and who had been warned in reviews that he (and his publishers) faced certain economic ruin and religious damnation should he continue navigating the literary course set by *Moby-Dick* and *Pierre*? Furthermore, how does so conspicuous an allusion to the disappearance of obscure persons and texts function in a historical narrative that dwells on the fates of the unheralded figures who fought valiantly for the Revolutionary cause but received neither distinction nor recompense? Rather like some of Phillis Wheatley's odes, *Israel Potter* closes not by resolving its vexed areas of inquiry but by returning to precisely those unresolved, perhaps even heightened, ideological conundrums and by parading the implications of their state of tense irresolution.

This passage quite clearly expresses some of Melville's hostility and bitterness concerning his own rapidly declining literary fortunes. After his literary reputation and fortunes had been in steady decline since the publication of *Moby-Dick* and *Pierre*, Herman Melville wrote *Israel Potter* in what is commonly regarded as a last-ditch effort to recapture a readership that had responded enthusiastically to Melville's narratives of South Seas adventures. As Walter Bezanson terms it, "the two years between the publication of *Pierre* in the summer of 1852 and the first installment of *Israel Potter* in the summer of 1854 seem to have been a difficult and ambiguous time for Melville" (178). Melville turned, in response to these difficulties and ambiguities, to a generic fusion of biographical and historical fiction, one capacious enough to enable him to pursue many of the social, philosophical, and ontological conundrums that had driven much of his fictional project since the publication of *Typee,* but one also with the more commercially viable, lively, and familiar adventures of a historically specific hero. In

May of 1854, having had his "The Two Temples" rejected by *Putnam's Monthly Magazine* for "offending the religious sensibilities of the public," Melville promised to submit "some other things, to which, I think, no objections will be made on the score of tender consciences of the public"; in June he submitted the early chapters of *Israel Potter* for publication first in the magazine, then in book form (the first time he had proposed this more lucrative arrangement), engaging that "the story shall contain nothing of any sort to shock the fastidious. There will be very little reflective writing in it; nothing weighty. It is adventure" (*Correspondence* 261, 265, 636). In some respects, *Israel Potter* was his own attempt to come back into print, to revive his own life, and to strengthen his place in American literary history.

It is, perhaps, due to remarks like the one to Putnam that critics have considered the novel, as Richard Chase quite representatively declares, "a lighthearted and unpretentious book, falling partly within the picaresque tradition" (176). However, rather like his reference to the ill-fated *Pierre* as "a rural bowl of milk" (*Correspondence* 219), Melville's own promotional remarks introduce into *Israel Potter* the authorial doubleness that he attempted to sustain in order to produce another narrative capable of straddling two rhetorical fences, one generically familiar and domestic, the other generically unstable and meditative. In this sea narrative, as in *Moby-Dick,* "meditation and water are wedded forever." In fact, Melville's earliest reference (December 18, 1849) to this project as "the Revolutionary narrative of the beggar" already insinuates a powerful level of critique. Referring to Melville's phrasing as "ungrammatical," Walter Bezanson assumes that Melville *must* mean a narrative of the Revolutionary soldier who fights in and then descends into pauperism following the war (186), certainly a reasonable plan for a popular literary project. However, while Melville certainly *is* capable of ungrammaticality, he might genuinely want to write a *revolutionary narrative,* that is, one which in its thematics and level of ideological critique pits itself radically against American popular political and historical opinion. From one angle, in fact, *Israel Potter* is a generically predictable and ideologically consensual project, from another a literary and historical discourse of profoundly disturbing proportions. Melville's turn to the historical is really a return to many socio-ideological issues already embedded within much of his novelistic output and progressively central to his short fiction in *The Piazza Tales*, written at much the same time as *Israel Potter*.

Within *Israel Potter* Melville articulates a shrewd commentary on the economy and the economies of history and literary history, one complicated by the fact that the historical personages who populate Israel Potter's narrative include Benjamin Franklin, John Paul Jones, Ethan Allen, and, by virtue of literary echoes, Ralph Waldo Emerson and Henry David Thoreau—all figures whose influential places in American history and literary history were personally and consciously managed and promoted. In *Israel Potter*, Melville critiques an economy that requires the suppression of anything resembling the "full historical record" in order to package and arrange a historical narrative in an acceptable (both politically and aesthetically) commodity. The problem, as Melville sees it, is that for the likes of Franklin and John Paul Jones to achieve historical prominence and enduring political and literary fame, the labors and accomplishments of others must be erased from the public record. In this case, Israel Potter performs many of the dangerous tasks for which Franklin and Jones are commonly (even in many of today's school textbooks) attributed full responsibility. The task of the historian, Melville might argue, is the painstaking reconstruction of the erased margins of history in order to tell something like "more of the truth," or perhaps a "different," if not the "real truth." I argue that Melville's conclusion actually hedges by suggesting that Potter's "little book" *faded* out of print, and that Melville's own book actually reveals the economy by which books are *forced* out of print by other books whose claim to "the truth" is more marketable. Melville saturates the narrative's most pressing thematics with the dynamics and pressures of economic equations, which, in virtually every instance, expose an insidious inertia underlying ("beneath," in David Reynolds's sense) both the literary production of the so-called American Renaissance and the narrativization of American history. *Israel Potter*'s representation of American history, literary history, the intimate linkage between American nature and American experience, and, ultimately, the much-heralded American character frames each of these thematic constellations within a horizon, not of moral righteousness, but of economic power.

iii

Melville introduces the dynamics of literary economy early in the preface to *Israel Potter* and, thus, frames the entire narrative (including his introductory, authorial qua editorial remarks) with the economy of literary history. In his several-paragraph dedication to the Bunker Hill Monument, Melville quickly divulges his conclusion. Discussing how he discovered the original Potter biography, Melville encapsulates the fate of his source:

> Shortly after his return in infirm old age to his native land, a little narrative of his adventures, forlornly published on sleazy gray paper, appeared among the peddlers, written, probably, not by himself, but taken down from his lips by another. But like the crutch-marks of the cripple by the Beautiful Gate, this blurred record is now out of print. From a tattered copy, rescued by the merest chance from the rag-pickers, the present account has been drawn. (vii)

Positioned so conspicuously at the very beginning and very end of *Israel Potter,* these passages recounting the publishing fate of Israel Potter's original narrative constitute not only a noticeable frame for Melville's narrative, but a frame from which a history of Melville's book (perhaps any book) can be inferred. We recall that, in his final paragraph, Melville mentions both that Potter's "little book . . . faded out of print," and that Potter "died the same day that the oldest oak on his native hills was blown down" (169). If we take the falling of a tree as a moment enabling the harvesting of one of the raw materials for papermaking, Potter's death and his narrative's fading out of print correspond precisely with the creation of the materials for the composition of other books about other lives. Melville, no less than Henry David Thoreau, projects a zero-sum "economy"; money, resources, and discursive space spent on one life are exhausted and unavailable for any others.

The introductory reference takes on greater meaning, then, when we notice that Melville "rescues" Potter's original narrative from the "rag-pickers," those who would collect rags (and unwanted books) for the paper mills and for trunk makers, who recycled the materials from old books as trunk linings. Melville's picking the book up from the ragpickers, then, preserves the identity of Potter's narrative by preventing it from becoming the paper for the representation or cartage of some other life. The reference to the "sleazy gray paper" that supposedly bore the ink traces of Potter's biographical narrative underscores both the forlornness and the niggardly presentation of the original biography. But this account is fabricated. As Hennig Cohen demonstrates, the paper of Melville's copy of *Life and Remarkable Adventures of Israel R. Potter* was, in fact, "normal for its period, fairly white rather than gray and inexpensive though hardly sleazy" (*Israel Potter* 349). By intentionally cheapening the quality of the original publication, Melville suggests that, even in its initial appearance, Potter's literary offering was disadvantageously produced and marketed, an economic and technological handicap capable of offsetting whatever credibility entering the world of print circulation may have lent Potter's narrative claim to a pension. Canonicity, Melville suggests, is far more complex than simply going into or "fading" out of print; aside from any and all questions of public taste and literary quality, it cannot be separated from the hard facts of literary economics and papermaking technologies. In both the prefatory and concluding passages, Melville offers a complex of literary recycling involving natural process (the growth and falling of trees), technological production (the manufacture of paper goods), and economic cycle (books going into and "fading" out of print). While exposing such a dynamic, Melville's own narrative nonetheless obscures the logic by suggesting that, in both cases, random naturalistic process rather than any conscious economic workings governs the entire complex. Just as trees do fall when they extend well past their maturity, ragpickers simply collect whatever they are given, presumably books and old clothes that have outlived their usefulness. According to Melville's explicit rendering, "fading" might well be an adequate term for the life-history of books.

However, throughout his own version of Israel Potter's life, Melville foregrounds an alternative economy, one very much in the service of human agency. Ragpickers, to be sure, function as components in an economic and social ensemble that relegates the humble and contemptuous livelihood of gathering rags to the lower rungs of the social ladder. So, while the final reference to Potter's book fading out of print posits a naturalistic metaphor for the economic fate of his narrative, Melville's first such reference—technically prior to the emergence of the narrative proper—discredits this evasive logic by proleptically insinuating the naked facts of both a cultural and a social economy. While the "representative man" of American popular culture, whether in a Franklinian, an Emersonian, or an Algerian mode, might well undergo the mythic transformation "from rags to riches," Melville's "Revolutionary narrative of the beggar" stages the suppressed underside of this "American dream." Melville figures Israel Potter's story with a difference, "from rags to rags"; that is, from the rags and various tattered disguises Potter dons to escape discovery during his long exile in England to the rags his obsolete little book joins (or would have joined) as a discarded book suited only for disposal.

In fact, after Israel exchanges clothes for the first time (in order not to be seen in "the dress of an English sailor") Melville departs from Trumbull's original narrative when he significantly notes, "Little did [Israel] ween that these wretched *rags* he now wore, were but suitable to that long career of destitution before him; one brief career of adventurous wanderings: and then, forty torpid years of pauperism" (19; my emphasis). Melville's revision of Trumbull's passage changes little other than the appearance of the clothes Israel gets from the older man; in the original, the farmer trades Israel his "church suit," his best, albeit a motley, patched affair (314–15). The primary difficulty for Trumbull's Potter is the tightness of the ill-fitting suit he receives. Melville transforms the clothes to work clothes (not Sunday reserve) with gaping knees; they render Israel as they rendered their rustic wearer "the very picture of poverty, toil and distress. His clothes were tatters" (19). In addition to these early references, Melville regularly punctuates *his* narrative with allusions to rags (and, in some cases, tatters), describing, in all cases save one, Potter's impoverished apparel.[3] Moreover, of these various moments, only the last corresponds to Trumbull's original narrative, when Potter himself is reduced to collecting old rags to survive difficult economic times. Each of the others reinforces Melville's oppositional work on the quintessential myth of American subjectivity overcoming oppressive odds en route to economic success and ontological stability. Melville revises his source significantly to make Israel's first suit of borrowed clothing conform to the ragpicker's heap from which he supposedly rescues that source.

Throughout this "Revolutionary narrative," Melville represents a used or secondhand (at least) rag pile of a social, cultural, and natural world. This is a narrative world in which all components function in the service of some other sector or logic, with the entirety of *Israel Potter* as the largest and most conspicuous such entity. Of course, Melville announces as much when he declares that his work "with [only] a change in the grammatical person, . . . preserves, almost as in a reprint, Israel Potter's autobiographical story" (vii). Melville's *Israel Potter: His Fifty Years of Exile,* thus, advertises its distance from any original, prerepresented historical events. There was a soldier named Israel Potter who performed certain feats during and after the Revolutionary War. There was a biography written by Henry Trumbull based on the oral narrative of said Israel Potter concerning his exploits. There is now Melville's own extension of this lineage. But Melville immediately complicates this already circuitous representational scheme by mentioning yet another set of narratives that he has evidently consulted, "the volumes of Sparks" (viii), in which the name of Potter, remarkably to Melville (the Editor), does not appear. As John Samson documents in his brilliant *White Lies: Melville's Narratives of Facts,* Melville does, indeed, owe a significant debt to the biographies of Jared Sparks, but he owes equally as much to historical and biographical works of Ethan Allen, George Bancroft, James Fenimore Cooper, Nathaniel Fanning, Benjamin Franklin, Richard Hildreth, and Robert C. Sands, among others.[4] Melville's *Israel Potter* represents, then, a complex intertextual relay for numerous literary and historiographical texts, as well as a meditation on the scene of literary-historical discourse. Melville's own narrative stages the dialogical struggle within and for representation directly and aggressively. By so doing, he frees his own work from any pretense of precise historical accuracy, though not, I will argue, from historical truth.

My focus will be on Melville's negotiation of two representative lives, those of Benjamin Franklin and Ralph Waldo Emerson, with passing reference to his treatment of John Paul Jones and Ethan Allen. While Melville's rewriting of Potter's narrative engages a number of other texts with a number of other motives and revisionary schemes, the lives, texts, and receptions of Franklin and Emerson impact directly on Potter's fate with peculiar force. Specifically, the economy revealed by *Israel Potter* is a complex of historical, ideological, and literary issues based on thematics derived from the self-representations of Franklin and Emerson. While Franklin quite obviously occupies a major, if problematic, place in *Israel Potter,* Emerson and transcendentalism exist as a focus of Melville's critique more subtly and allusively, though quite as significantly as Franklin. These two figures merge to represent compatible perspectives on nature, history, and self-representation and -promotion. However unlikely the convergence of Franklin (the utilitarian intent on mastering nature and creating history) and Emerson (the idealist intent on signifying nature and surviving in history), their views and the angles they work prove equally antithetical to the interests of Israel Potter and his place within both the natural world and the (literary) historical record.

Though readers agree that Franklin plays a pivotal role in *Israel Potter,* Melville scholars have regarded that role variously, often irreconcilably. William Dillingham argues for a wholly virtuous and admirable reading of Franklin, consistently at the expense of Potter, a doltish and opaque bumpkin incapable of grasping the complexities of the venerable Franklin's profound moral import and solidly heroic character. From Dillingham's perspective,

> Israel's exposure to Benjamin Franklin, John Paul Jones, and Ethan Allen does not alter his limited understanding of the nature of true liberty. Time and again Melville departs from his source and invents such episodes in order to show Israel repeatedly failing the test of self-knowledge and, consequently, moving toward that terrible state of death-in-life that results from a lack of personal identity. (288)[5]

Walter Bezanson casts Melville's representation of Franklin as "dominantly comic," but "so complex and informed as to suggest considerable study of Franklin's life and writings" (192). Richard Chase characterizes Melville's attitude toward Franklin as "humorously hostile. . . . Franklin is at once a likable, fairy-tale philosophizer and charlatan" (178), softening the impact of this putative indictment by limiting his critique to Franklin's charlatanism. More recently, critics have turned their attention to Franklin's more sinister role in Melville's text, highlighting more devious traits in Franklin's character. Judith Hiltner, for example, refers to Franklin's (and Jones's) "abandonment" of Potter as well as to the absence of any genuinely patriotic motives informing Franklin's conduct. John Samson examines Franklin's discursive identity as Melville would have known it, dwelling on Franklin's apparent insouciance toward the poor and the oppressed. Samson concludes that

> Melville's Franklin is akin to Jacob and Hobbes: the former acquired his brother's birthright by taking advantage of Esau's extreme hunger (Gen. 25), while the latter developed a philosophy of self-interest that culminated in the totalitarian Leviathan.
> (187)

Finally, H. Bruce Franklin and Carolyn Karcher anticipate Samson's critique of Franklin with brief analyses of *Israel Potter* as proletarian text, both critics exposing the suppression of working-class contributions to the Revolutionary cause (Franklin 62–63; Karcher 102).

While I sympathize with Samson's, Franklin's, and Karcher's line of thinking, I am less interested in taking sides on Benjamin Franklin's role in *Israel Potter* than I am in exploring Melville's analysis of the founding father's role in the literary and historical economy of the United States—in other words, I want to consider the representational inertia that has accrued to the figure of Benjamin Franklin in the popular memory. *Israel Potter* may well hold the likes of Franklin culpable for certain inequities endemic in American social life, but it seems equally plausible that it merely observes the naturalistic, nearly mechanical, operations of a literary economy that is without any guidance or regulation from an "invisible hand" and, thus, renders such metaphysical questions out of order. In fact, one of the great remaining issues in Melville criticism (especially in *Israel Potter* and later works) is Melville's contribution to, perhaps his invention of, the genre of naturalism, in which, as many generic theorists believe, questions of morality, ethics, fairness, and the like are rendered moot by the inexorable and often brutal workings of natural process. Israel Potter may be victim of the subtle connivings and manipulations of unscrupulous opportunists, but he may equally be, like Theodore Dreiser's Carrie Meeber almost fifty years later, merely "a waif amidst forces."

Most discussions of Franklin's role in *Israel Potter* focus exclusively on those chapters in which the "venerable sage," as Melville calls him, figures explicitly in the narrative action. But there is a vast array of less direct ways in which Melville insinuates Franklin's many voices and beliefs into *Israel Potter.* One such introduction occurs early in the novel, when Potter embarks as a trader among the Native Americans. Melville characterizes his industry and independence:

> One fancies that, had it been summer, Israel would have travelled with a wheelbarrow, and so trundled his wares through the primeval forests, with the same indifference as porters roll their barrows over the flagging of streets. In this way was bred that fearless self-reliance and independence which conducted our forefathers to national freedom. (9)

The suggestion that Potter may have paraded his goods via wheelbarrow, of course, echoes one of the more famous moments from Franklin's *Autobiography.* Defining his own industriousness and rationalizing his methods ("to show that I was not above my Business"), Franklin notes:

> I sometimes brought home the Paper I purchas'd at the Stores, thro' the Streets on a Wheelbarrow. Thus being esteem'd an industrious thriving young Man, and paying duly for what I bought, the Merchants who imported Stationary solicited my Custom, others propos'd supplying me with Books, & I went on swimmingly. (68)

Franklin's entire narrative articulates the theory and virtues of industry quite explicitly, and this passage obviously functions as a seminal moment in the *Autobiography* (not to mention in its subsequent reception and canonization). But the workings of this passage are remarkable even beyond whatever pragmatic or utilitarian ethos the autobiographer desires to impart.

Of primary interest is the fact that this wheelbarrow vignette precedes the character Franklin's appearance in Melville's text by some years of narrative time and by five chapters. Franklin's "presence" in *Israel Potter* is thus implied via this allusion significantly before any explicit discursive representation of Franklin's character. For Melville as "editor" of this revisionary telling of Potter's story, Franklin exists as part of a cultural archive, a flexible body of quotations available for citation, much like the sayings of Poor Richard constitute a substantial part of Potter's and John Paul Jones's lexicon and moral encyclopedia within *Israel Potter*'s middle chapters. The accessibility and recognizability of Franklinian discourse is itself remarkable, given that, as William Shurr points out, "no version of the *Autobiography* anything like what we now read was published until the 1840s" (435). Franklin's allusive entry into Melville's version of Potter's biography also figures prominently in *Israel Potter*'s commentary on the economy of literary history, precisely by signaling the fact that Franklin's text(s), by virtue of their immediate and profitable marketability (their remaining *in* print), are generally and conveniently available for citation. One can fall back, so to speak, on Franklin's sayings and on canonized moments from his life history—they constitute, to an unspecifiable degree, the rhetorical archive of American culture. By contrast, by commenting that Potter's little book "faded out of print" Melville dramatizes American culture's repressive construction of a barely recoverable political unconscious.

Moreover, that Franklin's language occupies such a privileged role in Melville's America by no means occurred accidentally, but rather by the careful management and consolidation of Franklin's reputation, by Franklin himself as well as by his contemporaries and by subsequent filiopietistic brokers in cultural currency. Beginning with the publication of his *Autobiography*, Franklin coordinated a careful and opportunistic public-relations mechanism intent on protecting and disseminating his image to posterity. Franklin himself introduces his text as the conduit of a life "fit to be imitated" (1), while Benjamin Vaughn affirms, in a letter Franklin includes as one of the transitional passages bridging its first and second parts, that the style (and substance) of Franklin's text will quite likely "induce more men to spend lives fit to be written" (188).[6] Both of these accolades, of course, attempt to specify the proper reception of Franklin's narrative by casting the sage as both a rhetorical and an ethical exemplar. Similarly, as Benjamin Vaughn also notes, any such intervention, any preemptive rhetorical posture, necessarily carries a polemical and, in the terms I am using, an economic dimension. In urging Franklin to continue his autobiographical project, Vaughn offers both positive and negative incentives: "your history," he summarizes, "is so remarkable, that if you do not give it, somebody else will certainly give it; and perhaps so as nearly to do as much harm, as your own management of the thing might do good" (185). This might be what Michael Warner has in mind when, in discussing how Franklin's represented life shares many of the features of books, he remarks that "although Franklin has been (at least since Weber's *Protestant Ethic and the Spirit of Capitalism*) the exemplary figure of modernity, his exemplary modern subjectivity can be read as a very special cultural articulation of printing" (75).

Vaughn's reading of Franklin's problematic historical status could hardly have been more to the point, although he was wrong to suggest that Franklin had to manage and promote his image to posterity single-handedly. As Michael Warner, among others, points out, Franklin did not have to look far to find detractors. Franklin's enemies, for example, "portrayed him as lecherous and greedy, but above all as 'designing'; a common theme in anti-Franklin literature is the connection between his self-concealing designs and his manipulations of letters" (Warner 90). That Warner has recourse to a genre specifically designated as "anti-Franklin literature" suggests the pervasive and, at times, virulent struggles for representational dominance, struggles that, as John Samson demonstrates, were international in scope. In his attempt to consolidate an acceptably favorable historical representation of Franklin (and others), the nineteenth-century filiopietistic historian par excellence, Jared Sparks, consciously attempts to mold and cast the reputation of revolutionary hero. In each case, the reputation is a response to British aspersions: for instance, Sparks, in his "Continuation" of Franklin's *Autobiography*, controverts "a late English writer" who "insinuates" that Franklin ignored his poor relatives. (Samson 177)

William Shurr has suggested that the triumphant construction of Franklin as "American Hero" continues even into the present, arguing that "Franklin biographers often purge all events that cast doubt on Franklin's status as American saint" (446). However much criticism Franklin had (and has) come under, and however potent the charges of his detractors, the positive, "patriotic" version of Franklin managed to achieve an ascendency, certainly by Melville's time. Walter Bezanson comments on the obvious success of Franklin's promotional efforts in his discussion of Franklin's prominence as a cultural icon:

> In mid-nineteenth-century America it was impossible to escape Franklin: only Washington, archetypal father of the Republic, surpassed him as cultural hero. If Parson Weems, who had planted Washington's cherry tree in the garden of national morals, was unable to do as much for Franklin with *The Life of Doctor Benjamin Franklin* (1815), it was because the shrewd Doctor had gotten there first. (191)

This is in many ways Melville's point as well, not merely about Franklin's promotional opportunism, but about the very nature of historiographical discourse and public opinion in general. In his frequent turns to Franklin's Poor Richard motto, "God helps them that help themselves" (54, 61, 115, 118), Melville highlights the self-serving nature of autobiographical representation as well as the commonly (and perhaps unavoidably) partisan nature of all biographical and historiographical writing.

Melville's peep at Franklin's Parisian life encompasses a wide angle of critical vision, at times one nearly prophetic of subsequent trends in American cultural thought. To be sure, Melville's reading of the sage's identity, his cleverness, and his ambiguities emerges without any necessary reference to Franklin's relationship with Potter, but largely by virtue of authorial commentary in which he represents Franklin as a satanic lord of the flies (39), as a union of "the apostolic serpent and dove" (a characterization reminiscent of the Reverend Falsgrave from *Pierre*), as a "tanned Machiavelli in tents" (46), and as a savvy, worldly-wise hustler who, knowing the world, "could act any part in it" (48). Melville also represents Franklin throughout *Israel Potter* as a figure of unparalleled pomposity and duplicity, constantly lecturing and correcting young Potter's blunders, while commandeering the few creature comforts Potter's temporary French abode offers. Indeed, if, as R. Jackson Wilson has argued, Franklin himself cunningly posed so as to achieve any number of different effects in his many respective portraits (21–25), Melville's multifaceted narrative portrait ultimately challenges the tradition of visual representations of Franklin as well, just as his themes take on the composite cultural *idea* of the sage.

But Melville also insinuates a much more damaging level of critique via implicit comparisons that emerge between the illustrious Franklin and the beggarly Potter, as well as by data from a historical record that was frequently (in Melville's time as well as in ours) ignored, if not suppressed. Issues of the respective degrees of genuine patriotism of these two Revolutionary figures, and, more personally, of their relationships with their immediate family members, punctuate Melville's debasing of Franklin's currency as originary cultural icon. Melville's critique seems aimed most directly at those trends in filiopietistic historiography which served to establish and consolidate Franklin's (and Jones's) identities as "founding fathers," as *the* exemplary embodiments of distinctively American selfhood, a selfhood which had undergone trials and triumphed under martial, cultural, and ambassadorial pressures. *Israel Potter* presupposes a readership already wedded to the dominant, hegemonic vision of Franklin's identity as founding father par excellence. Without such a culturally optimal patina of associations informing his public's internalization of Benjamin Franklin, most of Melville's overt parodying of Franklin's self-importance, his dogmatism, his solicitousness, his condescension, as well as his apparent manipulation of the ignorant and provincial Potter, is incomprehensible. Melville's text, in other words, requires a canonical and normative, if not a stable, image of Franklin in the popular mind. *Israel Potter* is, in this respect, parasitical on Franklin's *Autobiography,* as well as on much of the Franklin corpus. From that basis, Melville's text goes on to cast Franklin and Potter in ways that consistently destabilize that very Franklinian image.

The statesman's credibility and patriotism receive special attention in Melville's critique. In embellishing Franklin's promise to assist Potter's return to the new Republic, Melville targets the sage's disingenuousness. Franklin was known to couch his celebrations of America's divine mission by referring to the new America as a home for any and all deserving refugees. He prayed to the Almighty to "perfect his Work, and establish Freedom in the new World, as an Asylum for those of the Old, who deserve it" (*Papers* 29: 431) and termed the Revolution "a glorious task assign'd us by Providence" (*Papers* 24: 7). John Samson calls our attention to another pertinent essay of Franklin's that we can reasonably suppose Melville to have read. In "On the Price of Corn, and Management of the Poor," Franklin's attitudes toward the poor are particularly relevant to the sage's treatment of Israel Potter: "I think the best way of doing good to the poor is, not making them easy *in* their poverty, but leading or driving them *out* of it" (*Works* 2: 358). As Samson notes, Franklin expresses the same sentiment throughout the volume (180).[7] Highlighting the contradictions between Franklin's early assurances to Potter and the exile's subsequent descent into wretchedness as well as between Franklin's theoretical dedication to alleviating the miseries of hardworking people and his actual reneging on his promise to Potter, Melville exploits the hypocritical gap between Franklin's public persona and his actual conduct throughout *Israel Potter.*

Concerning Franklin's highly vaunted patriotism, Melville is no less severe. As Judith Hiltner observes, one of Melville's important revisions of Trumbull's original life of Potter was altering "his primary source to make his protagonist appear more naively patriotic" (43). In addition to his many perilous endeavors in battle and in espionage work, Potter regularly reaffirms his commitment to American ideals, American rhetoric (especially in his casual audience with King George), and American freedom. However much Melville complicates the young Potter's motives for going to war, the Potter that we experience directly involved in European adventures is uncompromising in his loyalty to the colonial cause. Indeed, after Israel's dialogue with George III, in which the monarch's kindness and geniality alter Potter's prejudices about him, Melville's narrator hypothesizes that "had it not been for the peculiar disinterested fidelity of our adventurer's patriotism, he would have soon sported the red coat; and perhaps under the immediate patronage of his royal friend, been advanced in time to no mean rank in the army of Britain" (32), thus preemptively alleviating his decades of poverty and obscurity.

Potter's loyalty contrasts strikingly with the absence of any comparable expressions of nationalistic pride on the parts of Franklin and John Paul Jones. Again, as Hiltner remarks, throughout the entire scene involving the three characters, "neither Jones nor Franklin ever refers to the elevated and celebrated cause of the revolution" (43). In a revisionist reading of Franklin's *Autobiography,* Shurr has questioned the degree of Franklin's authentic patriotic involvement in ways that bear significantly on our reading of *Israel Potter.* According to Shurr, Franklin's motives for residing on the Continent during the entirety of the war involve many unsavory possibilities. Shurr presents four:

> 1) during the Revolutionary War, Franklin himself asked to be sent to France, the safest place for a revolutionary should the weak armies of the rebellion fail . . . ; 2) while the compatriots fought the war, the supposedly "busy" Franklin actually enjoyed long stretches of leisure, playing with his press and sporting with the ladies of the court; 3) as for the armaments contracted for and provided, they were guns that had been retired from the French army, bought for little by Franklin's agents and sold for a considerable profit; 4) Franklin may even have been playing on both teams not only during the 1760s and 1770s while colonial agent in England but also during the Revolutionary War while serving as American agent in France. It is a matter of record that information Franklin received in France found its way to the office of the Secret Service in England, where he himself and one of his associates had code names. (446–47)

Melville could not have known about Franklin's perhaps having served as a spy during the Revolution, but it is possible that Israel Potter may have been that historical associate also with a code name and conceivably even in the employ of British intelligence.[8] These possibilities should subject Franklin and Potter to the harsh light of retrospective clarification; they also highlight the extent to which Melville inserts his counterhegemonic historiographical project into a highly problematic and contested historical record. As Shurr makes increasingly clear (and critics such as John Samson reiterate), "the actual Franklin needs to be decanonized" (447). In *Israel Potter* Melville anticipates this recent clarion call among Americanists by almost 150 years.

Israel Potter's final chapters contain a wealth of domestic details from Potter's family life during his long years in London, details capable of deepening the range of Melville's protracted dismantling of Franklin's claims to primacy in the American historical record. That Melville compresses decades of Potter's life into a few pages in no way detracts from the resonance and allusive force of his representation of Potter's life. In fact, largely by virtue of its numerous resonances with facts of Franklin's life and adventures, this penultimate chapter scatters a plethora of "loose ends" requiring extratextual reference for comprehensibility. Of Potter's marriage, for example, we learn only that, having saved nearly the amount of money needed to secure passage across the Atlantic,

> as stubborn fate would have it, being run over one day at Holborn Bars, and taken into a neighboring bakery, he was there treated with such kindliness by a Kentish lass, the shop-girl, that in the end he thought his debt of gratitude could only be repaid by love. In a word, the money saved up for his ocean voyage was lavished upon a rash embarkation in wedlock. (162)

Thus, Potter's commitment to his family complicates his possible return: "he could only embrace the facilities for a return here furnished [by the consul], by deserting a wife and child; wedded and born in the enemy's land" (162). He, of course, refuses to do so; instead he supports his family by working a variety of jobs, surviving the fluctuations of available manpower impacted either by English war with France or by peace as best he can by mending chairs, making matches, and collecting various bits of nails, broken glass, and, most significantly—given Melville's account of saving Trumbull's *Life and*

Remarkable Adventures from the "rag-pickers"—old rags and bits of paper (163). In spite of the glut of workers periodically flooding the streets of London during times of peace, and in spite of having out of necessity to live in the sewers (also with unemployed soldiers), Israel Potter, Melville forcefully points out, "the American, never sunk below the mud, to actual beggary" (165). Eventually, ten of Potter's eleven children ("born to him in certain sixpenny garrets in Moorfields" [162]) and his wife die, but, throughout many long years of destitution, Potter remains united with his sole surviving son, "the spared Benjamin of his old age" (166). Potter, Melville suggests, spends many long days and nights talking with his boy, entertaining him with "tales of the Fortunate Isles of the Free," to which Benjamin "listened, night after night, as to the stories of Sinbad the Sailor" (166). And when he finally returns to the old family homestead, now only ruined remains, Potter fades into a reverie of his family past:

> "*'Father!'* here," raking with his staff, "*my* father would sit, and here, my mother, and here I, little infant, would totter between, even as now, once again, on the very same spot, but in the unroofed air, I do." (169)

In these hallucinatory remarks, Potter reenacts the security of parental care and domestic stability, but he also provides a moment of union, not only between him and his parents, but between his surviving son and himself. In this moment, the Potter name spans three generations of males, although the possibility of that name surviving into the future seems tenuous, as neither Melville's nor Potter's original narrative entertains the possibility of Benjamin Potter's future as a father of his own children.

I dwell on these final pages and their truncated account of the final decades of Potter's life to establish the endurance of the bond between Israel Potter and his wife and children. Nowhere is there any suggestion of instability within the Potter household, however mean and impoverished that household became. Furthermore, Melville's narrative implies a Potter whose dedication to wife and children requires not only that he forego his dream of returning to America, but also that he struggle in the meanest of jobs foraging for their support. Melville intensifies the pathos of Potter's story by fictionalizing the homely details of the aged soldier's squalid years of exile and by anchoring his representation of Potter's family life as the sole constant in his otherwise moorless wanderings. Through the securing and losing of employment, through the birth and loss of children, and through the marrying and losing of his wife, Potter dedicates his life during these decades of exile to his family. But embedded within the account of these homely details resides one of Melville's sharpest areas of implicit critique. Clark Davis, in fact, bases his discussion of *Israel Potter* on what he characterizes as Potter's commitment to an Ishmaelian center of domestic felicity, including Potter's remaining true to his goals of heart, family, and hearth. Davis reads Potter's drive to return home, for example, as an energy that "restates the centrality of home and hearth in the quest pattern of Israel's life" (183), and he argues that Potter is delayed in returning to the United States for so long because "in marrying and attempting to produce a family in England, he was also attempting to create a substitute home" (184). While perhaps merely bathetic in isolation, Potter's suffering and perseverance with his family highlight by contrast the absence of such commitment on the parts of both Benjamin Franklin and John Paul Jones.

For example, as Samson remarks, both of Potter's more famous contemporaries "were notorious for their sexual exploits" in their own times, an issue that generated some testiness in even their most committed acolytes, Jared Sparks, Nathaniel Fanning, and Robert C. Sands (196). In *Israel Potter*, Melville heightens their notoriety by frequently exposing the sexual adventurism driving Franklin and Jones, with similar opportunistic "gallantry" also informing his brief portrait of Ethan Allen. Franklin, for instance, ogles and perhaps even enjoys the sexually vital chambermaid assigned to Potter's room in Paris, while John Paul Jones gropes virtually every woman that comes near him and gratuitously interrupts his military campaign to vindicate himself with the Duchess of Selkirk after his troops loot her estate. Melville manipulates these cases to foreground their high, often absurd humor, but, from an angle consistent with Potter's titular claim to narrative centrality, Franklin's and Jones's sexual exploits and insatiable cravings contrast starkly with Potter's own miserable fate, dating back as far as Potter's first love, "Jenny," having married another suitor while Potter was off establishing his economic security with the expectation of overcoming parental resistance to the match. Potter's constancy and dedication (both to "his mountain Jenny" and to his eventual English wife) come to naught, even as Franklin and Jones enjoy sumptuous sexual interludes while "fighting for American freedom" in Europe.[9]

Melville, it could be argued, merely projects throughout *Israel Potter* the tawdriness and duplicity he reads in Franklin's representation of his sexual and marital circumstances in his *Autobiography*. Just as Melville can truncate his account of the Battle of Bunker Hill on the excuse that "everyone knows all about the battle" (13), he similarly relies on Franklin's reputation as a womanizer to underwrite his own oblique writing of the history of the sage's sexuality. In his *Autobiography*, Franklin's own representation of women in general is fraught with contradictions. On the one hand, he can in theory advocate the education of women to enable them better to assume important civic and business responsibilities should their spouses die (96), and on the other, he can in practice use female pseudonyms to disseminate unpopular opinions and subordinate women as marginal players in the service of his self-promotion—his wife first introduces the luxurious and, to Franklin, extravagant china and sterling silver dinnerware into their house (76)—or of his sexual desire: he admits that, in his youth, he "hurried . . . frequently into Intrigues with low women that fell in [his] way" (70).

Franklin's marital affairs pose problems of their own. His commonlaw wife, Deborah Read Franklin, suffered greatly as a result of Franklin's rumored indiscretions as well as his failures to write her regularly, though over one two-year period he is known to have exchanged over 130 letters with Polly Stevenson, his admirer, scientific protégée, and, possibly, paramour (Randall 172). Furthermore, the artist Charles Willson Peale personally caught Franklin fondling and kissing an amorous young girl perched on his lap when he visited the sage in hopes of a letter of recommendation (Lopez and Herbert 27). Even before his marriage, Franklin all but ignored his engagement to Deborah Read, noting in his *Autobiography* that his friend Ralph "seem'd quite to forget his Wife & Child, and I by degrees my Engagements with Miss Read, to whom I never wrote more than one Letter, & that was to let her know I was not likely soon to return" (43). The two young men were, according to Franklin's own admission, spending so much money on plays and "other Places of Amusement" that Franklin's expenses on pleasure "constantly kept" him "unable to pay [his] Passage" back to the colonies (43). Here Franklin contrasts dramatically with Potter. Whereas Israel Potter's sense of debt and gratitude prompt him to spend the money he has saved for return passage home on a wedding, we witness quite the opposite in Franklin. He squanders funds, ostensibly salted away for his return, on various entertainments, among which almost certainly number his frequent intrigues with "low women."

"Franklin," as Shurr reminds us, "was a notoriously absent husband; he lived apart from his wife, mostly in London, for 25 of their 44 married years" (445), and cohabited with at least one woman while having affairs with numerous others. Even while ostensibly "at home" in the colonies, Franklin "was never very good at staying at home. . . . In fact, he spent eight of the first twelve months at home [from London] away from home" (Randall 186). Franklin's wandering affected his wife so powerfully that her mental health deteriorated rapidly while Franklin spent much of the mid-1760s in England. Franklin had usually written cursory notes once a month, but in 1765 he simply stopped. "For weeks," writes Randall, "in letter after worse-spelled letter, Deborah had poured out her loneliness to him" (201):

> I have wrote several letter to you one almoste everey day but then I Cold not forbair saying sumthing to you [about] publick afairs then I wold [destroy] it and then begin a gen and burn it a gen and so on. . . . All is well att home. . . . No body but my self at home. . . . As ever yours till Deth, D. Franklin. (Oct. 8, 1765, *Papers* 12: 300–304)

Franklin's second agency to England caused him to be gone when his wife suffered the paralytic stroke that eventually took her life. Her anguish at Franklin's long absences is clear in William Franklin's letter to his father notifying him of Deborah's death:

> She told me when I took leave of her on my removal to Amboy, that she never expected to see you unless you returned this winter, for that she was sure she should not live till next summer.

I heartily wish you had happened to have come over in the fall, as I think her disappointment in that respect preyed a good deal on her spirits. (Dec. 24, 1774, *Papers* 21: 400–402)

Aside from his obvious and frequently publicized transgressions of conventional standards of marital fidelity, the circumstances surrounding Franklin's common-law marriage with Deborah Read are hardly the stuff that the "family values" so central to the 1992 presidential campaign are made of.

Similarly, Melville casts Potter's relationship with his children, especially his one surviving son, not only against his own depiction of Franklin but also against the nearly sacrosanct image of Franklin current in antebellum American culture. Once again, Melville's economical representation of Potter and son revises Trumbull's *Life and Remarkable Adventures* in careful and resonant terms. In Trumbull's account, Potter refers to his surviving son as Thomas. While Melville certainly capitalizes on the biblical "Benjamin of his old age" (166), his use of the name surely reintroduces Benjamin Franklin, the text's only other Benjamin, into the condensed final pages of his counternarrative. Both Potter (via Trumbull) and Melville recount an impoverished though mutually supportive bond between father and son. The Thomas of Trumbull's account works diligently to aid his ailing, aged father in his manual labor, often working by himself when Potter grows too ill or hungry (376–88). Virtually every paragraph of his account of these difficult London years is punctuated with gestures and remarks of paternal tenderness and dedication ("my little son," "my dear child"). Melville, while condensing these forty years into one brief, penultimate chapter, nonetheless maintains both the emotional tenor of Trumbull's text and the sense of quiet desperation that drives Potter and son. In fact, the only solace available to Potter in Melville's narrative exists in storytelling, a discursive substitute for actual physical comfort and familial nurture:

In his Moorfields' garret, over a handful of re-ignited cinders (which the night before might have warmed some lord), cinders raked up from the streets, he would drive away dolor, by talking with his one only surviving, and now motherless child—the spared Benjamin of his old age—of the far Canaan beyond

the sea; rehearsing to the lad those well-remembered adventures
among New-England hills, and painting scenes of nestling happiness and plenty, in which the lowliest shared. (166)

Whereas bachelor, heirless Ishmael, even up to the time of writing
his narrative, takes to the sea as a substitute for suicidal pistol and
ball (*Moby-Dick* 3), widower and father Israel takes to storytelling
with his loving son to exorcize his own dolorous hypos. Benjamin
reciprocates the affection and solicitude he receives from his father
by struggling to secure passage back to America for himself and his
father: "By his persevering efforts he succeeded at last, against every
obstacle, in gaining credit in the right quarter to his extraordinary
statements" (166). Desperate, exhausted, and often starving, the two
Potters remain emotionally committed, each lending whatever assistance the other may need.

The historical Franklin's relationship with his own sons offers a
remarkable contrast to the bond between Melville's fictionalized Potters. Franklin was, of course, capable of moments of tenderness. For
example, he recounts the loss of a young son in his *Autobiography* in
touching language: "In 1736 I lost one of my Sons a fine Boy of 4 Years
old, by the Small Pox taken in the common way" (99). While Franklin
does not embellish the passage with emotional language, the mere
mention of the loss of a beautiful and vivacious four-year-old child
elicits sympathy, especially given Franklin's litotic, though resonant,
characterization of him as "a fine Boy." However, while I am tempted
to project emotional lushness into Franklin's remarks, his rhetoric
and the narrative milieu of his reference to the loss of his son certainly truncate whatever parental emotional charge the passage may
have. For one, this paragraph follows one in which Franklin discusses
returning home to Boston to make amends with his family, whom he
deserted when he set off on his own to Philadelphia. Moreover, immediately before those remarks, Franklin muses on the possibilities
of foreign-language instruction in colonial schools, and immediately
after the mention of his toddler's death, he moves on to a lengthy discussion of his Junto, without ever returning to the loss of his little boy
(98–99). Even within the passage, however, it is never clear whether
Franklin actually feels the loss of his son, or simply deploys this

particular autobiographical moment in the service of inculcating a sounder, more scientifically viable approach to vaccination. Franklin's failure to disclose *this* son's name certainly seems peculiar, and may suggest that, rather than expressing deep, personal loss, this passage's primary intent is to depersonalize the entire event in the interest of abstract public service. Franklin's "fine Boy," then, slips into an allegorical and representative realm, more an exemplar than a flesh-and-blood toddler. As Franklin himself contextualizes the remark,

> I long regretted bitterly & still regret that I had not given it to him by Inoculation. This I mention for the Sake of Parents, who omit that Operation on the Supposition that they should never forgive themselves if a Child died under it; my Example showing that the Regret may be the same either way, and that therefore the safer should be chosen. (99)

It might well be futile to attempt to discriminate the personal from the public, rhetorical Franklin, but we can remark nonetheless that in this particular passage in the *Autobiography* the blurring of familial, ontological, and rhetorical identities gives readers some pause concerning the depth of Franklin's fatherly feelings.

It is, however, Franklin's relations with his other son, the "Dear Son" the *Autobiography* explicitly addresses, that figure most problematically in relation to Melville's *Israel Potter.* While Franklin's relationship with William proceeded on relatively good terms for much of William's youth, by the mid-1750s, "each year [William] became less attracted to his father's artisan friends and more closely linked to his father's rivals" (Randall 73). These tensions continued to mount almost without abatement, flaring during the Revolutionary War and culminating in Franklin's disinheritance of William in his will, which included the final insult: "the part he acted against me in the late war, which is of public notoriety, will account for my leaving him no more of an estate he endeavored to deprive me of" (*Works* 10: 493–510). As Shurr has demonstrated, Franklin's animosity toward his illegitimate son was pervasive, constituting an illuminating subtext for much of Franklin's life and writings.

Shurr's biographical/generic analysis of Franklin's *Autobiography*, in fact, makes a strong case for viewing the first part of that classic text as a protracted and often sadistic attack on the "Dear Son" to whom it is very specifically addressed. For example, Shurr argues that many of Franklin's references to money and the paying of debts, such as his discussion of the Quaker merchant Denham (50–51), are pure inventions intended to prod William into paying his own debts to his father. Furthermore, Shurr notes, almost all of Franklin's letters to his son remind the son of these debts: "some of the letters included long itemizations; some of the itemizations even included school clothes purchased three decades earlier" (440). Franklin's financial obsession is only one facet of his ongoing tensions with William. As early as his first paragraph, Shurr argues, Franklin begins his assault on William by referring to his fantasy of being able to correct some faults and to "change some sinister Accidents & Events of [his life] for others more favourable" (2). Born out of wedlock as he was, the fruit of one of Franklin's "Intrigues with low women," William could hardly but have been insulted by Franklin's foregrounding of his illegitimacy through the reference to William's *sinister* origins—the bar sinister being the heraldic mark of illegitimacy—and by Franklin's dismissal of his birth as an "accident" (444–45). But Franklin's vitriol exceeded mere verbal assaults, however public they may have been. Again as Shurr points out, Franklin "knew of and permitted the torture of his son William for two hundred and fifty-two days in a rebel prison in Litchfield, Connecticut. He knew that William's wife was dying at the time and that William himself was close to death, yet he did nothing to aid either" (447). Indeed, as Randall documents, while Franklin was blandly insouciant concerning William's incarceration and ill-treatment, he was actively involved writing letters to David Hartley, an influential friend in Parliament, protesting "all the horrors of imprisonment" for Americans held in Britain, focusing especially on his abhorrence "that our people are not allowed the use of pen or ink, not the sight of newspapers, nor the conversations of friends," the same deprivations he knew William suffered under (453).

I dwell on these instances of familial treachery and sadism largely to highlight the obvious discrepancy between the affection and dedication characterizing Israel Potter's represented relationship with his wife and son and the betrayal and hostility commonly understood to have defined Franklin's familial roles. By virtue of his condensed

penultimate chapter, Melville casts his narrative fully against the unsavory, and often highly publicized, images of Franklin coexisting
with the sage's consciously managed and defended place in the pantheon of American "founding fathers." However, Melville's *Israel Potter* pushes for an even more intimate level of critique. In many instances within Melville's narrative, Franklin's relationship with Israel
Potter reenacts scenes of authoritarian dominance and exploitation
from Franklin's bio-historical record. One such cluster recalls Franklin's ambiguous and contradictory relationship to the slavery question
in eighteenth-century colonial Philadelphia. As Paul L. Ford points
out, Franklin printed the first two antislavery tracts during the 1740s
(204); furthermore, Franklin paid great "attention to the antislavery
movement" (Shurr 447) for many years. But Franklin himself not
only owned a personal slave, for whom he never made any attempt
at redemption, but also invested in slave ships and owned numerous
slaves when elected president of the Pennsylvania Abolition Society
(Shurr 447). Franklin also published the following advertisements in
his own newspapers:

> "A Likely Young Negro Wench, who is a good Cook, and can
> Wash well is to be disposed of. Enquire of the Printer hereof."

> "To be Sold, A Likely young Negroe Fellow, about Twenty-six
> Years of Age, suitable for any Farming or Plantation Business,
> having been long accustomed to it and has had the Small-Pox.
> Enquire of the Printer hereof."

> "To Be Sold, A Lusty, young, Negroe Woman, fit for Country
> Business, she has had the Smallpox, and Meazles. Enquire of the
> Printers hereof." (Ford 319–20)

All of this activity, of course, ran contrary to Franklin's professed
Quaker principles, a contradiction heightened by the overt sexual
violence suggested in Franklin's physically designating one woman
as "Lusty" and "young," stressing, thereby, her suitability for either
breeding or rape, the sexual exploitation he encodes in the euphe-
mistic "Country Business."

Focusing on Franklin's own activities within the eighteenth-
century colonial slave trade enables us to return to his encoun-

ters with Israel Potter with a new understanding. Many of their exchanges, for example, are characterized by Franklin's contradictory yoking of solicitousness and goodwill toward Israel with imperious condescension, including his lectures to Potter on proper boot heels, pronunciation, and the virtues of drinking water as opposed to wine, but, more importantly, in his lecturing Potter on the dangers of sweets, cognac, and voluptuous French maids while commandeering the same vices for himself. More specifically, Franklin's duplicity within Melville's narrative resonates with his callous treatment of his own son. After Potter informs Franklin that he needs no loan for his return trip, joking, "No interest, Doctor, I hope," as he returns coins to Franklin's hand, Franklin offers only the following withering retort: "My good friend, never permit yourself to be jocose upon pecuniary matters. Never joke at funerals, or during business transactions" (43). While Franklin's humorless response is consistent with Melville's depiction of him throughout these passages, the resonance of this and other monetary allusions with his strained economic relations with William suggests an affinity between the sage's dealings with Potter and with his son. More insidiously, Franklin's absolute control over Potter's entire stay in Paris similarly recalls some of the more unsavory moments from his own history. For instance, after Franklin deprives him of several pleasant appurtenances, Potter remarks that "every time he comes in he robs me" (53), and Franklin himself comments on Potter's virtual enslavement, "Business before pleasure, my friend. You must absolutely remain in your room, just as if you were my prisoner" (43). Both scenes of dispossession restage Franklin's own history of domination, *both* in his control and manipulation of his slaves *and* in his apparently bland indifference to his own son's imprisonment and torture.

Franklin's use of Potter as a courier trafficking in critical intelligence also figures in the elaborate scheme of critical sociohistorical allusions at work in *Israel Potter*. Squire Woodcock recruits Potter to serve as mediary between his group of Englishmen friendly to the colonial cause and the Paris-based Franklin. While the English trio and Franklin all, of course, run certain risks stemming from the delicate espionage work in which they are engaged, nonetheless, it is Potter whose life is directly endangered by his repeated crossings of the

Channel and by his carrying secret information hidden in a false boot heel. Woodcock and Franklin both stress the danger Potter faces and caution him to proceed accordingly. However, while Potter is hidden away, disguised, and transported from coast to coast, Franklin resides in the Latin Quarter or at "his country retreat at Passy" (48) in modest, though strategically chosen and tactically revealed, simplicity. As Melville comments,

> The frugality of his manner of life did not lose him the good opinion even of the voluptuaries of the showiest of capitals. . . . Not only did he enjoy the homage of the choicest Parisian literati, but at the age of seventy-two he was the caressed favorite of the highest born beauties of the Court; who through blind fashion having been originally attracted to him as a famous *savan,* were permanently retained as his admirers by his Plato-like graciousness of good-humor. (48)

It is Franklin, of course, who comes down in history as the diplomat par excellence during the Revolutionary War, though it was, at least in Melville's retelling, Israel Potter who performed many of the dangerous tasks crucial to Franklin's fame. A similar scenario lies behind one of the most celebrated and represented moments of American scientific history, Franklin's kite-flying electricity experiment. Contrary to the popular iconography of Franklin risking life and limb in the glorious service of science, it was actually his "Dear Son," William, who performed the deed. William was the only volunteer willing to scale roofs to install Franklin's primitive lightning rods; further,

> when Franklin was ready for his climactic experiment to draw the lightning from the clouds with the aid of a kite and a key, it was William who designed and built the kite and three times raced across a cow pasture in an electrical storm to get the kite aloft while Franklin stood safe in a shepherd's shed nearby. (Randall 62)

Once again, the popular historical record falsifies the entire scene, usually granting sole recognition to Franklin for the work actually performed by others. Once again, Melville represents Israel Potter in a manner which implicitly links his fate with that of Franklin's son, both of whom suffered anonymously in the service of Franklin's notoriety and historical preeminence.

What emerges with special irony from Melville's highly condensed scheme of historical representation is Franklin's enduring (certainly in Melville's time, and largely in our own) image as quintessential "founding father." Superimposing the homely details of Franklin's actual domestic history onto his metaphorical and mythicized status as national founder, Melville, by virtue of the humble and squalid endurance of Israel Potter, draws our attention to the dysfunctional nature of the actual and mythico-nationalist families over which Franklin presides as putative head (of household or of state). Furthermore, Melville provides the narrative data necessary to establish homologies between the deception and duplicity by which the dysfunctional family conceals the psychodrama and physical brutality lurking beneath the facade of its domestic normalcy *with* the historiographical and ethical contortions necessary for the post-Revolutionary construction and consolidation of mythical "founding fathers" by their scions in mid-nineteenth-century American culture. The peep behind the fraudulent iconography of filiopietism may not penetrate the "naught beyond" that Captain Ahab realizes might lurk behind the pasteboard mask of physical appearances (164), but it may expose the "charnel-house" (195) which Ishmael speculates may lie beneath the painted harlot of the American past.

iv

Ralph Waldo Emerson enters *Israel Potter* obliquely, but unmistakably, in the same early paragraph in which Melville introduces Franklin. Elaborating on his echo of Franklin's wheelbarrow vignette, Melville refers to the definitive Emersonian trope and title, "Self-Reliance": "In this way was bred that fearless self-reliance and independence which conducted our forefathers to national freedom" (9). By the 1854–55 publication of *Israel Potter,* Melville's readership could hardly have processed the phrase "self-reliance" without its conjuring up the still influential figure of America's most internationally recognized rhetorician and spokesperson. Melville's allusion here is remarkable in that it projects the Emersonian virtue of self-reliance

anachronistically. That is, neither did Revolutionary political rhetoric construct colonial political rights in such terms of self-reliance,
nor does Emerson's essay of that title campaign for any nationalistic
or geographic agenda—that was the political work of "The American
Scholar" address first delivered at Harvard University in 1837. Emerson's work in "Self-Reliance" (1841) was primarily ontological and
philosophical, not patriotic and nationalistic, although certainly not
without some degree of nationalistic residue from his Phi Beta Kappa
oration. By adding this passage to Potter's rather focused account of
his wilderness prowess and business acumen, Melville revises Potter's
ostensibly self-serving plea for a government pension into an inci-
sive commentary on the mythology of the American character. In so
doing, he constructs his own apparently consensual version of the
American dream of hard work and success with specific reference
to two of the young Republic's paragons of rhetorical and practical
virtue, Benjamin Franklin (as we have seen) and Emerson. Oddly,
Emerson as a specific historical and cultural referent disappears from
Melville's narrative after this one early, significantly placed and culturally loaded allusion, although one could argue that any reference
foregrounded so visibly and so anachronistically nonetheless pressures the subsequent narrative. I believe that such is the case with
Melville's reference to Emerson. The cameo appearance of Melville's
contemporary in what is otherwise so densely (if also fictionally)
historically based a narrative serves not only to insinuate Melville's
multidimensional historical perspective into his "Revolutionary narrative," but also to provide a specific marker for his version's complex
representation of "American nature."

From its initial paragraph to its final sentence, *Israel Potter* exposes
the inadequacy of transcendentalized visions of nature as an "other"
world, as a terrain purely and transcendentally "beyond," but compatible with and nurturing of human desire. Melville quite frankly
challenges the transcendental ideal of "man in the open air," calmed,
refreshed, and reconnected with utopian, not yet corrupted, cosmic
energies. In Melville's narrative, nature exists in virtually every passage as an always subordinate and already colonized, industrialized,
and economized territory, either neutral or inimical to human aspira-
tion.

We can clarify Melville's antitranscendentalist work in *Israel Potter* by journeying back to one of his first and best-known pokes at Emersonian natural optimism. In one of *Moby-Dick's* more famous passages, Ishmael reflects on the dangers of losing oneself in transcendental-like reveries while on duty atop the masthead. Overly philosophic whalemen are bad bets for raising whales, for, while there may be shoals of whales within eyeshot,

> lulled into such an opium-like listlessness of vacant, unconscious reverie is this absent-minded youth by the blending cadence of waves with thoughts, that at last he loses his identity; takes the mystic ocean at his feet for the visible image of that deep, blue, bottomless soul, pervading mankind and nature; and every strange, half-seen, gliding, beautiful thing that eludes him; every dimly-discovered, uprising fin of some undiscernible form, seems to him the embodiment of those elusive thoughts that only people the soul by continually flitting through it. In this enchanted mood, thy spirit ebbs away to whence it came; becomes diffused through time and space; like Wickliff's sprinkled Pantheistic ashes, forming at last a part of every shore the round globe over.
>
> There is no life in thee, now, except that rocking life imparted by a gently rolling ship; by her, borrowed from the sea; by the sea, from the inscrutable tides of God. But while this sleep, this dream is on ye, move your foot or hand an inch, slip your hold at all; and your identity comes back in horror. Over Descartian vortices you hover. And perhaps, at mid-day, in the fairest weather, with one half-throttled shriek you drop through that transparent air into the summer sea, no more to rise for ever. Heed it well, ye Pantheists! (159)

Melville's passage rewrites the oft-noted (and often parodied) passage from early in Emerson's *Nature:*

> In the woods is perpetual youth. Within these plantations of God, a decorum and sanctity reign, a perennial festival is dressed, and the guest sees not how he should tire of them in a thousand years. In the woods, we feel we return to reason and faith.

> There I feel that nothing can befall me in life,—no disgrace, no calamity (leaving me my eyes), which nature cannot repair. Standing on the bare ground,—my head bathed by the blithe air and uplifted into infinite space,—all mean egotism vanishes. I become a transparent eyeball; I am nothing; I see all; the currents of the Universal Being circulate through me; I am part or parcel of God. (38–39)

Ishmael's meditation proposes a potent corrective to the blithe denials of early Emerson in a variety of ways—direct echoes (transparent air/transparent eyeball, inscrutable tides of God/plantations of God); parallel thematics ("loses his identity" / "all mean egotism vanishes . . . I am nothing"); and compatible imagery (the literal ocean of *Moby-Dick* / the liquified nature of Emerson's "head bathed by the blithe air" and "the currents of the Universal Being").[10]

Consider *Israel Potter*'s opening sentence, not insignificantly also the site of Melville's first departure from Potter's narrative:

> The traveller who at the present day is content to travel in the good old Asiatic style, neither rushed along by a locomotive, nor dragged by a stage-coach; who is willing to enjoy hospitalities at far-scattered farmhouses, instead of paying his bill at an inn; who is not to be frightened by any amount of loneliness, or to be deterred by the roughest roads or the highest hills; such a traveller in the eastern part of Berkshire, Mass., will find ample food for poetic reflection in the singular scenery of a country, which, owing to the ruggedness of the soil and its lying out of the track of all public conveyances, remains almost as unknown to the general tourist as the interior of Bohemia. (3)

We might first comment on the Thoreauvian echoes scattered throughout the passage. The resistance to being "rushed along by a locomotive" and "dragged by a stage-coach" recalls Thoreau's assaults on the frantic pace of Concord life as well as on the absurd economy of railroads, including the emasculating luxury of rail accommodations (79), the actual inefficiency of rail travel (96), his discussion of the Fitchburg Railroad in "Sounds," his comment that he "would rather ride on earth in an ox cart with a free circulation, than go to heaven in the fancy car of an excursion train and breathe a *malaria* all the way" (80), and his summarily acerbic aphorism "We do not ride on the railroad; it rides upon us" (136).

However, as significant as Melville's apparent echoing of one of *Walden's* areas of critique is this paragraph's representation of nature as a territory already inscribed within the general categories of travel and tourism. Here, Melville registers experience of nature as inseparable from one's mode of "paying his bill," again a concern revived from *Moby-Dick's* weighing of the general merits of going to sea as a sailor against going as a fare-paying tourist, a debate Ishmael decides on behalf of "getting paid" as opposed to paying. *Israel Potter's* opening paragraph proposes a similar approach to nature, traveling "in the good old Asiatic style," but one which nonetheless concedes that any encounter with the putative American wilderness (however much its exotic foreignness creates within the observer the "sensation of being upon some terrace in the moon") is always subject to economic demand and already "mapped out [even] in its beauty" (3). Cartographic and economic figures, in other words, already overlay the heavily promoted freshness of westward travel. The region's principal inhabitants include "horses, cattle, and sheep," and, though wild and remote, its soil cannot sustain farming, as all "arable parts have long since been nearly exhausted" (4). In short, Melville's nature cannot be imagined in terms other than those of human interest, including cartographic representation, agricultural exploitation, and economic opportunism.

Needless to say, Melville here communicates a vision antithetical to the nature wherein Emerson can become a "transparent eyeball" and feel his head "bathed by the blithe air" (39), and to which Thoreau can confidently retreat to discover and test a realm of pure natural Otherness, inimical to the lives of quiet desperation and economic confusion of the marketplace of Concord. In the ensuing descriptions of Israel Potter's native grounds, Melville continues his counternarrative to transcendentalized nature, reducing the entire scene to the aesthetic vocabulary of "picturesqueness" (4) and continuing his refusal to represent nature neutrally. For example, "each tuft of upland grass is musked like a bouquet with perfume," "the balmy breeze swings to and fro like a censer," and "you behold a hawk sallying from some crag, like a Rhenish baron of old from his pinnacled castle"

(5). The metaphors in these and other descriptive passages function to consolidate the narrative's vision of nature unthinkable outside the terms of human culture and intervention, here including a catalog of the cosmetic (perfume), the religious (censer), and the historical/political/oppressive (Rhenish baron). This dimension of *Israel Potter* also confirms Robert Zaller's argument that in Melville, nature

> stands in mysterious dialectical relation to man, often at cross purposes to him, delaying, denying and ultimately dissolving all his acts, but sometimes speeding and assisting them, a fate which verges on will but never finally declares itself. Separated only by the thin edge of consciousness from total immersion in it, man seems a creature half in, half out of Nature, his desires only rarely distinct and lucid enough to be distinguished from Nature's half-purposive dreams. (616)

The same basic metaphorical dynamic informs the great majority of all references to a natural world throughout *Israel Potter.* From somewhere in the English Channel as Israel first voyages from England to France, for example, "the white cliffs of Dover resembl[ed] a long gabled block of marble houses. Both shores showed a long straight row of lamps. Israel seemed standing in the middle of the crossing of some wide stately street in London" (66–67). When he is escaping from Squire Woodcock's Brentford estate, a line of fog, a grove of dwarfish trees, and some tall tree trunks take on two aspects for Israel. First, "the vapor wore the semblance of a deep stream of water, imperfectly descried; the grove looked like some closely-clustering town on its banks, lorded over by spires of churches," and, second, "the whole scene magically reproduced to our adventurer the aspect of Bunker Hill, Charles River, and Boston town, on the well-remembered night of the 16th of June" (76). In each of these examples, Potter perceives nature saturated with human, ideological residue, as from the point of view of various oppressive subject positions—the economic privilege of London's wealthiest avenues, the tyrannical religious sway of churches "lording" over towns, and recollection of the Battle of Bunker Hill with all the Revolutionary fervor against British tyranny as well as with its human carnage.

Melville further undermines transcendentalized nature by frequently reversing the metaphorical relationship between vehicle and tenor, and by recasting wastage, exploitation, and destruction in vocabularies and dynamics derived from nature. John Paul Jones's nautical exploits provide a representative example. After being reduced to little more than scraps by Jones's cannons, the English ship *Drake*

> seemed now, above deck, like a piece of wild western woodland into which choppers had been. Her masts and yards prostrate, and hanging in jack-straws; several of her sails ballooning out, as they dragged in the sea, like great lopped tops of foliage. The black hull and shattered stumps of masts, galled and riddled, looked as if giant woodpeckers had been tapping them. (113)

The titanic struggle between the *Bon Homme Richard* and the *Serapis* furnishes similar dynamics. As the *Serapis* circles around Jones's *Bon Homme Richard,* the English ship made "lounging advances now and then, and as suddenly steering off; hate causing her to act not unlike a wheeling cock about a hen, when stirred by the contrary passion" (122). Judith Hiltner has offered a compelling reading of such passages as these. As she argues, "throughout the novel Melville develops simultaneous patterns of imagery associating Israel with a patriotic, naive, provincial, agrarian and idealistic American youth on the one hand, and with extinction, immurement and imprisonment on the other" (42). "A close reading of *Israel Potter,*" she suggests, "also reveals a consistent pattern in which rural imagery is metamorphosed into that of urban institutions, or in which imagery of a benign and pastoral nature slides into sinister forms of civilization" (47). Regarding Israel as the virtual personification of what she regards as the agrarian dream of the Pilgrims and the founding fathers, Hiltner concludes that

> the persistent "sliding" between imagery of the rural and the urban blurs the distinction between "rural America" and "civilized England," subverting the geographic direction of the narrative line, which seemingly conducts Israel from the former to the latter. (49)

Hiltner's emphasis, like those of John Samson and other politically focused critics of Melville, is on Melville's supposed cynicism concerning the outcome and implications of the Revolutionary War. I agree with her argument (as well as with Samson's), but I also believe that a different perspective on Melville's nature imagery in *Israel Potter* can illuminate a different dimension of his thinking: his commentary on nature's subversion within a profoundly unnatural cultural economy. The workings of both representational schemes are compatible. Whereas Hiltner focuses on Melville's thinking about America in relation to its continuing (and counter-Revolutionary) affiliations with a transatlantic identity it believes it has shed, I am working to ferret out Melville's thinking about America's failure to embrace its own self-declared political and environmental ideals.

Melville punctuates his critique of Emersonian idealism (a consistent target for Melville from *Moby-Dick* through *Pierre* and *The Confidence-Man*) with one of his most remarkably allusive and evocative passages. In "Israel in Egypt" (ch. 23), Melville ushers Israel into his final forty-five years of exile via a thirteen-week stint as a brickmaker, using elaborate description of the wretched environs to conclude his commentary on Emersonian nature. Indeed, by suggesting that the "mill stood in the open air" (154), Melville anticipates F. O. Matthiessen's well-known designation of Emersonian (and Whitmanian) nature, "man in the open air." For Israel Potter, however, the scenario (as with his lessons in Franklinian optimism) turns sour:

> For thirteen weary weeks, lorded over by the taskmasters, Israel toiled in his pit. Though this condemned him to a sort of earthy dungeon, or grave-digger's hole while he worked; yet even when liberated to his meals, naught of a cheery nature greeted him. The yard was encamped, with all its endless rows of tented sheds, and kilns, and mills, upon a wild waste moor, belted round by bogs and fens. The blank horizon, like a rope, coiled round the whole. (155–56)

The next paragraph expands upon the despair inherent in Israel's situation by intensifying the bleak aspect and oppressive conditions under which he labors, the entire sequence assuming a rhetorical grandeur, historical resonance, and philosophical pessimism reminiscent of the best passages in *Moby-Dick*. Quite significantly, Melville's refusal of Emersonian "nature thinking" is insinuated in the phrase "naught of a cheery nature greeted him," pitting the ramifications of Potter's lived experience against the powerful, colonizing force of Emerson's *Nature*, with its encyclopedic vision of a veritable cornucopia of spirit, commodity, language, and so forth. Contrasting with Emerson's nature as a terrain fully compatible with human interests and as a relay for human spiritual desire (recall the entire natural context of Emerson's famous "transparent eyeball" iconography), nature here imposes a series of protonaturalistic and truncated limits over Potter's life. Potter and the other reminders of human presence are situated at the center of a series of concentric circles, the "wild waste moor" completely rimmed by "bogs and fens," themselves surrounded by a "blank horizon, like a rope, coiled round the whole." Like both the dead wall of Moby Dick's head and the brick surfaces of Bartleby's "dead wall reveries," this matrix of barriers stands in sharp contrast to Emerson's "circles" of overlapping significance and to Thoreau's magic circles of Walden. Not life-giving and empowering, Potter's boundaries are wild, belted, blank, and constricting. The strangulation implied by the rope coiled, like a hangman's noose, around the whole not only suggests the deterministic edge of natural limitations, but, to refer to an earlier segment of our argument, again translates natural phenomena into human instrumentality. The horizon as coiled rope recapitulates the entirety of *Israel Potter's* revisionist assault on Emersonian nature as medicinal salve and philosophical consolation. Furthermore, the elaborately detailed visual impression of the scene offers its own repudiation of Emerson's radiant passage. Recall that Melville's iconography casts Potter as the submerged center of a landscape consisting of three concentric circles—waste moor, bogs and fens, blank horizon. With his protagonist pinned in the center of three concentric circles, perhaps Melville is suggesting Israel Potter, not as "transparent eyeball," but as "opaque pupil." Potter clearly has not internalized the liberating rhetoric and personal bravado of either Franklin or Emerson; as a result, he exemplifies the potency of their respective strategies of self-representation and aggrandizement.

v

While Melville's perspective on these issues is unique, neither the thematics of character nor those of nature require his intratextual theorization. The "idea" of an/the American character had been of vital interest both ideologically and literary-historically for over two hundred years. Likewise, the discursive representation of "American nature" so predominated colonial and early Republican literary production that in 1836 Emerson's *Nature* was not an originary text so much as a forceful recolonizing of deeply contested turf. Nevertheless, Melville's articulation of these terms from the perspective of the generalized economy governing their operations and representations initiates a new dynamic with a new vocabulary for literary and ideological consideration. Within *Israel Potter,* Melville extends his recognition of a deep economy to its furthest reaches in his examination of the terms and priorities of nineteenth-century discursive practices. If Melville's exposé of the economy constructing our apprehension of the natural world is more disturbing than his similar examination of the lives and fortunes of dominant historical celebrities, his argument that we have access to the past (a subject of intense and public rhetorical bravado during Melville's middle years and central to Potter's narrative) only via the economically driven reproduction of American historical writing must surely have struck a jarring chord amidst the patriotic fervor of the American public and historiographic community.

As I have argued, the concluding passage of *Israel Potter* propels a refiguration of the economy of cultural production from a variety of angles. The same flexibility characterizes its critique of the discursive practices of midcentury American historical and literary production, including perspectives on American history, on biographical and autobiographical representation, and on the workings of literary history as well—what we now commonly call canon formation and maintenance. *Israel Potter's* critique of these forces takes two angles: (1) proposing an alternative "truth" of American history by reintroducing into the narrative of American history the exploits and heroics of common, forgotten soldiers, and (2) clarifying the underlying discursive economy that, quite likely, frustrates any attempt to tell "the whole truth," whether from the point of view of an oligarchical ruling class or of the oppressed working class. To write history, Melville insinuates, is necessarily to align oneself with some exclusionary narrative scheme. We should recall Melville's initial description of Israel's homeland, with its many reminders of desolation, ruggedness, and virtual inaccessibility. Melville continues that description by adding that "at the present day, some of those mountain townships present an aspect of singular abandonment. Though they have never known aught but peace and health, they, in one lesser aspect at least, look like countries depopulated by plague and war" (4). The ruggedness of the terrain, the isolation of the locale and its inaccessibility by "public conveyances," and the uncommon quality of the country—one not ordinarily the venue of tourist entertainment—all suggest an unknown, nearly alien, outback beyond the interest or abilities of common travel. Melville uses this descriptive overture partially to invoke the ruggedness and the heroic wilderness sensibility and temper "of the men of the Revolutionary era" (5), but these paragraphs accomplish something more as well. Rather like Thoreau in *Walden*, Melville describes a milieu that, by virtue of its nearness and its elemental simplicity, is almost unknown and easily overlooked, nearly inaccessible in its nearness because of the conventions and economics of agriculture, tourism, and landscape aesthetics of Melville's era. Paradoxically, it registers as *unheimlich*—foreign and unfamiliar.

To suggest a possible level of theoretical interest in this "descriptive" passage, I would like to invoke one of my favorite passages in American historiographical literature. In 1928, Arthur M. Schlesinger outlined in pertinent terms what he perceived to be the primary difference between the perspective of the social historian and that of the literary intellectual:

> What first impresses the social historian is that his fellow delver in the literary field has been mainly interested in the picturesque, the unusual, and the super-excellent; the same preoccupation, it is well to recall, was the dominant complex of the historian himself a generation ago. . . . The point of view has changed from the heavens above to the earth below. It is now recognized that many of the mighty movements that have affected the destiny of

man had their origins in obscure places; they gathered strength in hidden valleys and along dusty highways, and were carried through to success by the united efforts of hordes of nameless men and women. (Foerster 160–61)

In addition to clarifying the respective scholarly epistemologies of the historian and the literary scholar, Schlesinger's encapsulation nicely echoes some of Melville's primary interests in *Israel Potter*. Schlesinger's paean to the "hordes of nameless men and women" extends the Revolutionary focus of Melville's prefatory remarks directed to "His Highness, the Bunker-Hill Monument," which Melville as "the Editor" dubs "the Great Biographer: the national commemorator of such of the anonymous privates of June 17, 1775, who may never have received other requital than the solid reward of your granite" (viii). Schlesinger's methodological claims similarly resonate with Melville's. Both participate in the effort to refocus our historical vision so as to enable our recognition of the common and ordinary, the Israel Potters, as opposed exclusively to "the picturesque, the unusual, and the super-excellent," the Franklins, Joneses, and Allens of Melville's version. Finally, both draw on geopolitical metaphors to communicate how one's focus needs to be altered, and where one must look to revise the historical record. Both Potter and the significance of his acts, Melville and Schlesinger might agree, have their origins in obscure places; they gathered strength in hidden valleys and along dusty highways that every battle monument commemorates not only as a specific site and moment of conflict, death, victory, and loss, but as a "tomb of unknown soldiers" as well. As early as his 1850 review-essay on Hawthorne's *Mosses from an Old Manse,* Melville was ruminating on this theme with specific reference to Hawthorne, but with implicit insight into his own plight and into the plights of Israel Potters everywhere. Contemplating the failure of the American reading public adequately and enthusiastically to embrace native authors, Melville alludes to this "lack of recognition" in pregnant terms:

Believe me, my friends, that Shakespeares are this day being born on the banks of the Ohio [in Israel's case, the Housatonic]. And the day will come, when you shall say who reads a book by an Englishman that is a modern? The great mistake seems to be,

that even with those Americans who look forward to the coming
of a great literary genius among us, they somehow fancy he will
come in the costume of Queen Elizabeth's day,—be a writer of
dramas founded upon old English history, or the tales of Boccac-
cio. Whereas, great geniuses are parts of the times; they themselves are the times; and possess a correspondent coloring. *It is
of a piece with the Jews, who while their Shiloh was meekly walk-
ing in their streets, were still praying for his magnificent coming;
looking for him in a chariot, who was already among them on an
ass.* (*Piazza Tales* 245–46; my emphasis)

Here, as in the Christ imagery with which he so frequently robes
Israel Potter, who has, among other symbols, a cross of scars on his
chest, Melville uses Christ's commonness, humility, and anonymity
to suggest the unacknowledged presence of genius or heroism among
us. As he puts it early in *Israel Potter,* "from the field of the farmer,
[Israel] rushed to that of the soldier, mingling his blood with his
sweat. While we revel in broadcloth, let us not forget what we owe
to linsey-woolsey" (13).[11]

Melville's critique of American historiography is multidimensional.
John Samson, Daniel Reagan, and Peter J. Bellis have all contributed to our understanding of Melville's critique of prevailing historiographical practices; I will restrict my present discussion to two
elements: his questioning of the very nature of historical data and
his suggestion that the dominant practice of historical discourse is
always one of forgetting and repression of "the whole truth." Whereas
history, in Melville's view, has functioned to eliminate disorder, Melville's retelling of a historical narrative, itself of dubious authenticity,
serves to reintroduce, even to exaggerate, the confusion surrounding
events from the most banal to the most extraordinary. Such a discursive intervention into a culture's historiographical practices both disrupts and problematizes some of that culture's most protected myths
about its own origins.

One of Melville's most striking challenges to the authenticity of in-
herited historical traditions quite paradoxically takes the form of his
refusal to narrate commonly valorized incidents from the putative
historical record. In fact, on two crucial occasions, Melville either ab-

breviates or otherwise warps two of the most famous remarks, learned by schoolchildren ever since, from famous Revolutionary battles. It is only by assuming a consensus of beliefs and of battlefield quotations that Melville can define Potter's place at Bunker Hill as glibly as "Suffice it, that Israel was one of those marksmen whom Putnam harangued as touching the enemy's eyes" (13). The same holds with his reordering of John Paul Jones's famous "I have not yet begun to fight" (128), which Melville places in the final desperate and demoralized moments of the battle between the *Bon Homme Richard* and the *Serapis* rather than much earlier in its action. This revision, of course, contributes to Melville's portrayal of Jones as borderline psychopath rather than true-blue American hero, but it also calls the very details of history into question, as does his Hawthornian passage (reminiscent of "My Kinsman, Major Molineux") on the rising moon as stagehand. In his gloss on this revisionist tendency in *Israel Potter*, Peter J. Bellis argues that, by "turning the [*Serapis/Bon Homme Richard*] encounter into heroic theater, [Melville] suspends the issue of historical accuracy and aims instead for dramatic force" (615) and, further, that "Melville's aesthetic objectives run directly counter to the historian's here. He can establish dramatic and textual coherence only by turning away from the terrible disorder of history" (616). I disagree on both counts. Bellis assumes that historical reality is itself known or knowable, not that Melville is competing for the very status enjoyed by historical discourses in his own time. First, Melville's objectives don't necessarily pivot on as rigid a distinction between "aesthetics" and "history" as Bellis argues; Melville isn't struggling against the discourse of historiography, but, more pointedly, against a historical economy that would simplify the complexity of historical representation. Second, Bellis's reliance on a formulaic and melodramatic reference to the "terrible disorder of history" completely misses Melville's focus. It is *disorder* that he is trying to reintroduce so as to defamiliarize a complex ensemble of events and forces that have, via their historical transmission, been simplified and calcified as accepted truths. Melville isn't replacing "terrible" historical disorder with glazed aesthetic smoothness—he is inserting a counterversion of the same events, which, even while drawing on familiar sources and quotations, destabilizes our sense of those events we think we know most comfortably. By rewriting a narrative that had previously "faded out of print," Melville recovers a source of disorder, its aesthetic production and distribution notwithstanding.

In fact, Melville's first elision of direct historical narration foregrounds this angle of his critique. Rather than exploit the dramatic potential of narrating the Battle of Bunker Hill, Melville deploys only this shorthand version: "but everyone knows all about the battle. Suffice it, that Israel was one of those marksmen whom Putnam harangued as touching the enemy's eyes" (13). Furthermore, he continues with a brief but lively description of the hand-to-hand combat in which Israel receives the first of his sword wounds that will eventually constitute a cross of scar tissue on his chest. Melville's gesture here is remarkably complex, revealing, through his narration of secret conversations, unacknowledged heroics, conflicted motives, and bizarre turns of fortune that *nobody* really knows *anything* about the Revolutionary War, its principal combatants and covert operations, and its outcomes relative to poor, unknown foot soldiers such as Israel Potter. Melville's narrator here parodies the consensual nature of historical knowledge and its sedimented distortions, by highlighting not only their inadequacies, but also the filiopietistic conventions of their transmission.

The entire question of historical "accuracy" may, indeed, be moot, and Melville may simply be asking us to recognize that our narratives of history are nothing more than stories formalized and canonized by an American public eager for confirmation of its own heroic past. As Michael Kraus and Davis Joyce argue, historians such as Jared Sparks and Parson Weems "told the American people what they wished to hear about their past. Important factors in the nation's early history, however, including economic factors, were inadequately considered by these 'filiopietistic' historians" (92). This bias, Kraus and Joyce contend, pervaded the filiopietistic tradition in American historiography with which Melville is struggling. For example, "in his editing of *The North American Review,* as in his later editing of the letters of famous men, Sparks revealed a fatal weakness—he was timid about offending those in high places" (93). This popular bias affected not only the range of the historical record early historians were willing to document, but also the accuracy of their accounts of those personages and events:

> For both authors [Sparks and Weems] the lives of great men, particularly Washington, were sermons exhorting lesser mortals to nobler personal achievement. Not all aspects of Washington's life, nor all his words, were fit to be sermons, and rather than exhibit Washington's human frailties, Sparks edited his language to fit the image that America worshiped. (96)

As John Samson makes abundantly clear, Melville's work in *Israel Potter* examines and critiques the implications of these filiopietistic prejudices, especially by having Potter finally return to his native shores on July 4, 1826, not coincidentally the day on which both Thomas Jefferson and John Adams died, fueling what Michael Kammen has termed "a popular impulse that for a time verged upon being a cult of ancestor worship" (17–18).

But Melville isn't simply charging inaccuracy in the historical record. His own historical narrative gratuitously and aggressively plays fast and loose with the "truths" of both Israel Potter and America's Revolutionary past. Most obviously, Melville regularly and substantially departs from Trumbull's narrative of Potter's life, claiming a revisionary freedom wildly incommensurate with his prefatory assurance that his narrative "preserves, almost as in a reprint, Israel Potter's autobiographical story" (vii). Of course, Melville swerves from Trumbull's Potter by reincarnating his Potter in western New England rather than Rhode Island. More importantly, Melville foregrounds his own unreliability as an introduction to the global problems of historical verification and authenticity. The tale of *Israel Potter's* intertextual matrix is a tale of historical deletions, elisions, lies, frauds, and patent fictions. Henry Trumbull's own reputation for historical writing was none too secure. In fact, David Chacko and Alexander Kulcsar label Trumbull "one of our early and most prolific literary liars," pointing out that "by the time he met Israel Potter in 1823, Trumbull had reached a new low: one of his apprentices . . . had been arrested on the streets of Providence for 'selling obscene books and pamphlets' to the youth of the town" (367). Their research reveals that Trumbull's (and perhaps Potter's, for all we know) version of Potter's initial voyage aboard the *Washington* is abbreviated and edited (no mention being made of the mutiny aboard ship) so as virtually to falsify the "event that was the real watershed of Potter's life. In fact, the story of the *Washington* is an epic tale of anti-heroism—a bad ship with a bad captain, a bad crew, and worse luck" (375).

But this skein of intertextual inaccuracy goes much deeper, implicating not only the so-called filiopietistic historians Weems and Sparks, but Benjamin Franklin and Melville's transcendentalist contemporaries as well. Franklin, for example, manufactures lies about the Quaker merchant Denham, in order to encourage his own son to pay his debts to his father (Shurr 440). Both Sparks and Robert C. Sands, Franklin's and Jones's biographers respectively, struggle to affirm their particular versions of their subjects' lives, usually against competing British narratives. John Samson notes that Sparks

> consciously attempts to mold and cast the reputation of revolutionary hero. In each case, the reputation is a response to British aspersions: for instance, Sparks, in his "Continuation" of Franklin's *Autobiography,* controverts "a late English writer" who "insinuates" that Franklin ignored his poor relatives; and in the preface to Jones's narrative, Robert C. Sands attacks the English edition, whose editor reveals "his own monarchical and English prejudices" by impugning the character of Jones. (177)

Melville's narrative even dramatizes John Paul Jones challenging popular versions of his own barbarism. During a confidential chat with Potter, Jones denies the "sad stories" told about him. "To this hour," he complains,

> they say there that I,—blood-thirsty—coward dog that I am,— flogged a sailor, one Mungo Maxwell, to death. It's a lie, by heaven! I flogged him, for he was a mutinous scamp. But he died naturally, some time afterwards, and on board another ship. But why talk? They didn't believe the affidavits of others taken before London courts, triumphantly acquitting me; how then will they credit *my* interested words? (91)

All renditions of the truth, *Israel Potter* implies, can only be articulated in "interested words"; no source, primary, secondary, or oral, can be trusted. Indeed, *Israel Potter* is littered with references to the biased and prejudicial nature of what passes as "historical knowledge." Israel's personal encounter and friendship with King George III leaves him "with very favorable views of that monarch. . . . Yet hitherto the precise contrary of this had been Israel's opinion, agreeably to the popular prejudice throughout New England" (32–33). Melville's narration of the famous confrontation between Jones's *Bon Homme Richard* and the *Serapis* anticipates Stephen Crane's *The Red Badge of Courage* in its representation of the chaotic swirl of battle that later gets formalized, systematized, and falsified. He begins with a stark admission of discursive impossibility:

> Never was there a fight so snarled. The intricacy of those incidents which defy the narrator's extrication, is not ill figured in that bewildering intertanglement of all the yards and anchors of the two ships, which confounded them for the time in one chaos of devastation.
>
> Elsewhere than here the reader must go who seeks an elaborate version of the fight, or, indeed, much of any regular account of it whatever. The writer is but brought to mention the battle, because he must needs follow, in all events, the fortunes of the humble adventurer whose life he records. Yet this necessarily involves some general view of each conspicuous incident in which he shares. (120–21)

At the conclusion of this titanic struggle, the narrator further complicates the proceedings by admitting, "So equal was the conflict that, even after the surrender, it could be, and was, a question to one of the warriors engaged (who had not happened to see the English flag hauled down) whether the Serapis had struck to the Richard, or the Richard to the Serapis" (129), again suggesting the subjective, variable, and often fortuitous (not to mention ambiguous) nature of historical recollection. When John Paul Jones sends his schizophrenically polite letter to Lady Selkirk to apologize for his charges' ransacking of her estate, the narrator notes:

How the lady received this super-ardent note, history does not relate. But history has not omitted to record, that after the return of the Ranger to France, through the assiduous efforts of Paul in buying up the booty, piece by piece, from the clutches of those among whom it had been divided, and not without a pecuniary private loss to himself, equal to the total value of the plunder, the plate was punctually restored, even to the silver heads of two pepper-boxes; and, not only this, but the earl, hearing all the particulars, magnanimously wrote Paul a letter, expressing thanks for his politeness. In the opinion of the noble earl, Paul was a man of honor. It were rash *to differ in opinion with such high-born authority.* (110–11; my emphasis)

Stressing the selectivity of historical discourse, the triviality of what commonly passes as historical knowledge (the catalog of booty, including "the silver heads of two pepper-boxes," and the gentlemanly exchanges of pleasantries), and the importance of control over the reception of historical data (in the phrase I have emphasized), this passage establishes the generally random, but not arbitrary, nature of the transmission of the past. But because they appear only two pages before one of Melville's most pointed critiques of historiographical exclusivity, these rather casual omissions take on more significance. This chapter concludes by directly addressing the relay from event to historical discourse and the corresponding fame accruing to those agents designated as instrumental: "This cruise made loud fame for Paul, especially at the court of France, whose king sent Paul a sword and a medal. But poor Israel, who also had conquered a craft, and all unaided too—what had he?" (113). Indeed, Melville's claim finally to be disclosing "the secret history of the affair" (115) of Franklin's securing the ship to be named the *Bon Homme Richard* might function as an index to *Israel Potter's* thesis on the secrecy, in terms both of the multiple unknowable or mutually exclusive perspectives, and of the covert machinations integral to the unfolding of historical action and to the discursive translation of actions into the archive we generally refer to as history. Of course, there are secrets, and there are secrets, some indicative merely of information that is not (or not yet) known, others actually participating in the covert machinations that history can't but falsify in order to appear palatable. All partake in the general economy of prejudicial and self-promoting rhetoric, not in the noiseless transmission of objective historical data.

This is the crux of Melville's meditation on the working of historical discourse, and it is why his protagonist emerges with such uncanny resonance. One slight measure of the impact Melville's "Revolutionary narrative" may have had is, not so oddly, registered in the initial reception of *Israel Potter.* As Walter Bezanson remarks, "no American review noted that Israel was nearly run down by the patriotic car near Faneuil Hall on the Fourth of July" (217). Given the favorable initial reception of the narrative, praised, as Bezanson notes, "for its masculine style, Yankee wit, and alleged patriotism" (216), the reviewers' silence on this rhetorically and typographically highlighted (and most disturbing) image that opens the final chapter indicates deep denial on the part of a reading public and reviewing elite of one of *Israel Potter's* harshest truths. Daniel Reagan has argued convincingly that Melville's approach in *Israel Potter* contests the biographical theories of Emerson, Thomas Carlyle, Jared Sparks, and frequent contributors to *Putnam's, Harper's,* and other periodicals in the middle decades of the nineteenth century. Reagan marshals revealing passages from Emerson, Carlyle, and others, all indicative of their theoretical animadversion for "the common, the low, and the mean" that Emerson quite paradoxically elicits in "The American Scholar." Quite apropos for our discussion of *Israel Potter,* Reagan cites Emerson, who notes in "The Uses of Great Men" that "enormous populations, if they be beggars, are disgusting, like moving cheese, like hills of ants, or of fleas—the more the worse," and also that "the worthless and offensive members of society, whose existence is a social pest, invariably think themselves the most ill used people alive, and never get over their astonishment at the ingratitude and selfishness of their contemporaries" (quoted in Reagan 269). Reagan summarizes contemporary historiographical theory in terms useful for this argument:

> Three assumptions held by the School of Carlyle about the nature and purpose of biography make the common man a victim and tool of history. First, by valuing ideas more than the creation of material civilization, Carlyle and Emerson ignore

the common man's role in shaping the world. Second, by arguing that only great men are appropriate subjects for biography, they condemn the common man to anonymity and exclude him from the world's memory. And finally, by encouraging readers to ignore outward conditions and search for inward greatness, they trivialize the very forces that define and limit the lives of common men. (273)

Indeed, Melville calls attention to the common blindness to and conscious suppression of the contributions of "the common man" in his penultimate chapter: "Why at one given stone in the flagging does man after man cross yonder street? What plebeian Lear or Œdipus; what Israel Potter cowers there by the corner they shun?" (161). Anticipating, almost prophetically, twentieth-century recognitions of lower- or working-class contributions to civilization and culture, from Arthur Miller's "Tragedy and the Common Man" to Thomas Pynchon's wraithlike figures illuminated only fleetingly by the headlights of speeding midnight traffic, Melville heightens our awareness of the costs of historical and literary-historical myopia and hero worship. His Israel Potter, perpetual type or figure without readers keen enough to realize his anti-type or fulfillment, *is* that figure that lurks invisibly, unacknowledged and unrewarded, in the margins of historical discourse.

Melville does not restrict to the level of the individual his analysis of the erased, suppressed, and otherwise forgotten agents of historical change. The complete title under which the first two serial installments of *Israel Potter* were published in July and August of 1854 was *Israel Potter; or, Fifty Years of Exile: A Fourth of July Story.* While Walter Bezanson speculates that both the inclusion and removal of the "Fourth of July" subtitle "may have been made in the [*Putnam's*] magazine offices, without consulting Melville" (209), to highlight the timing of its appearance, it is also possible that Melville titled his "Revolutionary narrative of the beggar" rather aggressively at first, and then backed off, perhaps in an attempt to comply with his promise "that the story shall contain nothing of any sort to shock the fastidious" (*Correspondence* 265). Whatever the reason, the subtitle, by virtue of its largely cynical gloss on the accompanying narrative, suggests that Melville's largest agenda was a critique of the trivialization and manipulation of America's patriotic myths and ideals. In this respect, the reference to Fourth of July can be read as Melville's rejoinder to various moments of rhetorical bravado, such as Thoreau's establishing his base at Walden Pond on the Fourth of July. Whereas Thoreau believed that our lives would emerge in their transcendental potential *if* we could only work through the proper "economy," and Emerson urged us to practice self-reliance as the only viable strategy for self-liberation, *Israel Potter* exposes the harsher, less forgiving, and more materialist economy that strangles even so diligent and self-reliant a figure as Potter. Melville's narrative should also be read in the context of those Fourth of July celebrations of working-class solidarity that Michael Kammen and Philip Foner discuss as arising during the 1820s. As Kammen notes,

> By the later 1820s, also, the Fourth of July had come to be regarded as a day with special significance in the minds of working-class people: a day for renewing the Spirit of '76, for dramatizing working-class demands, and for rewriting the Declaration to restore the rights employers "have robbed us of." It was a day for such toasts as "The Working Men—the legitimate children of '76; their sires left them the legacy of freedom and equality. They are now of age, and are laboring to guarantee the principles of the Revolution." Why such strident claims? Because the feeling had arisen among labor circles, especially at the close of the decade, that workers were increasingly being exploited by capital; that even though the "leathern aprons" [or Israel Potters] had played a major role in making the Revolution, its idealistic goals were not being enjoyed by their children and grandchildren. (45)

From the point of view of the common laborer or soldier, then, the Revolutionary legacy rather pathetically consisted of fraud, exploitation, and dispossession, interestingly echoed in Melville's Potter returning home to frenzied celebrations and then being able to find no trace of his heritage, his family all supposedly having moved west, the Potter name more or less forgotten.

But while Potter ostensibly belongs among the conquerors, the victorious colonial army, his fate quite clearly coincides more with the Other of American militarism and expansion, the victims whose lands were confiscated and whose families were murdered as the colonies broke from England and eventually roamed west over what Francis Jennings rightly calls "widowed" (15), not "virgin," land.[12] In this respect, *Israel Potter* recapitulates and foregrounds a theme of dispossession that had lingered on the margins of mainstream literary production in the United States since colonial times. Early Protestant settlers marshaled plausible scriptural and communal rationales for their brutalization and exploitation, whether of antinomian, Quaker, or Pequot. By the time of Melville's writing, the issue for him, as for at least one earlier generation, was the slaughter and removal of Native American tribes from areas prime for white settlement and agriculture. Every time Potter is represented as a prisoner, every time he is cheated or betrayed, every time he dutifully fulfills his part of an implicit contract without receiving due compensation, and every time he performs some deed of heroism without recognition, his fate exposes the scandal of the unstable (perhaps fraudulent) ethical and political bases upon which mythic constructions of American exceptionalism rest, echoing homologous travesties such as broken treaties with Native Americans as well as spectacles of abusive power and exclusionary violence exercised against American minorities.

While it is understood that Melville worked closely with James Fenimore Cooper's *History of the Navy* (1853), I would like to offer three passages from Cooper's *The Prairie* (1824) as important glosses on Melville's work in *Israel Potter.* In these scenes, which I consider to function as a triadic core of *The Prairie's* commentary on the westward-expansionist policies and practices of the United States, Cooper registers the ostensibly "naturalistic" erasure of the carnage and tragedy as inseparable from "the opening of the West." In a seemingly banal coda after a buffalo stampede, Cooper notes that

> The uproar which attended the passage of the herd was now gone, or rather it was heard rolling along the Prairie, at the distance of a mile. The clouds of dust were already blown away by the wind, and a clear range was left to the eye, in that place,

where ten minutes before there existed a scene of so much wild-
ness and confusion. (205)

While Cooper certainly is capable of environmentalist themes (Natty
Bumppo regularly castigates the waste and immorality of unsound
ecological practices), he does not contextualize this scene so as to
highlight its potential commentary on the near extermination of the
American buffalo; indeed, he is writing before that particular chapter of North American ecological tragedy. Rather, the scene accentu-
ates the wide expanses of the prairie and its apparently inexhaustible
resources, although bee-hunter Paul Hover's relish for roast buffalo
hump and his craving for one every day certainly hints at the extermination to come. In the context of two later scenes, however, even
this passage takes on greater significance. When Mahtoree and his
Sioux followers rapidly move their camp just prior to the final battle
with their Pawnee enemies, Cooper returns to similar language:

> During this summary and brief disposition of things, the disap-
> pointed Agent of Mahtoree and his callous associates were seen
> flying across the plain in the direction of the retiring families,
> and when Ishmael left the spot with his prisoners and his booty,
> the ground which had so lately been alive with the bustle and
> life of an extensive Indian encampment was as still and empty
> as any other spot in those extensive wastes. (329)

In other words, where there once had been thriving native civiliza-
tions, dense with elaborate and ancient social and cultural codes, now
there exists only prairie, with no hint of a former civilization visible
to daunt the westward flow across the Mississippi. An entire people
can vanish without a trace.

This line of thought culminates in the final battle between the two
warring tribes of Native Americans, exacerbated, of course, by the
influx of Ishmael Bush and his family, survey teams, and the nearby
American military presence:

> The day dawned, the following morning, on a more tranquil
> scene. The work of blood had entirely ceased, and as the sun
> arose its light was shed on a broad expanse of quiet and solitude.

The tents of Ishmael were still standing, where they had been last seen; but not another vestige of human existence could be traced in any other part of the waste. Here and there, little flocks of ravenous birds were sailing and screaming above those spots where some heavy-footed Teton had met his death, but every other sign of the recent combat had passed away. The river was to be traced far through the endless meadows by its serpentine and smoking bed, and the little silvery clouds of vapor which hung above the pools and springs were beginning to melt in air, as they felt the quickening warmth, which, pouring from the glowing sky, shed its bland and subtle influence on every object of the vast and unshadowed region. The Prairie was, like the heavens after the passage of the gust, soft, calm, and soothing. (341)

Completing *The Prairie's* defamiliarizing of western expansion, this passage supplements the previous one—where there had been fierce warfare and immense bloodshed and loss of life, there now only stand the tents of white itinerants. The history of westward movement need not, these passages suggest, address or historicize the bloody extermination of the region's original inhabitants; their cultures and the wars that eliminated them have left no trace. In fact, the prairie is, after the racial genocide of native peoples, cleansed and rendered more habitable (soft, calm, and soothing) for western settlers. Cooper's naturalistic language in these passages diminishes to the point of complete obliteration of the human agency essential to render a once populated and differently civilized environment the rightful turf for agricultural, mining, and other economic and military interests from the East.[13]

What I am suggesting, then, is that Melville's concluding reference to Israel Potter's original narrative ("it faded out of print—himself out of being—his name out of memory") and his final sentence ("He died the same day that the oldest oak on his native hills was blown down" [169]) both resonate with the predilection of American historiography to elide the violence and human costs inherent not only in the workings of history (here primarily in armed struggle, covert espionage, and intelligence operations) but in the discursive violence inherent in the historical representation of the past, in both cases by relegating human loss and tragedy to the naturalistic course of trees falling and traces fading. Like Cooper, Melville continually fuses and confuses the workings of nature with the workings of human agency and exploits the homogenization and misrepresentation of the historical record that results. Melville's highly charged naturalistic language of "fading" is duplicated by the opening paragraph of an anonymous 1855 *North American Review* essay on George Bancroft's historical work:

> One by one they totter and die, . . . the remnants of that sturdy race in whose ears the drums yet beat, in whose eyes the colors stream, as they tell to the children of their children the story of the Revolution, of its battles and its trials. It becomes us to save what is fading from the memory of men. ("Causes of the American Revolution" 389–90)

The echoes are remarkable; the only problem here is the reviewer's faith in the rhetorical reconstruction of a Revolutionary legacy. This reviewer's hunch is that those stories fading from the memories and oral traditions of sturdy men can be preserved in the written record of historical scholarship. Unfortunately, the fate of Potter's own "little book," itself originally dictated to Henry Trumbull, suggests that the economy governing the marketing of historical stories is closely linked with an economy that might argue, say, that the Pequots "faded" out of New England.

vi

I would like to close this chapter by suggesting a possible autobiographical dimension of *Israel Potter,* however discordant so intimate and personalized a chord may strike with the ideological and historiographical thrust of the present discussion. In Melville's case, however, and especially in the case of *Israel Potter,* these two discursive realms—that of cultural critique and that of autobiographical revelation—merge in noteworthy ways. Critics of *Israel Potter* have turned to autobiographical speculation with some regularity. Some of what follows will summarize and follow these leads; some will argue for an

entirely new way of understanding Melville's own grasp of our contemporary truism that "the personal is the political."

The inquiry into the autobiographical suggestiveness of Melville's
"Revolutionary narrative" has ranged from the very general to the
highly specific and from the stylistic to the psychological. Melville's
revisions of his source works have drawn attention from a number of
scholars. Walter Bezanson calls our attention to, perhaps, Melville's
earliest and most obvious alteration of his "source" for this novel:
"as he began to write *Israel Potter* Melville made two important decisions: to take the narrative role away from Potter, and to change his
birthplace from Cranston, Rhode Island, to the Berkshire region near
Pittsfield" (186). This change gave him the opportunity to situate
his pseudohistorical protagonist in the western Massachusetts environment he had come to know intimately since his move there in
1850. George Dekker has commented on Melville's representation of
the nightmarish London in *Israel Potter*'s final chapters. According to
Dekker,

> this vision of London was not fueled by contemporary accounts,
> Potter's or others', of the late-eighteenth-century city which the
> historical Israel Potter entered towards the end of the American
> War of Independence. It was prompted by the early Victorian
> city which Melville himself visited in 1849 and by [a] passage
> from Benjamin Haydon's *Life*. (192)

More specifically, Melville draws directly from his journal entry of
Friday, November 9, 1849, and revises Potter's original narrative account of his own entry into London. While Potter's journal mentions
only the year of his entry into the English metropolis, Melville dates
his arrival quite specifically in chapter 24, significantly titled "In the
City of Dis":

> It was late on a Monday morning, in November—a blue Monday
> —a Fifth of November—Guy Fawkes' Day!—very blue, foggy,
> doleful and gunpowdery, indeed, as shortly will be seen,—that
> Israel found himself wedged in among the greatest every-day
> crowd which grimy London presents to the curious stranger.
> (158)

Melville's own journal provides the matter for much of this description as well as for his brief account of Potter's day. After a description of his early morning ramblings, Melville recounts his thoughts:

> While on one of the Bridges, the thought struck me again that a fine thing might be written about a Blue Monday in November London—a city of Dis (Dante's) clouds of smoke—the damned &c—coal barges—coaly waters, cast iron Duke &c its marks are left upon you, &c &c &c (14)

The repetition functions on a number of levels, including the time (late morning in November), the Dantean allusion, the color blue, and the general attribution of a nightmarish cast to the entire area. As Peter Bellis notes in his discussion of this passage, "in resurrecting an episode from his own life, [Melville] darkens and ironizes it, suggesting both a radical alienation from his own experience and a veiled identification with his protagonist" (618). Melville thus sandwiches his retelling of Potter's story with extended and highly resonant geographic detail drawn almost exclusively from his own travels and associations, not from Potter's.

If we pursue the leads of still two other discussions of *Israel Potter,* we are ushered into a more pervasive doubling of Potter's and Melville's experiences. John Samson offers a generalized sense of the autobiographical subtext of Melville's narrative:

> Melville, seeing in Potter's narrative these ambiguities [concerning the ideology and accomplishments of the Revolution], heightens them with some help from the other narratives, and thereby offers a critique of problems—the poverty he personally experienced, the slavery, the acquisitive nationalism, and the rationalizing religiosity—evident in his own day. (176)

Kenneth Dauber draws a much more elaborate set of correspondences between Melville's life and the story of his titular hero:

> Melville, in the alienation of his authority for self-representation, represents himself as an other. His "I" becomes, "with a change in the grammatical person," a "he." His autobiography becomes biography or, even, fiction, at any rate something objectified.

Now Melville's personal situation, standing, as it were, behind Israel Potter's, is clear. For the neglect accorded Potter, we may read the neglect accorded Melville after *Pierre*. For Potter's reception upon returning to "his native land," we may read Melville's reception, after turning from stories of the sea to stories of land. In his exaggerated description of the narrowness of the circulation of Potter's own tale—a book not quite so unknown as Melville claims—we may even read the exaggerated sense Melville had of the narrowness of circulation of his own works, despite the following he to some extent continued to have. (217)

Readers may balk at the directness of Dauber's associations, but I think he is on the right track, especially once we recall that Israel Potter and Herman Melville shared the same birthday. In fact, while both the frontispiece and the first sentence of Trumbull's *Life and Remarkable Adventures* declare Potter's birthday as August 1, 1744 (Trumbull 286, 291), Melville nowhere indicates his protagonist's birth date. This elision seems all the more noteworthy when we consider that Melville *does* play off the title page's announcement of Potter as "a native of Cranston, Rhode-Island" (Trumbull 287), also on the frontispiece (286), a biographical fact which Melville aggressively changes to resituate Potter in his own Berkshire Mountains. One could argue that Melville was interested in establishing a thorough set of correspondences between himself and his historico-fictional character, but one which he advances as obliquely as possible, often via mere similarities, and certainly one perceptible only to those readers familiar with Melville's biography and economic crises. We might even posit that, as Hawthorne addressed his family's complicity with the darker moments in seventeenth-century Boston and Salem in his stories, Melville similarly struggles with the complications and complicity of his own Revolutionary ancestry in *Israel Potter* as well as in *Pierre,* again, albeit indirectly.

I would like to suggest that Melville consolidates and enhances these generalized parallels with a final flourish of intimate and yet unexamined homologies between Potter and himself. In the last few chapters of *Israel Potter,* Melville strews allusions to two works which he either completed or brought to near completion but never published, perhaps never seen by anyone other than a reader at Harper and Brothers. The fate of these two books, one most likely a novel entitled *The Isle of the Cross* and the other "another book—300 pages, say—partly nautical adventure, and partly—or, rather, chiefly, of Tortoise Hunting Adventure" (*Correspondence* 250), resonates with the alienated and deprived fate of Melville's Potter. Melville's "tortoise-hunting adventure" book has a curious history. Melville first mentions it in a letter dated November 24, 1853, and gratefully acknowledges receiving an advance of three hundred dollars on December 6. However, Melville sends two later inquiries to Harper and Brothers, one dated February 20, 1854, another on May 25 of that same year, before, finally, and in a tone of exasperation, sending the third and last inquiry concerning his project's reception on June 22, a letter that Melville concludes, "be so good therefore by an early reply to releive [sic] my uncertainty" (267). Unwilling to continue without any prospect of remuneration (he refers to the possibility of forwarding sections before adding, "but even this is not unattended with labor; which labor, of course, I do not care to undergo while remaining in doubt as to its recompence" [267]), Melville apparently prepares to proceed with *Israel Potter*, the proposal for which he had sent to Putnam only two weeks before this final missive pertaining to his tortoise book. Melville, I offer, alludes to the tortoise-hunting adventure early in chapter 24, "In the City of Dis," by concluding a paragraph on the sordidness and squalor of London with the following passage:

> The black vistas of streets were as the galleries in coal mines; the flagging, as flat tomb-stones minus the consecration of moss; and worn heavily down, by sorrowful tramping, as the vitreous rocks in the cursed Gallipagos, over which the convict tortoises crawl. (159)

In addition to contributing to his squalid portrait of London, this passage includes the seemingly gratuitous reference to the mysterious "convict tortoises crawl[ing]."[14] While never referred to as a convict, Potter is designated scores of times as a prisoner, a prisoner of war, and a slave, while he is also confined, impressed, enclosed, restricted equally numerous times. Not only does this passage resonate with the sense of Potter's futility and imprisonment throughout *Israel Potter*, but it also directly echoes Melville's specific language from his February 20 letter to the Harpers, which he concludes by suggesting that he "shall be in New York in the course of a few weeks; when I shall call upon you, & inform you when these proverbially slow 'Tortoises' will be ready to *crawl* into market" (257; my emphasis).

While we might speculate that Melville's economic and publishing difficulties stemmed largely from his failure to finish his proposed book of three hundred pages on tortoise-hunting adventures, there is another, more mysterious, moment from his publishing history, a second narrative equally at play in *Israel Potter*'s final pages. Compelling evidence exists to suggest that Melville had discussed at length with Hawthorne, researched, written, and submitted a novel that was eventually known as *The Isle of the Cross* by about May 22, 1853, the day his daughter Elizabeth was born.[15] Further, "the *Springfield Republican* of 11 June 1853 under 'Pittsfield Items' reported that 'Herman Melville has gone to New York to superintend the issue of a new work'" (*Correspondence* 249). The trouble is that Melville never published this work that biographical evidence increasingly suggests he had, in fact, finished. In a letter of May 22, 1853, Melville's cousin Priscilla Melvill asked his sister Augusta, "when will the 'Isle of the Cross' make its appearance? I am constantly looking in the journals & magazines that come in my way, for notices of it" (Parker 11). The only hard evidence for Melville's attempt to publish it also contributes to the enigmatic nature of that work's non-history. In a letter to Harper and Brothers dated November 24, 1853 (the same letter in which he proposes the tortoise-hunting narrative), Melville alludes to "the work which I took to New York last Spring, but which I *was prevented from printing at that time*" (250; my emphasis). Within this devious phrasing lurk various questions regarding the fate of Melville's manuscript—was it rejected outright? were there legal problems regarding Harper's liability for a story involving a living person? was Melville simply put on hold, as the phrase "at that time" might indicate? Hershel Parker's speculation that "Melville apparently did not feel afterwards that the Harpers had rejected *The Isle of the Cross* but that he somehow had been 'prevented' from publishing it" (13) may be as close as we can get to answering these questions. What we do know is that during these wranglings with the Harpers Melville was actively planning and working on *Israel Potter,* the project he first mentions in a journal entry of December 1849, in which he discusses poring over many "ancient maps of London . . . in case I serve up the Revolutionary narrative of the beggar," and buying one (*Journals* 43).[16] Given the consensus that *Israel Potter* was intended to initiate Melville's return to literary popularity and, perhaps, economic gain, it is certainly unlikely that the setbacks he apparently endured regarding both the tortoise-hunting adventure and *The Isle of the Cross* were not on his mind as only the most recent—along with the rejection of "The Two Temples"—economic failures in his rapidly declining literary fortunes following the complicated publishing and review histories of *Moby-Dick* and *Pierre.*

Melville integrates his bitterness over these two thwarted attempts at publishing substantial works of fiction into the very fabric of Potter's own disillusionment and sense of futility. Melville punctuates the aged Potter's return to his native country with numerous moments of withering irony, pathos, and tragedy. Melville plays up the ironic perspective by having Potter, whose own heroics are obviously forgotten, land on the Fourth of July, 1826—remarkably, both the fiftieth anniversary of the signing of the Declaration of Independence and the day on which both John Adams and Thomas Jefferson die—and by having him nearly killed by a triumphal car flying a banner proclaiming:

BUNKER-HILL.

1775.

GLORY TO THE HEROES THAT FOUGHT!

The entirety of the final chapter emphasizes Potter's failed attempt to secure a pension, the desperation of his final days, and the ignominious closure of his existence, which is coupled with reminders of his own narrative "fading out of print." Quite significantly, Melville's June 1853 visit to New York to secure publication for *The Isle of the Cross* coincided with his own attempt to secure a political position— not the pension that Potter petitions for, but a political appointment, most likely in a consulate. Melville, Hawthorne, and many of their associates occupied much of early 1853 in the first protracted attempt to secure a political appointment for the needy Melville, but it was not until the second half of June that Lemuel Shaw decisively ended their campaign (Leyda 1: 468–76). As Parker summarizes the fate of the New York trip, "Melville returned to Pittsfield without a political appointment and apparently without any prospects for printing *The Isle of the Cross*" (13). We could conclude that their shared failures in securing economic assistance from the government constitutes a final biographical dimension to *Israel Potter*, but I would like to pursue this issue a bit further.

Israel Potter's final chapter begins and ends with references to Potter's scars. "His scars proved his only medals" (169), Melville notes in the final paragraph, but Melville closes the chapter's second paragraph by referring to Potter as "the bescarred bearer of a cross" (167), this cross apparently referring to two intersecting sword wounds, one from Bunker Hill and one from the fight with the *Serapis,* on Potter's mutilated chest. This image, laden with poignance, forges a biographical conjunction between Potter's historical fate and Melville's immediate cultural fate, for what was Melville himself following the recent depression of his literary fortunes and the rejection of two full-length works, one of which is entitled *The Isle of the Cross,* other than himself the "bescarred bearer of a cross"? The reference, in other words, does double duty, representing Potter struggling for recognition and recompense from the government, yet also signifying Melville, similarly bearing a *Cross* to the Harpers' door in his own struggle to recover his waning popularity. Whereas Potter "was repulsed in efforts, after a pension, by certain caprices of law" (169), Melville's own attempt to secure a consulship and to publish *The Isle of the Cross,* a work he "was prevented from printing at that time," meets with a similarly ambiguous and, perhaps, inexplicable foil. The actual reasons for both failures are probably gone forever in the welter of lost historical records.

Women, then, have not had a dog's chance of writing poetry. —Virginia Woolf, *A Room of One's Own*

Emily Dickinson's poem "I started Early – Took my Dog –" presents us with another kind of loose end altogether by announcing the presence of a dog in the high-visibility position of the final word in the poem's first line, only to abandon the dog immediately thereafter. While I take poem #520 to be one of Dickinson's most compelling and certainly one of her most complex feminist works, the fact is, however, that the overwhelming majority of critics, including those who investigate Dickinson's postromantic or posttranscendentalist poetics of nature, do not discuss the poem at all. Those who do read "I started Early – Took my Dog –" (as opposed to those who merely mention it) tend to stress its negotiation of a variety of themes—sex; death; Dickinson's supposed renunciation of life; or an encounter with nature, the unconscious, or some unspecified overwhelming force. Most critics, moreover, synthesize a number of these analytical paradigms within their interpretations.[1] Even those critics who do discuss poem #520 tend not to grapple with the structurally (and, I will contend, thematically) significant question of what happens to her dog.[2] Unlike other loose ends that emerge at or near the conclusions of the works we have been examining, this lost dog presents a different kind of absence, one which is conspicuous throughout a work in which its presence is only fleetingly alluded to and then simply dropped. I would like to pursue this textual enigma doggedly, so to speak, as a strategy both for reading poem #520 and as an occasion to pursue some of the implications of important feminist approaches to Dickinson's poetry and its responsiveness to pressing

issues in literary history and feminist thought. Margaret Homans suggests that "Dickinson derives her unique power from her particular
way of understanding her femininity, and . . . her work is as complex
and profuse as it is . . . because she is able to put behind her problems of identity that make Dorothy [Wordsworth] and Brontë linger
over the same theses and issues in poem after poem" (165). Homans's
argument is tempting, but, I feel, optimistic; I don't read Dickinson
as ever having put any fundamental question "behind her." In fact, I
would go so far as to argue that in "I started Early – Took my Dog –,"
a poem which Homans does not engage, Dickinson's work is so complex and so fraught with loose ends that it demonstrates little if not
the impossibility of resolving questions of gendered identity.

The text begins "I started Early – Took my Dog – / And visited the
Sea –," but, while important enough to be mentioned as the speaker's
companion in the poem's first line, the dog simply disappears from
the narrative of this work, which has been read variously as adventure, as trauma, and as initiation rite. In one basic, literary respect,
this loose end, the vanishing of Dickinson's dog, problematizes the
privilege of poetic beginnings which initiate not only poetic but narrative schemes of importance. As Peter Rabinowitz argues,

> our attention during the act of reading will, in part, be concen-
> trated on what we have found in these positions [beginnings *and*
> endings], and our sense of the text's meaning will be influenced
> by our assumption that the author expected us to end up with
> an interpretation that could account more fully for these details
> than for details elsewhere. (59)

We may, of course, be puzzled by various narrative details or ensembles of data—by the possible meanings of the "mermaids" or
"frigates" in this poem—but, according to Rabinowitz's calculus, our
perplexity at the disappearance of Emily Dickinson's dog conflicts
with important structural imperatives of poetic interpretation and,
by virtue of so flagrant a violation of Rabinowitz's "rules of notice,"
should generate a commensurate hermeneutic gesture on our parts as
readers. To be sure, Dickinson's poems frequently transgress ordinary
poetic conventions, leaving loose ends not quite accommodated by

the expansiveness of her verse narratives. The issues and images of her beginnings, however, tend to persist as central concerns for her poetic texts. Dickinson's beginnings establish contexts, locate scenic environments, address interlocutors, pose questions, raise issues, articulate problems, declare fractured identities, assert certainties, suggest ironies, but virtually all introductory moments in Dickinson remain thematically operative for the duration of the poem, and are usually generative of those poetic worlds. For example, the bird in "A Bird came down the Walk –" remains the center of that poem's focus, and in "I know that He exists" the existence or nonexistence of God drives this problematic meditation. Her poems rarely provide total (frequently even satisfactory) closure, but the nature of Dickinsonian ambiguity hinges predominantly on provocative, resonant, and problematic terms—either on an excess of meaning, detail, and allusion or on the absence of certitude or finality—but rarely on amputation, fragmentation, or disappearance, although the disappearance or absence of God (in one case the amputation of his right hand), of tradition, of self, of lover, or of hope often provides the thematic core for Dickinson's poetic interrogations.

How do we figure the significance of the dog's capitalized presence in the poem's first line? What breed of dog is it, and male or female? Is this one of the few poetic excursions on which Dickinson allows her beloved Carlo to accompany her? And, if so, how could a dog which Dickinson described in a letter to Thomas Wentworth Higginson as "large as myself" (*Letters* 2:404) simply vanish? Is *this* hound as fluffy and lovable as my keeshond, Cubby-Bear? How do we understand the identity of the speaker to be modified, qualified, strengthened, or in some other way constructed with reference to the dog (that is, is Emily Dickinson's dog her best friend and/or "man's best friend")? How do we account for its absence (or at least for Dickinson's silence about it) by the conclusion? When and how does it vanish, if vanish it has, within the narrative of the speaker's encounter with a masculinized and aggressive sea? And why is the disappearance of the dog not reported as a dilemma? The poem seems blithely and disturbingly unaware of its vanishing. I think that all these questions can be answered to the satisfaction of those concerned with animal as well as with human rights. In fact, the problematic status of Emily Dickinson's dog may well provide us with an angle for approaching both one of Dickinson's most aggressively feminist poems and her thinking about nature, culture, and sexual identity. My reading of "I Started Early – Took my Dog –" will deal most directly with the question of Dickinson's pet near its own conclusion, but traces of the dog will everywhere inform its progress and concerns.

ii

This poem begins with a two-stanza statement of the speaker's announcement of her visit to the sea followed by what seems to be the sea's reaction to her presence, at this point apparently on the shore. The first two lines,

> I started Early – Took my Dog –
> And visited the Sea –

provide the only occasion for a declaration of motive, goal, or rationale for the "visit," and, of course, no such declaration appears. Rather than clarification, the speaker provides only a statement of enigmatic fact, recalling the earliness of this venture, but not a specific point of departure, although we might assume that the terminus of the poem, the "Solid Town" of the concluding stanza, doubles as a point of origin. I would offer that in this poem Dickinson enacts what Myra Jehlen calls "America's primal scene, Columbus arriving on an unknown shore" (2), though with the crucially gendered difference that her female persona elicits. Here we have no confident conquistador, no rapacious army of voyagers hungry for material gain, but a young woman testing the waters of one of her culture's dominant tropes. More tentative than the invincible male explorers driven by dreams of glory and gold, the speaker in this narrative provides no information concerning the exact nature of this "visit," though the possibilities the reader can construct for this poem's speaker include such scenarios as a casual early-morning walk accompanied by her dog, an excursion of some ambiguous nature on which the dog might accompany her for protection, and, in an Emersonian or Thoreauvian vein, a latter-day examination of or experiment with nature, perhaps even

Dickinson's problematic consideration of "where she lived and what she lived for"; that is, *her* Walden. In fact, two possible definitions of the word "visit" invite the latter reading, incorporating the sense of "an instance (or the action) of going to a place, house, etc., for the purpose of inspection or examination" along with the verbal form "to go to (an institution) for the purpose of seeing that everything is in due order; to exercise a periodic surveillance or supervision over, or make a special investigation into (management or conduct)" (*OED*). The poem gives no indication in its earliest stanzas that this range of the term "visit" seems operative, but the more we pursue this work's conundrums both within its textual boundaries and within several cultural contexts, the more this reading of Dickinson's "visit" reveals about her poetic work.

What does happen as soon as the speaker reaches the sea is that, far from maintaining any objective distance from the ocean, she becomes associated with, even identified as, actual or mythical creatures of nature.

> The Mermaids in the Basement
> Came out to look at me –
>
> And Frigates - in the Upper Floor
> Extended Hempen Hands –
> Presuming Me to be a Mouse –
> Aground - upon the Sands –

The ambiguity in these lines is forbidding, and critics have reached little consensus concerning the nature of the mermaids or the frigates and their hempen hands.[3] We can observe, however, that both images cast the speaker as a creature of nature, diminished and not fully human. The image of the mermaids evokes the mythical half-woman, half-fish, and, while the mermaids come out to look at the speaker and, hence, cannot easily be identified with her, they usher into the poem the possibility that, as woman, this Dickinson speaker is strongly identified with this subhuman element.[4] The next stanza intensifies this possibility when the speaker is explicitly naturalized as "a Mouse" by the frigates. In other words, we can trace a descent from the human to the animal in these first two stanzas, with the figure of the mermaids functioning as a pivotal and transitional image, suggestive, perhaps, of some mutation in the original human presence of the poem's beginning. As she nears the sea, the speaker, we might argue, loses her specifically human identity and begins a process of diminution, of bestial transformation.

The shifting terms of this poem's articulation of the relationship of the human (or the cultural) and the sea (or the natural) also informs the poem's architecturalization of the sea, organizing it conveniently into the common domestic units of ordinary housing structures. So, while the speaker's human identity erodes, the sea and its creatures take on human characteristics. It is important, also, that both the mermaids, by virtue of being half-human, and the mouse (as in the deprecatory adjective "mousey") can suggest human diminishment or insignificance. Furthermore, the connotation that the frigates are "presumptuous" in their diminution of the speaker highlights the arrogance and dominating perspective attributed to them. To return briefly to Myra Jehlen's argument, Dickinson's poem might actually invert Jehlen's notion of "Columbus arriving on an unknown shore" by casting herself as a metaphor for those native peoples victimized by colonial appropriation. In fact, while I will be pursuing a reading primarily concerned with Dickinson's thinking about gender and sexuality, Jehlen's image enables us to maintain a colonial and racialized subtext for Dickinson's poem. What begins as an apparently ordinary walk on the beach becomes very quickly an ontologically threatening event in which the speaker perceives her humanness slipping into a subhuman form commonly regarded as a nuisance or insignificant and, in this specific instance, threatened. The poem intensifies this level of threat through mutually canceling images of mermaids and frigates. While both are, of course, human constructions, one imaginative and the other material, mermaids function in traditional mythologies as partial explanations for the loss or destruction of ships and the madness of sailors, who, rather than remaining in control of their ships, drown while swimming to join the mild and tormenting half-women, half-fish. On the other hand, both moments—the undefined gaze of the mermaids and the presumptuous groping of the frigates—do not actually constitute the speaker's identity, but stand as her hypotheses concerning the Other's perception of her being, imposed constructions of female identity from some yet unspecified locus of discursive energy. The imposition of these constructions gains significance throughout the rest of "I started Early – Took my Dog –" and constitutes a major source of thematic conflict.

We can accept the ultimate ambiguity of these images while still granting a powerful sexual subtext inherent in them. In both cases the speaker of Dickinson's poem is situated in a potentially weakened (or perhaps covert) sexual position. The coming up of the mermaids from their basement quarters could signal the rising of a subordinate group (they live below the stairs while the frigates are in the "Upper Floor"); while normally "kept down," these mermaids rise up in this instance.[5] Furthermore, their gaze, their "looking at" the speaker on the sand, is at least partially homoerotic, especially if we read the "coming out" of the mermaids as a declaration of sexual rather than simply of social emergence and if we read the speaker's early starting in the poem's first stanza as a youthful, perhaps prodigious or premature, gesture of some initiatory importance. The frigates' assumption of the speaker's vulnerability further constructs her as a weakened self, in this case one to be groped for with hempen hands, at least partially suggestive of fettered bondage or the strangling grasp of a hempen noose. The act of "extending" these hempen hands fuses the potentially violating intentions of these frigates with their equally possible and decorous "extending" of courtesies to the speaker imagined to be weak or in need of assistance. Whether "extended" out of concern, decorum, or predatory opportunity, these hempen hands carry at least an implicit threat of restriction and bondage, especially since there has been no indication of the speaker's being in any actual danger at this point in the poem.

For both the mermaids and the frigates, then, the speaker on the sands is translated into an object for visual or physical appropriation, though it is important to contrast the possibly liberatory implications of the mermaids with the potentially (or at least partially) demeaning and inhibiting gestures of the putatively masculinized "Hempen Hands." Whether the object of the female gaze or of the male grope, the speaker has suddenly entered a realm quite beyond the ostensible "walk on the beach" ease of the poem's opening. But the difference in these modes of objectification and possible appropriation needs to be remarked as well. We should recall that the gaze of the mermaids is more integrally and less threateningly recounted by virtue of its relatively intimate placement with the emergence of the poetic speaker. It need hardly be said as well that, while not utterly without demeaning or objectifying potential, the gaze, even that of the voyeur, is objectively less damaging than would be the physical violation or bondage potential in the extending of the "Hempen Hands."

One advantage of working through this line of thinking concerning both mermaids and frigates is that it better prepares us for the opening line of the third stanza:

> But no Man moved Me – till the Tide
> Went past my simple Shoe –
> And past my Apron – and my Belt
> And past my Bodice – too –

Unless we grant some sexual dynamic to the initial vision of the mermaids and frigates, the contrast and the intimate personal impact of this line makes little sense. It would contrast with nothing, regardless of whether we stress "Man" as the agent or "moved" (or both) as the focus of the line. Whereas the sexually charged symbols of the first two stanzas function at an oblique and, perhaps, merely potential level, most of this poem's readers have focused on the sexual overtures inhering in the heightened physicality and nearly pornographically fetishistic specificity of the poem beginning in the third stanza. Here, the rising of the water is measured with relation to the speaker's body as coded in the culturally significant semiotics of clothing: shoe, apron, belt, and bodice, with each accessory demarcating a specific and fetishized position on the speaker's body. Furthermore, the hypnotic repetition of the word "past" in three consecutive lines (the final two using the conjunctive "And past") suggests a paralyzed and static subject whose only recourse is to gaze at her own body being overwhelmed. This shift contrasts with the early stanza's casting of the poem's speaker as the object of the Others' hypothetical gaze, but it also heightens the poem's drama of seduction and violation. In either or both scenarios the speaker is again rendered a passive victim in a scene of intensified aggression relative to the voyeuristic drama of the first two stanzas.

The escalating tide functions more threateningly than this inventory of sexually charged accoutrements would indicate, however. The potential of the sea entirely to engulf the subject is clarified in the next stanza:

> And made as He would eat me up –
> As wholly as a Dew
> Upon a Dandelion's Sleeve –
> And then – I started – too –

The threat in these lines of the speaker's total absorption culminates the logic of the poem up to this point. Imaged as a drop of dew, the speaker is rendered even more minuscule than in the earlier moments as a "mouse," and her total engulfment by the sea finalizes the gradual rising of the seawater in the previous stanza. However, the gargantuan proportions of this opposition—ocean versus drop of dew—suggest that no metaphor for the speaker's self at this point could plausibly oppose the encroachment of the ocean. She might as well be Lake Superior; the outcome would be the same annihilatory absorption by the immense forces of the ocean. The visual and physical specificity of this drop of dew (using the article "a") similarly recalls the paralysis of the previous stanza and echoes the hypervisuality and implied paranoia of poem #328 ("A Bird came down the Walk –"), in which the puzzled onlooker can note with great and, as I read it, disturbing precision, "And then he drank *a* Dew / From *a* convenient Grass" (my emphasis). In this poetic world, the incredibly large threaten the incredibly tiny.[6]

But the addition of "Dandelion's Sleeve," with its echo of the catalog of the speaker's clothing and accessories, contributes to the metaphorical instability of the poem. Whereas the speaker could be metaphorized as a mouse in the first stanza and a drop of dew in this one, here also the flower/weed is represented in terms which, while botanically correct, also imply the "sleeves" of human clothing. This poem's human subject can be metaphorized in natural terms, while constituents of nature can simultaneously take on attributes of the human worlds of architecture (basement, upper floor), apparel, and trade or war (frigates). The trafficking between human and natural worlds foregrounds an important facet of the poem's work through its first four stanzas and up to its concluding two. We will return to this slippage after finishing our initial summation of some of the poem's dynamics.

This fourth stanza concludes not with this image of a comparatively infinitesimal drop of dew, however, but with the line "And then – I started – too –," echoing the poem's first two words by isolating the "I started," and freeing the subject from the static and immobile state she has seemingly been in since her arrival at the sea. But to what extent does this repetition of "I started" merely repeat its sense from the first stanza, and to what extent might its repetition depart from that initial register? These two moments share important ranges of meaning. The initial "I started" signals the poem's genesis and, to that extent at least, indicates a moment of initiatory movement, a beginning before which no poem existed, although that silence prior to the poem's first line remains unexamined and, perhaps, unexaminable. Both occurrences signal a beginning of sorts, but, while we can argue that the poet's inaugural articulation "I started" brings that subjectivity to life out of some unspecifiable state prior to verbalization, only the second such "start" seems to be a response to some specific, because examined, ontological threat. This responsive moment also constitutes an important difference between the two. Whereas the first "I started" signals the poet's apparently unprovoked and unproblematic desire to undertake a visit, the second moment clearly is a response to some external threat and carries the further connotation of "start," as in to be startled or "to discover [something] suddenly, to wake up, [or] to escape" (OED). The 1862 composition date for this poem also enables us to read "started" within a context capable of highlighting its responsiveness to the confinements and oppression peculiar to a slave culture, in this case reimagined by Dickinson to include the oppression of American women, even in the North. Frederick Douglass, to cite just one example, refers to his and his companions' planned escape from slavery as their "intended *start*" (94) in his 1845 *Narrative*. Whichever of these ranges we attribute to Dickinson's "start," another important difference between these repeated phrases resides in their demarcation of action and direction. The first initiates a journey toward the sea, the second a retreat from the sea, now newly perceived as a threatening Other rather than the scene of a pleasant stroll. We might also read this as an additional variation on the poem's psychosexual dynamic. Following the fairly explicit sexual maneuvering attributed to the sea in the poem's central stanzas, gestures in response to which the poem's speaker can only look on in motionless passivity, the poem's second "I started" could also signal the speaker's own sexual awakening, the first moment of her active response to the sea's overtures. This possibility, then, suggests an alternative beginning to that of the speaker's retreat, especially since the details clarifying that this second start is, in fact, an escape or retreat from the sea are not disclosed until the final two stanzas. The poem's punctuation—the fact that the fourth stanza is closed with a final dash—strengthens this suggestion, though, given the vexations of Dickinson's own punctuation scheme as well as the stylistic normalization of the Johnson edition, we can only hazard guesses of this nature. On the other hand, we might not force ourselves to choose between these two incompatible ranges and, instead, link them to construct a highly ambivalent moment in which the speaker, once fully aware of the sexuality implicit in her rendering of the sea's advances, is caught between and committed to both possible inclinations: terrified flight *and* responsive participation, refusal and acquiescence. That this ambivalence responds to and mirrors the structural instability of the poem's metaphorical trafficking between the human and the natural indicates the thematic consistency of Dickinson's meditation on the condition of women in nineteenth-century American culture.

However, the poem does not itself negotiate, much less provide the semantic clarifications necessary to resolve, these alternatives. They remain mutually possible, perhaps mutually constitutive of the speaker's riven subjectivity up to this moment in the poem. That the final two stanzas imply rather strongly (though not at all definitively) that the speaker indeed rejects the sea's advances and escapes to safety nevertheless does not clarify or guide our reading experience through the first four stanzas. When we return to this discussion, however, I will qualify, if not reject, the readerly relativity implied in this scenario. Despite the value we tend to attribute to the "freshness" of our reading experience, any first reading is exploratory, but our "reader

response" would be pathetic indeed if our interpretive procedures remained limited to the infinite ignorance that accompanies our first
encounter with the narrative. Every subsequent reading reads with
foreknowledge of the poem's entirety, and, especially in the case of so
focused and limited a work as this brief poem, the tensions, turns,
ambiguities, and structural and thematic twists aren't nearly as surprising as in initial readings, though this is not to imply that they are
less vexing.

The ambiguities proliferating in the poem's central stanzas carry
over to the concluding eight lines. The penultimate stanza functions
as a transition from the middle stanzas' representation of the sea's advances in highly sexualized terms to the final image of separation,
withdrawal, and the speaker's refuge in the "Solid Town":

> And He – He followed – close behind –
> I felt His Silver Heel
> Upon my Ankle – Then my Shoes
> Would overflow with Pearl –
>
> Until We met the Solid Town –
> No One He seemed to know –
> And bowing – with a Mighty look –
> At me – The Sea withdrew –

The stutter at the beginning of the fifth stanza resituates the source
of the ambiguity embedded in the speaker's "starting" within the sea's
movement and her response to it. That the sea "followed" the speaker
might, as in the case of her "starting," indicate that it continued
its pursuit of her. The speaker's repetition of the pronominal "He,"
then, alerts us to her continuing terror even as she escapes the immediate site of her vulnerability. However, that the sea's sexualized
motions now follow those of the speaker can also signal a transformation on the part of the sea from sexual aggressor to responsive
partner. This development confronts us with the possibility that the
speaker's sexual urges and energies, once awakened or started, out-
strip those of the previously aggressive sea and exceed them in desire
and enjoyment. In this case, the repeated "He" serves to discriminate
the speaker's state of arousal from that of the sea; that is, whereas

the speaker "started," the sea could only "follow" her lead. The sea's following "close behind" similarly supports both possible readings, again tending to cast both speaker and sea in symbiotic intimacy.

The speaker's potential dominance of these lines, even in the midst of her retreat, produces a revision of the poem's initial fetishistic imaging. Previously it was the speaker and her apparel represented as isolated accessories—"Apron," "Belt," "Bodice"—not to mention the poem's initial staging of her as the object of the voyeuristic gazes of both mermaids and frigates. Here, while the speaker defines herself in terms of her "Ankle" and "Shoes," she also domesticates and limits the previously irresistible and overwhelming force of the sea within the phrases "His Silver Heel" and "Pearl," both of which transfer the fetishistic specificity previously reserved for the representation of her own body to the body of the sea. Even with the final image of her shoes "overflow[ing] with Pearl," suggestive of the ejaculatory culmination of the sexual act begun in the third stanza, the appropriation of the male emission as an object of female ownership (pearls or jewelry) recasts the entire drama of the poem within terms more compatible with, or at least potentially less hostile to, female desire and fulfillment. Even if we read the image of her shoes overflowing with pearl as one of male sexual climax, the speaker nonetheless represents that climax as equally female—it is her shoes that overflow, suggesting the possibility that her desire, however generated, culminates in its own dripping fulfillment.

The first word of the poem's final stanza delimits the entire ensemble of these possibilities. The finality implied by "Until We met the Solid Town" can simultaneously terminate the speaker's escape, the sea's continuing pursuit of the speaker, and the apparently mutual moments of sexual climax hinted at in the image of her shoes overflowing with his pearl. The sea's suddenly traversing whatever distance separates the poem's two locales poses a spatial problem, but, however one accounts for the sea's new ability to extend up to the boundaries of the solid town, the final stanza polarizes the poem's world into two realms, the one natural, fluid, surging, and surprising (though inhabited and characterized by the appurtenances and rituals of culture) and the other significantly "Solid" and civilized. The stability implicit in this image of the "Solid Town" as a barrier beyond which the sea does not extend, however, weakens as the poem performs one final set of ambiguous twists. The boundary of the "Solid Town" may appear daunting and absolute, but the poem carefully designates the sea's departure as a result, not of some impenetrable boundary, but of unfamiliarity: since the sea seems to know no one, it departs. The boundary between culture and nature in this poem, as it was in the trafficking between nature and culture in the poem's beginning, is itself fluid and variable, not in any way stable or inherent. The sea's final departure further strains the ambiguities established throughout the poem's final four stanzas. The "Mighty look" of the sea is tempered by its apparent conformity with social niceties represented in its "bowing" upon departure. Again, an image from poem #328, "A Bird came down the Walk –," provides a useful intertext. In that work, the perception of the seemingly incompatible and contradictory actions of the bird, who in one moment eats a worm raw only to hop out of the way to allow a beetle to pass in the next, puzzles and almost paralyzes the onlooker. The sea's power and rapacity in "I started Early – Took my Dog –" exists simultaneously with its courtesy and conformity with the ritual codes of the speaker's culture.[7]

The culmination of the poem's sexual drama resides in the final word. Suggestive both of the sea's ultimate departure from the speaker and of the terminal gesture of a completed sexual act, the term "withdrew" (along with the politeness implied by the sea's "bowing") complicates our final understanding of the sea, although both of these possibilities cast the sea in the role of active participant, if not of aggressor. Either of these possibilities needs to be reread within the poem's designation of the motivation for the sea's withdrawal. That departure responds not to any expressed wish or desire of the speaker's but rather to the sea's discovering itself on alien and unfamiliar territory in the "Solid Town." Even the "bowing" of the sea, while potentially an act of courtesy, could conceivably indicate the arched-back posture of sexual rapture so common to visual representations of both male and female orgasms. The poem's conclusion represents the sea's "withdrawal," in other words, as an act in no way necessarily concerned with or responsive to the desire of the speaker. In fact, the "Mighty look" cast by the sea upon the speaker in this final withdrawal slants the poem in the direction of representing the sea as aggressor. This mighty look returns us to the other looks directed at the speaker early in the poem. In every case, those gazes fixed the speaker as an insignificant and objectified Other for visual appropriation (as oddity to the mermaids and as mouse for the frigates). The mightiness of this final gaze, furthermore, recapitulates the act of diminution and presumption characteristic of the frigates by asserting its power and the speaker's passivity. Whatever responsive gestures and whatever the pleasures the poem implies the speaker may have enjoyed, this final moment reasserts her body as an object for consumption, not her potential equality (perhaps superiority) as fully involved participant.

Up to this point, I have focused on the poem as a drama of significant, perhaps life-determining, human and sexual experience in which the speaker encounters the sea (and its personified inhabitants). The terms of this drama begin in apparent innocence, and move through the mysterious encounter with the mermaids and ambiguous grasping of the frigates to the protracted and highly sexualized exchange with the sea. The ambiguities informing each of these episodes prevent us from arriving at any certitude with regard to their precise register, but the play of these ambiguities remains fairly consistent, casting the speaker in what is always a two-sided and at times mutually constitutive dialectic of passivity and action, complicity and resistance, participation and violation, courtesy and hostility. It is difficult, if not impossible, in other words, to determine whether the mermaids' gaze is friendly or demeaning, whether the frigates' extended hands intend violation or rescue, whether the sea's rising over the speaker's body implies sexual opportunism or mere naturalistic process, whether the speaker's starting (and the sea's following) implies fear, surprise, or response (and courtesy, pursuit, or response), or whether the sea's final bowing and withdrawing indicates acquiescence to the speaker's wishes, retreat from alien territory, or satisfied culmination to an act of sexual aggression. It is equally problematic to determine just where the speaker comes from, what significance her starting early has for the poem, what her return to the solid town represents, and what impact this experience has on her life. The latter may be especially important if, as the first line suggests, this poem records some early, perhaps formative, experience.

We can't even reach a degree of relative interpretive certainty that the poem is anything other than the record of a child's vivid memories and hyperbolic account of a walk on the beach. With respect to the sexualized action of the poem in particular, we can't be sure whether whatever sexual drama the poem represents stages the speaker's violation, her erotic participation, or her successful resistance of the sea's unwelcome and seemingly traumatic threat. However, any reading we may attempt must certainly address the poem's generative loose end: where, amidst all this activity and all these ambiguities, is her dog?

iii

Given the potential irreducibility of many of the poem's images and the rampant circulation of its contradictions, we might examine the conditions of this poem's possibility, the conditions of its production, the generic and thematic parameters that render it nonetheless producible and readable. I would suggest that there are at least two decisive sets of generic circumstances that we need to bring to our reading of this poem. The most local of these generic and cultural ensembles involves Dickinson's place within American literary discourse and the "authorization" of her poem by preexisting narratives—specifically, the ways in which the work of this poem draws on and generates images and tensions common to nineteenth-century American literary production. Broader, and not absolutely (or desirably) separable from the first, are the ways in which Dickinson's poem stages the crucial and recurring concerns of women's lives and literary work. I would like to emphasize the interrelatedness of these two concerns by tracing the important connections between this poem in which a woman is nearly engulfed (and we assume drowned) by the power of the sea and texts such as Nathaniel Hawthorne's *The Blithedale Romance* and Kate Chopin's *The Awakening,* both of which drive inexorably toward the drowning death of women, or texts such as Elizabeth Stoddard's *The Morgesons* and Harriet Beecher Stowe's *The Minister's Wooing,* in which women's responses to powerful sea surges serve to test the limits and possibilities for women's thought and conduct. In these instances, as in the case of Shakespeare's Ophelia, the waters which claim their female victims function as dual metaphors, for the desires pursued by the female characters *and* for their cultural construction as bodies of water, fields of fluid desire for entry and appropriation by opportunistic males who both define and subjugate women as flowing and malleable territories for colonization.

Within the context of mid-nineteenth-century American literary production, Dickinson's "I started Early – Took my Dog –" revisits what many scholars of American literature regard as one of the ur-themes of nineteenth-century American literary culture: the entry into and examination of the natural world, often integral with the conscious or implicit repudiation of the confines of various cultural assumptions.[8] That the examination and valorization of these moments underwrite numerous critical perspectives on what we often call the "American Renaissance" suggests the cultural centrality of Dickinson's work in this poem.[9] Briefly summarized, one of the definitive moments in American literary texts is the protagonist's (fictional or nonfictional) entry into, exploration of, and internalization of the values of a realm of nature, either actually or symbolically undefiled by human social existence. While not all of these excursions involve the exploration of what Melville's Ishmael refers to as "the watery part of the world" (3), those encounters do proliferate, and the specifics of Dickinson's poem direct us to them. In this context, however, "I started Early – Took my Dog –" performs a revisionary reading and strategic reappropriation of cultural discourse; it is one way in which Emily Dickinson examines, engages, dismantles ("visits" in the sense of overlooking or supervising), and smuggles the thematics of several influential precursor texts. Both Joanne Feit Diehl and Mary Loeffelholz have contributed to our understanding of the revisionary, antiromantic and antitranscendentalist, agenda inherent in Dickinson's "nature poetry," and I would like both to draw on their demonstrations and to revise their own findings by reading Dickinson's poem through various contemporary discourses. According to Diehl, Dickinson struggles most consistently against the romantics, recasting their thematics even while she accepts their centrality. "Like the Romantics," Diehl suggests, Dickinson "writes quest poems, for they seek to complete the voyage, to prove the strength of the imagination against the stubbornness of life, the repression of an antithetical nature, and that 'hidden mystery,' the final territory of death" (*Dickinson* 161). For Dickinson, however, unlike both her English and American precursors, "nature becomes an antagonist, a deeply equivocal mystery, certainly exquisite at times, but with an exotic power that withholds its secrets as it dazzles," and, perhaps more to the point of our present discussion, "nature becomes not a sacred ground but a place that fails to protect, from which she must withdraw to ask other kinds of questions" (163). Loeffelholz pursues the implications of Diehl's reading when she posits that Dickinson's nature poems

> most often tell stories of blocked quests into nature, blocked initiations into erotic knowledge; mysterious dangers, uncertain and perhaps secret profits from their questers' ventures; they parody, fracture, condense, and diminish better-known romantic and transcendentalist precursor texts. (8)

Dickinson

> demonstrates to herself that she cannot write, or does not wish to write, poems that literally repeat male poets' encounters with nature. Yet these poems of blockage, failed language, and ambiguous quest objects, in their sometimes halting, often opaque way, repeat and critique the contradictions and liabilities of Emerson's account and other romantic accounts of natural poetic origins. These contradictions emerge most clearly around the gender of the romantic speaker, and so pertain to the woman poet particularly. (8)

Diehl has also read Dickinson's work in the context of the sublime and has come to importantly related conclusions. As opposed to its role in the work of her male contemporaries, including Emerson and Whitman, for whom ecstatic merging with the sublime constituted the essential epiphany of poetic experience and production, "in Dickinson's work . . . the Sublime operates as a compressed and consolidated mode wherein power, whether from the landscape or external consciousness, threatens the poet as it infuses her with its presence" (*Women Poets* 28).

Significantly, Emerson's famous description of his entry into nature dramatized in *Nature,* while not explicitly an exploration of a body of water, renders the human experience of nature as well as the essence of the natural world in terms suggestive of great fluidity:

> Standing on the bare ground,—my head bathed by the blithe air and uplifted into infinite space,—all mean egotism vanishes. I become a transparent eyeball; I am nothing; I see all; the currents of the Universal Being circulate through me; I am part or parcel of God. . . . In the wilderness, I find something more dear and connate than in streets or villages. In the tranquil landscape, and especially in the distant line of the horizon, man beholds somewhat as beautiful as his own nature. (39)

As what must be one of the most discussed moments in all of Emerson, this passage is surely familiar, and I will comment only on its relationship to Dickinson's poem. For Emerson, the entry into nature is one of infinite expectation, infinite possibility, infinite mirroring and recognition, and infinite growth and expansion, both of nature and of the human nature that constitutes its furthest development. However, the many resonances between this passage and Dickinson's poem (suggestive even of conscious reworking of Emerson) highlight the decidedly vagrant understanding of Dickinson's approach. Both Emerson's virtual apotheosis in nature and Dickinson's near disappearance and her dog's vanishing within nature delineate the moment of the self's entry into nature as simultaneously the entry of nature into the self. In passages that resemble Dickinson's, Emerson constructs the meeting of self and nature as a contrast between the realm of nature and that of social form ("In the wilderness, I find something more dear and connate than in streets or villages"), as a highly fluid experience ("head bathed," "currents of the Universal Being circulate through me"), as a highly optical moment ("transparent eyeball," "I see all," "man beholds"), and as one of nearly obliterating potential ("all mean egotism vanishes," "I am nothing," "I am part or parcel of God").

Despite its shared components with Dickinson's poem, Emerson's passage quite significantly casts these moments in near total opposition to what Dickinson will later do. Whereas for Dickinson, returning to the "Solid Town" protects the endangered subject, for Emerson —indeed, for much romantic and transcendentalist writing—the rejection of "streets" and "villages" is a virtual prerequisite enabling the perception of beauty and intimacy between human life and nature. Whereas for Dickinson, the fluidicizing of her being translates into near annihilation as a drop of dew disappearing within the ocean, in Emerson, the fluidicizing of being generates the ultimate clarification of one's proper orientation within the created world. Whereas for Dickinson, the optical intensity of her poem slides into the voyeuristic fetishizing and appropriating of her entire body—she becomes the objectified target of various gazes (which themselves become violating grasps)—in Emerson, he as transparent eyeball becomes the optical center of a subjectified world in which all creation radiates outward from him and becomes the object of his totalizing gaze. He emerges, despite the apparent loss of self, as the ontological, spiritual, and philosophical locus from which all life and all meaning emanate. Finally, whereas for Dickinson, the threat of obliteration terrifies the subject with sexual violation, perhaps even death, in Emerson, the translation of individual ego into universal being again signals refinement and escape from the limiting parameters of social categorization. In every instance, what constitutes opportunity and possibility for Emerson triggers isolation, fear, violation, and danger for Dickinson. This tension may even account for resonance between Emerson's "Each and All," in which the "pearls" created by ocean waves add significantly to the beauty of the scene, and Dickinson's poem, in which the froth of "Pearl" is implicated in the ocean's predatory stalking of the speaker.

Thoreau's Walden experience recapitulates, albeit with important local differences, many of these Emersonian postulates. Most importantly, for Thoreau the encounter with the body of water comes complete with the polarization of nature and society, the highly visual apprehension of nature and life (although Thoreau complements such optically rich moments as counting the number of bubbles in a square inch of Walden ice with a nearly equal sensitivity to tactile and aural stimuli), and the fluidicizing of experience (indeed, the seasonal and daily transformations of Walden translate for Thoreau into a categorical affirmation of human change). The primary revision is the apparent absence of the obliterative moment for Thoreau, although we might argue that, in leaving Walden for the more lives he has to live,

Thoreau seizes even this moment of self-transformation (conceivably the destruction of his Walden self) as a moment of self-transcendence. Significantly like Emerson and significantly different from Dickinson, the ensemble of Thoreau's experiences at Walden generates a refinement and clarification of human perception, possibility, and potential. Thoreau as subject is constituted and strengthened by virtue of his encounter with Walden. Thoreau's "solid bottom" (378), which he insists is everywhere as a *point d'appui* from which philosophical investigation can begin, is located in nature, but the "Solid Town" in which Dickinson's speaker finds refuge stands in counterdistinction to the threatening realm of nature. As Cynthia Griffin Wolff characterizes Dickinson's posttranscendentalist poetics,

> No serious poet could afford to ignore the transformation of poetry that had been wrought by the British Romantic poets and especially by Wordsworth, who in his most hopeful moods had postulated that man and nature might have a benign, reciprocal relationship. Dickinson was not an Emersonian transcendentalist, either; however, any American poet who wished to be "Representative" was constrained to address Emerson's optimistic assessment of the meaning a poet would discover in the landscape. In short, as an artist working in the aftermath of these attitudes, Emily Dickinson became a new kind of "nature poet," one who could articulate the ambiguity and latent violence that mankind must constantly confront in the course of ordinary existence. (282)

Of course, Herman Melville's Ishmael offers a powerful counterpoint to this transcendentalized encounter with the watery world of nature. More like Dickinson's in some obvious respects, Ishmael's nature emerges as more problematic, contested, and potentially rapacious than the *Nature* of Emerson or the nature of Thoreau. For Ishmael, to go to sea is to encounter not only the "watery part of the world," but the fluid, internal regions of oneself, moments which, if not identical to Thoreau's, certainly anticipate his dictum that one should become

> the Mungo Park, the Lewis and Clarke and Frobisher, of your own streams and oceans; explore your own higher latitudes,—

with shiploads of preserved meats to support you, if they be necessary; . . . Nay, be a Columbus to whole new continents and
worlds within you, opening new channels, not of trade, but of
thought. (369)

A few well-known and significant passages should adequately sum up
this facet of Ishmael's oceanic thinking. In *Moby-Dick's* earliest pages,
Ishmael contrasts the desperation and entrapment experienced by "all
landsmen; of week days pent up in lath and plaster—tied to counters,
nailed to benches, clinched to desks" with the pervasive allure that
drives "crowds, pacing straight for water," and makes them "get just
as nigh the water as they possibly can without falling in" (4). "Why
is almost every robust healthy boy with a robust healthy soul in him,
at some time or other crazy to go to sea?" Ishmael asks, and "why
upon your first voyage as a passenger, did you yourself feel such a
mystical vibration, when first told that you and your ship were now
out of sight of land?" (5). Indeed, the global yearning to get near, but
not too near, the water leads Ishmael to conclude, "yes, as every one
knows, meditation and water are wedded for ever" (4). I would like
to pause and remark on just two elements in these passages to which
I will return. For Ishmael, this migration to the oceans is the purview
of "robust healthy boy[s]" rather than of girls, however robust and
healthy they may be, and it is tinged with sexual overtones, implied
in Ishmael's phrase "wedded forever" and by his subsequent "marriage" with Queequeg, a sexual charge quite remarkable given the
near total absence of women in *Moby-Dick*. Dickinson's revision of
Melville's (and, for that matter, transcendentalism's) basic thesis concerning "man in the open air" plays significantly off these elements.

As is commonly rehearsed in Melville criticism, Ishmael's grasp of
the magnetism of the sea complicates whatever simple associations
we may attribute to it. It is in this respect that Ishmael's complex
grasp of the ocean most clearly anticipates important constituents
of Dickinson's. Whereas Emerson's entry into the world of *Nature's*
nature is blithely untroubled by naturalistic or ontological peril, and
whereas Thoreau constructs Walden Pond as a seamless and philosophically stable mirror within which humanity, once properly sensitized, views its true potential reflected, Ishmael grants all-consuming,

all-absorbing annihilatory Otherness to characterize the world of the sea. Of central importance for our discussion of Dickinson's poem, the very departure from land and entry into an aquatic world is fraught with danger. Ishmael reminds us and repeatedly stages the truth that "there is death in this business of whaling—a speechlessly quick chaotic bundling of a man into Eternity" (37), beginning with his meditation on the drowning of Narcissus, expanding into his and other mourners' meditations in Father Mapple's chapel, and continuing up to the concluding spectacle of carnage.

This peril is especially acute for those who approach the ocean with a philosophical agenda or predisposition. As Ishmael characterizes the dangers of ocean gazing in "The Mast-Head,"

> lulled into such an opium-like listlessness of vacant, unconscious reverie is this absent-minded youth by the blending cadence of waves with thoughts, that at last he loses his identity; takes the mystic ocean at his feet for the visible image of that deep, blue, bottomless soul, pervading mankind and nature. (159)

Ishmael punctuates this lesson to the pantheists, who would confuse human self with naturalistic environment, with the hypothetical drowning of one who loses track of the crucial parameters of human consciousness. For Ishmael, as we have seen for Dickinson, to go too far into the sea is, quite simply, to court the same peril that claims Narcissus, who, as Ishmael cautions us in the first chapter, "because he could not grasp the tormenting, mild image he saw in the fountain, plunged into it and was drowned" (5). The crucial difference for Dickinson is that "the watery part of the world" threatens her existence even at its shallowest. There is no indication in this poem that she ever intends to wade out more than a few yards into the surf.

In addition to enumerating the dangers that obviously inhere in the business of whaling, Ishmael's commentary posits the sea as inherently double, inherently complex, inherently deadly, often despite its placid and lovely appearance. We cannot forget, while reading *Moby-Dick,* that "beneath the loveliest tints of azure" glide its "most dreaded creatures," who "prey upon each other, carrying on eternal war since the world began" (274). Furthermore, in a proleptic inversion of the utopian analogies that Thoreau discovers between nature and human nature, Ishmael makes explicit his belief that this "universal cannibalism of the sea," this rapacious, deceptive, subtle, and remorseless force of nature, exists in "a strange analogy to something in [the human soul]" (274). Melville's ocean (as metaphor for the global forces of nature) quite clearly exists as a decisively different arena for human thought and action than do constructions of nature in Emerson and Thoreau. It can kill, and it can, as in the case of Pip, drive insane one who descends too far into its depth and secrets.

Just as the myth of Narcissus presiding over the whole of *Moby-Dick* embodies the threat of Thanatos, it also elicits the lure of Eros. In its erotic charge, Melville's ocean and the oceanic feelings elicited in Ishmael bear significantly on Dickinson's drama of sexual emergence and ontological terror. For example, Ishmael describes his early intimate experience with Queequeg as precipitating "a melting in [him]" and feels his "splintered heart and maddened hand," once "turned against the wolfish world," soothed and relieved (51). Ishmael characterizes the intimacy generated by this "melting," this fluidicizing of his inner hardness, as a version of marriage, replete with the pleasures of the marriage bed. This scene, which has, of course, received extensive critical attention, makes explicit the homoerotic, if not copulative, implications of Ishmael and Queequeg's intimacy:

> How it is I know not; but there is no place like a bed for confidential disclosures between friends. Man and wife, they say, there open the very bottom of their souls to each other; and some old couples often lie and chat over old times till nearly morning. Thus, then, in our hearts' honeymoon, lay I and Queequeg—a cosy, loving pair. (52)

The eroticism implicit in this and other moments between Ishmael and Queequeg returns periodically. From his vision of "young Leviathan amours in the deep" (388) to the visionary "insanity" he feels when squeezing globules of whale sperm while "looking up into [other sailors'] eyes sentimentally" (416), Ishmael represents moments of love, tenderness, and eroticism in terms of fluidity, melting, and malleability. This strategy is partly motivated by Ishmael's persistent narrative resistance to Captain Ahab's "iron will," but it resonates throughout the narrative, including numerous moments with no explicit intranarrative polemical register.

For all his differences with more orthodox transcendentalists, Melville's vision of the ocean without and the oceans within shares several important similarities that constitute something like a polemical adversary for Dickinson's work in "I started Early – Took my Dog –." First, for Emerson, Thoreau, and Melville, the entry into and examination of nature is, virtually without exception, the right and responsibility of males. These worlds are populated exclusively by men, and the images and metaphors deployed in their writings represent nature, water, and whales as mysterious spaces to be plumbed, penetrated, and mined for intellectual and cultural (if not for monetary) capital. Second, all three (and many other contemporary figures) represent nature in feminine terms. Both Emerson's nature and Thoreau's Walden are feminine, and the entry into these fluid realms constitutes the generative moments of many of their most influential texts. Melville/Ishmael may not represent the ocean in such clearly feminine metaphors, but the erotic charge associated with voyaging suggests that the masculine observer's interest in the business of whaling (perhaps in all capitalistic venture, as Dreiser will later explore) is tinged with erotic as well as with monetary appeal. Finally, these writers negotiate the encounter with nature (always cast in heightened visual terms) for their aggrandizement (spiritual, epistemological, philosophical) alone. It is a commonplace in Emerson and Thoreau criticism to address the paradoxes associated with their insouciance toward social existence and with their boundless egotism, often called self-confidence, self-reliance. While Melville's ocean is decidedly more dangerous a venue for philosophical voyaging than is either Emerson's nature or Thoreau's Walden Pond, it nonetheless remains raw material for human (male) expansion and appropriation: "meditation and water are wedded for ever" (4). And, while Ishmael may bemoan his inability ever to complete his grasp of whales or the composition of his whale book, he remains committed to the task and carefully, at times lovingly, documents the stripping, cutting, boiling, and eating of the spoils of the whaling business. If nature is imagined as feminine by these writers, it is a feminine Other wholly subordinate to untrammeled masculine desire.

We discover a decidedly different reading of seas if we turn to women writers of the American Renaissance. In two notable texts, *The Minister's Wooing* (1859) and *The Morgesons* (1862), Harriet Beecher Stowe and Elizabeth Stoddard depart significantly from the male representation of the sea and parallel Dickinson's feminist revision of the American masculinist poetics of nature. Stowe's narrative in particular resonates with the erotic intensity and danger I have focused on in Dickinson's poem. As Stowe's youthful protagonist, Mary Scudder, and her French counterpart, Virginie de Frontignac, stroll along the ocean in an attempt to get Madame de Frontignac's mind off her potentially adulterous passion for the novel's ultimate seducer, Aaron Burr, the two eventually find themselves threatened by a rapidly rising tide. Prior to any intimation of danger for these two women, Stowe describes the sea in terms significant for our discussion: "A fresh breeze of declining day was springing up, and bringing the rising tide landward,—each several line of waves with its white crests coming up and breaking gracefully on the hard, sparkling sand-beach at their feet" (464). While the young women play at Shakespeare's *The Tempest* to pass the time, Burr himself unexpectedly appears and, as the two attempt to avoid him, remarks that their

> very agreeable occupations have caused time to pass more rapidly than you are aware. I think you will find that the tide has risen so as to intercept the path by which you came here. You will hardly be able to get around the point of rocks without some assistance. (466)

In an attempt to forego Burr's offer, Mary looks around but finds

> a fresh afternoon breeze driving the rising tide high on to the side of the rocks, at whose foot their course had lain. The nook in which they had been sporting formed part of a shelving ledge which inclined over their heads, and which it was just barely possible could be climbed by a strong and agile person, but which would be wholly impracticable to a frail, unaided woman. (467)

Mary agrees to allow the suave Burr to help her up, but Virginie at first adamantly refuses even to acknowledge the rake's presence.

While Virginie faces out to sea, a wave breaks over her feet, prompting Burr to warn: "There is no time to be lost . . . there's a tremendous surf coming in, and the next wave may carry you out" (468). The dynamics of this scene reproduce those of Dickinson's poem with remarkable thoroughness, suggesting, almost, that Dickinson's poem is a gloss on Stowe's prose meditation. Important in these passages is the convergence of Burr's arrival with the danger posed by the sea, suggesting the affinity between Burr and the ocean as dangers to "a frail, unaided woman." The threat of being washed away, the cool urbanity of Burr, and the sexual threat posed by him all anticipate the physical and sexual drama enacted in Dickinson's poem. Without the male presence, the seaside is a playground for the two young women, but the second he arrives it is transformed into a threatening and potentially deadly torrent. Add to these parallels Madame de Frontignac's strained and ambivalent feelings toward Burr, and Stowe's narrative captures the delicate position of Dickinson's speaker as well as of her own, both stranded between a rock and a hard place or, more appropriately, between the devil and the deep blue sea.

Elizabeth Stoddard's *The Morgesons* comes closest to staging the drama of the sea as threat and as seductive force played out in Dickinson's poem more than any other novel prior to Kate Chopin's *The Awakening*. Throughout Stoddard's novel, Cassandra Morgeson's vitality, her originality, and her individuality are all gauged in relation to her responsiveness to the salt sea. For example, early in her life Cassandra remarks that, "whichever way the circumstances of my life vacillated, I was not yet reached to the quick; whether spiritual or material influences made sinuous the current of being, it still flowed toward an undiscovered ocean" (77). As she matures, Cassandra's attitudes closely follow the forces of the sea:

> A habit grew upon me of consulting the sea as soon as I rose in the morning. Its aspect decided how my day would be spent. I watched it, studying its changes, seeking to understand its effect, ever attracted by its awful materiality and its easy power to drown me. By the shore at night the vague tumultuous sphere, swayed by an influence mightier than itself, gave voice, which drew my soul to utter speech for speech. (142–43)

As far as I know, Stoddard's novel is the first in American literary history to define a female protagonist in terms of this intimacy with nature, especially with the sea. Following the death of her mother late in the novel, Cassandra undergoes an initiatory experience on the seashore in a passage that, like the one in Stowe's *The Minister's Wooing*, anticipates some crucial themes from "I started Early – Took my Dog –." As she walks along the beach following her mother's death, Cassandra narrates the following experience:

> The wind was coming; under the far horizon the mass of waters began to undulate. Dark, spear-like clouds rose above it and menaced the east. The speedy wind tossed and teased the sea nearer and nearer, till I was surrounded by a gulf of milky green foam. As the tide rolled in I retreated, stepping back from rock to rock, around which the waves curled and hissed, baffled in their attempt to climb over me. I stopped on the verge of the tide-mark; the sea was seeking me and I must wait. It gave tongue as its lips touched my feet, roaring in the caves, falling on the level beaches with a mad, boundless joy!
>
> "Have then at life!" my senses cried. "We will possess its longing silence, rifle its waiting beauty. We will rise up in its light and warmth, and cry, 'Come, for we wait.' Its roar, its beauty, its madness—we will have—*all*." I turned and walked swiftly homeward, treading the ridges of white sand, the black drifts of seaweed, as if they had been a smooth floor. (214–15)

The intensity of Cassandra's response to the sea in this passage is of a piece with the general intensity of her passions and of her eccentricities. It is in the erotic charge of the sea's encroachment upon her body, as well as in her narration of the physicality of the sea in corporeal terms ("tongue," "lips") and in the entire drama of a woman pursued by a turbulent and rising tide, that Stoddard's drama anticipates Dickinson's. The affinities in these passages, in fact, cast interesting light on the letter Thomas Wentworth Higginson wrote to his wife after meeting Emily Dickinson for the first time. Her household and life struck Higginson as so bizarre that he could come up with only one analogy: that his wife "could understand the [Dickinson] household [and the poet herself] if she had read Mrs. Stoddard's novels" (Stoddard xii).

But if Stoddard's narrative anticipates the psychosexual dynamics of Dickinson's poem, Cassandra Morgeson's response to the sea seems to differ from that of the speaker in "I started Early – Took my Dog –" in its wild affirmation of life and in its role in inspiring Cassandra's maturing self, a self now in greater possession of its destiny after the death of her mother. We need to recall, however, that the sea, however powerful a metaphor for Cassandra's psychological and social emergence, nonetheless remains a male environment, a male possession. Cassandra may gaze constantly at the sea and may plan to build a house all of whose windows face seaward, but it is men who possess the sea through their economic activity and the mobility that seems strictly a male prerogative in *The Morgesons*. Cassandra's father, Locke Morgeson, owns a fleet of merchant ships that covers the globe, and at one point she even asks him "how far out at sea his property extended" (129). Also, both Ben and Desmond Somers traverse the Atlantic either for amusement or to dry out from their alcoholic benders in Spain. Cassandra, while mobile on land, never ventures to sea prior to her marriage trip to Europe with Desmond. The issue of possession, literally who possesses whom and what, informs much of Stoddard's novel, and the narrative stops short of affirming a central role for women in this culture managed primarily by male entrepreneurs.[10] This tension between Cassandra's chutzpah and the sea's control by male economic interests actually reemerges in Dickinson's poem, a point to which we will return.

Dickinson's ocean needs to be resituated with respect to these writers and their major themes. Dickinson casts her drama of a woman's visit to this surprisingly masculinized nature in two implicit polemical registers: (1) in response to the male cultural hegemony over the representation and the colonization of nature; and (2) in a closely related response to the sociopolitical hegemony of American politicians and their drive to buy, annex, conquer, or steal lands over the whole of North America. For these antagonists, nature is nearly wholly Other—an undefiled locus of value within which one is capable of being refined prior to one's reinsertion into civic society. Central to Dickinson's vision is her anticipation of more recent notions of the constructedness of all human institutions, even those which may strike us as obviously or naturally "natural." Thus, the only ways in which "I started Early – Took my Dog –" represents the supposedly natural venue of the sea is through the colonizing, human constructions and metaphors "Mermaids," "Basement," "Frigates," "Upper Floor," "Hempen Hands," "Man" (for sea), "eat me up" (for absorption), "Silver Heel," "Pearl," "bowing," and so on. Her anthropomorphizing, architecturalizing, and otherwise "clothing" of the sea foregrounds the "unnaturalness" of this realm of "nature." For Dickinson, as for many current feminist thinkers, the very construction and maintenance of categories such as domestic/social, culture/nature, and woman/man (and the hierarchies implicit within them) are already deployed in the service of male dominance over culture. If, as Jane Tompkins argues, Harriet Beecher Stowe's argument with masculinist politics and racial thinking required the total reconceptualization of historical and political life from a woman's point of view,[11] Dickinson similarly postulates that the tradition of nature thinking at least as far back as Jonathan Edwards and the Puritans is itself determined by male priorities, constructed within the values and sociopolitical parameters of male hegemony. To encounter nature, even woman naturalized as animal (mouse) or body of water (dew), is to encounter an always already male construct, even though that construct may be feminized as "Mother Nature," as an "Earth Mother," or by the common designation of feminine pronouns for bodies of water. In this respect, I would amend the claims made by Diehl and Loeffelholz, who, too simply, I believe, posit the nature investigated in so many of Dickinson's poems as essentially neutral. Not only does Dickinson challenge the poetic deployment of "nature" in canonical "nature writers," but she argues that neither male nor female poets ever encounter an essential or neutral "nature." Of course for the female poet, the masculinely colonized realm of nature is more forbidding because more saturated by the masculinist residue of prior male representational constructions.

Furthermore, by personifying the sea as male in this poem, Dickinson recasts one of her culture's most common assumptions: the association of women with nature and the corresponding attribution of men with the civilizing work of culture, the "solid town" of social practice. In dismantling and exposing the masculinist logic of this common ensemble of cultural metaphors, however, Dickinson also reveals the insidious power relations inscribed within them. In other words, the cultural work of "I started Early – Took my Dog –" both clarifies the semiotics of masculinist hegemony from within the terms of the culture and, in the course of this clarification, stages Dickinson's repudiation of those culturally constructed hierarchies. From this point of view we can begin to recover some of the cultural work of Dickinson's poem, and to unpack the semiotics of gendered power issues encoded within it.

iv

Dickinson's poem represents the problematic status of woman figured as a fluid field by her culture, and both recovers and anticipates an ongoing crisis in the construction of female identity. While we have just examined the specific context of cultural production in Dickinson's own era, we now turn to the recent and vital examination of similar stereotypes by those working in the fields of feminist cultural studies, sociology, and anthropology. In fact, we might now reread the omnipresence of male interests in many writers of the American renaissance, their representation of male travel, expansion, surveillance, and conquest of nature as well as of culture, as a historically and geographically specific version of a much larger, gendered sociopolitical dynamic. In a study that has determined much of the trajectory of recent inquiry into the subordination of women, Sherry B. Ortner has offered the following influential anthropological perspective:

> woman is being identified with—or, if you will, seems to be a symbol of—something that every culture devalues, something that every culture defines as being of a lower order of existence than itself. Now it seems that there is only one thing that would fit that description, and that is "nature" in the most generalized sense. (72)

Ortner's formulation "that women are seen 'merely' as being *closer* to nature than men," accounts for what she refers to as the "pan-cultural devaluation of women, for even if women are not equated with nature, they are nonetheless seen as representing a lower order of being, as being less transcendental of nature than men are" (73). While Ortner's hypothesis has been challenged from a number of perspectives, specifically those citing cultures in which her thesis does not have the explanatory force that it does in most Western cultures, her position continues to determine much of the debate concerning the oppression of women in many cultures, even those which tend simultaneously to glorify and to devalue the social and cultural practices of women.[12] Ortner isolates three interlinked relationships constituting this cultural construction:

> (1) woman's *body and its functions,* more involved more of the time with "species life," seem to place her closer to nature, in contrast to man's physiology, which frees him more completely to take up the projects of culture; (2) woman's body and its functions place her in *social roles* that in turn are considered to be at a lower order of the cultural process than man's; and (3) woman's traditional social roles, imposed because of her body and its functions, in turn give her a different *psychic structure,* which like her physiological nature and her social roles, is seen as being closer to nature. (73–74)

Ortner's hypothesis helps situate some of Dickinson's work on woman in and as nature in "I started Early – Took my Dog –." Specifically, it enables us to understand the motivation, or rather the absence of motivation, of the poem's speaker. That no reason is given for her "visit" to the sea suggests the "naturalness," or at least the inevitability, of such an eventuality, though such a "natural" phenomenon needs to be grasped as cultural belief, not as biological imperative. Similarly, the designation of this visit as "early" assumes that such a visit would occur by implying that the only unknown is its timing. Whether we emphasize the initial "I," which would single out the speaker in relation to when and how other women started; or whether we emphasize the "Early," which, again, designates the timing of the speaker's visit, the poem's initial line grants a looming expectation, if not necessity, to the eventual visit of the speaker to the sea. In other words, all women, we might read the first line as implying, make this journey, perhaps as an initiation into this culture's construction of female identity. This particular journey, then, does not depart from some rite of passage; it is only that this speaker, this particular woman, embarks prematurely. Such a journey, if indeed it does embody a cultural tradition of projecting specific characteristics onto women, represents something like a woman's confrontation with her destiny, or, more correctly, with the destiny her culture has designated for her.

There are other possibilities for this first line. Should we emphasize "started," we can grasp the poem as a rejoinder to a hypothetical warning to the speaker not to be out too late, after dark perhaps. Acknowledging the danger facing a woman out alone, Dickinson's speaker might be defending her conduct, as in "I *did* start early." The same may be true if we emphasize "Took," and the speaker might again be responding to a reprimand that she *should have* taken a dog or merely reminding her audience that she *did* take her dog for protection. But where did her caution—her early start, her dog for protection—get her? The convergence and proliferation of these possibilities suggest that no woman can safely explore the already masculinized territory of nature. The terrifying conclusion that such a reading leads to is that no woman, however circumspect her demeanor, however careful her preparations, however cautious her proceedings, or however firm her resolve, is safe alone.

The physicality of this speaker's confrontation with the sea and its inhabitants corresponds with another of the constituents that Ortner posits as merging into a larger set of assumptions concerning the subordination of women. From the initial gaze of the mermaids and grasp of the frigates' hempen hands to the gradual and bodily gauged rising of the sea, Dickinson's poem renders its speaker primarily as a body either on display or available for appropriation (by frigate or by sea). That the speaker's body is diminished and bestialized as that of a "Mouse," or dismembered and fetishized as individual and specific bodily zones, merges with the overarching diminution of women once constructed in accordance with the hierarchy of men=culture=privileged and women=nature=subordinated. The representation of the speaker's body via specific objects (shoe, apron, belt, bodice) also suggests the saturation of the poem by the logic of pornographic representation. Murray S. Davis formulates a helpful definition in *Smut: Erotic Reality/Obscene Ideology*. Drawing implicitly on the work of Richard von Krafft-Ebing, whose *Psychopathia Sexualis* remains a standard resource in the field of fetishism, Davis posits that

> *Fetishism* is the term for activity in which a person seeks sexual satisfaction from things rather than from beings. Not just any thing can be a fetish, however; only those things associated with, but dissociated from, beings. Fetishistic sex objects are the subvital slices of vital wholes, whether inorganic segments (like shoes) or organic segments (like feet). (134)

In a note to the above passage, Davis adds,

> Many men regard [garter belts] as sexier than more modern female underclothes because they appear to cut the genital region off from the torso and legs, transforming it into a stage set that draws the attention to where the action will take place. (272)

Most legal statutes against pornographic materials, in fact, include some variation of the following prohibitions: "women's body parts— including but not limited to vaginas, breasts and buttocks—are exhibited, such that women are reduced to those parts" (quoted in *Pornography and Sexual Violence* 3).[13] Linda Williams adds that in hard-core pornography, the definition of women (and men) through sexually specific body parts "has operated in different ways at different stages of the genre's history" but stresses the centrality of the genre's tendency "to privilege close-ups of body parts over other shots; to overlight easily obscured genitals; to select sexual positions that show the most of bodies and organs. . . . The principle of maximum visibility operates in the hard-core film" (48–49).

The poem's offering up of its speaker's body as an object for visual appropriation and in disjointed sections, then, is tantamount to participating in the metaphorical dismemberment of women characteristic of pornographic representation as defined by these theorists. While not explicitly concerned with pornography as such, Krafft-Ebing's still authoritative *Psychopathia Sexualis* (drawn upon repeatedly by expert witnesses in the insanity trial of murderer-cannibal Jeffrey Dahmer) underscores the antipathetic nature of clothing and body-part fetishism. Noting that fetishism usually "occurs in the most various forms in combination with inverted sexuality, sadism, and masochism" (221), Krafft-Ebing devotes significant discussion to shoe and apron fetishes in particular, highlighting the violence and other criminal threats to women by virtue of the reduction and transformation of their beings to specific articles of apparel (218–80). The dynamic of the poem's violation of the speaker, thus, progresses from the mermaids' gaze casting the speaker as object of visual pleasure through the frigates' presumption of her as bestial and insignificant (perhaps in need of rescue) to the fetishizing of the speaker's body and, once the first three functions are performed, absolute domination of the speaker's body. Once dehumanized, the poem's speaker cannot but be victimized. That this victimization has gone unattended in Dickinson criticism is made the more remarkable by the persistence of feminist readings of the entire Dickinson corpus.

While Ortner provides a theoretical basis from which to investigate the psychosexual dynamics of Dickinson's poem, her thesis does not explicitly account for its suggestion of physical violence. This is not to say that we could not deduce violence, both physical and psychological, as inherent, perhaps even inevitable, within a set of assumptions that casts women in a manifestly subordinate, trivialized, and bestialized position, only that Ortner's essay does not specifically cross over into that inquiry. However, many thinkers have pursued such implications, whether from the perspective of the violence implicit in pornographic representations of women as fetishistic objects (see much of Andrea Dworkin's work, for example) or from that of the debasement of women's identity in the workplace and in the culture in general (the heavily covered legal/legislative vindications of William Kennedy Smith and of now–Supreme Court Justice Clarence Thomas in 1991 on charges of rape and sexual harassment respectively being recent cases in point). In midcentury, Simone de Beauvoir, for one, assessed the physiology of femaleness with conclusions that account more forcefully for the violence against women endemic in Western culture: that "the female is the prey of the species" (372) and that the female "is more enslaved to the species than the male, her animality is more manifest" (239). Neither Ortner nor de Beauvoir would validate the corresponding masculinist conclusions that women *are* in fact of a lower nature than are men, but both acknowledge that the physical traits which characterize and differentiate women from men can be and have been interpreted in ways that consolidate masculinist dominance in many cultures.

Klaus Theweleit's *Male Fantasies: Volume 1: Women Floods Bodies Histories* (1987) investigates the cultural construction of women as bodies of water and the violence inhering within that image with far more emphasis on the persistence of male fantasies and male violence against women. While Theweleit specifically studies the fantasies of fascists between the two world wars, he proceeds in a manner that accounts for more diverse phenomena and a more diverse cross section of human behavior. Barbara Ehrenreich boldly clarifies the larger scope of his study in her foreword to *Male Fantasies*: far from isolated, historically and politically specific acts of symbolic violence, "these acts of fascist terror spring from irreducible human desire" (xii). She continues:

> For if the fascist fantasy—which was of course no fantasy for the millions of victims—springs from a dread that (perhaps) lies in the hearts of all men, a dread of engulfment by the "other," which is the mother, the sea or even the moist embrace of love . . . if so, then we are in deep trouble. But even as I say that, I am reminded that we who are women are *already* in deep trouble. As Theweleit says, the point of understanding fascism is not only "because it might 'return again'," but because it is already implicit in the daily relationships of men and women. Theweleit refuses to draw a line between the fantasies of the Freikorpsmen and the psychic ramblings of the "normal" man. . . . Here Theweleit does not push, but he certainly leaves open the path from the "inhuman impulse" of fascism to the most banal sexism. (xv)

Theweleit understands the semiotics of women represented as fluid bodies of water complexly, stressing both physiological and mythical dimensions. What may have a partial biological determination reemerges in mythic form in the consciousness of men, who face the possibilities of the fluidity, the disorderliness, the expansiveness, and the chaos of life stripped of or prior to the imposition of boundaries, rules, and organizational regimentation with terror and who react to such threats to masculinist fantasies of order (banal or fascist) with unrestrained and sadistic violence. As Ehrenreich summarizes, whether in the political Other of communism or in the erotic Other of boundless female sexuality, the fascist, and, by Theweleit's implication, the male, respond to the "joyous commingling" (xv) with loathing, with walls, with lonely dread. He needs to "occupy" both militarily and sexually the threatening space of female Otherness, reducing by his presence its flexible and fluid horizons. In Theweleit's study, male loathing and loneliness merge as the psychic basis for atrocities of unspeakable sadism. In a fully compatible manner, Dickinson's poem exposes the woman as nature construction as preliminary to subordinating and appropriating her both visually and physically.

Theweleit's anatomy of male fantasies furnishes a valuable perspective for Dickinson's reading of women's danger in "I started Early – Took my Dog –." In several summaries of literary representations of woman as watery territory, Theweleit's remarks provide important perspectives for our study. "Since around 1700 and the beginning of the Enlightenment," Theweleit postulates,

> writers applied the name "woman" to anything that flowed, anything limitless; in the place of God, the dead transcendence, they set the female sex as a new transcendence that finally abolishes lack. The earth became a limitless woman: life, thy name is woman; woman, thy name is vagina; vagina, thy name is ocean, infinity.
>
> In other words, they used, or misused, the fluidity—the greater malleability and as yet unspent utopian potential of femaleness, a desiring-production that is fallow, undirected, not yet socially defined, and thus remains in closer proximity to the unconscious; a life of emotion, rather than of intellect (that cruel, demarcating product of the constraints that beset men's bodies)—to encode their own desire, their own utopias, their own yearning to be free of boundaries, with the notion of an "endlessly flowing woman." (380)

One function of Dickinson's poem is to establish boundaries, breaking her world into flowing ocean and solid town. In so doing, Dickinson tests out the construction of ocean as woman and woman as ocean, a proposition which, while potentially liberating and at least partly responsive to anthropological and psychoanalytic theory, has become appropriated within masculinist hegemony over cultural space and boundaries, permeated by the exclusionary cast of male territoriality.[14]

Theweleit also theorizes and globalizes the masculine colonization of land, sea, and women that Dickinson's poem responds to in American transcendentalist literature, especially those examples we have already discussed by Emerson, Melville, and Thoreau:

> A river without end, enormous and wide, flows through the world's literatures. Over and over again: the women-in-the-water; woman as water, as a stormy, cavorting, cooling ocean, a raging stream, a waterfall; as a limitless body of water that ships pass through, with tributaries, pools, surfs, and deltas; woman as the enticing (or perilous) deep, as a cup of bubbling body fluids; the vagina as wave, as foam, as a dark place ringed with Pacific ridges; love as the foam from the collision of two waves, as a sea voyage, a slow ebbing, a fish-catch, a storm; love as a process that washes people up as flotsam, smoothing the sea again; where we swim in the divine song of the sea knowing no laws, one fish, two fish; where we are part of every ocean, which is part of every vagina. To enter those portals is to begin a global journey, a flowing around the world. He who has been inside the right woman, the ultimate *cunt*—knows every place in the world that is worth knowing. And every one of those flowing places goes by the name of Woman: Congo, Nile, Zambezi, Elbe, Neva ("Father Rhine" doesn't flow—he is a border). Or the Caribbean Sea, the Pacific, the Mediterranean, *the* ocean that covers two-thirds of the earth's surface and all its shorelines, the irreproachable, inexhaustible, anonymous superwhore, across whom we ourselves become anonymous and limitless, drifting along without egos, like "masses of rubble," like God himself, immersed in the principle of masculine pleasure. (283–84)

While these male texts do not specifically articulate the sexual power suppressed by their covertly imperialistic appropriations of nature, they stake that territory (whether as Emerson's nature in the abstract or Melville's "watery part of the world") as literally a "no woman's land." Dickinson's speaker confronts the mythical "woman in/as water" and discovers that this woman is actually a male construct carrying the sedimentation of male desire and rapacity. This woman, in other words, is already "occupied" by man. Dickinson's work addresses and tries to extract woman from this equation. Once she is colonized by male desire, the "withdrawal" of masculinist ideology from woman doesn't leave her unaffected; in fact, for the woman, desire is always jeopardized by masculinist heterosexual construction.

v

But how do we resolve this level of critique, given the rampant ambiguities that characterize this poem? The narrative itself seems not to provide anything like unambiguous resolution to any of its numerous contradictions and paradoxes. Before searching in earnest for Emily Dickinson's lost dog, I would like first to return to Simone de Beauvoir and her writings about women's early sexual initiations. I have paid special attention to the sexual ambiguities rife within "I started Early – Took my Dog –." While the poem stages an entire ensemble of contradictions and unresolved themes, I am operating under the assumption that the primary contradiction among these is that troubling the speaker's response to the sea. As we have seen, it is difficult to argue decisively one way or the other whether the speaker responds passionately to the sea's erotic overtures. Just how the speaker is "moved" by this man, and just what she means when she asserts "I started – too" are questions answerable in a variety of ways. While we can expose the poem as a rape scenario in which the speaker is violated or at least threatened with sexual violation, the range of readings for those critical scenes makes it equally possible that she eventually responds with some enthusiasm to this not-so-subtle seduction, that she "started" to enjoy and, in fact, to initiate sexual behavior ("He followed – close behind").

De Beauvoir's The Second Sex offers some clarification for this vexed series of moments in Dickinson's poem. In her analysis of youthful sexual initiations, de Beauvoir argues that, given the manifestly subordinate position of women in Western culture, the initial sexual encounters of women tend to be fraught with contradictory impulses. According to de Beauvoir, whereas males tend to be the active, almost predatory, creatures in Western culture,

> the young girl, on the contrary, is courted and solicited in most cases; even when she first incites the man, it is he who then takes control of their relations; he is often older and more expert, and admittedly he should take charge of this adventure, which is new to her; his desire is more aggressive and imperious. Lover or husband, it is for him to lead her to the couch, where she has only to give herself over and do his bidding. Even if she has mentally accepted this domination, she becomes panic-stricken at the moment when she must actually submit to it. (380–81)

De Beauvoir elaborates on the physicality involved in such encounters in terms strikingly appropriate for Dickinson's poem:

> To be gazed at is one danger to be manhandled is another. Women as a rule are unfamiliar with violence, they have not been through the tussles of childhood and youth as have men; and now the girl is laid hold of, swept away in a bodily struggle in which the man is the stronger. She is no longer free to dream, to delay, to maneuver; she is in his power, at his disposal. These embraces, so much like a hand-to-hand tussle, frighten her, for she has never tussled. She is used to the caresses of a fiancé, a comrade, a colleague, a civilized and polite man; but now he takes on a peculiar aspect, egotistical and headstrong; she is without recourse against this stranger. It is not uncommon for the young girl's first experience to be a real rape and for the man to act in an odiously brutal manner; in the country and wherever manners are rough, it often happens that—half consenting, half revolted—the young peasant girl loses her virginity in some ditch, in shame and fear. (382–83)

In Dickinson's poem, the young girl might even lose her virginity on the beach. De Beauvoir's entire passage sheds valuable light on the dynamics and problematics of Dickinson's poem as well as on some areas of pornographic representation. As Linda Williams argues, the male dominance of the production of pornography results in the fact "that so much early hard-core fantasy revolves around situations in which the woman's sexual pleasure is elicited involuntarily, often against her will, in scenarios of rape or ravishment" (50). Moreover, de Beauvoir's distinction between being "gazed" at and being "man-handled" echoes the dilemma of Dickinson's speaker, who, gazed at by the mermaids and groped both by the frigates and the sea, undergoes both modes of appropriation.

De Beauvoir enables us to return to this poem's central conundrum, the stressed position of the speaker in "I started Early – Took my Dog –." The complex dialectic between what I am calling her resistance and her compliance, her paralysis and her fascination with the sea's rising to cover her body, her repulsion and her attraction, her terror and her desire, may well point us toward the complications of women's sexual experiences in a society in which males have consolidated their hegemony not only over social and political life, but over psychological, physical, and sexual practices as well. It is this vision of nature as construct that explains Dickinson's architecturalizing the ocean (the realm of nature in this poem) into "Basement" and "Upper Floor," and which accounts for fluid trafficking between human life and the naturalistic lives of animals ("Mouse" and, as we shall see, "Dog"). "I started Early – Took my Dog –" thus stages the arena of male cultural and social hegemony while simultaneously performing an immanent critique of it, exposing both the watery and unsubstantial foundation of her culture's subordination of women and the lordly domination and repressed hostility inherent in masculinist propriety ("And bowing – with a Mighty look").

We still have the matter of Emily Dickinson's lost dog, the poem's most significant "loose end," to address. What I would like to suggest is that the disappearance of the dog from "I started Early – Took my Dog –" provides a perspective from which to extend these and other conclusions concerning this poem's sexual-political commentary. We should note that dogs are very rare in Dickinson's poetry, mentioned in only six other poems.[15] We might therefore argue for the importance of this dog simply by virtue of its presence, but, as I remarked at the beginning of this chapter, this particular dog appears only once in the poem and in a high-priority position at that. Both Ortner and de Beauvoir theorize woman's position in Western culture as one of diminishment and subordination to the level of nature, and de Beauvoir explicitly equates this subordination with bestialization.[16] Dickinson's poem, as we have seen, revisits this scenario in two respects, first by diminishing its speaker as a mouse and then by assaulting its female protagonist with the cultural construction of woman as water, albeit in a form which exposes the male interests consolidated by such a construction. Dickinson's very composition of such a "nature" poem, then, requires that she enter into a dialogue with her culture about the nature of American nature, a dialogue in which the terms are, as we have seen, loaded against the case of women. Whether as mouse, as stranded maiden in need of help, or as victim of the sea's aggression, Dickinson's speaker everywhere registers the subordination of women not only within the parameters of the English language and the genre of American nature writing, but in American society as well. We might disregard the dog as mere anomaly in the poem, as a creature whose disappearance is of little matter. We might equally posit the dog as an essential component of the speaker's identity, in which case her silence about its disappearance might represent her trauma over her experience by the sea. However, we might find the naturalization of the poem's human subject even earlier in the poem, in its initial designation of her starting with her dog. From its initial line onward, we might argue, this poem examines the cultural construction of woman under the sign of the dog; that is, woman cast as inferior and animalistic bitch. It stages the degradation of women in a culture that regards them as somewhere between nature and the male of the species, with specific focus on male sexual opportunism exercised over the bestialized woman.

If the speaker in "I started Early – Took my Dog –" goes to the beach with her dog, she goes as woman constructed within her culture as bitch. And if she encounters there the degradation and violation inherent in a masculinist culture that so designates women, we might read her returning without this dog as her own personal and hard-fought transcendence over the construction of woman as animal. In this case, the disappearance of her dog is a sign of her having encountered and triumphed over the various ways in which nineteenth-century American culture subordinates and degrades women. She returns to the solid town, a place where the sea knows no one and must depart, a citizen in a community, albeit an imaginary one, beyond gendered prejudice and institutionalized sexism. The poem clearly differentiates between the "Solid Town" and the watery realm of violation and peril, and it equally clearly positions the speaker within that town at the poem's end. Given the number of women whose drowning concludes the many nineteenth-century American literary texts in which women actively seek out identities of their own invention and construction, women such as Hawthorne's Zenobia, Crane's Maggie, Chopin's Edna, the very fact of this woman's survival is itself significant. The dog, once *some* index of her identity, vanishes, and Dickinson's speaker returns, in the manner of Cassandra Morgeson, fully cognizant of her culture's limitations and of her triumph. "I started Early – Took my Dog –" could then be read as an examination and repudiation of the semiotics of gendered hierarchy and male domination, one of Dickinson's most forthrightly feminist poems and one rigorously critical of masculinist hegemony.[17]

While I have been suggesting that this dog simply vanishes and have read the poem as a sign of feminist resistance to male domination, it is also possible to modify that position, arguing instead that Emily Dickinson's dog doesn't disappear at all. More precisely, it undergoes a metamorphosis, merges with the sea in a powerful convergence of two of the poem's definitive symbols of the construction of cultural hierarchies. This amalgam of woman/dog/sea functions as an alternative index to Dickinson's thinking about sexual politics in "I started Early – Took my Dog –." I refer specifically to the following lines from the penultimate stanza:

> And He – He followed – close behind –
> I felt His Silver Heel
> Upon my Ankle – Then my Shoes
> Would overflow with Pearl –

Along with the sexual energies contained within this stanza may exist a representation of the sea reimagined as a dog obeying a command "to heel," which, as anyone who has a dog knows, means for the dog to "follow close behind," literally at one's heel.[18]

Could we now read the poem as the drama of a woman who confronts and tames the very idea of nature within which her culture has subordinated her being? But casting the sea, once aggressive and potentially violating, as obedient dog doesn't quite completely respond to all of the poem's difficulties. It does provide support for the reading I advance above, in which the speaker "visits" the sea, figures out the cultural dynamics of female subordination, and returns once she has shed (or at least "mastered") the degrading designation of woman as bitch. However, this pursuit continues, and the sea later withdraws and departs. I think this complication requires us to reproblematize our final reading, to recognize in the poem again the dialectic of mutually constitutive oppositions without resolution. In this reading, the speaker is still being dogged by her dog, plagued by the difficulty of ever fully escaping the construction of her identity by a male culture. Here "to dog" takes on a sinister meaning, suggesting a pursuit with the intention of harm, as an assassin might dog a victim or a detective might dog a suspect. Dog and ocean merge in one aggressive complex, a currish personification of the hostility and oppression common to patriarchal culture still pursuing and still threatening Dickinson's speaker. And since the poem's voice is still enmeshed in whatever sexual drama the poem stages at this point, this dogging suggests, perhaps, the final inextricability of this woman and her culture's semiotics of gender subordination. Furthermore, the fusion of sea and dog in the poem's final stanzas calls our attention to the intimacy of this construction, its centrality to this culture's definition of woman.

Merged thoroughly with the speaker's beloved pet, the sea, a symbol of irreducible ambiguity throughout the poem, now figures even more intimately in this woman's life, figures as an image of the all-permeating cultural baggage she bears, as an index to the fractured identity of woman in a patriarchal culture. Both domesticated and wild, both friendly and hostile, this pet may dog the steps of the speaker, even as she finds refuge in the "Solid Town." A similar penetration of speaker by her culture's assumptions pervades the entire poem. As I remarked earlier, the many moments of personification and anthropomorphism in the poem are all generated by the speaker herself. They are not merely her passive record of some objective reality. It is she who imagines the mermaids staring at her, she who imagines the frigates presuming her to be a mouse on the sands, she who documents the sea and its actions in sexually charged terms. That this speaker's very imagination constructs her world as a threatening arena of misogyny and violence against women testifies to the internalization of sexism and subordination nearly paralyzing American women. Like an anorexic gazing in horror at a mirror in which she sees herself only as a grotesque violation of what she takes to be her culture's idea of svelte beauty, the speaker in "I started Early – Took my Dog –" inhabits a world in which she figures primarily as the prey of a culture characterized in its sexual (as well as in its business) dealings by rapacity and violence. The sea might choose to withdraw from her, but she, the poem suggests, cannot withdraw from her culture's definition of women. In all its gendered and sexual complexity, Dickinson's poem thus exists as symptom of the bestialization and resulting domination of women in a patriarchal culture.

There is one final possibility to consider in the case of Emily Dickinson's lost dog. Perhaps there is no dog in "I started Early – Took my Dog –," even at the beginning of the poem. Not, in any case, a canine creature as the speaker's companion. The poem might recount the drama of the speaker going to the sea armed only with her poetic vision and sensibility, referred to here self-deprecatingly as her "doggerel." Once the poet's voice emerges out of the prenarrative silence and once the poem announces her and its presence in the self-conscious first line, any subsequent references to her dog(gerel) would be redundant. So imagined as the expression of Dickinson's deeply felt and variously expressed ideas about her own femininity, the poem's articulation and continuing presence stand both as sign and as symptom of the status of women in patriarchal society and literary culture. The terms of the poem's debate remain relatively constant—the speaker encounters and is assaulted by the sea, and the terms of that encounter remain equally problematic at the stylistic, thematic, and cultural levels of signification. However, without whatever protective function a canine "dog" might have been intended to serve, the speaker embarks with her ability to resist the domination of her being by masculinist cultural values by virtue of her poetic vision—shrewd, penetrating, and fully capable not only of exposing the woman as nature construction for what it is, but of redressing the subordinate status of woman simply by coming into existence. Read in this way, Dickinson's poem challenges the legitimacy of the thematics and values inscribed within the works of writers such as Emerson, Thoreau, and Melville. She also challenges them generically; rather than Thoreauvian "bragging for humanity," or speaking in the lamentation of Emersonian jeremiad, the hyperbole of Melvillian metaphysics, or the "barbaric yawp" of Whitmanian rhapsody, Emily Dickinson poses only her "doggerel" as a subtle and self-deprecating, yet nonetheless powerful, countervoice to the various male constructions of the American Renaissance. This litotic gesture challenges the rhetorical bravado of the voices meant to silence her own by means of the apparent innocence and humility of its voicing.

I would like to extend this line of thinking for just another moment, and suggest an equally intimate relationship between Dickinson and her dog—one of virtual identity. Indeed, many of Dickinson's allusions to her own Carlo indicate that she commonly projected her own intimate emotions into her faithful pet. As large as his mistress and, hence, a plausible double for some of her emotional states, Carlo was used as a vehicle for expressing Dickinson's embarrassment, and, quite revealingly, her sadness, as when she writes to her Norcross cousins that "Carlo is consistent, has asked for nothing to eat or drink, since you went away" (Sewall 634), or to Mr. Bowles that, after his sailing for Europe,

> it is a suffering, to have a sea—no care how Blue—between your Soul, and you. The Hills you used to love when you were in Northampton, miss their old lover, could they speak—and the puzzled look—deepens in Carlo's forehead, as Days go by, and you never come. (*Letters* 2:416)[19]

Indeed, while I grant that this is extreme, Dickinson's notorious and mysterious letters to "Master" might in fact consciously adopt the persona of a dog dutifully addressing her absent "master." These letters, which, as Richard B. Sewall rightly judges, provide "the seedbed, the matrix, of dozens of her poems" (520), communicate Dickinson's profound devotion to "Master" and her restless desire to hear "her master's voice," revealing, as Cynthia Griffin Wolff suggests, her "all-too-human discomfort in suffering love's insecurity" (409). As in the poem's earliest lines, Dickinson may, in the "Master" letters, offer herself up strategically in bestialized form in order more dramatically to communicate her dedication and loyalty to the hypothetical addressee of the three letters. Given the potential gender neutrality implicit in any dog's devotion to its "alpha," such self-deprecating posturing on Dickinson's part would also eliminate the need for us to speculate on whether "Master" might have been a male or a female lover.

However we conclude our search for Emily Dickinson's lost dog, her encounter with the aggressive, potentially violating, force of the sea stages a powerful psycho-ontological drama that exposes the masculinist values encoded within her culture's constructions of nature and of the residual "male" and "female" identities inherent within that construction. To equate women with nature and natural process is already to encode them within terms and categories constructed from, within, and for the sociosexual priorities of American men. The sea, nature, or Walden Pond may exist as territories to be explored, conquered, colonized, and exploited in the service of masculinist hegemony. Emerson, Thoreau, and Melville may all discover ontological and philosophical revelations about the truths of their characters (whether essentially benign and conducive to human strivings or essentially contradictory, if not the "universal cannibalism" of Melville's sea) largely because American nature has been constructed and maintained as male turf. Male discourses have saturated "nature" with the sociopolitical and cultural desires of American males at least since the earliest European explorations and conquests and at least since the earliest promotional verses luring Pilgrims to a utopian terrain of unprecedented fertility. For Dickinson as American woman, on the other hand, to "visit" nature, to encroach—however tentatively— onto male territory, is to be ogled, groped, assaulted, attacked, and perhaps raped, by the full force of the psychosexual residue peculiar to the masculinized constructions of North American "nature." Her ostensibly simple walk on the beach turns very quickly into a threatening discovery that these waters run red with aggression and violence. From Dickinson's perspective, what Ishmael refers to as "the universal cannibalism of the sea" is not some abstract universal in "human nature" but rather the culturally specific denigration of and violence against women. This speaker may escape and return to the "Solid Town," but her survival may be counterpointed, not only to the drownings of the fictional women we have discussed, but also to the drowning of Margaret Fuller, the transcendental voice most irksome to Emerson, and of whose body (along with those of her husband and little boy) Thoreau, sent on a recovery mission by Emerson, was unable to find anything more than a button.

"The Jolly Corner," one of Henry James's latest and most demanding short works, presents a remarkable example of the loose ends in a work of "high-culture" literature unraveling its entire representational scheme. In many ways an anomaly in the James corpus, "The Jolly Corner" negotiates a dual narrative, one focusing on Spencer Brydon's pursuit of and encounter with his spectral Other, and one significantly, though subtly, attentive to the concerns, priorities, and desires of Alice Staverton, Brydon's longtime friend and soul mate. While Brydon's tale dominates the narrative and generates most of its issues and themes, Staverton's counternarrative and counterdiscourse are no less important and may actually overwhelm the story of her friend, despite the imbalance of narrative time allotted to their respective and interrelated concerns. In the tale's final scene, Spencer Brydon recovers consciousness (after swooning at the sight of his double) in Staverton's lap. In sharp contrast to the complex and sometimes violent imagery of Brydon's experience throughout the extraordinary middle section of the tale, the mood of the brief, concluding section is mild and conciliatory. Significantly, it is Alice Staverton, not Brydon, who dominates that final scene, both physically and verbally. The barely conscious Brydon is aware, as he comes to, of his head "pillowed in extraordinary softness and fainly refreshing fragrance . . . and he finally knew that Alice Staverton had made her lap an ample and perfect cushion to him" (478).

Throughout this section Brydon and Staverton engage in a remarkably conventional and sentimental dialogue. Brydon, for example, remarks,

"Yes—I can only have died. You brought me literally to life. Only," he wondered, his eyes rising to her, "only, in the name of all the benedictions, how?"

It took her but an instant to bend her face and kiss him, and something in the manner of it, and in the way her hands clasped and locked his head while he felt the cool charity and virtue of her lips, something in all this beatitude somehow answered everything. "And now I keep you," she said.

"Oh keep me, keep me!" he pleaded while her face still hung over him: in response to which it dropped again and stayed close, clingingly close. (480)

It is under the sign of such sentimentality, itself jarring in James's work, that Brydon and Staverton exorcize the tale's specter in their final exchange, ostensibly eliminating the haunting presence that had generated Brydon's protracted hunt for his alter ego. Agreeing that the wraith he confronted was not the alter ego he had feared encountering, Brydon concludes, "He has a million a year. . . . But he has n't you." Staverton quickly, though stutteringly, adds, "'And he is n't—no, he is n't—*you!*' . . . as he drew her to his breast" (485). The tale ends with this embrace, projecting this emotionally lush and intimate final scene into an implicitly romantic future. The problem is, however, that in "The Jolly Corner," as in the other works we are considering, this conclusion not only fails to resolve the narrative's generative socio-ideological problematics in any meaningful way but actually, through its own forceful imposition of *some* conclusion, highlights the reality that its own strategy for reconciling the tale's stresses actually reinscribes them more disruptively within the final narrative moments. The embraces and breathlessly uttered promises that stop "The Jolly Corner" create the illusion that the intimacy of loving physicality and mutually articulated pledges of fidelity, the power of isolated, interpersonal union (reminiscent of Hester Prynne's declaration to Dimmesdale that their love "had a consecration of its own" because they "felt it was so, [they] said so to each other"), can in themselves insulate the story's protagonists from the endemic social and cultural ruptures that characterize the social discourses of the tale and that hover just beyond its margins. The belated psychosexual communion of Brydon and Staverton (she has waited thirty-three years for Brydon's return from Europe) is thus offered almost ritualistically as a panacea for Brydon's narcissism and Staverton's passivity, a union that transcends whatever social contingencies have deflected their attentions away from each other. However, rather than transcending, through their bonds of love, the fractured histories of Brydon's and Staverton's struggles, James's conclusion forcefully suppresses unresolved narrative energies in a desperate and self-contradictory imposition of aesthetic order.

Just as James's characters enter the narrative with thirty-three years of different and, according to the plot of the story, incommensurate experiences, so this tale's conclusion itself splits into two entwined and, at times, tensely antagonistic frames of reference. The final scene suggests one ensemble of implications for Spencer Brydon, while exactly the same scene strains for a decidedly alternative "conclusion" for Alice Staverton. In the terms I have been using, therefore, "The Jolly Corner" unravels into two unique sets of "loose ends," one exposing the historical and class specificity of Spencer Brydon's psychohistory, and another emerging from the particulars of Alice Staverton's gendered representation within James's narrative scheme. This is not to argue that Brydon's own narrative is not itself marked by gender issues, only that the primary motivation of his identity within James's tale is situated more suggestively within the discourses of late-nineteenth- and early-twentieth-century economic and class relations. To be sure, Brydon's own phallic and bellicose affiliations and imaginings mark him as rampantly male, and his similarities with other late Jamesian male narcissists press for an analysis of James's late work on maleness and its discontents (or perhaps, more appropriately, its dysfunctions).[1] In "The Jolly Corner," however, Brydon articulates his concerns in terms resonant with the figures of economic and urban transformation, quite likely in an evasion of deeper sexual anxieties but worthy of analysis in their own right. What we will examine, then, are the various dramas staged within "The Jolly Corner" and how their multiple irresolutions by tale's end expose alternative narratives lurking just around the jolly corner.

ii

When Spencer Brydon recovers consciousness at the conclusion of "The Jolly Corner," neither he, nor Alice Staverton, nor the reader knows quite what he has experienced or just what, if anything or anybody, he has confronted at the foot of the stairs in the family home of his childhood. So complex and enigmatic is the narrative of Spencer Brydon's encounter with his spectral Other that critics have variously read the presence Brydon confronts and rejects in the jolly corner as Brydon's past self, his potential self, his ideal self, his animal self, his unrecognized self, his repressed self, his hidden self, his mutilated ego, the beast in his jungle, the repository of his repressed fantasies, fears, or compulsions, the Jamesian (authorial) unconscious, the embodiment of figurative language run wild, William James, even an actual human—an agent hired by Alice Staverton to frighten Brydon.[2] While such critical perspectives are normative and establish suggestive relationships between "The Jolly Corner" and other Jamesian narratives, I believe it is important to distinguish between characters such as George Stransom in "The Altar of the Dead" and John Marcher in "The Beast in the Jungle," whose situations are rendered primarily in the privatistic terms of abstract anxiety or sexual trauma, and Spencer Brydon, whose nervous return to New York is represented in, at least in terms of James's work, uncharacteristic historically specific detail, primarily in the first and third sections of the tale. Our consideration of Brydon's encounter will focus on those sections, with occasional reference to the tale's extended second section, not to allow those pages that "constitute one of the peaks of Henry James's art . . . to speak for themselves," as Tzvetan Todorov does in his reading of "The Jolly Corner," but to suggest some social and historical analogues for those tropes and energies that enliven these passages of intense introspection and subjective quest. What such a historicizing of James's tale suggests is not a mirror of a stable and coherent moment in history, but a social text that represents through its own flux and contradictions an arena of social and historical flux, even struggle. Indeed, this late James narrative represents, among other things, a transitional moment in American social and cultural history —the disruption of traditional "genteel" values by the emerging structures and discourses of technology, urbanization, and consolidating capital—while it also examines critically some characteristic subjective (and male) responses to such change. The "loose ends" of "The Jolly Corner," the mystification and ruptures precipitated by Brydon's denial of his Other in the final moments of the second section and throughout the third section of James's tale, open this claustrophobic narrative to the influx of social and historical tensions, virtually inverting the narrative perspective within which Brydon has been constructed. When Brydon is confronted by his Other at the bottom of the stairs, this encounter transcends any putatively subjective experience or identity crisis and, by virtue of the implications embodied by this wraithlike presence, transports Spencer Brydon well beyond the familiar confines of his family home and situates him squarely in the highly contested public sphere of early modern urban United States. The interpretive projects I allude to above clearly respond to important narrative signals, but they also confirm, rather than challenge, Brydon's perspective on his experience. It is precisely this perspective that James's text, in fact, discredits.

To prepare ourselves for Brydon's meeting with his Other, we need, above all, to grasp the extent to which Brydon and the world of the tale are defined in explicitly economic and social terms. To be sure, many Jamesian protagonists find their worlds marked by financial prospects, but primarily insofar as money (or the lack of it) functions as a catalyst for greater imaginative experience. We don't experience them making or spending money, though we do witness a vague contempt for an exchange economy. Donald L. Mull correctly, I think, defines the role of money in many James narratives when he notes that "money abounds [in the early tales]; and though the financial motif is often less than integral to the story, its fundamental interest attends those relations into which it enters and the attitude among the characters which it engenders" (15). In "The Jolly Corner," however, finances provide more than an implicit environment in which characters move; they define the cultural moment as well as the characters' personalities, their potentialities, even their dreams.

The first section of "The Jolly Corner" sets up Brydon's return to the United States from a thirty-three-year sojourn in Europe and the renewal of his friendship with Alice Staverton. Most of this section dwells, however, on Brydon's revulsion before the face of a recently industrialized and modernized New York. In this topsy-turvy world, Brydon feels, "Proportions and values were upside-down; . . . the 'swagger' things, the modern, the monstrous, the famous things, . . . were exactly his sources of dismay" (436). Brydon takes in three decades of the most materially significant change New York has ever seen, and he feels as though it would take a century to adjust to "the differences, the newnesses, the queernesses, above all the bignesses, for the better or the worse, that at present *assaulted* his vision wherever he looked" (436; my emphasis). Brydon imagines the matrix of economics, physical transformation, and social upheaval that constitutes modern New York variously as "bristling," "harsh," "vulgar and sordid," "awful," "rank," "monstrous," and "base" (438, 441, 447, 449, 469). Nothing of this modern spectacle had ever, Brydon feels, spoken to any "need of his spirit" (470). Amidst this Babel, it is in terms resonant with economic tropes that Brydon remembers the route to Alice Staverton's flat

> better than to any other address among the dreadful multiplied numberings which seemed to him to reduce the whole place to some vast ledger-page, overgrown, fantastic, of ruled and criss-crossed lines and figures—if he had formed, for his consolation, that habit, it was really not a little because of the charm of his having encountered and recognised, in the vast wilderness of the wholesale, breaking through the mere gross generalisation of wealth and force and success, a small still scene where items and shades, all delicate things, kept the sharpness of the notes of a high voice perfectly trained, and where economy hung about life like the scent of a garden. (439)

Brydon returns, in short, to a world in which he perceives traditional values and proportions as under siege by the crudely palpable facts of modern economic reality and urban materiality. Brydon sees Staverton's frugality and traditionalism (her values) as a repudiation of the permeation of life by economic exchange values, so that Staverton's "economy" stands as the antithesis to the "rank money-passion" (449) and cash nexus of the economized modern life Brydon finds so repellent.

Brydon, as we learn, owns two structures, the incomes from which motivate his return from Europe and guarantee his future financial stability, just as they and other family assets have underwritten his decades of indulgence in Europe. Their significance for Brydon figures largely in his representation of a polarized modern New York. Located in a quiet district, the jolly corner resonates with memories of his early childhood and family life. Described variously as "good," "better," "ample," "superlatively extended," and "consecrated," the jolly corner is associated with the personal and intimate—it is "the opposite extreme to the modern" (466) and Brydon's haven from the "harsh actuality of the Avenue" (447). The modern, on the other hand, defines Brydon's other property, a high-rise apartment building under renovation to maximize its economic potential, and in most ways the antithesis to the jolly corner. Whereas the jolly corner is kept neatly maintained and quietly traditional, Brydon's skyscraper, located "two bristling blocks" west, is "already in course of reconstruction as a tall mass of flats" (438). To Brydon, his apartment building, like the entire world of cultural change that hovers just beyond the tale's main dramatic action, is associated with the "queernesses" and the "bignesses" of the "dishonoured and disfigured" (441) metropolis to which he returns. The jolly corner stands, in Brydon's scheme of things, like Alice Staverton's flat, as an alternative to the world of cultural change. The contrast between the two structures makes concrete the binary opposition in "The Jolly Corner" between economies and economics (private frugality versus public values), between traditional values, spirit, and sentiment on the one hand, and money and modernity, with all its material trappings, on the other.

The identity crisis dramatized so thoroughly in "The Jolly Corner" begins to take shape amidst the contradictions of Brydon's response to modern American culture. Early on in the tale, Brydon registers the subtle, internal difference triggered by his return and exposure to the urban forces of contemporary New York:

> He had lived his life with his back so turned to such concerns and his face addressed to those of so different an order that he scarce knew what to make of this lively stir, in a compartment of his mind never yet penetrated, of a capacity for business and a

sense for construction. These virtues, so common all round him now, had been dormant in his own organism—where it might be said of them perhaps that they had slept the sleep of the just. (438)

Indeed, despite his traumatized flinching before the face of modernized New York, Brydon, responding to these wiggles deep in his consciousness, enjoys loafing about the renovation site of his skyscraper "secretly agitated, . . . ready to climb ladders, to walk the plank, to handle materials and look wise about them, to ask questions, in fine, and challenge explanations" (438). All this in spite of his revulsion. In fact, Brydon's personal, financial interest in the successful gentrification of his property seems to overwhelm his aesthetic and, at times, seemingly moral contempt for the very disruptive alterations he confronts. Brydon's anxieties about who or what he might have become cannot be grasped in the abstract—his split self corresponds to his representation of a rupture in the social world of contemporary New York. Brydon's "problem" is larger than the shape his own life might have assumed—it resembles, in fact, the shock of a displaced cultural aristocracy before the modernity of the United States in the midst of industrial and economic transformation. Brydon recoils from the new facts of New York, a world he simply cannot make sense of: "Everything was somehow a surprise" (435) to Brydon upon his return. Spirit, sentiment, and a broad array of privatistic modalities are, according to Brydon, under siege by the crudely palpable facts of urban economic existence. To be sure, his dilemma is told in James's highly psychologized language, but that same putatively intrapsychic rhetoric should not deflect our understanding of its irreducibly social function.

This rigid stratification of Brydon's psyche and of the tale's two architectural venues suggests that in his construction of Spencer Brydon and "The Jolly Corner" James stages a split in American culture for which critics have offered a number of models. For George Santayana, the "genteel tradition" model, for example, suggests senile femininity: essentially passive, decorous, and, most damagingly, "apart from the ongoing business of society" enervating American high culture. Santayana offers an architectural trope for this split strikingly appropriate for "The Jolly Corner":

> The truth is that one-half of the American mind, that not occupied intensely in practical affairs, has remained, I will not say high-and-dry, but slightly becalmed; it has floated gently in the back-water, while, alongside, in invention and industry and social organization the other half of the mind was leaping down a sort of Niagara Rapids. This division may be found symbolized in American architecture: a neat reproduction of the colonial mansion—with some modern comforts introduced surreptitiously—stands beside the sky-scraper. The American Will inhabits the sky-scraper; the American Intellect inhabits the colonial mansion. The one is the sphere of the American man; the other, at least predominantly, of the American woman. The one is all aggressive enterprise; the other is all genteel tradition. (13, 39–40)

In this image, Santayana criticizes a split nearly coincidental with Brydon's dichotomous vision of modern New York split between an emerging economic and urban order, encapsulated in the image of *his* skyscraper, and the cultural and sentimental haven of the jolly corner.[3]

The split in Brydon's world can be traced back to some earlier Victorian antecedents. John Ruskin, for instance, touched on this phenomenon in its English bourgeois form, referring to "the true nature of home" as "the place of peace; the shelter, not only from all injury, but from all terror, doubt, and division. . . . So far as the anxieties of the outer life penetrate into it . . . it ceases to be a home; it is then only a part of the outer world which you have roofed over and lighted fire in" (quoted in Millett 98–99). To another English critic, the Victorian family was "a tent pitch'd in a world not right" (Houghton 345). Brydon's existence within this polarized world has earlier parallels in Dickens's Mr. Wemmick (whose house quite literally is his castle) and in Mark Rutherford's autobiographical persona, both of whom cultivate a dissociation of their "personal" lives from their social existences so that their "true" selves should not be stained by contact with crude economic realities. That Brydon's sense of self corresponds as much to a Victorian English model as it does to that model's genteel American counterpart suggests the international range of the cultural and economic transformations represented in "The Jolly Corner" as well as both James's own peculiar international stance and that of his semiautobiographical character, the expatriate Brydon. James's own *The American Scene* articulates many of the reactions characteristic of Brydon in "The Jolly Corner."

This domestic milieu provides an interesting perspective on James's text. The American family responded to industrialization and urbanization by playing off society at large in two contradictory ways, mirroring the split in American culture with its own stereotyped divisions, while at the same time assuming an arguably new identity against the new social order. According to Christopher Lasch, the concept of the family as a "haven in a heartless world," emerging in the nineteenth century, granted "a radical separation between work and leisure and between public life and private life" (6–7). This polarization was not simply a difference; like Brydon's image of modern New York, it carried a rigorously coded social, moral, and ethical charge as well. According to Lasch (in a restatement of Marx's description of commodity fetishism from chapter 1 of *Capital*),

> the products of human activity, especially the higher products of that activity such as the social order itself, took on the appearance of something external and alien to mankind. No longer recognizably the product of human invention, the man made world appeared as a collection of objects independent of human intervention and control. (7)

The emotional response to the putative hostility of this social world was the glorification of private life and of the family, which "represented the other side of the bourgeois perception of society as something alien, impersonal, remote, and abstract—a world from which pity and tenderness had fled in horror" (8).

Lasch's commentary succinctly defines Brydon's outlook. The social order may appear alien, and may appear to transcend human intervention and determination, but *is*, in the final analysis, not only the product of human invention, but, in Brydon's case, a function of his own investment strategy. Brydon's contradictory revulsion before the financial matrix of modern life points to a precariously sustained antithesis between the imaginary self Brydon would like to be and the economic basis for the entrepreneurial self he actually is. Brydon may define himself against the material forms of modern New York and may condemn its disfigured economic appearance, but he remains thoroughly, though contradictorily, implicated in that order. Indeed, he is not just a cog in an inhuman machine, but one who through his property ownership and renovation (he is, after all, a landlord seeking to maximize his capital investment) constitutes an essential ideological brace for that world. Brydon is a living contradiction, at one level repulsed by the urban landscape and economic climate of his world, at another invigorated by the excitement of his engagement and capital returns. Brydon's detachment from the material source of his wealth lies at the root of his detachment from the the social order in general and his contempt for the ledger-book matrix that he himself superimposes on his world. Brydon can't reconcile the personal (the world of "spirit") with the social (the world of enterprise and industry), even though his own life aggressively and intimately yokes those spheres. Brydon fails, one might say, to recognize his own presence (in the sense of his economic interests) in a world that he perceives as alien and hostile to his human or cultured "interests."

While Brydon thinks of himself as separate from this grotesque new world of disfigured ledger pages (he *is not* what modern New York *is*), this binary opposition on which Brydon structures his identity begins collapsing, even in the tale's early pages. We have already mentioned Brydon's excitement over the "lively stir in a compartment of his mind never yet penetrated, of a capacity for business and a sense for construction." But "The Jolly Corner" also elsewhere stages the tense irresolution of Brydon's contradictory impulses. Most directly, Brydon's past and his future prospects depend on his two pieces of property, which he appropriates and mobilizes in his own metaphorically ruptured account of New York. Alice Staverton articulates just such an interpenetration of Brydon's imagined oppositions when she remarks to Brydon, who is badgered by others to renovate the jolly corner as well as the high-rise: "In short you 're to make so good a thing of your sky-scraper that, living in luxury on *those* ill-gotten gains, you can afford for a while to be sentimental here!" (444). Whereas Brydon would like to maintain both his sense of his own identity and the jolly corner as distinct from the cash nexus of modern culture, Staverton foregrounds the interpenetration of such imagined oppositions. Brydon's retreat from the world is sustained by the rent income from his skyscraper: one needs to be able to *afford* sentimentality. James provides no specific information on Brydon's income, but there is little doubt that Brydon can well afford the luxury of sentiment. Although data on rents from the period is very sketchy, Robert Higgs provides some useful figures: "in Chicago's central business district, the square mile surrounding State and Madison streets . . . the value of the land increased during 1873–1910 [a period corresponding almost exactly to that of Brydon's stay in Europe] from about $72 million to about $600 million, an amazing increase of over 700 percent" (66).

Brydon's own version of this opposition contrasts the jolly corner as a transeconomic haven of personal values with the "beastly rent-values" (444) that his other property earns, an association of rent values with beastliness that figures prominently in the tale's denouement. We should now note, however, the contamination of Brydon's discourse by the language of rent values even as he designates the financial gains earned by private property as "beastly." These images mark Brydon's contradictory deployment of a heavily economized vocabulary both to demonize the very idea of the economic and to insulate himself from his complicity in the economic realities to which he returns. After all, it is precisely those "beastly rent-values" that have underwritten Brydon's long stay in Europe and that will guarantee his future economic security, enabling him to "shelter" the jolly corner as a "consecrated" world elsewhere. The tensions straining at the two discourses available to Brydon and the extremeness of their paradoxical yoking suggests something bordering on the schizophrenic in Brydon's understanding (or lack thereof) of his own unexamined presence.

In this respect, both Brydon himself and the jolly corner embody the contradictions definitive of another late Jamesian locale, the world of Portland Place and Eaton Square in *The Golden Bowl*. In "The Consuming Vision of Henry James," Jean-Christophe Agnew makes an important point about that late novel:

The world of Portland Place and Eaton Square cannot be more distantly removed from the crude and callous transactions of the marketplace (the place where Adam [Verver] made his millions), yet it is nonetheless a world saturated with the imagery of the market, a world constructed and deconstructed by the appreciative vision. (94)

As Agnew illuminates (97), the market metaphors that infuse the later works define a medium in which characters are subtly, but fully, reified, transformed from verbs into nouns, from active human agents into commodities to be appropriated within a realm of culture inseparable from the market. "The Jolly Corner" can be read, in part, as a much shorter, though roughly synonymous, investigation into the mutually constitutive "opposition" between the realms of culture and finance.

The collapse of Brydon's imagined opposition between the world of culture and the world of economic and social change is suggested in a number of other ways. For one, Brydon draws heavily on financial metaphors throughout the tale. His identity crisis, for example, is precipitated primarily by his sense of "a compartment of his mind never yet penetrated, . . . a capacity for business and a sense of construction." Brydon first feels these stirrings as he oversees work on his high-rise apartment building: he feels ready to "really 'go into' figures" (438). He never becomes conscious, however, of the relationship between his figurative language and the social and economic contexts of his existence. Just as Brydon feels energized by the work being done on his skyscraper, he tends to define the jolly corner in opposition to the cash nexus of modern New York, though again in a language permeated by economic imagery, once even referring to his two properties as "his main capital" (437). Because of his contempt for the world of enterprise, Brydon refuses to consider renovating the jolly corner; any reason for doing so would "be inevitably a reason of dollars," and he adds with unqualified disdain, "There are no reasons here [in America] *but* of dollars" (446). In one final example of Brydon's largely unconsciously contradictory relationship to the "facts and figures" of modern New York, he first imagines the alter ego which he will pursue through the tale's long second section in suggestive terms: "He knew what he meant and what he wanted; it was as clear as the figure on a cheque presented in demand for cash" (456). Thus, despite his revulsion from the economic matrix of the life to which he returns, Brydon's own discourse is marked, in the form of economic figures and tropes, by the very financial realities against which he defines himself. Eventually, these contradictions and their economic basis constellate in the appalling figure Brydon encounters in the jolly corner.

In a more sinister vein, Brydon commodifies his friend, Alice Staverton. We have already seen that Brydon contrasts Staverton's frugality to the crass and oppressive ledger-book values he superimposes on the urban landscape to which he returns. However, Brydon also "values" Staverton in other ways. Early in the tale, he reflects that "she was as exquisite for him as some pale pressed flower (a rarity to begin with), and, failing other sweetnesses, she was a sufficient reward of his effort" (440). The terms of Brydon's statement—Staverton is imagined as a precious piece of property; she exists *for* Brydon as a *reward* for his efforts—are important in a number of ways. For one, they recall John Marcher's commodification of May Bartram, who "might have been a lily too—only an artificial lily, wonderfully imitated and constantly kept, without dust or stain, though not exempt from a slight droop and a complexity of faint creases, under some clear glass bell" (James 98–99). Brydon's and Marcher's visions suggest a common appropriative tyranny that "values" a feminine Other only in terms that aestheticize and commodify her. The specific terms of Brydon's vision also parallel his desire to figure himself beyond economic determination. Casting Staverton as "some pale pressed flower" (another form of fetishized, aesthetic calcification) functions for Brydon as another strategy to project some valued commodity (in this case, a human being) into a realm beyond the ravages of change. Brydon would, then, "preserve" both the jolly corner *and* Alice Staverton, fixing them in time and valuing them precisely in relation to their distance from a world of social transformation.

Brydon's commodification of his friend also represents what Agnew has termed the "consuming vision." As Agnew notes, "the only thing Jamesian characters actually produce are effects. A person's effects are always contrivable, alienable, acquirable in James's fictive world"

(84). In the late novels especially, market metaphors "are more than mere conceits or occasional tropes. They define the very medium . . . in which the characters and their relations dissolve" (97). Brydon, in representing Staverton as an *object* to be won as "reward" for his efforts, literally "invests" her with attributes that transform her into a thing to be acquired, valued, displayed as any other cultural commodity, deployed as cultural capital. While this is a common scenario in James's work, this case is different: whereas characters like Christopher Newman, Chad Newsome, or Adam Verver all assume their appropriative visions as legitimate extensions of their economic privilege, Brydon's "consuming vision" is fundamentally at odds with his understanding of himself.

iii

It is, of course, Brydon's understanding of himself, his past, and his future that is examined in his encounter with and rejection of his Other. Brydon's narrative, his story, culminates in two loose ends, one concluding the second section of the tale, and the other in his final conversation with Alice Staverton. We need to examine those intimately related moments in terms of the protracted psychological dynamic through which James's tale represents Brydon and his "interests." As I have mentioned, readings of "The Jolly Corner" tend to confirm the merely subjective and hypothetical implications of Brydon's vision, but that confrontation with the "ghost" can also be read in a manner consistent with the rest of the tale's representation of the social and economic transformation of the United States. At the very moment Brydon encounters his spectral other self, the meeting registers on his consciousness in suggestive terms:

> The penumbra, dense and dark, was the virtual screen of a figure which stood in it as still as some image erect in a niche or as some black-vizored sentinel guarding a treasure. . . . It gloomed, it loomed, it was something, it was somebody, the prodigy of a personal presence.
> . . . He had been "sold," he inwardly moaned. . . . Such an identity fitted his at *no* point, made its alternative monstrous. . . .

It came upon him nearer now, . . . for the stranger, whoever he might be, evil, odious, blatant, vulgar, had advanced as for aggression, and he knew himself give ground. Then harder pressed still, . . . he felt the whole vision turn to darkness and his very feet give way. His head went round; he was going; he had gone. (475–77)

Even before the actual meeting, Brydon had imagined the figure as "a creature more subtle, yet at bay perhaps more formidable, than any beast of the forest" (456–57), and as "the fanged or the antlered animal" that "bristled there—somewhere near at hand" (461–62).

The horror of such suggestions and the ghastly visage of the Other have not, however, gone unanticipated. Nearly every term associated with *this* figure has already been applied to Brydon's revulsion before the transformed appearance of modern New York. The figure recalls the "beastly rent-values" on which Brydon lives. Its "bristling" in wait for Brydon similarly recalls not only the location of his skyscraper "two bristling blocks" west of the jolly corner, but also the "bristling line of hard unconscious heads" (455) over which Brydon imaginatively projects himself into the "real" life of his sentimental home. References to the figure as looming, erect, and rigid (475) also suggest Brydon's skyscraper, a tall mass of flats—early in the tale he goes to "see how his 'apartment-house' was rising" (440). Nearly all of Brydon's adjectives in this description of the alter ego, especially "vulgar," reconfigure earlier comments on modern New York as "vulgar and sordid" (438), and on society in general, as witnessed in Brydon's slur against "some vulgar human note" (469). In referring to this figure as "monstrous," Brydon also recalls a word used throughout the tale to denote his vision of modern life as new and base. Brydon, we remember, describes his dismay before the "monstrous" things in modern life (436). In early conversations, Brydon and Alice Staverton agree that the self he might have become is "quite huge and monstrous," to which Brydon adds, "Monstrous above all! . . . quite hideous and offensive" (450), merging with the proliferation of "beast" images as well as with Brydon's contradictory understanding of himself (he also imagines himself as a "monstrous stealthy cat" [458] capable of frightening his formidable Other).

It is especially significant that the presence is denoted by the word "figure," a term so resonant, not only with the sense of the "figurative," as Deborah Esch illuminates, but with its economic connotations as well. After all, Brydon feels ready to "really 'go into' figures" (438); he sees New York as a "vast ledger-page, overgrown, fantastic, of ruled and criss-crossed lines and figures" (439); he even pictures his alter ego as "as clear as the figure on a cheque presented in demand for cash" (456). Even negatively, Brydon's skyscraper is on a street he characterizes as "dishonoured and disfigured in its westward reaches" (441), disfigured, we can surmise, by being so thoroughly inscribed with monetary figures. The intimate details of the presence, his "grizzled bent head" and the hand missing two fingers "which were reduced to stumps, as if accidentally shot away" (475–76), also represent the "disfigured." Again, despite Brydon's denial of his alter ego, the violence of these images also corresponds with Brydon's early conception of what he might have become: "If I had waited I might have seen it was [possible to have pursued another life], and then I might have been, by staying here, something nearer to one of these types who have been hammered so hard and made so keen by their conditions" (449). In a sense, then, what Brydon sees in the figure at the bottom of the stairs is a figure—a dollar sign writ large, an image of modern, capitalist man caught in the cross fire of incommensurate worldviews, aesthetics, and discourses. As this scene and the second section of "The Jolly Corner" conclude, the significance of this "figure" for the tale and for Brydon takes one final turn. Before the violence and vulgarity of this figure, erect and bristling, blocking his exit from the jolly corner, Brydon lapses into unconsciousness quite appropriately to an auctioneer's call: "He had been 'sold.' . . . His head went round; he was going; he had gone" (476–77).[4] In this final turn, Brydon passes out imagining the impossible—not only that his being has been auctioned off, but that the jolly corner itself has been invaded and divided into lots.

Of primary importance to Brydon's fate in this tale is his repeated rejection of the significance of this Other for his own life. While Brydon perceives the visage of the Other with terrifying clarity—"No portrait by a great modern master could have presented him with more intensity"—he insists on the unfathomable gap separating his

being from this other "man of his own substance and stature" (475).
James represents Brydon's response in complex detail, beginning with
the figure moving his hands to reveal his face:

> The hands, as he looked, began to move, to open; then, as if
> deciding in a flash, dropped from the face and left it uncovered
> and presented. Horror, with the sight, had leaped into Brydon's
> throat, gasping there in a sound he could n't utter; for the bared
> identity was too hideous as *his,* and his glare was the passion of
> his protest. The face, *that* face, Spencer Brydon's? — he searched
> it still, but looking away from it in dismay and denial, falling
> straight from his height of sublimity. It was unknown, incon-
> ceivable, awful, disconnected from any possibility—! He had
> been "sold," he inwardly moaned, stalking such game as this:
> the presence before him was a presence, the horror within him a
> horror, but the waste of his nights had been only grotesque and
> the success of his adventure an irony. Such an identity fitted his
> at *no* point, made its alternative monstrous. A thousand times
> yes, as it came upon him nearer now — the face was the face of a
> stranger. (476–77)

Brydon follows his immediate and fleeting recognition, "the bared
identity was too hideous as *his,*" with despair and desperately reiter-
ated repudiations, "looking away from it in dismay and denial." His
rapid mobilization of his arsenal of repressive and projective mecha-
nisms, however, can't alter the truth of the matter. Even his dismissal of the figure on the grounds that it doesn't resemble his present
appearance rings false and exposes the superficiality of his self-
understanding. Predicated as it is upon the truism of naturalism that
environment determines existence, "The Jolly Corner" discredits any
assumption that appearances can indicate character. Brydon's Other,
as alternative Brydon or actual, essence of, Brydon, resonates too
thoroughly with the facts and history of his life for any shallow (and
transparent) denial to protect Brydon's fragile and conflicted self. In
his final words, appropriately enough, Brydon distinguishes himself
once and for all from the grizzled figure at the bottom of the stairs:
"He has a million a year," he intones. "But he has n't you" (485).
Throughout the tale up to this final turn of the economic screw, Bry-

don's self-image depends on his figuring himself beyond economic determination, above the sordid concerns of financial transaction, though, paradoxically, also in terms of acquisitive practices—the final distinction pivots on what each character *has*. He is not, to his way of thinking, the figure he meets, despite the monetarization of his discourse, of his relationship with Alice Staverton, or of the actual financial means on which his life is predicated. Brydon believes he can keep his genteel identity permanently and ultimately separate from the very financial facts that underwrite his life in Europe and in New York. Just as Brydon doesn't recognize himself in his financially saturated language, finally he fails to accept that the figure he confronts is a figure for that side of his existence that contradicts the image he is willing to entertain. He thus attempts to keep separate from his consciousness not only one of its figurative constructs, but an essential component of his actual lived social and economic existence.

If the term "figure" is thus of central importance to reading Brydon's tale within a historical and economic context, it is important to note that this economic use of the term exists in a dialogue of sorts with "figure" in a different sense. "The Jolly Corner" is, Deborah Esch argues, "a tale that turns upon the consequences, for character, narrator, and reader of 'strange figures' lurking in the text in the guise of familiar idioms" (588). Brydon cannot decipher the figure because "he cannot tell (or admit) the difference between its literal and figurative senses. He has forgotten, if he ever knew, that the figure of his *alter ego* is a figure by virtue of the linguistic process of figuration" (595). Esch's foregrounding of the primacy of Brydon's metaphorical "figurings" of his alter ego has implications far beyond those she advances. Her focus on the process of figuration within "The Jolly Corner," for example, does not account either for its various manifestations or for the economic implications that proliferate throughout the tale. Brydon, in fact, consciously images himself in a variety of "figurative" postures. He views himself as a simpleton on stage, as Pantaloon tricked by Harlequin at a Christmas farce (460), as a hero "almost worthy of an age of greater romance" (464), as a conductor beginning a symphony, and as an author. He even compares the figure he meets at the jolly corner to the work of a great painter. These moments are consciously marked by Brydon as moments of figuration.

When Brydon first brings up the idea of what he might have become, for example, he comments to Alice Staverton that "it 's only a figure, at any rate, for the way I now feel" (449). And at a moment of an imaginary sword fight he realizes that "the light he had set down on the mantel of the next room would have to figure his sword" (464). In other words, Brydon is hyperaware of the figurative nature of his quest, of how self-conscious he is of his dilemma in aesthetic terms, whether parodic or epic. Brydon's figurative processes *do* get out of hand, but not owing to any inherent instability of his figurative system or to his "forgetfulness." His figures of speech spin away from him precisely because they are meant to postpone, if not to displace, his increasingly troubled sense of his complicity in an economic world he loathes and fears. Thus, Brydon's denials of his Other, a denial central to most readings of the tale, are, in one important sense, another example of his persistent strategy of condemning the economic reality to which he returns from Europe. It is noteworthy that it is the *appearance,* rather than the meaning or some attribution of essentialistic traits, that Brydon condemns in both New York as an economic landscape and in his ghostly Other as an image with any possible significance for his life. Neither conforms to his aesthetic desires.

These two senses of the "figures" of "The Jolly Corner"—on the one hand, the artistic sense, and on the other, the economic sense—are more important than the homonymous pun. Brydon's "figures" are not simply abstract or unmotivated tropes. His increased anxiety before the figures of modern existence and the blinding split in his rhetorical constructions of character and city merge to precipitate his figurative adventure—his adventure of and in figuration. His figurative practices function, in part, as a strategy to elicit an image of the self he feels he might have become, though Brydon elides the actual figure he figures by rejecting the significance of that Other. However, the data of Brydon's social and economic complicity in the new economic order around him belies his sense of his separateness from that world, and the figure he encounters collapses both senses of figure (as money and as metaphor) into his inescapable human presence— the human figure he encounters. Any reading that accounts for this Other needs to consider the possibility that this figure isn't simply an image of Brydon's personal unconscious, but an image of, speaking very loosely, Brydon's political unconscious. One needn't even agree with Fredric Jameson's pronouncements that "there is nothing that is not social and historical . . . [and] that everything is 'in the last analysis' political" (20) to agree that there is *something* in "The Jolly Corner" that *is* social and historical, even political. One might even argue that the ghostly presence wandering the empty rooms of the property on the jolly corner has more in common with the specter Marx and Engels witnessed haunting Europe than it does with other Jamesian ghosts. In any case, whereas Brydon finally rejects any significance the specter has for him, James's text suggests that the rejection is, to borrow again from Jameson, a strategy of containment, a fiction Brydon must impose on his experience in order to force a coherence onto his own life and to shut out the truth of his history. This is not to suggest that James was necessarily aware of the extent to which he gives fictional form to some of Marx's critique of reification and commodity fetishism, but rather that the discourse of James's text exists in a complex network of social discourses in turn-of-the-century United States.

What does such a reading suggest about James's own relationship with his figures, rhetorical and economic? The ideology of James's text is far from simple, far from stable, and many questions about James's relationship to American culture remain to be answered. Is Brydon's dilemma a sign of James's own grasp of a rupture in American life or a symptom of his own alienation from the material facts of a rapidly modernizing world? Does James's notion of realism resemble that of William Dean Howells—"fashioning serious fiction as an anodyne for the rifts he observed in the social fabric, the growing tensions between old and new ways of life" (Trachtenberg 191)— or does James focus instead on exposing and examining those rifts? Whatever ideology we ascribe to James, what relationship does it have to the ideological disruptions performed by particular texts? I would like to suggest that "The Jolly Corner" (along with many other James narratives such as *The Bostonians* and *The Golden Bowl*) exists complexly both as naive and as critical representation of the crises and ruptures of the culture of its genesis. That is, the terms of subjectivity in "The Jolly Corner" are radically social, historical, and economic. The tale of Brydon's quest for his Other seems to represent James's assault on the possibilities of a unified subject; it also seems to enable its own deconstruction.

iv

So far, we have dwelled almost exclusively on the male character in James's tale. To be sure, "The Jolly Corner" spends an inordinate amount of narrative time on Brydon's history, Brydon's finances and properties, Brydon's questions and issues. "The Jolly Corner," in fact, has been regarded as solely and obviously an examination of Spencer Brydon's character and crisis, and James criticism has marginalized Alice Staverton, viewing her as an appendage to the tale's "hero." Quentin Anderson is representative when he regards Staverton as

> the first full illustration of what the girl (or, in this case, middle-aged woman) who becomes a man's conscience does for him. Her acceptance of his human limitation is in no way censorious. Nor is it coercive . . . [she rather] tames this lowest element of human nature to divine uses. (181)

Other critics offer hope that Spencer Brydon will achieve a sense of psychic wholeness "through [this] woman's unselfish, all-comprehending love," or view Staverton as "the integrating spirit, the principle of divine love which makes selfhood possible in the fullest sense," as a "prize" for Brydon, as an "all-forgiving, all-accepting mother figure," embodying the "redemptive power of love," and as an "example for the reader of the tale" (by virtue of her understanding the complex figurative reality of Brydon's vision).[5] And even Mary Doyle Springer's *A Rhetoric of Literary Character: Some Women of Henry James* continues to marginalize Alice Staverton as a "frame character" whose "most important function is to be sensitively aware of those muffled vibrations of [Brydon's], and so sympathetic that she can divine 'his strange sense' of what he is about to confront and thus give her sanction to the strangeness" (119). And lest we exaggerate the importance of such a role, Springer cautions that we should consider the possibility that even the worthiest of frame characters are always less worthy than the protagonists they frame. Spencer Brydon gets his worth, yes, partly because we see that he enjoys the concern and love of a woman who knows how to live better than he does. But the accolades for bravery go to him—to the one who faces, in physical and spiritual darkness, the problem of who he might have been, with all its direct bearing on who he is now. They have their roles—the wise Alice Stavertons and Ralph Touchetts who only stand and wait—but the richness of character and moral worth reveal themselves best where the battle is hot, in acts and in the extended "action" which is reserved to the protagonist. (122–23)

Such readings share the view that the tale valorizes Brydon's priorities, while valuing Staverton primarily insofar as she validates his identity. Such readings do not take as problematic either the uncharacteristic sentimentality of the final scene or the appropriative implications of Staverton locking and keeping Brydon.[6]

Nonetheless, while viewing Staverton as a passive sounding board for a man's ideas rather than an active participant in the narrative action may be normative, it is not, I feel, correct and should not go unexamined. In fact, Alice Staverton's role in "The Jolly Corner," like so much of that tale, is an anomaly in James's canonical short fiction. Staverton, no less than Brydon, is situated in a complex historical and political world that, in her case, defines and constrains her options, priorities, and rhetorical strategies. The historical frame of James's tale encompasses the latter half of the nineteenth century (Brydon leaves the United States as a young man at about the time of the Civil War and returns just after the turn of the century), and James's representation of Staverton draws extensively on representations of women from early- to late-nineteenth-century Anglo-American discourses. I will also be drawing on texts even earlier than this explicit chronology (but, for the most part, coherent with the characters' plausible prenarrative biographies) in order better to suggest popular representations of women and women's political status that would constitute the discourse of women's power informing the historical reference of James's text. Such a focus reveals James's tale not as a mirror of a stable and coherent moment in history but as a text that represents, through its own flux and contradictions, an arena of social and cultural change.

This new perspective on Staverton's role in "The Jolly Corner" can productively follow the methodological revisions called for by feminist historians and literary critics. For example, Judith Fetterley argues that "the first act of the feminist critic [explicitly of American culture, but implicitly of all cultures] must be to become a resisting rather than an assenting reader" (xxii) of all texts that have become sedimented with masculinist critical priorities. The historian Carroll Smith-Rosenberg defines her own revisionist project by arguing that the major limitation of traditional historiography inheres in its viewing women as only acting roles in a male script:

> It fails to look for evidence of women's reaction, of the ways women manipulated men and events to create new fields of power or to assert female autonomy. . . . [Women's historians] see history as an ongoing struggle between women and men actors for control of the script, a struggle that ultimately transforms the play, the players—even the theater itself. But if we reject the view of women as passive victims, we face the need to identify the sources of power women used to act within a world determined to limit their power, to ignore their talents, to belittle or condemn their actions. (17)

To draw on Smith-Rosenberg's metaphor, Alice Staverton is more than a supporting actress in this tale; she is fully Brydon's cultural, if not his social and financial, equal. In three senses in particular—her actions, her imaginative boldness, and her rhetoric—she signals the complex historical dialectic marking the emergence of a new political strategy for American women. Historicizing Staverton's role throughout the tale, and particularly in the final section, helps us not only to grasp her place in the tale's social world, but also to account for the bizarre shift in James's tone and to avoid the masculine priorities that characterize much criticism of this tale.

V

It is important to note that Staverton is remarkably like Brydon in many ways. Both characters respond with dismay to modernity and its economic and cultural upheavals, to the shock of the new. Upon his return to New York after a thirty-three-year sojourn in Europe, Brydon stands repelled by the altered face of modern urban life and defines both himself and Staverton in opposition to modern life. He finds solace amidst modern disorder in two places: in his family home—the "jolly corner" of the title—and in Alice Staverton's flat, which he values as "a small still scene where items and shades, all delicate things, kept the sharpness of the notes of a high voice perfectly trained, and where economy hung about life like the scent of a garden" (439). Similarly, Alice Staverton's quarters in Irving Place, roughly like the jolly corner in their seclusion and in their associations, are *her* haven from New York life. As Brydon defines her,

> His old friend lived with one maid and herself dusted her relics and trimmed her lamps and polished her silver; she stood off, in the awful modern crush, when she could, but she sallied forth and did battle when the challenge was really to "spirit," the spirit she after all confessed to, proudly and a little shyly, as to that of the better time, that of *their* common, their quite far-away and antediluvian social period and order. (439)

Like Brydon's, Staverton's world seems a regressive one, opposing the "awful modern crush" at every crucial point. Her solitude, her quaintly anachronistic dusting of relics and trimming of lamps, and the arcane knowledge she shares with Brydon of their "antediluvian" past all suggest that Alice Staverton, like Brydon, is a genteel warrior against modernity.

Throughout "The Jolly Corner," we should recall, the two properties Brydon owns—his high-rise apartment house and his family home—represent two conflicting sets of values in American culture, an aggressive commercial life versus one of high ideality and culture, and serve as two poles around which many of the tale's other oppositions cluster. Santayana's tropological reading of the American skyscraper versus the colonial mansion figures as a metaphor for Brydon's two properties and also for the split within his own consciousness, embodying the contrast in "The Jolly Corner" between sentiment and traditional values on the one hand, and industrialization and modernization in general on the other. However, Santayana's image also offers a vantage point from which to reimagine Alice Staverton's role in what otherwise seems so patently Brydon's story.

A new constellation for the family emerged along with this perceived split in American culture. Many of the terms and contradictions associated with this domestic milieu inform the terms and contradictions represented in Alice Staverton's role in "The Jolly Corner." The American family responded to the emerging urban, industrial order by more systematically defining itself as a humane and consoling alternative to the world of ruthless and mechanized enterprise. This localized split, however, played off society at large in two contradictory ways—assuming an arguably new identity as what Lasch refers to as a "haven in a heartless world," while at the same time mirroring the split in American culture with its own stereotyped division of labor. John Ruskin, we recall, referred to the "true nature of home" as "the place of peace; the shelter, not only from all injury, but from all terror, doubt, and division" (quoted in Millett 98).[7] The Reverend Charles Burroughs articulated a version of this ideology in *An Address on Female Education,* in which he communicated this vision to young women in his audience:

> It is at home, where man . . . seeks a refuge from the vexations and embarrassments of business, an enchanting repose from exertion, a relaxation from care by the interchange of affection: where some of his finest sympathies, tastes, and moral and religious feelings are formed and nourished;—where is the treasury of pure disinterested love, such as is seldom found in . . . a selfish and calculating world. (quoted in Cott 64)

The woman's place in this domestic matrix was complicated by her being designated as the guardian—often the virtual embodiment—of the values associated with home and the family. The gendered terms of this ideological milieu permeate even technical and economic discourses of Victorian Anglo-American culture. According to the industrialist Peter Gaskell,

The moral influence of woman upon man's character and domestic happiness, is mainly attributable to her natural and instinctive habits. Her love, her tenderness, her affectionate solicitude for his comfort and enjoyment, her devotedness, her unwearying care, her maternal fondness, her conjugal attractions, exercise a most ennobling impression upon his nature, and do more towards making a good husband, a good father, and a useful citizen, than all the dogmas of political economy. (165) [8]

Gaskell's explicit contrast of the domestic and maternal role played by women with "all the dogmas of political economy" provides a powerful analogue to James's vision of the ideological work of gender in late-Victorian America; both imagine the realms of public and private life in tenuous opposition. According to Eli Zaretsky, in the nineteenth century,

> the housewife emerged, alongside the proletarian—the two characteristic labourers of developed capitalistic society. Her tasks extended beyond the material labour of the family to include responsibility for the "human values" which the family was thought to preserve: love, personal happiness, domestic felicity. . . . The split in society between "personal feelings" and "economic production" was integrated with the sexual division of labor. Women were identified with emotional life, men with the struggle for existence. (36)

Of course, "The Jolly Corner" is about neither housewives nor proletarians, but Gaskell's and Zaretsky's remarks nevertheless illuminate Alice Staverton's status in the world of "The Jolly Corner." Alice Staverton's role as guardian of human values takes the form of her quaint domesticity, her trimming of candles and polishing of lamps. It also appears in her urging Brydon to humanize the jolly corner by living in it and in her pillowing and cushioning him at the tale's conclusion. Her role as emotional guardian is reinforced by her nearly clairvoyant reading of Brydon's feelings. She has dreams in which Brydon's alter ego appears to her, suggesting the depth of her capacity to understand and accept.

The imagery associated with Staverton (and with the jolly corner) also situates her within the context of genteel and sacred Victorian womanhood. Harriet Beecher Stowe, for example, articulated the sanctification of the American housewife in *The Minister's Wooing* (1859): "priestess, wife, and mother, there she ministers daily in holy works of peace, and by faith and prayer and love redeems from grossness and earthliness the common toils and wants of life" (356). As Walter Houghton defines it, "the Victorian home was not only a peaceful, it was a sacred place," and a woman's place within that "temple of the hearth" was sanctified as well. Her "everyday relations and duties [within] the family were the most divine because they [were] the most human" (346–47). In a similar vein, Lasch argues that husbands and wives escaped from the "highly competitive and often brutal world of commerce and industry" by finding "solace and spiritual renewal in each other's company. The woman in particular would serve, in a well-worn nineteenth-century phrase, as an . . . angel of consolation" (5). Magazine literature and other popular literary genres throughout the nineteenth century voiced similar ideological platitudes. As early as 1830, the *Ladies' Magazine* issued a typical panegyric on the virtues of the model woman:

> See, she sits, she walks, she speaks, she looks—unutterable things! Inspiration springs up in her very paths—it follows her foot steps. A halo of glory envelops her, and illumines her whole orbit. With her, man not only feels safe but is actually renovated. For he approaches her with an awe, in reverence, and an affection which before he knew not he possessed. (83–84)

As Ann Douglas comments, the woman was "of value because she [was] able to work a religious transformation in man; she represents nothing finally but a state of susceptibility to very imprecisely conceived spiritual values" (52).

So nearly priestly a function of "womanly guidance" received "scientific" support in medical literature of the age, which often suggested that a woman's mysterious internal organs determined her behavior, though this position was usually used to subordinate women to the more rational male of the species. For example, in *The Sexes Here and Hereafter* (1869), William Holcombe, a physician, noted that

Another proof of the inferiority of woman is the wonderful secre-
tiveness . . . which she possesses. . . . Woman's secrecy is not
cunning; her dissimulation is not fraud. They are intuitions or
spiritual perceptions, full of tact and wisdom, leading her to con-
ceal or reveal, to speak or be silent, to do or not to do, exactly
at the right time and in the right place. (337)

Of course, poetic works such as Coventry Patmore's *The Angel in the
House* and Tennyson's *The Princess* provide literary representations of
the sexual division of labor characteristic of mid- and late-nineteenth-
century Anglo-American culture as well as of the sacred aura imposed
on women by male ideologues. As Carol Christ comments on these
poems, "woman possesses a purity, a self-sufficiency, a wholeness, but
man, for Tennyson as for Patmore, is disjointed, never at peace" (Vicinus 154).

Such vague, religious associations, in fact, characterize Alice Staverton's role throughout "The Jolly Corner." Brydon himself asserts her
redemptive powers when, upon waking up in Alice's lap, he refers
to the "mystifying grace of her appearance" (439) and when he asserts, "Yes—I can only have died. You brought me literally to life. . . .
only, in the name of all the benedictions, how?" (480). Brydon's other
spiritualized terms for Staverton's agency—virtue, charity, and beatitude—only confirm the divine role she plays for him.

At this point one might conclude that Staverton's role in "The Jolly
Corner" is normative—that she represents trivialized genteel femininity and that the jolly corner and a "woman's sphere" are roughly
synonymous zones. Staverton could be seen, then, as the angel of the
jolly corner (a divine and consoling alternative to the beastly specter
that confronts Brydon), as an agent of the love implicitly absent
from Brydon's "chilled adolescence," or as a successful May Bartram
who triumphs where her predecessor had failed. These interpretive
options correspond roughly to the prevailing critical assessments of
Staverton's role—as a divine center of love, as an image of maternal
care and affection, or as a sensitive auditor for Brydon's privileged anguish. But if critics of "The Jolly Corner" have responded to these significant narrative details, they have tended to abstract and/or mythi-
cize them rather than to situate them historically, and consequently

have simplified the very attitudes they attempt to elucidate. In fact, the very genteel traits Brydon associates with his childhood home as a strategy for escaping from contemporary realities function in exactly the opposite fashion for Staverton. That is, they are, perhaps paradoxically, signs of her engagement with and manipulation of the very forces of modernity Brydon shrinks away from. One might argue that Brydon is "feminized" (or at least constructed as weak and passive) by his affiliation with the discourses and habits of gentility. Quite the contrary, Staverton is "masculinized" (or at least empowered in ways commonly assumed available only to men) by her mobilization of a rhetoric and praxis associated with Victorian femininity. Brydon's characterization of the world he returns to as "topsy-turvy," in other words, is right on the money, although certainly not in the ways he intends.

vi

While Staverton does embody a suggestive array of traits definitive of the trivialized bourgeois matron, she both deploys those traits strategically and also strains against the conventions in a manner that marks an important departure from an earlier mode and signals the emergence of a new strategy of feminine politics. As critics of the "cult of domesticity" have argued, the notion of a "woman's sphere" had the virtue of opening certain religious and political options to women, but it also contained them within a sphere distinctly separate and not equal. Nancy F. Cott, for one, notes,

> the canon of domesticity did not directly challenge the modern organization of work and pursuit of wealth. Rather, it accommodated and promised to temper them. The values of domesticity undercut opposition to exploitative pecuniary standards in the work world, by upholding a "separate sphere" of comfort and compensation, instilling a morality that would encourage self-control, and fostering the idea that preservation of home and family sentiment was an ultimate goal. (69)

Cott also suggests that this implicit weakness of domestic resistance was appropriated by male ministers: "In their sermons of the 1830's the theme of order in family and society took precedence, vividly emphasizing the necessity for women to be subordinate to and dependent on their husbands" (158). It is important to note that the narrative moments situating Staverton within the so-called cult of domesticity tend to be either remarks made by Brydon or perspectives mirroring *his* priorities—they are not remarks made by Staverton nor are they perspectives consistent with how we see her independently of Brydon's commentary. We can, then, profitably shift our focus to Staverton's own words and actions in order to fashion our understanding of her role in the tale.

Staverton is not simply a feminine version of the tale's male protagonist—her differences from Brydon are many and significant. In one important respect, Staverton's status as a single woman in turn-of-the-century United States distinguishes her, though such unmarried women were regarded as problems for a male economy, not successes as New Women. According to Lasch, a rising divorce rate and a falling birthrate among "better sorts" in late-nineteenth-century American cities constituted a national problem. While Theodore Roosevelt addressed the "problem" of sluggish birthrates among middle-class white women (Lasch 8–9), medical science was representing the unmarried woman as a significant health risk. According to Carroll Smith-Rosenberg and Charles Rosenberg,

> the maiden lady, many physicians argued, was fated to a greater incidence of both physical and emotional disease than her married sisters and to a shorter life-span. Her nervous system was placed under constant pressure, and her unfulfilled reproductive organs—especially at menopause—were prone to cancer and other degenerative ills. (336)

Apparently, single men were a hardier breed. Even while reading such warnings as ideological prescription rather than "scientific" description, however, we can situate the supposed dangers Alice Staverton, and other women like her, were risking as a powerful challenge to Brydon's imagining himself in danger on a "big-game" hunt (a veiled allusion to Roosevelt's own "vigorous" pursuits?). Indicating that single women were perceived as a "problem" on the other side of the Atlantic, the British manufacturer W. R. Greg complained of

an enormous and increasing number of single women in the
nation, a number quite disproportionate and quite abnormal . . .
who, not having the natural duties and labours of wives and
mothers, have to carve out artificial and painfully sought occu-
pations for themselves; who, in place of completing, sweetening,
and embellishing the existence of others, are compelled to lead
an independent and incomplete existence of their own. (436)

To this extent, women were, paradoxically, blamed for a perceived
decline in birthrates and crisis in family (and in England, class) stability even while they were pitied as victims of recent economic and
industrial transformations. Staverton's ability to weather such ideological assaults on the viability of single womanhood is at least a partial indication of her ability to withstand potentially hostile trends in
public opinion while adhering to her own image of her life. Staverton's apparent physical health in the midst of traumatic urban change
is even noted by Brydon when he remarks that her physical appearance "defied you to say if she were a fair young woman who looked
older through trouble, or a fine smooth older one who looked young
through successful indifference" (439–40).

Staverton's strengths and inner resources as well as her adaptability
to cultural and social transformation are represented directly in a
variety of other ways. While distinctly "genteel" and refined (though,
perhaps, embattled), she nonetheless operates actively within modern New York on its own terms. For example, she stands off from
the modern crush when possible, but "she sallied forth and did
battle when the challenge was really to 'spirit'" (430), and she rides
the streetcars and confronts "all the public concussions and ordeals"
(439). She admires both Brydon's skill in debating a construction
company representative as well as the knowledge of building techniques he exhibits. Staverton again demonstrates a greater imaginative response to New York and to Brydon's potential when she suggests to Brydon that, had he only remained in New York, "he would
have anticipated the inventor of the sky-scraper" (440), words that
eventually precipitate Brydon's search for the other self he might have
become. Staverton, we realize, is capable of articulating an alternative history for Brydon, one in which she understands the kind of

aggressive enterprise, invention, and complicity in a new economic and urban order that Brydon feels is only monstrous and ugly.

She also demonstrates a bolder imagination by envisioning in her dreams the grizzled self Brydon might have become had he stayed in New York, while Brydon, we recall, faints away at the hideous sight of this alter ego. As Staverton attempts to reeducate Brydon concerning the identity of his Other in the tale's final moments, her question as to why she shouldn't have liked the "black stranger"

> brought Spencer Brydon to his feet. "You 'like' that horror—?"
>
> "I *could* have liked him. And to me," she said, "he was no horror. I had accepted him."
>
> "'Accepted'—?" Brydon oddly sounded.
>
> "Before, for the interest of his difference—yes. And as *I* did n't disown him, as *I* knew him—which you at last, confronted with him in his difference, so cruelly did n't, my dear—well, he must have been, you see, less dreadful to me." (484)

The important difference in this and other similar exchanges is that where Brydon polarizes his identity from that of his Other (and the jolly corner from his skyscraper), Staverton attempts to undo the imagined opposition between Brydon and the self he might have become. Both Staverton's recurring dreams of this grizzled figure and her explicit remarks about accepting him, then, suggest the extent to which she has confronted the competitive and potentially disarming forces of cultural and social transformation. Brydon rejects this vision; Staverton integrates it.

We can return to the architectural trope for Brydon's real estate for a final illustration of this point. Remember that, when Brydon imagines an absolute split between the jolly corner and his soon-to-be-gentrified high-rise, Staverton challenges his distinction between these two worlds when she remarks to Brydon, as he is badgered by others to commercialize the jolly corner in addition to his apartments: "In short you 're to make so good a thing of your sky-scraper that, living in luxury on *those* ill-gotten gains, you can afford for a while to be sentimental here!" (444). Staverton has an unflinchingly realistic perspective; she understands that one needs to be able to *afford* to be sentimental. Rather than representing antithetical worlds, Brydon's two properties, in Staverton's vision, are mutually constitutive of a new urban formation in which the interrelationship of culture and economics is no longer veiled or deniable but made manifest. Whereas Brydon's vision is one of unresolved and antagonistic polarities, Staverton grasps and argues for the interpenetration of the tale's two worlds. Any self-respecting "angel in the house" would almost certainly fear to tread this path toward a new urban, industrial order.

In *Disorderly Conduct: Visions of Gender in Victorian America*, Smith-Rosenberg provides a useful historical paradigm for Staverton's divergences from an earlier domestic model. During the 1870s and 1880s, Smith-Rosenberg notes,

> a new bourgeois woman had emerged. Confident and independent, a self-created urban expert, she spearheaded bourgeois efforts to respond creatively to the new city and the new economy. In the process of working for herself and other women, she had begun to demand equality in education, in employment, and in wages. Certain of her own abilities, she began again to demand the vote, so as to implement her new social visions more effectively. In short, she had politicized gender. (175)

I do not intend to suggest that Alice Staverton fully embodies the traits Smith-Rosenberg attributes to this new female crusader or that she represents an unambiguous and stable image of women in turn-of-the-century United States. Staverton is in some respects too patient (she waits thirty-some years for Brydon's return) and too passive (it is possible that she imagines a union with Brydon as the fulfillment of her life). She nonetheless represents in her actions as well as in her response to a new economic and social order some of the traits Smith-Rosenberg cites as definitive markers of this New Woman. Staverton also represents some of the historically specific options made available to women following the power and labor shortages brought on by the Civil War. Women entering public activity following the war acquired experience in industrial organization and political mobilization, and by so doing recognized not only their independence but their ability to effect social change as well. Mary Jo Buhle describes the memberships of popular women's clubs as many "well educated and leisured" women who were otherwise "deprived of serious social intercourse" (56); such social memberships and activities enabled women to empower themselves, both socially and politically.

This instrumental role is most significantly represented in Staverton's speech. Staverton's apparent lack of a decisive (or at least an unambiguous) voice may be the result of her being subordinated in a position so manifestly dictated by the male hegemony over mass culture. That we see her more than we hear her in the tale may suggest that Staverton counters the dominance both of men and of voice represented in "The Jolly Corner" with an array of tactics meant to preempt Brydon's own attempt to control the world through his own economic and political practice. Her problem is that Brydon simply does not comprehend any of her statements, even those of assurance, support, or acceptance, because they are articulated from a position alien to his own social, economic, and gendered perspective. However, while Staverton's direct role is limited to the first and third sections of the tale, where she exists primarily as a discursive presence that confounds Brydon as much as her physical presence consoles him, she might also be understood as the precipitating agency in the narrative, motivating even the protracted and stylistically demanding account of Brydon's search for his Other in the second section of "The Jolly Corner." For example, after she broaches the topic of what Brydon might have become had he only stayed at home, his growing obsession with his potential alter ego produces in him a defensiveness that makes him bristle and interpret her assurances as challenges. Moreover, after Staverton intimates that, though "quite huge and monstrous," Brydon's other self would not have been entirely contemptible, Brydon asks, "You'd have liked me that way?" to which his friend gently responds, "How should I not have liked you?" Entirely missing the implied reconciliation as well as the imaginative strength in Staverton's answer, Brydon wrongly concludes, "I see. You'd have liked me, have preferred me, a billionaire!" Staverton immediately once more counters, "How should I not have liked you?" (450), but the point is lost on Brydon. He is incapable of comprehending the discourse of a feminine Other.

"The Jolly Corner" concludes, however, with an embrace and a pledge of unity to seal Staverton's and Brydon's apparently shared understanding of Brydon's relationship with his Other, not with a further exacerbation of their rhetorical impasse:

> Then, "He has a million a year," he lucidly added. "But he has n't you."
> "And he is n't—no, he is n't—*you!*" she murmured as he drew her to his breast. (485)

Staverton's hesitation in this final sentence along with her many remarks earlier in the tale suggest that Brydon's identity is not so simply separated from that of his Other. In addition to having seen Brydon's Other twice in dreams (452), Staverton's understanding of this "ghost" and all its implications might be more familiar than the story can narrate. Indeed, such intimacy would align not only Staverton, but James as well, with an important history of characters in "ghost stories by American women." According to Lynnette Carpenter and Wendy K. Kolmar, ghost stories by American women represent a significant challenge to "the assumptions of men's work in the genre. . . . women often seem to develop their stories in conscious antithesis to men's stories" (10). Especially in terms of how they reject the dualistic thinking that would pit reason against unreason, science against nature, faith against doubt, and so forth, women writers of ghost stories bring an inherently deconstructive habit of mind to their tales and are "more likely to portray natural and supernatural experience along a continuum. Boundaries between the two are not absolute but fluid, so that the supernatural can be accepted, connected with, reclaimed, and can often possess a familiarity" (12). Rejecting rigid categories of reason and unreason also enables women to replace reason with sympathy: "the valuing of the quality of sympathy shows the affinity of these American women's stories with consolation literature, which, in keeping with the feminine ideology promulgated by the Beechers, privileged sentiment and feeling over reason and intellect" (13–14). As a result of this alternative orientation, women work beyond such responses as horror or terror before the supernatural and, instead, "realize their commonality with the ghostly women and children they encounter and are often called upon to understand and act upon the messages brought by those who haunt their houses"

(14). These generic constituents defined by Carpenter and Kolmar mesh almost exactly with Staverton's understanding of both Brydon and his spectral Other. Sympathetic and consolatory rather than defensive and denying, Staverton enacts the role most frequently given to women characters by women authors, and, by so doing, she is capable of a radically alternative response to the ghost. Moreover, she is capable of negotiating her own and Brydon's relationship with this Other in a manner that empowers her in her future dealings with Brydon. James's affinity with American women writers of ghost stories might well be another example of the vampiristic relationship Alfred Habegger argues characterized many of James's covert appropriations of themes and plots from women writers whose works he savaged in reviews. On the other hand, such similarities might also simply indicate a shared belief in the gendered differences between male and female characters, as Carpenter and Kolmar's anatomy of women's ghost writing draws heavily on conventional breakdowns of male and female interpersonal and social behaviors. On the other hand, Staverton's circuitous discourse also points to the possibility that, in these final lines, she may well be lying, agreeing with Brydon not because she actually shares his perception (we know, in fact, that in many specifics she doesn't), but because she realizes that by corroborating Brydon's interpretation she accomplishes a significant transformation of his priorities and her future.

vii

How do we account for what appears to be a lie, however, in the context of this tale's representation of gendered political struggle? We might refer to Marlow's lie to Kurtz's intended—a lie Marlow justifies as a strategy to protect the woman from a truth too dark for her to comprehend or bear. Staverton's prevarication would reverse the gender roles—here a woman protects an aging man from a truth too horrible for him to bear—but it also secures an emotional (and perhaps financial and political) victory for her. We might also turn to another late James work for significant intertextual resonance. Alice Staverton's subtle, yet authoritative and successful, verbal ministrations can be read as a later examination of what Maggie Verver accomplishes in

The Golden Bowl.[9] While very different in age, both Verver and Staverton operate in linguistically subtle and strategic ways to achieve and protect their visions of their lives and futures. Both do so by lying.

Elizabeth Allen's *A Woman's Place in the Novels of Henry James* is so compatible with my argument that I will briefly summarize her position on Maggie Verver in order to establish Maggie's relationship with her successor, Alice Staverton. Central to James's representation of women is the struggle between their existing as *signs* for male interpretation and consumption and as *selves* capable either of becoming interpreters of others or of mystifying (and thereby manipulating) the process whereby men transform women into grist for their masculinist interpretive mills. A woman's function in *The Golden Bowl*, according to Allen, is "to mediate experience for those [men] in control; to order either by representation, or by arranging existing appearances and making sense of them" (185–86). Maggie Verver succeeds largely by mastering the linguistic channels through which social (and domestic) reality is mediated and by mastering linguistic signs and the arrangements they are meant to signify; in this way she triumphs in controlling the delicate and, for women, potentially destructive dynamics of social *and* sexual intercourse. As Allen argues,

> If Maggie is to preserve social form and take her place within it . . . she has to function in recognizable forms, speak understandable language. The fact that this involves lying and deceit reminds us of the self-assertion that is simultaneous within this process of repair and conservation. Maggie pretends to be a fool, she pretends to be an unchallenged and unchallenging wife. . . . Her selfhood is asserted through concealment, her signification is that of opacity and mystery and she gains, if not the intimacy of being, for another, her self, at least the attention of the Prince. (195–96)

Allen's description of Maggie Verver's triumphant rearrangement of the domestic relations at the conclusion of *The Golden Bowl* touches on what I regard as Alice Staverton's similarly successful transformation of Brydon at the conclusion of "The Jolly Corner" in a number of ways. Both Verver and Staverton confront threats to their futures, and, after coming to understandings of these crises, both privately formulate strategies for combating them. Both deploy subtle verbal manipulations of the realities they share with the other characters — they articulate and promote versions of the past and present to insure that the future unfolds according to their terms. Finally, the strategies and successes of both women remain unknown to the men whose realities they were designed to disrupt. Completed just a few years after the publication of *The Golden Bowl*, "The Jolly Corner" can be read as James's projection of the verbal and gendered dynamics of his late novelistic work, replete with overt sexual and economic issues, into the work of his late tales, in which the characters' greater ages and barely examined social and financial statuses seem to mystify, if not to suppress, explicit questions of sexual and financial power.

In addition to furthering James's analysis into discursive strategies available to women, Staverton's oblique approach to cornering Brydon has analogues in the political discourses of disenfranchised women in the nineteenth century. Speaking about the paradoxical position of middle-class women in nineteenth-century America, Ann Douglas notes that a woman's future quite literally depended "on the willingness and ability of her male peers, increasingly absorbed in the tasks of settlement and competition, to recognize the values which their activity apparently denied" (223). Although women played active roles in political and social undertakings such as antiwar and temperance movements, Douglas reminds us "women were more likely . . . to evince their concern by less direct and conspicuous means" (83). For example, Harriet Farley, one of the editors of the *Lowell Offering*, advocated "picniques" over strikes as an appropriate vehicle for feminine protest against factory conditions. By way of rationalizing so delicate and arguably ineffective a strategy, Farley explained:

> To convince people, we must gain access to them: to do this we cannot assault them with opinions contrary to their own. We cannot harm them by revealing the deprivation which could suggest our rage and their danger. We must sugarcoat the proverbial pill. . . . we must "do good by stealth." (quoted in Douglas 83–84) [10]

Alice Staverton succeeds at winning Brydon to her point of view by precisely such nonconfrontational means.

If we read (as critics have tended to read) Alice Staverton's circumvention of direct confrontation ahistorically, her goals might appear simply regressive and domestic, and her apparent complicity in enabling Brydon to reject the significance of his Other could be read as a lie which caters to Brydon's vision. By historicizing the tale's complex representation of social and sexual struggle, however, we can also discern within this moment Alice Staverton's own deployment of the subtle political action that Farley advocates, suggested in the "way her hands clasped and locked his head," in her face staying "clingingly close" to Brydon's, in her assertion "And now I keep you" (480), and, finally, in the likelihood that she has transformed Brydon, has "won" him to her vision of his past and their future. Alice Staverton gently, though effectively, closes off Brydon's private search for his true self and opens him up to her ministrations, which, in sharp contrast to those of an "angel in the house," will escape domestic containment and extend into the realm of social and political organization. And, like Maggie Verver's "lies" in *The Golden Bowl,* Staverton's "lie" (as well as her clasping and locking Brydon's head) can also be regarded as thoroughly conscious, an exercise of women's historically specific political praxis calculated to generate a new social arrangement.

Ann Douglas argues that the mission of the heroine in women's historical novels in the nineteenth century "is to free the hero from history: she rescues him paradoxically from the historical novel, which she transmutes into a domestic tale" (221). "The Jolly Corner" begins in a complex historical world filled with the material facts of newly modernized and internally divided America and with Spencer Brydon's struggle to grasp his place in so contradictory a world. The tale ends with Staverton and Brydon falling into each others' arms, repudiating (or at least tabling) the potentially disruptive social significance of Brydon's Other, while possibly ushering in a newly feminized social order. Brydon's willingly accepting Staverton's agency in his life offers a fitting conclusion to the tale—Staverton has Brydon cornered, as it were, in the jolly corner.

This political struggle also registers in the generic flux of the tale. The first section of "The Jolly Corner" reads like Howellsian realism, replete with amply documented urban landscapes, architectural detail, and an account of the characters' lives amidst a volatile urban scene. The third section, on the other hand, reads like domestic romance, but romance with a political difference. Whatever emotional energies the final pages represent are framed within Staverton's subtly politicized operations in modern New York. It is not, then, completely accurate to argue that Staverton rescues Brydon from the historical narrative (as Douglas's model might suggest). More precisely, Staverton's words and actions initiate Brydon into a different historical experience, one that produces the generic transformations within James's tale. In this respect, Staverton's "lie" is not a sacrifice of the "truth" of Brydon's condition as much as it is a recasting of the very grounds of truth in an emerging urban order in which women are no longer subordinate figures.

viii

How does one account for the contradictions characterizing Staverton's role in "The Jolly Corner"? One might recall that the tropes situating her as the angel of the jolly corner are Brydon's, or at least come from a narrative voice representing Brydon's perspective, and that another view of Staverton emerges once we focus on *her* words and actions. I have argued that the array of differences in James's text can be approached from the perspective of gender analysis and sexual politics. We might also note, however, that Brydon's perspective corresponds not only to a male definition of a woman's role but to an earlier historical era as well, dating roughly from the time of his leaving the United States for Europe, or even before that. Staverton's "disorderly conduct" happens to correspond more closely with an image of women's power and priorities roughly coincidental with the tale's narrative present. Brydon represents his friend, then, in largely anachronistic terms. Staverton, despite some arguably arcane habits, presents herself in a grammar (of actions and words) both more contemporary and more complex. In terms of James's narrative, this difference points to the important implications of Brydon's and Staverton's respective histories. Brydon, absent from the United States for over thirty years, returns with outdated notions of cultural and social forces, of the urban landscape as well as of women's place. Like Julian West in Edward Bellamy's *Looking Backward*, Brydon confronts the present with the vocabulary of the past. Staverton, presumably as a result of her remaining in New York, embodies a variety of progressive skills and strategies. Like many a character in Howells or Dreiser, indeed, like many a realist author, Staverton is energized by the pulse of an active and changing American urban reality. In other words, James's text lies on the margins of the genre of naturalism, suggesting a close and crucial connection between one's material and historical conditions and one's ideological assumptions and conduct.

To shift briefly to a different vocabulary, Brydon's perspective corresponds roughly to what Raymond Williams terms "residual," while Staverton represents Williams's notion of "emergent," cultural forces. For Williams, any dominant cultural formation is characterized by "internal dynamic relations" and contains elements both residual of earlier forms and emergent of transformations to come. The "residual" means, in Williams's lexicon, practices and structures of feeling formed in the past but "still active in the cultural process, not only and often not at all as an element of the past, but as an effective element of the present" (*Marxism and Literature* 122). The emergent, on the other hand, marks "new meanings and values, new practices, new relationships and kinds of relationship [that] are continually being created," usually in "relation to the emergence and growing strength of a class" (123, 125). The differences inscribed within "The Jolly Corner" between Brydon and Staverton as well as between Brydon's view of Staverton and her own self-presentation suggest a dynamic of cultural and gendered struggle analogous to that which Williams argues characterizes any cultural moment.

Two recent feminist perspectives corroborate Williams's vision. Amidst the fluidity of late-nineteenth-century America, Elizabeth Allen notes,

> one might expect to find change, even progress, in the role and status of women. What one does find is a confusing mix of old and new ideology, of women as somehow more than anything the example of the new nation with new freedoms, and yet at the same time more than anything the constant amidst flux, the paragon of perennial domesticity and, again, social relations. (18)

Mary Poovey offers a compatible reading of such "uneven developments" when she argues that the ideological formation of mid-
Victorian England

> was uneven both in the sense of being experienced differently
> by individuals who were positioned differently within the social
> formation (by sex, class, or race, for example) and in the sense
> of being articulated differently by the different institutions, dis-
> courses, and practices that it both constituted and was consti-
> tuted by. (3)

Poovey's work also provides important insight into the difficulty of
identifying the roles that women played in the emergence of feminist
politics, when she addresses the likelihood that women working out
of the public view and "behind the scenes," as it were, were often as
important as more public spokeswomen for women's rights (21–22).
Such is, in fact, the cultural fluidity and historical stutter represented
by Alice Staverton's role.[11]

Alice Staverton's differences from earlier historical and literary representations of women's ideas and practices, then, can be read as
marking the emergence of a new set of strategies and options for
women. That those options are not yet consolidated in James's text
but exist in solution with an earlier, anachronistic view of Staverton
suggests the troubled history of any new area of political practice. In
fact, "The Jolly Corner" reinscribes similar fissures of these modern
social and historical upheavals within the tale's contradictory social,
material, and architectural tropes. Nothing exists simply or self-
identically in the world of "The Jolly Corner." We have in this late tale
an example of a shadow narrative, suppressed by virtue of its under-
determination throughout the tale, erupting from within the framework of James's dominant thematics, those centering on Spencer Brydon, and recasting the entire narrative. Whereas Brydon is remarkably
like other late narrators such as John Marcher from "The Beast in the
Jungle" and George Stransom from "The Altar of the Dead," in terms
of his extreme narcissism and the corresponding impact it has on his
potential heterosexual relations, Alice Staverton departs significantly
from virtually all other female characters in these so-called bachelor
tales. Whereas the majority of these characters wait passively in the

hope that the intensely solipsistic males of their desires will eventually acknowledge their love, Staverton shepherds Brydon through his own subjectivist crisis and, through her aggressive surveillance of his activities and engagement with his fate, enacts a transformative shift in his consciousness. The novelty of the tale's conclusion, therefore, stems not only from its departure from James's usual despairing closure, but also from the forceful intrusion of the largely unrepresented "disorderly conduct" of Staverton, conduct that we grasp, albeit imperfectly, only in the tale's final moments, when the conventional Jamesian conclusion fails to materialize *and* when Staverton's machinations successfully coalesce in her own empowerment.

6 "THE EASIEST ROOM IN HELL": THE POLITICAL WORK OF DISNEY'S *DUMBO*

Ah, *Dumbo;* sure be good to get my mind off things for a while.
—Robert Stack as General Stilwell, preparing to attend
a screening of *Dumbo* in Steven Spielberg's *1941*

The child's laughter is pure until he first laughs at a clown.
—Angela Carter, *Nights at the Circus*

During a momentary respite from his journey down the Mississippi with Jim, the King, and the Duke, Huck Finn goes to a circus in Arkansas. At one point Huck is surprised by an apparently drunken man who stumbles into the ring and insists on riding one of the circus horses, and he narrates the ensuing scene:

> The minute he was on, the horse began to rip and tear and jump, and cavort around, with two circus men hanging onto his bridle trying to hold him, and the drunk man hanging onto his neck, and his heels flying in the air every jump, and the whole crowd of people standing up shouting and laughing till the tears rolled down. And at last, sure enough, all the circus men could do, the horse broke loose, and away he went like the very nation, round and round the ring, with that sot laying down on him and hanging to his neck, with first one leg hanging most to the ground on one side, and then t'other one on t'other side, and the people just crazy. It warn't funny to me, though, I was all of a tremble to see his danger. (193)

Of course, every person at the circus save Huck knows that the entire scene is part of the circus's entertainment, and it is difficult not to wonder just how ignorant Huck can be not to catch on. The episode underscores one of Mark Twain's central points—that in the slaveholding world of the American South, every imaginable facet of existence is contaminated by the viciousness, the violence, and the total disregard for human life that can generate a form of amusement which pivots on a person appearing to be in mortal danger. That this circus scene is situated immediately after Colonel Sherburn's murder of Old Boggs and immediately before the King and the Duke's "Royal Nonesuch" foregrounds the connection between entertainment, profiteering, and cold-blooded murder in antebellum American culture.

Mark Twain's fictional world is one in which every segment of society is characterized, if not defined, by violence. Pap Finn, the King and the Duke, the riverboat criminals, Colonel Sherburn, and the entire crowd of Arkansas bumpkins duped by the "Royal Nonesuch" embody the most obvious forms of violence, exploitation, and oppression, physical, verbal, and psychological. Judge Thatcher, while a minor character, nonetheless presides over the entire politico-juridical order that sanctions the brutality of the slave economy and culture, and the otherwise "good and kind" characters such as the widow and Miss Watson, Miss Judith Loftus, the Grangerfords, and the Phelpses reinforce the cultural, social, and religious parameters of the slave system. Even Tom Sawyer is defined by games such as ambushing and killing racial Others and tying Jim "to a tree for fun," not to mention the elaborate and degrading rituals he forces Jim to submit to on the Phelps farm. This is an entire world defined by fraud, cruelty, and violence, and the only option available to Huck at the end of the novel is to "light out for the Territory" in hopes of escaping the corrupt civilization that has framed his and Jim's journey throughout the narrative. To remain within this culture and to be constructed in any way by its codes of behavior and literacy is perforce to be implicated in the rituals of violence and debasement of intelligence that define Mark Twain's anatomy of southern slave culture. Both the physical violence and the intellectual corruptions we witness have specific racist functions but also permeate virtually all relations in the novel, including the scenes of physical child abuse by Pap Finn and Jim and the cursing by the widow, who calls Huck "a poor lost lamb" and "a lot of other names too" upon his return at the novel's beginning. As in the scene in *Adventures of Huckleberry Finn* wherein Tom Sawyer can, in his childish preparation for adult racist violence and lynchings, tie Jim to a tree for fun, *Dumbo*, Walt Disney's 1941 animated classic, stages various images of violence and degradation in American culture and social unrest at a level palatable for children.

In fact, we might draw an extended comparison concerning the centrality of exclusionary violence, exploitation, and humiliation in the worlds of both *Huckleberry Finn* and *Dumbo*. While Leonard Maltin could define *Dumbo* as "the nicest, kindest Disney yet," adding that "it has the most heart, taste, beauty, compassion, skill, restraint" (53), *Dumbo* is in many ways not at all a film suitable for children, as is the case with much of Disney's animated work. More accurately, I believe, *Dumbo* is a film that, if suitable for children at all, caters to a desire for terror and pain eradicated only by a momentary and fragmentary resolution. I agree with Michael Wilmington, who has characterized *Dumbo* as a "heartrending portrait of pain, degradation, and despair" in which we "see the world as little Dumbo does, an arena of vast, painful, and at times, incomprehensible struggle" (77). In this respect, *Dumbo* and most of the Disney Studio's other animated classics function as threshold moments in the diverse and flexible genre of horror films; they may serve (as do Mark Twain's *Adventures of Huckleberry Finn* and *Adventures of Tom Sawyer*) to prepare children for horror, pain, perhaps even war, and for the socially significant (and perhaps necessary) construction of horror within cultural forms.[1] Such a claim comports with the critique of Disney mounted by Frankfurt School critical theorists as early as the 1930s. Theodor Adorno and Max Horkheimer, for example, focused on the sadistic strain in Donald Duck features: "Donald Duck in the cartoons, like the unfortunate in real life, gets his beating so that the viewers can get used to the same treatment." And, as Walter Benjamin noted in the mid-1930s, even the early Mickey Mouse films require their audiences "to put up comfortably with bestiality and cruelty as corollaries of existence" (quoted in Hansen 35). *Dumbo* is accounted for by Benjamin's critique quite well, requiring us to internalize the pain and exploitation it inflicts upon its baby protagonist. As we will see, the loose ends of Disney's classic even require us to identify with Dumbo and his mother as they blissfully elide the many issues of social and economic exploitation raised during the film's sixty-three minutes and the pair ride into a future in which they, at least, are no longer the victims of immediate and forceful institutional violence. *Adventures of Huckleberry Finn* and *Dumbo* both stage and elicit the "laughter of the cinema audience," which, as Adorno remarks in a letter to Benjamin, is "anything but good and revolutionary; instead, it is full of the worst bourgeois sadism" (quoted in Bloch 124).

Whereas Disney classics such as *Snow White, Sleeping Beauty,* and, more recently, *The Little Mermaid* pivot on threats to children and families posed by witches, dragons, evil queens, and other largely supernatural agents, *Dumbo,* while participating in the convention of children separated from their mothers so definitive of Disney films, has more in common with features such as *Bambi, Cinderella,* and the more recent *The Rescuers Down Under* and, with certain animated license, *Beauty and the Beast* and *Aladdin,* in which the locus of evil and pain is specified as more plausibly, or at least more recognizably, "real" and social. In *Bambi,* "man" in the form of voracious hunters and careless smokers threatens the baby creatures and the stability of the forest ecosystem; in *Cinderella,* greed and a fierce preference for her biological daughters drive the evil stepmother; and in *The Rescuers Down Under,* the poaching of endangered species and the abuse of children constitute the film's ecological and moral crises. The villains in *Beauty and the Beast* and *Aladdin* are characterized by their rampant machismo and sexism and human greed, respectively.[2] *The Lion King,* even with its complete elimination of any human presence, nonetheless represents the villainous Scar as power-hungry and loaded with resentment over his brother's position as "king." For all its lushly animated and brilliantly dramatized animal protagonists, *Dumbo,* like these films, hinges on and explores a decidedly human condition: life under capitalism on the verge of one of humanity's greatest crises, World War II. Like Mark Twain's circus, the circus in *Dumbo* is an inescapable and hellish environment characterized by greed, profit, dehumanization, and exploitation; it shares with films such as *The Rescuers Down Under* and *Bambi* a vision of life threatened by politicized human agency.

Dumbo, however, is utterly unlike these and all other Disney films in one crucial respect. Disney animated films conclude in every other case with the extermination of the source of evil and with the suggestion of better, if not halcyon, days ahead: the witch turned into a dragon is slain at the conclusion of *Sleeping Beauty;* Captain Hook is dispensed with by a crocodile and the children's rigid father is softened to conclude *Peter Pan;* in *The Little Mermaid* Ursula the sea witch is (like the witch in *Sleeping Beauty)* impaled, this time on a sharp ship's prow; the wicked stepmother is exposed, humiliated, and rendered powerless by Cinderella's marriage; the sinister poacher and the braggart, Gaston, fall to rocky deaths at the conclusions of *The Rescuers Down Under* and *Beauty and the Beast* respectively; and the Machiavellian political advisor, Jafar, receives his due when *he* is forced to live out at least ten thousand years squashed into a magic lamp at the conclusion of *Aladdin.* Hyenas devour the fratri- and regicide, Scar, albeit offscreen, in *The Lion King.* Even in the naturalistic world of *Bambi,* the coming of spring and the vision of a mature Bambi and Faline with their newborn twins, while not a guarantee of living happily ever after, signal a conclusion in which the primary adversaries seem to have been bested by the resilience of natural process and the triumph of true love. However traumatic and horrifying their central crises, Disney films generally conclude, in accord with comic conventions, with marriages, celebrations, and rebirths. But in *Dumbo,* the circus, portrayed throughout the film as an arena of pain, humiliation, thwarted desire, hierarchical elitism, incompetence, exploitation, and greed, emerges triumphant at the film's conclusion, and is significantly strengthened by Dumbo's ability to fly, which translates directly into his viability and profitability as an act. In fact, Dumbo, mocked, rejected, exiled, and abused throughout the film, comes to constitute the circus's *most* profitable act. The locus of evil is, therefore, not merely unchastened and unvanquished, but consolidated and further empowered—its dominant ideology is reinforced and reconstituted; its disciplinary and economic apparatus strengthened—by the very subject that had suffered most under its tyrannical operations.

The conclusion of *Dumbo* is troubled by far more than these loose ends, this decidedly uncharacteristic climax. Immediately preceding the film's final scene of Dumbo and mother reunited and enjoying what appear to be the plush amenities of a streamlined circus train car—their easiest room in this modernized and secular hell—a series of newspaper headlines registers the implications of Dumbo's uncanny ability to fly. Those headlines strain at the film's margins, linking this narrative world (complete with talking animals, impossible circus acts, and a range of fantastical images and motifs) with a social and political world hovering just beyond the narrative's boundaries. The headlines branch out to the worlds of insurance corporations, the Hollywood film industry, scientific exploits, and World War II. It is in light of these images of corporate hegemony and mass destruction that the blithe denials of *Dumbo's* conclusion require careful scrutiny. By introducing an excess of referential significance which cannot be contained within the parameters of the narrative's conventional frame, these headlines and the world they insert within *Dumbo* destabilize the very closure meant to resolve the film's generative crises. Again, once the primary narrative themes of Disney's film stray into the realm of the social world otherwise elided by *Dumbo,* that social world and the tensions elicited by the film's referential gestures infiltrate and recast nearly every dimension of *Dumbo's* fabulous circus kingdom. This film's anatomy of the world of the circus grasps the world of a social totality—offers the circus literally as a metaphor for social life itself—by its considerations of childbirth, child rearing, and family life, of the labor relations and the economics of circus life, of social and racial tensions within and surrounding the circus, and, ultimately, of the final escalation of these tensions into the theater of World War II. The film's opening with a squadron of storks delivering baby circus animals and closing with a newspaper picture of "Dumbombers for Defense" (a squadron of Dumbo-like bombers flying in exactly the same formation as the storks) frames this tale of infantilization, bestialization, and destruction. Dumbo's progress from victimized infant to bomber prototype, then, parallels the fate of hundreds of thousands of children who, because of their own oppressed socioeconomic condition, have few options other than to "be all that they can be" by becoming either protofascist enforcers of a new world order or simple cannon fodder in some mercenary action supporting "the moral equivalents of our founding fathers" (that is, the corrupt murderers known as the Nicaraguan Contras) or in a full-blown war, now commonly labeled with some exotic adventure moniker like "Operation Desert Storm." The rapid flash of "Dumbombers for Defense" and other news headlines in the film's penultimate scene connect the workings of the circus, particularly Dumbo's spectacular ability to fly, with a social world more connected to the film's audience than to the film's world itself. It is in the convergence of these frames of reference that the political work of Disney's film is visible.

ii

The circus constitutes the core of this film's social realm, and virtually all of the narrative action is staged within the domain of its mobile, transient, and artificial world. The components and the logics of this world constitute a realm of exploitation, pain, humiliation, and violence; in fact, every element of the circus's repertoire pivots on danger and violence. Dumbo, however, represents the circus in much greater depth than any mere focus on its acts could be capable of. Dumbo begins, not with a vision of the circus per se, but with the squadron of storks flying through a torrential storm to deliver a batch of baby animals to expectant circus animal mothers. In essence, this mass delivery constitutes one way the circus reproduces its capital (babies from heaven, so to speak), and the arrival of these new circus babies becomes integral to the health and operations of the circus throughout the film. For example, not only do we see the animals performing acts under the big top, but we also glimpse the new arrivals working along with their adult parents to prepare for the circus's departure from its winter grounds and to set up the circus in new locations. However, these initial images focus more abstractly on childbearing and on family life in general and reveal an ambivalence and set of contradictions with the later glorification of childbirth in the film that, as I will argue, is essential to the very idea of families and of life in the more comprehensive social world represented by Dumbo's circus. The voice-over accompanying the flashes of lightning and sheets of rain links the reliability and intrepidity of the storks with that of the mail service: "Through the snow, sleet and hail . . . Ever faithful, ever true; nothing stops him. He'll get through." This institutional context links the birth of children with the delivery of the mail in a dependable confluence of commercial and social reproduction, communication, and exchange. Even the eventual delivery of Dumbo to Mrs. Jumbo can only occur within the strict conventions of the delivery service: Mrs. Jumbo twice tries to open her bundle of joy only to be interrupted, once by the necessity of her signature on the delivery form and then by the stork's required singing of "Happy Birthday," which itself is interrupted when the stork requires Mrs. Jumbo to name the baby immediately in accordance with the song's logic. What we witness at the scene of Dumbo's "birth," then, is a dense and rigorous institutional apparatus that pervades and determines private and personal moments in a mother's life.

As the storks emerge from the inky gloom of the storm, the first song in *Dumbo* articulates a vision of childbearing and of family life rife with doubt and danger. In this song, childbirth, like death, is a great equalizer as it levels social classes with the common affliction of having children.

> You may be poor or rich,
> It doesn't matter which.
> Millionaires they get theirs,
> Like the butcher and the baker.
>
> So look out for Mr. Stork
> And let me tell you friend
> Don't try to get away
> He'll find you in the end
> He'll spot you out in China
> Or he'll fly to County Cork
> So you better look out for Mr. Stork.

Immediately following the song we witness the arrivals of various circus babies, each one of which is welcomed by a thrilled mother, with the exception of Mrs. Jumbo, who looks in vain for her expected infant.

This dissonance between the song's warning ("look out for Mr. Stork") and the visual impression of the blissful parents accepting their newborns into the fold initiates an ambivalence about children and childbearing that persists throughout the film. For example, after Mrs. Jumbo protects Dumbo from the taunts and physical harassment of a group of unruly kids (maternal behavior consistent with the visual glorification of childbirth and child rearing), she is lashed and, when she resists, isolated in solitary confinement and declared insane. The other female elephants comment on her unacceptable behavior, "Mother love covers up for a multitude of sins." Mrs. Jumbo's crime is obvious—the children who taunt her infant are entitled to harass and even to torture Dumbo by virtue of having paid their admission to the circus. As a group of them remarks: "You can't hide him from us." "We want laughs." "Sure, that's what we came for." Sanctioned entry into this circus's world entitles paying customers to harass and violate the circus personnel.

The furthest extension of this ambivalence is staged within the circus acts in which Dumbo is forced to play a part, ostensibly to earn his own keep after his mother is incarcerated for her angry defense of her child. At first he, as "the world's tiniest little elephant," is required to attempt a dangerous vault to the top of a "pyramid of pachyderms" perched atop a small ball. After he trips over his ears, upends the elephants and brings the big top crashing down, he is demoted to a clown and made the center of an act which depicts a baby stranded in the top floor of a burning house. The mother on the ground screams out for the other clowns, now dressed as firemen, to "save my poor baby; save my child," and, after they perform various acts of buffoonery demonstrating both their incompetence and their insouciance regarding the endangered child, Dumbo is spanked with a board and plummets out the window and into a tiny barrel of water far below. As in the other comedic moments of this circus's routine, this one hinges on emotional trauma and physical peril. Exploited and depersonalized (one of the clowns remarks that "elephants ain't got no feelings" and another agrees, adding "no, they're made of rubber"), Dumbo, as child, is reduced to a mere stage property in the service of the clown act. The contradiction of a film that simultaneously glorifies and sentimentalizes childbirth *and* punishes mothers for defending their young while also placing those young in great danger is never explicitly rationalized, but is rendered coherent, if only implicitly, by the circus's economic situation. Children and the parent-child bond are sacred to the circus world, but only insofar as they contribute to the circus's financial health. We see the baby animals set to work constructing the circus tents on what appears to be the morning after their births, and, in the film's first circus parade, Dumbo already functions as a baby beast of burden, pulling a tiny cart with a doll in it. Only slightly later, one of only two or three intimate moments shared by Dumbo and his mother (the other is when she is incarcerated) is violently (both visually and aurally) interrupted by the arrival of circus patrons demanding access to Dumbo. Once "mother love" gets in the way of business as usual for the circus, it becomes a matter for violent suppression and psychic censure.

Dumbo's nighttime visit to his mother's prison car further extends the film's representation of the contradiction between parent-child relations and the business of the circus. As we witness Dumbo's mother straining against her chains to reach her trunk through the bars to caress and cradle her child, we are given a panoramic vision of all the other mothers and newborns in the circus sleeping tranquilly together. Accompanying this scene is the audio backdrop of the song "Baby Mine," another celebration of motherhood and child rearing, which stands in heightened contrast to the pathetic vision of Dumbo and mother separated by the cage's bars and the car's forbidding sign: "Danger—Mad Elephant."

> Little one, when you play,
> Don't you mind what they say.
> Let those eyes sparkle and shine,
> Never a tear, baby of mine.
> From your head to your toes,
> You're so sweet, goodness knows.
> You are so precious to me,
> Cute as can be, baby of mine.

Of course, this privatistic vision of a loving mother and child pitted against the cruelty and jeers of the world proves ineffectual given the circus's locking up Mrs. Jumbo for attempting actually to practice "mother love." Even Timothy Mouse, Dumbo's only friend, draws on the film's reverence for motherhood twice in order to motivate Dumbo to cheer up and turn his ears into an act. Soon after Mrs. Jumbo is locked up, the mouse tempts Dumbo to become his friend by suggesting that the two of them together "might be able to get [Dumbo's] mother out of the clink," although we see no such effort made. Perhaps more compassionately, but no less disingenuously, the mouse cheers up a tearful Dumbo after his first plunge as an endangered baby in a burning house by ad-libbing the planned visit to Dumbo's mother. The film's early glorification of childbirth, then, is inseparable from its later exploitation of child labor and its punitive dealing with mother-child relations when they disrupt the profit motive of the circus. This aporia exposes the ideology of *Dumbo's* circus world by foregrounding the mutually exclusive realms of "mother love" and circus profits. For now, we can conclude that *Dumbo* glorifies childbirth insofar as it produces raw material essential to the productive forces of the circus.

iii

Dumbo does not represent the destabilization of the family and the violence pervading its world abstractly. In fact, the primary scene of violence—the simultaneous valorization and violation of the family and of the individual—functions as a basis for other areas of the film's exploration of American culture, specifically in its representation of working-class life, of American society preparing for World War II, and of the racism and racist exploitation close to the heart of this film's world. The circus's reduction of parent-child relationships to economic functions is *Dumbo's* most sustained and elaborately dramatized version of economic exploitation. But the film's commentary on issues of labor and working conditions develops these themes in a larger social arena. In fact, the very question of labor provides an intimate link between these two disparate areas of inquiry.

The origins and labor necessary to procreate children and create the illusion of the finished product of the circus industry are veiled in every case. Specifically, we see neither the labor of childbirth nor the labor of working men and women associated with the circus. Circus babies appear painlessly, without "labor" (and in some cases seem to take their mothers by surprise), from the formation of storks that opens the film. In addition to the superimposition of this myth of childbirth, the film further mystifies childbirth by consistently eliminating male circus animals from any domestic contexts. With the single exception of the father tiger present when its baby arrives, the only time we view adult male and female couples together is when they are either laboring to raise the circus tents or in the process of being transported together. Furthermore, in the sweeping sequence of the sleeping mothers and children that accompanies Dumbo's midnight visit to his mother in her prison car, no fathers are present. Whatever intimate bond apparently unites these animal parents seems meaningless once the fathers inseminate the mothers.

In addition to the mystification of the labor of childbirth, *Dumbo* similarly conceals from the circus audience the labor necessary for the construction of the circus. With the single exception of the circus parade, one of the few scenes in the entire film that takes place in midday, *all* work associated with the construction and maintenance of the circus takes place at night, under the big top, or offscreen. All the physical exertion necessary to construct the circus is concealed under the cover of night and an intense rainstorm. The workers charged with the erection of the circus tents are the roustabouts, mammoth shapes shrouded in black and obscured by the torrential storm. Along with the conscripted circus animals, these faceless workers construct the circus amidst physical perils of elaborately syncopated sledgehammering and brutally difficult pulling and hauling necessary to raise the circus tents. Both babies and the elaborately organized circus tents appear, as if by magic, in the morning sunlight.

The film's veiling of the reality of maternal and other forms of human labor coincides with the anonymity with which *Dumbo* represents the human workforce of the circus and the tedium and ennui of human life within the circus world. For example, *Dumbo* renders the impoverishment of the roustabouts' lives in the film's second song, which gives voice to a life of endless, unappreciated, and unrewarded work and a life of near slave labor without any intellectual or economic fulfillment.

> We work all day; we work all night,
> We don't have time to read or write,
> We're happy-hearted roustabouts.
>
> While other folks have gone to bed,
> We slave until we're almost dead.
> We're happy-hearted roustabouts.

We don't know when we get our pay,
And when we do we throw our pay away.
We're happy-hearted roustabouts.

It almost goes without saying that the intensity of rage and denial encoded within the roustabouts' song (and disguised as blissful contentment) is hardly the stuff of children's entertainment. The workers' internalization of class conflict and feelings of their own inferiority have more in common with proletarian protest than with animated escapism.

The impoverishment of the roustabouts' labor is matched by the resentment and bitterness of the army of clowns, the only other circus community explored in Dumbo. I will return to the specifics of the clowns' routines in the next section; what is significant for the present discussion is the clowns' degraded status in the circus's social hierarchy and their economic grievances. The clowns, like the roustabouts, remain virtually faceless throughout the film; we see them either disguised in full makeup or as shadowy silhouettes behind the canvas of their dressing tent. As Buffo the Great complains in Angela Carter's Nights at the Circus, the clowns' facelessness testifies to their diminished expectations and degraded existence: "under these impenetrable disguises of wet white, you might find, were you to look, the features of those who were once proud to be visible" (119). Our first exposure to the clowns' place within the world of Dumbo's circus comes from the commentary of one of the haughty elephants, who function as an index to the hypocrisy and cruelty of the circus. When the group gathers to discuss Mrs. Jumbo's incarceration, the elephants decide to punish Dumbo. One of them asserts that no further punishment is necessary because, as she struggles to report, "They've gone and made him a clown." It seems that, however difficult the lives of the elephants (we see them doing backbreaking work during the setting up of the circus and as its most spectacular act), the life of a clown is the nadir of the circus's social world. The clowns themselves express their own sense of rage and exploitation. Immediately after they successfully perform the baby-rescued-from-burning-house routine, they gather to celebrate their great popularity and bask in their thirteen curtain calls. In addition to many self-congratulatory remarks, one clown affirms, "They'll have more respect for us clowns now," and the others agree and decide to celebrate with a brisk round of drinking. Once drunk, the clowns decide to organize for more pay, claiming that their act "is worth real dough," and they exit singing "We're going to hit the big boss for a raise." Like the roustabouts, the clowns get no respect and little money, and they feel their oppressed condition severely, targeting the "big boss" as their adversary.[3]

Dumbo intensifies the bleakness of life within this circus by rendering it as a powerful, all-encompassing, and all-appropriating social arena driven relentlessly by a desire for greater novelty and a reduction of all human and animal worth to a profit motive. In fact, *Dumbo* explicitly thematizes the omnipotence and the inescapability of the circus in a number of ways. The first time we see the circus train pull out of its winter quarters, the ringmaster calls out "all aboard!" not only inviting viewers to participate in the illusion of this film but suggesting the all-inclusiveness of the circus: once you board this train and enter into the world of the circus, there is no exit—you're either on this circus train, or you're off it. Only slightly later, and in only the second time we see the circus during the daytime, the camera pans the many circus cars and acts. Eventually we come to the gorilla rattling the bars of its cage, and this fierce beast pulls loose a bar, opening up a gap large enough for it to escape. Confused by this opportunity and puzzled by its own accomplishment, the gorilla looks out in dismay before finally replacing the bar and resuming its charade of struggle. Timothy Mouse reinforces this theme when he takes Dumbo to visit his mother in the prison car. Partially to lift Dumbo's spirits, but partially to rationalize further the hegemony of the circus world, the mouse refers to the desolate and ramshackle car as a "cozy little place."

Dumbo, then, represents the world of the circus as one in which even those suffering most under its most oppressive apparatus cannot think through their suffering to any vision of liberation. More sophisticated than many now obsolete theories of ideology merely as "false consciousness," *Dumbo* renders the many ways in which a citizenry must needs rationalize and internalize impoverished conditions in order to maintain their lives in any satisfactory way. This image of totalizing confinement is echoed throughout *Dumbo*, as we see shadows and various other images of prison bars on Dumbo's mother, on the ringmaster's undershirt, on some of the pink elephants on parade, and elsewhere. Even the roustabouts' song with its mentions of futility and imprisonment confirms the bleak and truncated horizons of those within the confines of the circus. The view of the audience, then, participates in a virtual anticipation of Foucault's image of the panopticon, a prisonlike world in which all inmates are subjected to constant surveillance and from which there is no hope (perhaps no desire) to escape.

The conjunction of these themes enables us to make a case for *Dumbo* as a Disney feature critical of the labor conditions at the Disney Studio in the early 1940s. Reacting against poor wages, arbitrary wage scales, long hours, no overtime pay, exploitative use of "student" labor, no recognition in film credits, and Disney's own oppressive control, many Disney workers walked out on May 29, 1941.[4] As commentators have noted, *Dumbo* was largely completed during the strike at the Disney Studio, a period when Disney had had to lay off animators and had been "forced to seek outside capital through a public sale of stock in 1940" (Allen and Denning 90) in order to reduce operating expenses as a result of lost revenues caused by the disruptions and ravages of the war in Europe. The situation became so tense that Walt Disney himself retreated to Brazil in an attempt to allow the heated conditions to cool off. Later, as a founding member of the Motion Picture Alliance for the Preservation of American Ideals and a "very friendly" witness before the House Committee on Un-American Activities, he blamed the unrest on communist organizing efforts—although, as Richard Shale argues, "the evidence suggests that the issues of the strike were more economic than political" (20).[5] A direct connection between *Dumbo* and heated labor unrest has been advanced by Richard Schickel and by Michael Wilmington, both of whom argue that the figures of some of the drunken clowns are vicious caricatures of some of the cartoonists striking the studios (Schickel 265; Wilmington 78).

That the film may make critical gestures toward the strikers, however, responds to only one side of a complex dynamic. It can equally be regarded as a work containing a veiled critique of the conditions against which those strikers rebelled. According to Shamus Culhane, onetime Disney animator, in general Disney's "pursuit of perfection created a very tense atmosphere in the studio" (144). Describing an environment of "creative deprivation, which must have aroused vague feelings of hostility among the more innovative people in the studio" (420), Culhane draws a picture of a Disney at once a perfectionist who drove his workers and a paternalist who referred to his employees as "my boys" (238). One of the strikers, in fact, characterized Disney as an "egocentric paternalist" who, after the success of *Snow White,* reigned even more tyrannically over his workers (Brady 3). Constantly overseeing and interacting with his animators, Disney's relentless pursuit of perfection led him to meet constantly with each animator and to require detailed lists of corrections which themselves would be "subjected to the same minute scrutiny" (113). As Culhane describes the volatility of working at Disney,

> A picture would remain in a constant state of flux right through the final stages of production. Walt was known to make changes in a film if he wasn't satisfied with the audience reaction at a sneak preview! No wonder Disney had contempt for New York animators. We were totally unprepared to cope with such an avalanche of criticism and changes, technically or emotionally. (113)

Given such demands, conditions during the strike at Disney were highly complex and emotionally charged. According to Culhane,

> The emotions of strikers and non-strikers are often very complex. Some people who did not join the picket line were guilt-ridden because they were not sure whether they had remained loyal to Walt from conviction or cowardice. Others who had been in the strike were equally unsure. Had they been wise to pursue a course that had so disrupted the studio? (141)

Even those who remained working during the strike had stressed relations with and contested loyalties to Disney:

> The management fostered a feeling of isolation between the Disney Studio and the rest of the industry. Most of the younger animators had never worked anywhere else, and it was the nightmare of this group that they might someday get fired and be

forced to get a job at one of the "other" studios. This specter was so menacing that many people who were fired left the business altogether. Walt's pursuit of quality was a Juggernaut that claimed many victims. (Culhane 141)

Indeed, the bitterness of the strike and the rigidity of Disney's authoritarian style of management resulted in the Disney Studio losing many of its best animators, including "two of the men who had been prime movers in [Disney's] meteoric rise to greatness," Art Babbitt and Bill Tytla, the latter of whom created Dumbo. Furthermore, those who did remain excelled in bringing "the viewpoint and style that had already been set to an astonishing degree of perfection," but "they were not innovators" (Culhane 238). Culhane adds that motivation Disney-style amounted to "each artist [being] permitted—nay, commanded—to do his best possible work. The whip was applied only if an individual showed signs of wanting to express his own artistic needs" (421).[6]

As even those who stayed on the job had vexed relations with the Disney Studio, it seems possible to argue that *Dumbo* may offer a critical view of more than those on the picket line. Conditions may have been unacceptable there, but the alternatives were equally terrifying. Seen in light of these remarks, the film's double denial of "labor" (again, of childbirth and of the physical exertion necessary for the circus to operate), its many images of enclosure and prison bars (especially the gorilla who, once free, doesn't know where to go!), the roustabouts' song of brutally hard and mindless slave labor, and the clowns' outrage over their status and their compensation all converge in a subtle dismantling of the very conditions under which *Dumbo* was produced. Oddly, Disney's trip to Brazil may have facilitated this covert struggle within his little feature. As Richard Schickel notes,

Some say . . . that [the studio] functioned better than it ever had while the boss was absent. They point to the speed and ease and inexpensiveness with which a little film called *Dumbo* was finished in this period. There were no delays while Disney would wrestle over each story point, each gag, each piece of design that flowed from the artists' desks. (264)

Even while they were completing *Dumbo* in record time and, nearly, "for peanuts," those who stayed on the job at Disney were themselves of dubious loyalties. In view of Culhane's commentary on Disney's constant and tyrannical overseeing of his animators, we might even speculate that the animators, even while working as strikebreakers, enjoyed their newfound sense of creative freedom and capitalized on it by infusing this film, the only one not to have been rigidly supervised by Disney, with a subtle record of their grievances.[7]

The particular conditions of the strike at the Disney Studio not only account for the specific critique of oppressive labor conditions within *Dumbo*, but serve as the basis for, paradoxically, freeing up the creative process and the eventual finished product for the more general levels of social criticism contained within *Dumbo's* commentary on domestic issues, racism, and escalating violence. In other words, what begins as a very specific dimension of criticism comes to incorporate and to establish homologies among labor unrest and other forms of exploitation. The *Dumbo* animators, then, could produce a work that simultaneously criticized striking cartoonists *and* the management at Disney against whom they struck, while also articulating their critique in a vocabulary and in a set of images capable of containing other diverse ranges of social critique. Consider, for example, the film's representation of the ringmaster. One of the most contested issues during the strike was Disney's claim to ownership of all work done by his artists, including that done away from the studio on other projects. Recalling the atmosphere of the times, Bill Pomerance, business agent for the Screen Cartoonists Guild, defines the extremeness of the situation: "he had them tied up to individual contracts that we did away with. . . . He claimed that everything they drew belonged to him" (quoted in Allen and Denning 94). *Dumbo* revisits this atmosphere of exploitation when it has one of the elephants forming the "pyramid of pachyderms" complain at the ringmaster's long-winded and self-serving introduction of the act, "to hear him talk, you'd think *he* was going to do it." Only slightly earlier, after Timothy Mouse hears the ringmaster declare "I've got it, I've got an idea," he remarks that "He hasn't had an idea in years" and then whispers the idea for the "pyramid of pachyderms" into his ears as he sleeps. It is also, we should recall, the ringmaster who cracks the whip most viciously when Dumbo's mother departs from circus protocol and attempts to protect her child from the abusive children. In all of these scenes, the film's mockery of the ringmaster's authoritarian policing of Dumbo's mother, his lack of imaginative and intellectual power, and his aggressive self-promotion all double as covert critiques of Walt Disney himself.

The economic implications of this claustrophobic world emerge from various other scenes in which the circus, the ringmaster, and even Timothy Mouse immediately reimagine any and all moments of novelty and disruption in terms of their potential profitability. We first meet the mouse as he scavenges for leftover peanuts and whistles the "Casey Junior" song that accompanies the circus train's movement throughout the film, a gesture which I take to indicate his consensual participation in the circus's rituals. After Dumbo's exclusion by the other elephants, Timothy Mouse attempts to befriend the desolate little elephant and approaches him with what he intends as an act of sympathy and friendship, but which is actually a business proposition. Focusing on Dumbo's ears, the mouse reassures Dumbo of his worth and redefines his ears as "beautiful" and "decorative," before finally translating them into the corporate terms of the circus: "All we got to do is build an act . . . make you a star." That opportunity knocks quickly, and the mouse capitalizes on the ringmaster's abortive idea to imagine a spectacular act based on his "pyramid of pachyderms" notion. Within that concept, Timothy Mouse defines Dumbo as the "climax" the ringmaster was lacking and reassures Dumbo that "you're a climax." Dumbo's identity thus reduced to the climax of a new circus stunt is reinforced by the rapid repetition of the word "climax" at least ten times in the scene. The mouse demonstrates his financial vision again after Dumbo's first performance as the baby in the burning house. As he bathes a sobbing Dumbo after a performance, the mouse's consolatory remarks all hinge on Dumbo's potential. Reassuring Dumbo that he is "stupendous" and "colossal," he attempts to convince the little elephant that "you ought to be proud; you're a star." Dumbo's truly climactic performance, though, his first flight with the crows, also elicits a response from Timothy Mouse predicated on Dumbo's financial promise. When first struck with the reality that Dumbo must have flown up into the tree, the mouse responds, not with relief and joy at Dumbo's curse being re-moved, but with the vision of an entrepreneur: "The very things that held you down are going to carry you up, up, up!" While the mouse seems to show some genuine compassion and concern for Dumbo (he sheds a few tears at the tenderness of Dumbo's reunion with his mother), his uniformed attire and his richly dressed appearance in the "Manager Signs Hollywood Contract" newspaper headlines that appear following Dumbo's first public flight suggest that, in his on-going relationship with Dumbo, whatever friendship exists between them will always coexist, perhaps subordinately, with financial man-agement and promise. The mouse's primary style of relating to Dumbo is repeatedly to assuage whatever pain he is feeling with promises of greater prominence within the confines of the circus's business. In this respect, Timothy Mouse resembles Jiminy Cricket from *Pinoc-chio* (1940), in that both function as voices reintegrating the marginal and reaffirming the status quo. He also resembles the early Mickey Mouse. As Miriam Hansen notes,

> Mickey's perverse streaks were sanitized, his rodent features do-mesticated into neotenic cuteness; the playful, anarchic engage-ment with machinery was functionalized to comply with the work ethic; and outlandish fantasy gave way to an idealized, sen-timentalized world. And despite—and, perhaps, through—this process of normalization, violence and terror became a staple of the Disney films, including the features. (50)

That the film's primary friendship exists always under the sign of eco-nomic potential testifies to the total reduction of all human relations to their economic bases.

This potential is, of course, more crudely realized in Dumbo's rela-tions with others in the circus. We have already seen that the children regard it as their right as paying customers to degrade and humiliate Dumbo. The clowns recklessly raise the height of the platform from which Dumbo jumps, assuming both that elephants are made of rub-ber and won't feel anything and that the act will grow geometrically in popularity and compensatory potential as the platform rises. The most interesting of these scenes occurs as Dumbo first flies within the circus, dive-bombing and shooting peanuts at his former antagonists. The ringmaster recovers from Dumbo's knocking him over by proudly jumping to his feet, smiling, and pointing, ringmasterlike, at this spectacular new routine. Without missing a beat, he rapidly translates Dumbo's venting of his rage, his own near bodily injury, and an unprecedented natural phenomenon into the show business of the circus. The former social outcast and pariah Dumbo is immediately welcomed into the fold, and his momentarily threatening ability to fly is just as quickly integrated into the circus's appeal.[8]

Essential to the emotional ambivalence and social contradictions staged within Disney's film is the omnipresence of violence and exploitation which emerges as something like the defining essence of the world of the circus. The few moments of happiness and domestic tenderness following the introduction of Dumbo and the exposure of his ears all occur when Dumbo and mother are alone and insulated from any other representative of the circus, its labor force, and its workings. Immediately after Dumbo's gigantic ears are exposed, the chorus-like group of elephants, who repeatedly regroup to register the depths of the circus's cruelty, ridicule and denounce Jumbo Jr., rechristening him "Dumbo" (like all of the other reindeer who "used to laugh and call [Rudolph] names"). Indeed, every single time Dumbo comes into contact with the circus, he is laughed at, prodded, physically abused, and degraded. Reference to a few of these scenes will suffice. During the opening circus parade, Dumbo's appearance is greeted by growing laughter and insults, which sadden Dumbo and send him to his mother for protection. This abuse from the public reaches a crisis when several boys taunt and eventually grab Dumbo, precipitating Dumbo's mother's rage and her consequent incarceration as a "Mad Elephant." We have already commented on the cruelty and danger inherent in the acts Dumbo is forced to perform, but even Timothy Mouse, ostensibly Dumbo's closest friend and defender, participates in these communally coercive practices when he jabs Dumbo with a needle when the little elephant is reluctant to run toward a platform from which he will leap to the top of the "pyramid of pachyderms." This act echoes that of one of the clowns, who spanks Dumbo with a plank to force him off the platform from which he plummets as the baby saved from a burning house, and anticipates the scene in which Timothy Mouse and the crows join together to push Dumbo off a cliff when he learns to fly. Friend and foe alike, it seems, are dedicated to the smooth running of the business of the circus.

In addition to those acts of violence specifically directed at Dumbo, *Dumbo* registers the omnipresence of competitive violence in a variety of other ways. Images of loss, fear, and violence pervade the festivities and pomp of the circus parade, in which we view the clowns nearly smashing each other with their musical instruments and props and, in rapid succession, two forlorn characters desperately searching for something they can't find. During the nightmarish delirium tremens visions shared by Dumbo and Timothy Mouse—a hellish inversion of the daylight circus procession—the hallucinatory "pink elephants on parade" stomp on each other, splatter each other with cymbals, and career dangerously in speeding cars and boats, while Dumbo and Timothy Mouse can only watch this defamiliarized anatomy of the circus in stupefied terror. Elsewhere in the film, the other elephants participate in the general atmosphere of violence by degrading and exiling Dumbo from their ranks. They take a "sacred vow" that Dumbo "is no longer an elephant." Even the crows, who ultimately are instrumental in Dumbo's triumphant learning how to fly, first appear in the film by taunting, scaring, and insulting Dumbo and his mouse friend. Dumbo himself caves in to the violent ethos of the circus when he enacts his own violent revenge, gleefully dive-bombing and machine-gunning with peanuts his antagonists during his first surprising circus flight.

iv

The linkage of rampant violence and economic oppression central to Disney's *Dumbo* merges coherently with the film's negotiation of racial issues. Questions of racial identity, racial prejudice, and racist violence constitute, I believe, one of *Dumbo's* most compelling and complex representational schemes. While the most obvious and objectionable racial representation in *Dumbo* is the stereotyping of the crows near the film's conclusion, racially charged images pervade the film.[9] The crows, whose cleverness and concern for Dumbo are instrumental to his learning to fly, are crudely and thoroughly racist depictions of African American characters. The minstrel-show shuffling, heavily stereotyped speech patterns and accents, and general sense of community among the crows call attention to their Otherness. Most amazingly, the leader of this flock is designated in the film's credits as "Jim Crow," making explicit the film's representation of the crows in terms of the racist "Jim Crow" laws formalizing and guaranteeing unequal and oppressive conditions for African Americans in the first half of the twentieth century. Just as it is difficult to respond humorously to the prospects of a baby violently ripped from its loving mother and forced to participate in a circus act that puts it in imminent peril, it would require a truly perverse and inhuman bias to find unproblematic humor in such blatantly racist images as those associated with the Jim Crow mentality that led to institutionalized, rampant discrimination and violence against early-twentieth-century African Americans.

Aside from the specifics of the visual and aural imagery associated with the crows, Timothy Mouse's initial response to their questioning makes their identities explicit. After Jim Crow flies to the branch on which Dumbo and the mouse are sleeping off their drunken binge of the night before, he addresses Timothy Mouse as "brother rat." Objecting to this designation and to the crow's familiarity, the mouse responds, "Now listen here. I ain't your brother, and I ain't no rat." The racial polarization implicit in his repudiation of the crow's assumption of brotherhood is strengthened when Timothy then asks, "what are you *boys* doing down here anyway? Go fly up a tree where you belong" (my emphasis). The remarks differentiate the mouse from the crows within pervasive racial stereotypes, which resulted in separate sections of public buildings, restrooms, and buses designated as "where [they] belong." The denial of brotherhood, the condescending reference to "you boys," and the attempt to order them "back where they belong" all resonate with some of the more obvious forms of racist polarization from the Jim Crow era of *Dumbo*'s making, while also echoing the paternalism of Disney's references to his employees as his "boys."

The presence of the crows and their crucial assistance in Dumbo's flying (they use their own form of voodoo in providing a "magic feather" that they say will give Dumbo the ability to fly) converge with the film's comment on veiled labor, again suggesting a close affinity between the denial of the input of labor into the reproduction of the elephant species and the production of the circus. While it is quite clearly the crows who first suggest that Dumbo may have flown up into the tree, and while their machinations are instrumental in his eventual recognition of his uncanny talent, the film erases all traces of the crows' efforts by leaving them behind in the final scene. The train outpaces the crows, who have been hovering above it with Dumbo, and the film's final words are those of the crows, one of whom is bemoaning that he didn't even get an autograph from the now famous Dumbo. This concluding scene recalls significant and similar scenes from the film's earliest moments, one in which the stork who delivered Dumbo is violently left behind when his neck is caught on a postal hook next to the train tracks, and the others in which the labor both of childbirth and of the construction of the circus is veiled and/or denied. In other words, Dumbo's ability, already fantastical for an animated film, is mystified even within the world of the film by virtue of the crows' being left behind and, we assume, denied any acknowledgment in Dumbo's discovery.

That the African American contribution to this phenomenon would be erased is itself consistent with many perspectives on African American contributions to American culture in general. For example, John A. Williams's 1972 novel *Captain Blackman* presents a historical-fictional, at times documentary, vision of the ways in which African American contributions to American military campaigns and successes are intentionally and systematically erased from the historical record. In one of that novel's concluding hallucinatory reflections, Captain Blackman summarizes what has been a persistent theme in African American participation in America's wars, from the Revolutionary War to Vietnam, the withholding of proper recognition:

> Soldiering to him was just like any other gig black folks stumble into with white folks. A soldier should get the credit due him for being responsible for the most abrupt and drastic changes that can be affected on any society. Man, they sing about soldiers; give them land. Salt. Women. Money. Pensions. Medals (!). Allowances. They do the cats up in bronze. They look so noble, even the pigeon shit doesn't matter. But when they don't give you no

credit, they're not obligated to honor you one bit, or to give you one mothafucking thang, baby. (326)

Much of Williams's narrative plays on Blackman's alternating rage at the injustice of American military procedures and racist practices and his (and others') tenuously sustained "faith that his army would make up for its past misdeeds" (118). In Williams's novel, the hoped-for revaluation, recognition, and rewarding of the African American presence in American military history predictably never occurs.

To draw on an example from popular music, it is commonly acknowledged that the early success of the Beatles and other groups of the "British Invasion," including white American responses to the British influence on American popular musical culture, depended on the translation and domestication of originally black rhythm and blues tunes, harmonies, and songs, on their whitewashing (even in the process of paying homage to) the contributions of African Americans to American musical culture. For example, Pat Boone rerecorded and enjoyed chart-topping success with a "white-bread" version of Little Richard's "Tutti Frutti," Little Richard's original and far wilder version of which remained in relative (commercial) obscurity. The commercial fate of R & B innovator Big Mama Thornton provides another typical case. Because of the lack of marketing and distribution arrangements available to many African Americans in the midcentury recording industry, Big Mama was overshadowed in two noteworthy incidents. "Hound Dog," which eventually became one of Elvis Presley's greatest hits, was originally written by Leiber and Stoller for Big Mama. Although her fantastically rough and sultry rendition reached number one during 1953 on the Billboard R & B charts, the rise of Elvis and white rock and roll sent Thornton and scores of other African American artists plummeting into obscurity. Nor were the economic impacts insignificant; Thornton claims to have received only one royalty check (for five hundred dollars), although her "Hound Dog" sold over two million copies. Later, because of copyright complications, Big Mama lost all revenues for her song "Ball and Chain," which Janis Joplin (along with Big Brother and the Holding Company) made famous and profited from on the album Cheap Thrills (Gaar 1–4). Joplin's version is surely worthy of the attention and success it received—she, perhaps more than any white female vocalist, could throttle a blues tune for all it was worth. The dilemma posed by "covers" centers on the exploitation of original artists, not to mention on the flaccid versions of songs that eventually top the charts for white performers. As David Pichaske notes, "Play Little Richard's 'Tutti Frutti' back to back with Pat Boone's 'Tutti Frutti' to grasp what 'cover' really means" (38).

Dumbo's final scenes represent one of the earliest examples of this phenomenon. As we see the circus train speeding into some utopian future, the penultimate car carries the four elephants who had vexed and opposed Dumbo and his mother since the discovery of Dumbo's ears—singing a song earlier sung by the crows, "When I See an Elephant Fly." Originally sung with tremendous soulfulness, clever wordplay, and jive dancing, in the mouths of these elephants the song is denatured of all of its original appeal by the shallow and vapid vocal quality of the elephants as well as by their overly careful enunciation of the song's lyrics. The elephants' version further contributes to the film's homogenizing of all Otherness by reducing the original progression of solos, with the various and individualized crows' witty repartee and signifying on each other, to one chorus of undifferentiated and bland harmony. With the crows left behind, without even Dumbo's autograph, the reclamation of this song by the elephants most likely signals the absolute appropriation of the crows' original song and echoes the film's other representations of the elision of African American labors and contributions to the film's culture.

Virtually this same scenario was repeated in a 1980 *Saturday Night Live* skit. With Ray Charles as the guest musician that week, the original group of the "Not Ready for Prime Time Players" appeared as the "Young Caucasians," preparing for a big recording session in which they perform "a tribute to Negroes." Anxious to meet "Mr. Charles," the Young Caucasians, all snazzy in college-glee-club matching outfits, reveal the shallowness of their understanding of African American music as well as their provinciality and racism during their chat with him and their rendition of "What I'd Say," which they call "What I Would Say." Their version, of course, butchers Charles's original masterpiece with perfect enunciations, corrected grammar, soulless harmony, and stiffly and absurdly choreographed dance accompaniment. Ray Charles can only shake his head despondently as he endures this travesty, and, as he discusses his objections to the Young Caucasians' version of his song with his manager (Garrett Morris), the two can only conclude that, however bad their performance, there is the slim hope that their popularization might bring attention to Charles as an African American performer. Morris tries to impress upon Charles the dilemma they face: "You like it; I like it, but white folks just ain't ready for this."

The convergence of all these scenes attests to the pervasiveness and endurance of African American culture's grievance with its appropriation by the white American culture industry. The remarkable quality of *Dumbo*'s staging of this recurring scene of dispossession is the degree to which it foregrounds the operations of the appropriation of African American labor by white culture. Disney's film recovers this moment in various, mutually reinforcing areas, at the expense both of the crows and of virtually all laboring sectors of the circus's world.

V

For all the importance of *Dumbo*'s various representations both of these crudely stereotypical images and of the complex networks of appropriation and dispossession I have discussed, the film's most sustained and, I will argue, central representation of racial issues inheres in Dumbo himself. In one obvious sense, the suffering and humiliation Dumbo experiences as a result of a physical characteristic mirrors, albeit at a superficial level, the segregation, oppression, and anguish experienced by any racial, ethnic, gendered, or other minority by virtue of its physical Otherness. Dumbo's ears, then, represent such commonly stereotyped characteristics as the hair, lips, or genitals caricatured in racist depictions of African Americans; the height, eye shape, or skin color of Asians in similarly racist representations; or even the gross exaggerations of the noses and other facial features of the Irish in late-nineteenth-century political cartoons. We recall Phillis Wheatley's lines "Some view our sable race with scornful eye, / 'Their colour is a diabolic die,'" which we examined in chapter 2, as but one common expression of racist designations of the African American Others in late-eighteenth-century America, though the huge majority of slave narratives and substantial numbers of African American literary works stage similar moments.[10] But Dumbo's resonance with the oppression of minorities extends far beyond mere physical difference. Nevertheless, even the significance of Dumbo's ears takes on deeper meaning once pursued more rigorously, especially when situated with other elements of the film's representation of Dumbo's difference. It is to the question of Dumbo's ears as well as to his treatment by other characters in the circus and the ways in which such treatment echoes characteristically racist behavior in American culture that we now turn.

Once Dumbo's mother unwraps the bundle Dumbo arrives in, the other elephants share in her exuberance and remark in turn on how adorable Dumbo is and what a proud day Dumbo's birth signals. But when Dumbo sneezes and exposes his enormous ears, the other elephants react with shock, dismay, and horror. Their remarks are more significant than their physical reactions. Immediately upon seeing his ears, one elephant asks, "Is it possible?" and the other, "Isn't there some mistake?" They immediately mock his looks, justify their scorn, and rechristen the baby elephant "Dumbo," replacing his mother's choice of Jumbo Jr. While the first of these remarks could refer to the impossibility of any elephant having ears this large, the suggestion that a mistake has been made seems to accept the possibility of large ears, but just not for *this* elephant. What mistake could the second of these remarks refer to if not the possibility that this delivery should not have been made to this mother? Neither of the elephants asserts that no elephant can have such large ears, only that this particular elephant should not. All five of the female elephants onscreen at this moment, Dumbo's mother and the four antagonists, it is important to note, are marked by the small ears that characterize Indian elephants. Of course, the much larger ones represented by Dumbo's inordinately huge ears characterize African elephants. What the revelation of Dumbo's large ears most likely represents, then, is African heritage. In other words, the scandal of Dumbo's birth and the mistake referred to by the second remark is that of miscegenation. Dumbo's mother is scorned as a result of what must have been her copulating with an African elephant never present in the film, and Dumbo because of his mulatto status in this otherwise racially pure herd. Dumbo's ears, then, in addition to their general resonance with any physical characteristic singled out for racist attack, designate him quite specifically and quite literally as at least one-half African.[11] The film insinuates as much by having two different characters (one of the Indian elephants and Timothy Mouse) refer to Dumbo as "a freak." Given the physical index provided by his large ears and the exclusionary violence they elicit, I take these references to function homonymically as an allusion to Afrique, Africa. Of course, we never see Dumbo's father, but the historical Jumbo of P. T. Barnum circus fame was, in fact, a gigantic African elephant, whose relative domestication was unprecedented.[12]

Dumbo's subsequent treatment by the elephants and other elements of the circus consolidates this range of significance by further marking Dumbo as a racialized and "dehumanized" Other. Just as Timothy Mouse castigates the crows with racism-tinged remarks, the other elephants, as we have seen, turn on Dumbo immediately after his sneeze exposes his ears. Furthermore, once Dumbo's mother is locked up and declared insane, these elephants close ranks and violently exclude Dumbo from their circle. As the desolate baby elephant approaches them, his eyes filled with tears and his head drooping over his separation from his mother, the elephants remark, "I wouldn't eat at the same bale of hay with him," and, only slightly later, "pretend you don't see him." Both of these exclusionary acts, like Timothy Mouse's verbal sparring with the crows, resonate with the racist policies of America's Jim Crow era. The first, of course, again conjures up images of separate bathrooms, restaurants, beaches, buses, and other public spaces racially demarcated "White" and "Colored." In fact, as Lerone Bennett Jr. defines it, "the cornerstones of the great wall [of Jim Crow segregation] were two taboos: interracial eating and intermarriage. Anything approaching interracial eating was proscribed. Anything which might by any stretch of the imagination lead to intermarriage was interdicted" (221). Quite uncannily, and perhaps quite unconsciously, Dumbo stages two of the core prejudicial practices of America's own racial policies. Dumbo's mother, as I have argued, most likely is guilty of intermarriage, and the refusal of the other elephants to "eat at the same bale of hay" with Dumbo echoes with the brutal tones of American racist segregation. To look ahead a bit, Dumbo and his mother having their own railroad car at the end of the film similarly recalls the other primary area of Jim Crow exclusionary practices, Jim Crow railroad laws. Not just meals in white restaurants or tickets to a white opera house, but seats "in a 'white' railroad car . . . became enormously complicated legal processes involving policemen, layers on layers of lawyers and judges and the expenditure of thousands of dollars on legal fees" (Bennett 224). Every single southern state "beginning with Florida [the first locale of the circus in *Dumbo*] in 1887 enacted Jim Crow railroad legislation" (226). While they may have a fancy railroad car, Dumbo and his mother ride alone and at the end of the train, like privileged but segregated exiles.

The second exclusionary act—"pretend you don't see him"—anticipates the socio-ontological dilemma of Ralph Ellison's Invisible Man. As the excluded Other of the elephant community *and* as the exploited labor from which the well-being of the circus community is sustained, Dumbo's invisibility functions to guarantee his status without representation as well as the status of his oppressors, who will not have to see their own privilege reflected in his eyes. The ways in which Dumbo eventually achieves visibility similarly anticipate the fate of Ellison's protagonist. Like Invisible Man, Dumbo is forced to perform in the service of a larger, suspicious and exploitative, organization that plays on its subject's experiences of alienation and oppression in order to incorporate him, provide him with an ersatz moment of belonging and participation, and, ultimately, manipulate him for a "larger good" that ignores his own interests. That Ellison's representation of the "Brotherhood"'s self-serving manipulation of American blacks is itself a representation saturated with the growing anticommunism of large sectors of the African American community who believed that they had been tokenized by the Communist Party USA does not detract from the validity and resonance of this localized comparison.

The specific terms of Dumbo's exclusion, then, resonate with the tragic persistence of exclusionary racial violence throughout American history. But the rapidity with which Dumbo is excluded from his original social unit once his physical difference becomes known also echoes important moments from numerous African American literary narratives that explore the status of American racism through the experiences of a light-skinned person of African descent. In many such works, the African American passes as white and is welcomed into a social circle or personal friendship, but, once that person's African heritage, however minimal, becomes known, her once-valued qualities are immediately denied and she is quickly and rigorously rejected. Frances E. W. Harper's important *Iola Leroy; or, Shadows Uplifted* (1892) is one of many African American narratives that pivots on such scenes. Iola is a beautiful, compassionate, and intelligent young woman with some African blood from her mother's side, although she shows no visible signs of her African heritage. Through the course of the novel, Iola develops many friendships and associations—with individuals, with co-workers, and with employers—that all end rapidly and violently once her past becomes known. Harper works through these same dynamics in numerous other characters, and the theme eventually becomes so thoroughly self-conscious that characters play games and place wagers on the ability of light-skinned African Americans to pass as white. In one such case two doctors, Gresham and Latimer (Iola's suitors in the narrative), carry on a sustained deception in order to test Dr. Latrobe, who prides himself on his ability to spot (and reject) even the most diluted Negro blood. After Dr. Latrobe had come to respect and value the intelligence and medical opinions of Dr. Latimer, the revelation of the truth of the latter's racial background dawns upon Dr. Latrobe in a scene consistent with *Iola Leroy*'s major thematics. In a discussion of the generally degrading influence African Americans have on the postwar society and its citizens, Dr. Latimer remarks:

> "You have been associating with me at the convention for several days; I do not see that the contact has dragged you down, has it?"
>
> "You! What has that got to do with associating with niggers?" asked Dr. Latrobe, curtly.
>
> "The blood of my race is coursing through my veins. I am one of them," replied Dr. Latimer, proudly raising his head.
>
> "Yes;" interposed Dr. Gresham, laughing heartily at Dr. Latrobe's discomfiture. "He belongs to that negro race both by blood and choice. His father's mother made overtures to receive

him as her grandson and heir, but he has nobly refused to for-
sake his mother's people and has cast his lot with them."

"And I," said Dr. Latimer, "would have despised myself if I had
done otherwise."

"Well, well," said Dr. Latrobe, rising, "I was never so deceived
before. Good morning!" (238–39)

So exits the incensed Dr. Latrobe. In this respect, the abrupt about-
face by the elephants after learning about Dumbo's ears returns to
another primal moment in African American literary production.
Along with such other generic constants as the separation of families,
the denial of literacy skills to slaves, the mutually degrading effect
of social relations in a slave economy, and the detailed anatomy of a
slave culture and economy, this repeated drama functions as one of
the basic narrative constituents of African American literary culture's
analysis of racism and slavery. That *Dumbo* stages virtually the same
moment outside of any overt African American productive contribution can be regarded as evidence of the pervasiveness of the dynamics
of racist oppression in American culture *and* of the potency of cultural intentionality.

Dumbo's treatment at the hands of the clowns reinforces his oppressed status in the circus community while also meshing with
Dumbo's other racialized inquiry. To return to the critical scenes, we
should recall that Dumbo is demoted to the status of clown after
he precipitates the "pyramid of pachyderms" disaster. Now reduced
to the role of the baby in the burning house, Dumbo's first performance is so popular that the clowns receive thirteen curtain calls and,
after the performance, revel in their success. During their celebration
and plans to revamp their act for greater popularity, the question of
Dumbo's role elicits problematic remarks. After deciding that raising
the platform from which the little elephant jumps would result in
a corresponding increase in the act's popularity and profitability, the
clowns conclude that a platform one thousand feet above the floor
would produce optimal results. To counter one voice of concern
that they should be careful because they "might hurt the little guy,"
two clowns respond in rapid succession that "elephants ain't got no
feelings," and "no, they're made of rubber." Articulated shortly after

Dumbo is declared "no longer an elephant" by the four matronly elephants, these comments further reduce Dumbo to a subconscious thing, no longer one of the personalized and largely humanized creatures in the world of Dumbo's circus allegory. The process moves inexorably, beginning with the elephants' changing the baby's name from Jumbo Jr. to Dumbo (he is now an object of contempt rather than someone's son), through his being declared "no longer an elephant," defined as a "climax" (again instead of a living being), and demoted to the status of clown, to being reduced, even on the lowest social rung of the circus, to a nonliving mass of resilient rubber (even Timothy Mouse contributes to this trend when he urges Dumbo to "bounce right back" after one of his painful performances).

This denial of Dumbo's feelings and of his sentient nature represents the film's convergence with persistent trends in racist practice, which characteristically denies the humanity of racialized Others, typically recasting them as animals or things. We know, of course, that antebellum legal codes reduced African American slaves to the status of chattel, often treated as no better than animals or machinery. Frederick Douglass's Narrative (1845) frequently returns to this strategy throughout its analysis of the entire system of slavery. Slaves know "as little of their ages as horses know of theirs" (21); the children were called to a trough "like so many pigs, and like so many pigs they would come and devour the mush" (44); and, after being nearly broken by the slave driver Covey, Douglass spends his free Sundays "in a sort of beast-like stupor" (75). Douglass complicates this essential dynamic by demonstrating the dialectical extension of slave owners and drivers also being brutalized by their praxis, but his point—that slavery reduces human beings to a level of animal existence—holds. To kill or maim a slave wasn't inhumane so much as it was stupid for a slave owner to damage his own constant capital. In addition to such codes of institutionalized barbarity, the discourse of slavery and racism is rife with similar denials of the full humanity of targeted Others. The literature of the mid–nineteenth century, especially such noteworthy genres as the slave narrative and the literature of slavery (Stowe's Uncle Tom's Cabin, for example) and such individual works as Melville's "Benito Cereno," represents the drive of a slave culture to bestialize African Americans. To cite just the latter example, Melville stages the simultaneous infantilization and bestialization of Africans within the consciousness of his self-satisfied and obtuse Captain Amasa Delano, who thinks of Africans variously as "a shepherd's dog," as Newfoundland dogs, as a gentle doe nursing its fawn, as "unsophisticated as leopardesses; loving as doves" (*Piazza Tales* 51, 84, 73), and as other animals. This mental habit, we learn through the epistemological and ideological twists of Melville's complex narrative, both enables and is enabled by Delano's inability to think of the Africans as fully human. Delano also envisions the Africans as helpless children, sorely needing the civilizing influence of himself, Benito Cereno, and others involved in the trafficking in human life.

These two positions, the bestializing and infantilizing of African Americans, coincide in large measure with an ensemble of racist attitudes consolidated, according to Joel Williamson, by the mid–nineteenth and persisting into the twentieth century. Williamson defines the "Sambo model" that whites constructed of African Americans in terms pertinent to our discussion of *Dumbo*. During the final decades of slavery, whites "began to build a stereotypical image of the black person as simple, docile, and manageable. They labored hard to see all blacks as, essentially, perpetual children." This benign image, however, reveals only half of the predominant intellectual and emotional construct. This Sambo model actually yoked two mutually constitutive notions of African Americans in the white mind: "improperly cared for, he became bestial, an animal in human form and all the more dangerous because of his human capabilities. Properly managed, on the other hand, he was like a white child, and dear" (Williamson 15). *Dumbo* parcels out these traits between Dumbo and his mother, reducing Dumbo to the level of perpetual child ("the world's tiniest little elephant") whose smallness and helplessness are essential to his marketability within various circus acts, while representing Dumbo's mother as a creature whose rage and violence lie just beneath the surface of her demure conduct. Her rampage against those who would harm her child draws to the surface her essentially unmanageable behavior, which, given the rage for order and uninhibited profitability of the circus, must be assiduously excluded and disciplined before she can be reintegrated into the circus's mainstream. The demure behavior of Dumbo's mother at the film's beginning coupled with the frenzy she flies into to protect her child, more-over, also resonates with cinematic stereotypes of African American women characters in the first half of the century. As Michael Parenti summarizes, the black actor's "female counterpart was good-natured, motherly yet sometimes sassy, able to work but complaining about it, and employed as a cook, seamstress, or servant" (128). Dumbo's mother, it would seem, pushes each of these traits to its explosive extreme, with her shyness and exaggerated femininity quickly trans-formed into her ultra-"sassy" physical retaliation against the cruel children who torment her baby. Her unmanageableness, not un-relatedly, also raises the specter of Dumbo's African father, as African elephants have rarely been successfully broken and trained for circus performances.

We, of course, witness more brutal and sadistic enactments of the same attitudes in slave narratives and in other literary works, as well as in the social history of racism and racist assaults of threatening Others. Through its representation of a wide array of racist attitudes and practices, *Dumbo* recovers the history of racist violence and op-pression in the United States, from the legalized violence of antebel-lum cruelty to the hardly less institutionalized and hardly less overt persecution of Jim Crow America. According to Charles Carroll, in a religious publication entitled "The Negro a Beast" (1900), the Negro was quite literally an ape rather than a human being, an argument Carroll extended to blame the simian Negro for the biblical tempta-tion of Eve (Fredrickson 277). Of course, Thomas Dixon's notorious works *The Leopard's Spots* (1902) and *The Clansman* (1905) repeat-edly characterize freed African Americans as "black beast rapists" and dramatize the violent attempt to suppress these newly released and insatiable threats to white purity. *The Clansman* demonizes African Americans as "half child, half animal, the sport of impulse, whim and conceit, . . . a being who, left to his will, roams at night and sleeps in the day, whose speech knows no word of love, whose passions, once aroused, are as the fury of the tiger" (293). And in that novel's climac-tic rape scene, Dixon offers his paranoiac audience a vision of their worst, yet most thoroughly rationalized, racist nightmares: "a single tiger spring, and the black claws of the beast sank into the soft white throat" (304). Consistent with the besieged southern mentality generative of and responsive to Dixon's images, the representation of any potentially threatening racialized Other as animalistic, or at least not fully human, has also tended to justify atrocities committed against African Americans. Similarly, the clowns' denial of Dumbo's feelings facilitate their putting him in greater peril in their "baby in a burning house" routine.

The relationship between representing African Americans as animals and the violence perpetrated against them can be viewed as a subset of the dehumanization of the Other that commonly accompanies military campaigns of racial slaughter. Since the Puritans first defined the native populations as animalistic and demonic, American military campaigns have denied the full humanity of their enemies as an enabling strategy in their plans for extermination. As Reginald Horsman summarizes early campaigns against African Americans and Native Americans,

> The Indians could . . . be thrown off the land, mistreated, or slaughtered, because in rejecting the opportunities offered to them they had shown that they were sunk deep in irredeemable savagery. In practice, like the blacks, they were regarded as different human beings even when there was no general rationale to explain any racial differences. (104)

Robert W. Johannsen similarly argues that "behind the belief that the Mexican War constituted a stage in world progress were the ever-present and much touted beliefs in racial hegemony" (289). American propaganda's caricature of the animalistic "miserable Mexican" ("degraded mongrel races" and so forth [Horsman 238 and passim]), Johannsen continues, was instrumental to the common belief that "America's preeminence resulted from the purity of the race" as well as from its being spared "from that commingling with others which has multiplied degenerate thousands upon the earth" (290).

Virtually the same racialized rhetoric characterized American propaganda during World War II, the period of *Dumbo's* creation and initial popularity. As John W. Dower describes the Western perception of Asian enemies, "the Western Allies, for example, persisted in their notion of the 'subhuman' nature of the Japanese, routinely turning to images of apes and vermin to convey this. . . . Subhuman, inhuman, lesser human, superhuman—all that was lacking in the perception of the Japanese enemy was a human like oneself" (9). A story depicting the Japanese as "yellow monkeys" appeared in the *New Yorker,* and, of course, many Japanese Americans were detained in stockyards before being sent to the notorious West Coast detention centers. During a 1942 parade in New York City in support of the American war effort, one tremendously popular float depicted "a big American eagle leading a flight of bombers down on a herd of yellow rats which were trying to escape in all directions."[13] *Dumbo* participates in this routine metaphorical equation of the eagle as symbolic of the United States, while the bestialization of the Japanese as faceless vermin, herd creatures acting without thought or individuality, recapitulates the racist denigration of ethnic Others as subhuman animals incapable of thought or feeling. As Dower puts it in *War Without Mercy: Race and Power in the Pacific War,*

> The dehumanization of the Other contributed immeasurably to the psychological distancing that facilitates killing, not only on the battlefield but also in the plans adopted by strategists far removed from the actual scene of combat. Such dehumanization, for example, surely facilitated the decisions to make civilian populations the targets of concentrated attack, whether by conventional or nuclear weapons. (11)

Philip Slater applies a similar argument to American military campaigns during the Vietnam War. Historically, Slater argues, Americans have "had a disturbing tendency to see nonwhites—particularly Orientals—as nonhuman, and to act accordingly" (33). More specifically, during the Vietnam War, the technologies of mass destruction greatly facilitated the bestialization and destruction of ethnic Others:

> Governments have always tried to keep their soldiers from thinking of "the enemy" as human, by portraying them as monsters and by preventing contact ("fraternization") with them, and modern weaponry makes it very easy for anyone to be a mass killer without much guilt or stress. Flying in a plane far above an impersonally defined target and pressing some buttons to turn fifty square miles into a sea of flame is less traumatic to the

average middle-class American boy than inflicting a superficial bayonet wound on a single male soldier. The flier cannot see the women and children being horribly burned to death—they have no meaning to him. (41–42)

Indeed, the specter of death from forty thousand feet that Slater analyzes presses significantly on *Dumbo,* in that the little elephant is forced to jump from a platform one thousand feet above a tiny bucket of water, and later is highlighted in headlines announcing the setting of altitude records and the transformation of Dumbo's skill into "Dumbombers for Defense."

This reference to bombers attacking Asians figured not as individual human beings but either as the specific "little Japs" or the nameless "yellow hordes" brings us to the conclusive moment in *Dumbo's* representation of Dumbo as African American Other. It is Dumbo's uncanny ability to fly that constitutes the movie's climax—by discovering his ability to fly, Dumbo discovers the value of his identity, recovers his imprisoned mother, and secures both a respected place within the circus and the fame and fortune that accrue from his talent and its marketability. It is Dumbo's ability to fly that generates the entire sequence of newspaper headlines in the film's penultimate scene: "Elephant Flies," "Dumbo Sets New Altitude Record," "Dumbombers for Defense," and the other two ("Manager Signs Hollywood Contract" and "Ears Insured for $1,000,000") focusing on the economic implications of Dumbo's flight. Dumbo's ability to fly establishes him as this circus's greatest star and biggest box office draw, while at the same time rendering him a permanent fixture within a circus whose basic operations consistently devalue and degrade all its employees. Dumbo's flight paradoxically secures his place within the circus rather than enabling him to escape its brutalizing and humiliating confines.

But how can we read Dumbo's flying as integral to *Dumbo's* representation of racial issues? We need to recall that Dumbo's ears initially function to expose his heritage as partially African and that the revelation of those ears begins the painful series of humiliations, risks, and exclusions to which he is subjected. We need also recall that Dumbo first flies while stupefied with alcohol and that the ministrations of the obviously caricatured Jim Crow and his friends inspire Dumbo's successful attempt to fly consciously. It is my contention that Dumbo's flight represents a recurring theme in African American history; that is, that in order to deal with the stress and danger of racial oppression, African Americans have repeatedly been forced/inspired to excel physically in ways that guarantee them audience recognition and mainstream notoriety, if not acceptance. In his definitive *Black Culture and Black Consciousness: Afro-American Folk Thought from Slavery to Freedom*, Lawrence W. Levine characterizes the persistent myth of the "flying Africans" in pertinent terms:

> African-born slaves were associated with conjure and magical powers as exemplified in the frequently told stories of Africans who put up with the treatment accorded to them by whites in America as long as they could and then simply rose up and flew back to Africa. In some versions they delayed their escape until they could teach their American-born relatives and friends the power of flight as well. (87)

Dumbo's flight, of course, rescues him from the torture and humiliation foisted upon him by the clowns and the circus management, aligning his aerial feats quite coherently with the flying Africans legends wherein abused slaves simply flew out of their troubles. Levine's remarks concerning the transmission of the "power of flight" from African-born to American-born slaves also coincides with the fact that it is Jim Crow, putative leader of the crow community, who not only first suggests the possibility that "maybe [Dumbo] flew up" into the tree, but performs some conjuring of his own when he comes up with the gimmick of "the magic feather" to boost Dumbo's confidence. That Dumbo's flight guarantees his reunion with his imprisoned mother similarly functions as a metaphorical "home" of Dumbo's accomplishment; he may not return to Africa as did the flying Africans of legend, but his reunion with his mother is a powerful incentive as well as a utopian closure of his nightmarish ordeal of separation and enforced labor.

Toni Morrison recovers this scene near the conclusion of *Song of Solomon*, a novel that represents "flying Africans" using the power of literal flight to escape racial oppression and social misery. Milkman,

Morrison's protagonist, whose search for personal identity and cultural bearings moves *Song of Solomon,* finally discovers one of the
truths of his past and, implicitly, the communal past of African Americans. After a long and frequently excruciating journey to discover the
hidden treasure of his family's past (he thinks it is a cache of hidden
gold at the time), Milkman is initiated into the truth of his family and
racial origins. Susan Byrd, the one living source of his family's past,
discloses the fact that Solomon, Milkman's most distant known relative, was one of "those flying African children." Assuming that Susan
Byrd's reference to "flight" simply refers to "escape," Milkman is corrected when Susan Byrd reveals the legend of the "flying Africans":

> no, I mean flew. Oh, it's just foolishness, you know, but according
> to the story he wasn't running away. He was flying. He flew. You
> know, like a bird. Just stood up in the fields one day, ran up some
> hill, spun around a couple of times, and was lifted up in the air.
> Went right on back to wherever it was he came from. (322–23)

Milkman expresses his elation over this discovery as soon as he
reaches the home of one of his paramours. She asks what he could
possibly mean by his excited report that "The son of a bitch could
fly! You hear me, Sweet? That motherfucker could fly! Could fly! He
didn't need no airplane. Didn't need no fuckin tee double you ay. He
could fly his own self!" Milkman clarifies the implications of Africans
having the ability to fly:

> Oh, man! He didn't need no airplane. He just took off; got fed
> up. *All the way up!* No more cotton! No more bales! No more
> orders! No more shit! He flew, baby. Lifted his beautiful black
> ass up in the sky and flew on home. Can you dig it?
>   . . . he went back to Africa.
>   . . . He left everybody down on the ground and he sailed on
> off like a black eagle. "O-o-o-o-o-o Solomon done fly, Solomon
> done gone/Solomon cut across the sky, Solomon gone home!"
> (328–29)

Milkman's revelation, of course, clarifies the novel's numerous images
of flight—its proliferation of characters with bird (Byrd and Bird)
names, the cryptic song of the children of Shalimar, references to

Charles Lindbergh, and the novel's opening suicidal jump of Mr. Smith, who "had promised to fly from Mercy [Hospital] to the other side of Lake Superior at three o'clock" (3). More relevant for our discussion of *Dumbo*, Solomon's flight figures as a response to the oppression of life under slavery; through flight, the "flying Africans" escape the "cotton," "bales," "orders," and the "shit" of a life of forced slave labor. Significantly, Solomon flies "home," recovers his origins, and, like Dumbo (who "flies just like an eagle"), "sailed on off like a black eagle."

The association of black flight with the flight of eagles in all these examples suggests the coherence of the image in African American culture, and, as such, links these otherwise disparate representations. In fact, the Tuskegee Air Squadron, the first all–African American air unit in U.S. history, was known by a number of nicknames, including their self-chosen "Lonely Eagles," the label "Schwartze Vogelmenschen" ("Black Birdmen"), given them by Luftwaffe pilots, and "the Black Redtail Angels," used by other U.S. crews.[14] All such designations raise the problematic status of African Americans as American citizens existing under the patriotic banner of the bald eagle. The eagle central to these three examples functions, thus, as a stressed and contradictory representation, capturing and linking at once the yearning for escape and transcendence generated by the oppressed conditions of African American existence *and* the highly contested desire for belonging and participation within the social arena of American life.

Contemporary African American athletic stars, while no longer flying back to Africa, are nonetheless required to fly, but usually only within the safely demarcated confines of the basketball court, football field, or, for those differently gifted, the musical stage. As sports sociologists, sports columnists, university athletic directors, and common observers have long known, the lure of the fame and fortune associated with athletic stardom has had particular impact on young African Americans, especially those from urban ghettos, where "getting high" with sports is often perceived as the only alternative to "getting high" and getting killed with drugs and crime. There are still numerous universities at which the majority of African American students are affiliated with various sports teams and play before packed houses of screaming white fans, and the recent tendency of NBA franchises to move to new suburban arenas far from their "home" cities of Cleveland, Detroit, and so on, enabling largely affluent, white audiences to enjoy their talents in the familiarity of their own neighborhoods, further exacerbates the already strained racial relations in professional athletics.[15] Sportswriter and cultural critic Nelson George makes this point in a powerful discussion of African American men and basketball:

> At the dawn of the 1980s basketball had a full-fledged rep—one perpetuated by coaches and media and believed by way too many Black families—as the fastest way out of the ghetto. "The life" (a.k.a. street hustling in general and drug dealing in particular) had this rep, too. So did the music biz. The narrowness of these options is testimony to the alienation so many young people felt toward the more traditional, socially acceptable means of personal empowerment. (200)

As George comments, "by the late seventies the opportunity for an education at white schools via sports, something new just a decade before, was now commonplace. At many schools these athletes constituted the first large group of African-Americans on campus" (194).

The dreams of escape and success through basketball (or music or drugs) harbored by many of these young men are betrayed, George argues, not only through their own misplaced materialism or greed, but because of structural exploitation at the university level. After three decades of false promises and misguided hopes (only 20 percent of college football and basketball players graduate, and nearly 50 percent genuinely believe they will sign NFL or NBA contracts [George 216]),

> Black kids now understood the deal. . . . As soon as their eligibility was up, it was almost uniformly "see ya later" at a great many institutions of higher learning. Lacking cars, girls, a pro contract, or a degree worth anything in today's marketplace, the brothers wandered back to the 'hood. Most returning players don't turn to drug dealing, but too many do. The failure of these players following years of work at (and exploitation by) schools

lets folks back home know these men were just pawns in a game. (201)

The cocaine-related death of University of Maryland star and Boston Celtic first-round draft choice Len Bias in 1986 pays a tragic tribute to the complicated lure of drugs and sports stardom for African American youths.[16] From this perspective, Dumbo's first flying while in an alcoholic stupor might be more than a coincidental linkage of the highs provided by chemical intoxicants with those derived from physical excellence. In *Dumbo* every single moment of insight and inspiration—the ringmaster's idea to use Dumbo in the "pyramid of pachyderms" routine, the clowns' realization that they deserve a raise, and Dumbo's first flight—occurs when these respective characters are either dreaming or wildly drunk, suggesting that the confines of the circus truncates the horizons of life and thought for all its individual agents. Conscious existence, even that as incompletely theorized as that of the roustabouts, is simply intolerable.

The wide-ranging and diverse commercial representations of Michael Jordan, the superstar of the Chicago Bulls of the NBA, revisit this entire phenomenon, while erasing any sign of its contradictions. The spectacle of Jordan's play has, of course, received more accolades than our sports publications can handle. Jordan's leaping ability, however, has been uncannily drawn upon in various advertising campaigns, most spectacularly in footwear maker Nike's "Air Jordan" ads (some of which include and are directed by Spike Lee) and in campaigns by Coca-Cola. Both Nike and Coca-Cola capitalize on Jordan's jumping abilities by representing him in a variety of mind-boggling, gravity-defying leaps. The Air Jordan television spots and still photographs highlight Jordan's aviation skills both by virtue of their play on common airline names (Air Canada, and so on) and by capturing Jordan soaring well above all other figures in the visual field. In each case focusing on Jordan's ability literally "to fly," Nike ads show Jordan with his arms fully extended with the title "WINGS" spread across the top of the photo; "High Flying" over the amazed look of Mars Blackmon (Spike Lee); approaching the hoop at eye-level in a photo entitled "Hang Time"; and, finally, "In Orbit" with the caption reading "Michael Jordan has overcome the acceleration of gravity by the application of his muscle power in the vertical plane, thus producing a low altitude earth orbit."[17]

Nike's campaign directed by and featuring Spike Lee as Mars Blackmon features a "professor of aeronautics and astronautics" explaining Jordan's flying abilities. Two other ads feature Spike Lee, in one spot having his wish for Air Jordans granted by Little Richard as a genie, and then exclaiming, "Look mom I can fly," and in another in his bedroom showing a series of photos depicting Michael Jordan flying over the Capitol, the skylines of Los Angeles, New York, Paris, and Moscow, the Colorado Rockies, and the lunar Sea of Tranquility. The ads also cast Jordan, variously, as the guy getting the girl because of his Air Jordans and as a public-relations man explaining the curricular advantages of "Michael Jordan's Flight School."[18] Nike diversified its "flying Jordan" campaign with its spectacular Nike Town athletic-shoe complexes, at which a huge image of Michael Jordan hovers eerily in flight over the earthbound bargain hunters below. Similarly, a Coca-Cola television spot depicts Michael Jordan jumping so high to secure a can of Coke that he actually goes into orbit around the moon. The cleverness and popularity of the Nike and Coca-Cola campaigns are well known; their innovations (including bringing a director of the quality of Spike Lee) have revitalized an often redundant commercial climate. However creative their contributions, though, their work needs to be recognized as capitalizing on the highly complex and controversial status of African Americans in the athletic programs of American universities and North American professional athletics.

vi

It might seem extreme to extend the thematics of Disney's 1941 classic to speak to contemporary American culture and its racial tensions. However, like many cultural products that engage deep social and historical fissures, *Dumbo* functions as a relay, in this case escalating the dynamics of its critique and allowing us to recognize them within subsequent social and historical currents. Furthermore, the film itself verges on authorizing the rationale for such a hermeneutic gesture. Integral to the social and economic formation of the circus and the entire social world of *Dumbo* is a principle of escalation or inflation that governs its actions as well as its inner operations. For example, the itinerary of the circus begins in the winter grounds in Florida; its first shows are in smaller, apparently rural, towns, and we know that the final performance we experience in the narrative is in the "Big Town" (the circus sits against the backdrop of an urban cityscape) toward which the circus has been heading for the entire film. This movement from small to large also characterizes two central facets of the circus's operations. For one, the clowns, sensing they have made an enormous hit with the baby in the burning house routine, push the intensity of their act by raising the platform from which Dumbo jumps. Their crudely arithmetic and economic logic is as follows: "if they laugh when the elephant jumps from twenty-five feet, they'll laugh twice as hard if he jumps from fifty feet." The other clowns agree with this logic, but refuse to stop at a mere fifty feet and eventually settle on Dumbo's jumping from one thousand feet above the circus's floor, a height which, once we visualize it in the final circus act, we see would be sure to kill the baby elephant were he not magically to fly just seconds before impact. Second, this escalation of the height and danger of the act for Dumbo translates into the inflationary logic of the clowns' compensation. The clowns realize that "this is worth real dough," and after drinking heavily, leave together singing "We're going to hit the big boss for a raise." In all these cases, the world of the circus is revealed to be constantly in flux, resisting stasis and tending toward larger towns, higher and more dangerous acts, and higher salaries for the clowns themselves. This logic of inflation and escalation informs the film from beginning to end, culminating in the newspaper headlines flashed in rapid succession in the movie's penultimate scene, one of which documents Dumbo setting a new altitude record and another depicting Dumbo's manager signing a million-dollar contract (he goes from working for peanuts—literally—to seven-figure compensation). Perhaps the most apt representation of the film's theory of inertia and momentum, however, occurs in the "pink elephants on parade" nightmare. Near the conclusion of that hallucinatory tour de force two elephants skate gracefully, leaving beautiful and geometric designs in the ice. After just a few seconds, however, the elephants speed up, the music intensifies and merges with mechanical sounds, and, eventually, the elephants, now transformed into motorized boats and automobiles, career wildly and erratically across the screen before colliding in one gigantic explosion.[19]

Just as the newspaper headlines transgress the prior autonomy of this fantastical animated world and interject another, "actual-world" discourse of newspaper copy and headline rhetoric into *Dumbo,* the events and trends announced in those headlines, as well as the issues, themes, and dynamics from within Disney's filmic text, intersect with the social horizons of the film's historical world. This tendency was even remarked upon and bemoaned by Siegfried Kracauer when he complained about the film's turn toward socially realistic narrative and its too intimate involvement with the social and political world of its initial audiences. In one obvious example, the newspaper headline reporting Timothy Mouse signing a million-dollar Hollywood contract for Dumbo fuses the economic context of the production of *Dumbo* with the still spiraling trends in Hollywood salaries and budgets, an area of the film's representation which clashes with the actual strike conditions that troubled the Disney Studio during the making of *Dumbo.* We have already paid some attention to Dumbo's flying ability as an early representation of the attempt of the African American community (and before them the Jewish community) to transcend their oppressed socioeconomic conditions by excelling physically in athletic competitions. The contemporary scene of Dumbo's million-dollar Hollywood contract would, then, also include the astronomical salaries earned by professional athletes, now almost routinely playing for several millions of dollars a season. The flip side of this escalationary logic would also have to account for the many "crimes of fashion" in America's inner cities, where impoverished children kill each other for hundred-dollar-plus pairs of athletic shoes and official NBA clothing items, such as team or superstar jackets, ostensibly to identify with the high-flying heroes who endorse the products.[20]

Even within the explicit confines of the film, however, there exists a chilling and murderous set of possibilities. If we allow the trajectory of the film's inflationary and escalationary logics, does not *Dumbo's* representation of ever higher platforms and ever more dangerous acts and the headlines of "altitude records" and "Dumbombers for Defense" converge with Dumbo's bombing and machine-gunning his antagonists, his being ordered to "wave flags," and the comment that he "flies just like an eagle" to suggest something like an allegory of American militarism? The proliferation of eagle iconography at the time of *Dumbo*'s making and release was remarkable. Not only were virtually all newspapers and many magazines saturated with diverse depictions of American airpower, but the eagle, not surprisingly, emerged as the most reliable symbol for that rising military force. A cursory check of the June 29, 1941, Sunday edition of the *New York Times* (in which an early review of *Dumbo* appeared) found numerous representations, including a magazine special on the Polish Air Force entitled "Poland's Eagles," and a Budweiser Beer ad stressing the beer's affiliation with the American eagle. The crow's remark that Dumbo "flies just like an eagle" could hardly have been processed outside the rampant imaging of the eagle as patriotic symbol of America's participation in the global theater of World War II.

Very shortly after the release of *Dumbo*, the Disney Studio was transformed into an efficient propaganda machine for the American war effort, producing, usually at cost, numerous animated instructional, inspirational, public-service, and propaganda features, many of which urged the American populace to join in ("all aboard!") the war effort. All this was not without its impact on the studio. As Thornton Delehanty observed,

> in the commissary where only a short while ago the boys and girls of the Disney family used to come in at lunch looking very Greenwich Villagey and individualistic in their sports clothes and open-collared shirts, there is evident a startling change. Naval officers in uniform swarm over the place; the atmosphere is regimented. (131)

The regimentation evidently worked, as the Disney Studio produced over three hundred thousand feet of film in 1943, ten times its highest previous output. Delehanty informs us that "that does not mean a tenfold increase in employment; it means the boys and girls are working about ten times as efficiently" (132). If we recall the usually tense and demanding atmosphere at the studio described by Shamus Culhane, it is not difficult to imagine the great toll that the sped-up conditions and stress must have taken on the already disgruntled animators. But the Disney Studio had joined in the patriotic mission even earlier. "Long before Pearl Harbor," the Disney artists were designing creative insignia for air force planes flying over Burma into China, and the demand for such graphics grew to the point that the studio designated five people whose full-time work was the invention of such insignia (Delehanty 137). What I am arguing is that it is a very small step indeed from the bellicose imagery and implications of *Dumbo* to the explicit propaganda of *Victory through Air Power*.[21] Steven Spielberg's *1941* captures something approaching this fusion of Disney's talents and America's emerging military might. In one of the film's few moments not spent on the mounting chaos and panic just prior to Pearl Harbor, General Stilwell (Robert Stack) takes a few minutes out of his hectic schedule to attend a screening of *Dumbo*. Spielberg gives us a few glimpses of the general watching the film, one of which focuses on Stilwell's hearty laughter during the crows' singing, while another captures him sobbing quietly during the singing of "Baby Mine" accompanying Dumbo's midnight visit to his mother.[22] For General Stilwell, apparently, sentimental visions of motherhood are not antithetical to the slaughter of millions of young men.

And, if we allow ourselves to fuse the film's representation of altitude records, "Dumbombers for Defense," and patriotism with its representation of the bestialization and brutal treatment of racialized Others, the principle of escalation built into *Dumbo* leads us to tragedies like the Nazi Holocaust, the bombings of Hiroshima and Nagasaki, and later to the carpet bombing of Vietnam and Cambodia, atrocities that could only have been committed by humans who were incapable of believing that the people they slaughtered were themselves fully human. That the squadron of "Dumbombers for Defense" flies in exactly the same formation as do the baby-animal-delivering storks in the film's opening scenes suggests the claustrophobic milieu within which *Dumbo* stages and meshes scenes as antithetical as the birth of baby circus animals and the vaporization of Japanese men, women, and children, pushing the film's ambivalence about childbearing to include the horrible possibility of the extermination of the human species. Richard Shale has remarked that "at the Disney Studio one of the problems at the outset of the war was how to convert from the production of entertainment films to instructional propaganda films" (11). *Dumbo,* of course, is no instructional film in the common use of the term, but we can certainly conclude that, by *Dumbo*'s release in 1941, Disney had already begun producing something close to propaganda, but propaganda which also contained the seeds of its own demystification.

vii

Near the conclusion of Michael Wigglesworth's monumental *The Day of Doom* (1701), a work itself concerned with the disappearance of human life, Christ hears and dismisses the impassioned appeals of various categories of sinners, all destined for hell. Refuting the shabby logic of the various contingents' claims, Christ reaffirms not only scriptural clarity and logic, but also God's beauty, power, and justice in every decision. Among the most pathetic of these claims, and the final one to be addressed before "all, both great and small, / are silenced and mute" (stanza 182), is that of the reprobate infants, who died prior to any possibility for them either to be exposed to the gospel or themselves to influence their eternal fates. Claiming that they should not be held responsible for sins committed by Adam, or for any acts to which they couldn't possibly have consented, the infants are nonetheless sentenced in the following way:

> A crime it is, therefore in bliss
>   you may not hope to dwell;
> But unto you I shall allow
>   the easiest room in hell. (181)

Wigglesworth's poetic narrative never examines just how "easy" that room may be, and the infants are, nonetheless, consigned to the eternal and inescapable confines of hell.[23]

Dumbo revisits this primal scene of damnation and futility and represents a modernized and secularized version of the fate visited upon the infants in Wigglesworth's poem. In Disney's film narrative, the world of the circus replaces the hell of Wigglesworth's Calvinist vision, and this circus's routine operations generate and sustain a totalized and all-pervasive world every bit as hellish, painful, humiliating, and inescapable as Wigglesworth's hell. However, Disney's animated world departs from the Calvinist view of an eternal division between the regenerate basking in heavenly glory and the damned languishing amidst the horrors of Wigglesworth's post-Dantean hell by collapsing this opposition, enveloping the ideal within the horrible and rendering a world in which the circus represents a hell that encompasses the entirety of social and political life. In Wigglesworth's poem—indeed, in the broadest horizons of Calvinist theology—the prospects of eternal salvation, however remote one's chances of entering and however unimaginable in its Otherness, stand as an undeniable utopian terminus for the souls of the saved. In *Dumbo* we experience a hell without the saving alternative of a heaven, a hell not of transcendentalized religious and spiritual justification but of mundane social, racial, and economic oppression. To paraphrase Milton's Calvinist Satan, whose presence constitutes and delimits a hell wherever he might be, in Disney's *Dumbo*, where the circus is, is hell.

The fundamental difference between a narrative like *Huckleberry Finn*, with its circus and its representation of numerous acts of cruelty against helpless victims, and *Dumbo* is that the conclusion of Disney's film deprives Dumbo of the alternative of permanently leaving ("light-[ing] out for the Territory") and hence repudiating—or at least escaping—the corruption and violence of the circus. While to remain within his culture is, perforce, to be constructed by it, for Huck Finn there still remains territory open for his escape. In *Dumbo* that territory is either nonexistent, already colonized by the economic machine of Western culture, or precisely the territory to be attacked by the chilling "Dumbombers for Defense." The concluding scene of *Dumbo* happily reunited with his mother in their private, plush circus car, in *their* "easiest room in hell," reinscribes Dumbo within that world as its most famous, most privileged, and, we assume, most profitable act. That this scene concludes a movie in which every segment of the circus, with the single exception of Dumbo's mother, has violated Dumbo's dignity and endangered his life, and that it immediately follows his momentary revenge on the primary agents of his suffering (his attacking them by dive-bombing and shooting peanuts out of his trunk), destabilizes any closure this halcyon image is meant to provide. There is no indication whatsoever that the ethos of the circus has been altered, that its exploitation of human and animal labor has been redressed, or that the principles of violence that govern its theory of entertainment have been softened by the touching reunion between Dumbo and his mother. There is no reason to believe, in other words, that the circus has ceased being the hellish world we have witnessed for approximately sixty of the film's sixty-three minutes. Whereas in most of Disney's animated features the conclusions work to eradicate or to transform the locus of evil and cruelty, *Dumbo*'s conclusion performs the alternative work of co-optation, of integrating the film's two heroes within the world that has abused them. Dumbo and his mother seem unproblematically to merge back into the circus that has tortured, mocked, separated, and nearly killed them. It is *they* who are transformed, the film's primary agents of family love and coherence, by being assimilated into the brutal and dehumanizing world of the circus, now free to carry out its operations without any potential challenge from the perspective of the oppressed. Miriam Hansen defines the project of critical theory during the interwar years in pertinent terms. Frankfurt School theorists were concerned, she notes, with investigating "whether [the technical media] were giving rise to new forms of imagination, expression, and collectivity, or whether they were merely perfecting techniques of total subjection and domination" (28). I would only add that *Dumbo* achieves both goals in a convergence, however, that situates us as a video citizenry likely to "amuse ourselves to death," as Neil Postman's critique of television culture would have it.

And if what I am calling the film's principle of escalation accounts for *Dumbo*'s inner logics as well as for its intersection with trends in American social and political life, then the nightmarish world of *Dumbo* stands primarily as a warning of atrocities to come. From Dumbo's flag waving, the crow's comment that "he flies just like an eagle," his machine-gunning of the circus, and the image of "Dumbombers for Defense," *Dumbo* stages a culture building up for technological atrocities—holocausts of gas ovens and nuclear vaporization perpetrated against women, men, and children of numerous races. In spite of the cheery little tune that accompanies its movement, the circus train that rolls through Disney's animated classic and at the end of which Dumbo and his mother ride, unlike Phillis Wheatley's "angelic train" of racial unity, unlike the liberatory promise of the Underground Railroad, and certainly unlike the hippie/utopian "Peace Train" of Cat Stevens's popular song, may have far too much in common with the trains that, when *Dumbo* was made in 1941, were already carrying Jews to destinations with names like Auschwitz and Treblinka. And who knows—maybe one of the "Dumbombers for Defense" would be named Enola Gay or Bockscar.

Perhaps it is fitting that a book about "loose ends" should admit to its own loose ends, to the impossibility/difficulty of its own cessation. Is there any similarity among these loose ends or among the relationships between these conclusions and the dominant themes of their narratives? I don't think so, at least in terms neither of their content nor of the nature of the extratextual discourses that they usher into their narrative worlds. Functionally, however, they all serve as conduits via which their host narratives are infiltrated by social and historical issues which frustrate any attempt at narrative consolidation and coherence, problematizing and sometimes rupturing the narratives from which they dangle. I think these "loose ends," in so doing, can also be read as signs of the conflicted relationships between the creators of these works and their ostensible audiences, between the creators and their own thematics, and, between the creators and their own vexed identities. Cathy Davidson, Michael Gilmore, Kenneth Dauber, and Toni Morrison, to name only a few, all have recently analyzed the identities of American authors vis-à-vis the historical, economic, gendered, and racial struggles of their times. The works studied in *Loose Ends* variously revisit all of these ideological sites.

In fact, the bizarre positioning of each author or, in the case of *Dumbo*, entire collective of artists relative both to the production of their work and to their ostensible audience raises numerous problems of interpretation, especially those concerned with intentionality of any sort. Brown addresses *Wieland* to President Thomas Jefferson as a gesture of political assistance, yet the work highlights the historical-ideological residue and tendencies inherent within the (by 1800) increasingly valorized historical core of the Republic's past. According to Brown's calculations, these tendencies also just happen

to have brought the culture to the verge of self-annihilation. Phillis
Wheatley writes her poetry to, for, and sometimes at the orders of
her Euro-American owners and their elite social circle, but she stages
within those lyrics both the violence and horror of the slave trade
and the oppressed circumstances of her own violated subjectivity.
Her poems, regarded as performances little short of miraculous by
her condescending audience, expose the dominance, corruption, and
hypocrisy of that very culture. Herman Melville writes *Israel Potter*
as a desperate attempt to recover the audience for travel narrative
and adventure writing that had all but abandoned him after the publications of *Moby-Dick* and *Pierre,* yet he assaults the patriotic beliefs that potential audience holds dear by exposing the opportunism
and fraudulence at the heart of the new generation of Revolutionary
"founding fathers" and the shallowness of a public who would "buy"
their self-aggrandizing narrative programs. Emily Dickinson's poem
(with no immediate audience) begins with a casual stroll along the
beach, but by its own denouement has given voice to the ensemble of
psychological, cultural, and social forces that constitute the ideology
of patriarchy and its pervasive oppression of women. Henry James
obviously tries to reconsolidate the inviolability of human consciousness and sanctity of intimate domestic boundaries, yet "The Jolly
Corner" foregrounds the impossibility of such subjective units existing, let alone being consolidated, outside of pervasive cultural trends.
The Disney Studio's *Dumbo* is pitched at the usual Disney audience of
children and is replete with the wonders of animated fabulation, yet
it elicits not only the horrors, common to the genre, of children separated from their parents and abused by entrepreneurs driven only by
greed, but also the "real world" of racism, oppressed labor conditions,
and world war. And yet, despite their numerous solicitations for a
socially driven reception, these works, because of their ambiguous
referential schemes (Brown and Dickinson), their generic constraints
(Wheatley's poetry and *Dumbo*), or the writer's corpus within which
the specific text is imagined (James and Melville), have rarely been
read in ways that render the conflicts at their very cores visible, let
alone dominant.

   Just as each of these works stages a highly stressed drama of sociohistorical conflict, it also signifies within conflicted generic parame-

ters. Is Brockden Brown's *Wieland* gothic tale, sentimental romance, or historical allegory? Phillis Wheatley, we might say, has stolen the signifying potential of the conventional ode and conscripted it to her own oppositional practice, much as she was stolen from her own African home and sold into domestic slavery for Boston's economic elite. Melville's *Israel Potter* advertises itself as a faithful retelling of a preexisting Revolutionary narrative, yet spins almost out of control into both biographical and autobiographical discourses as well as into the discourse of oppositional ideology critique. Dickinson's recollection of a stroll quickly swirls into a recapitulation of an initiatory experience of profound psychosexual dimensions as well as a meditation on the gendered colonization of American nature. "The Jolly Corner" breaks into as many genres as it has parts, with its three sections generally identifiable as urban realism, protomodernist stream of consciousness, and sentimental romance respectively, with traces of both naturalist representation and ghost stories thrown in to boot. *Dumbo*'s appeal as a child's animated fantasy is quickly complicated as it incorporates moments from numerous "adult" genres, including proletarian fiction, racial epic, and wartime propaganda. As a result of such representational fluidity, these generic anomalies are quite capable of being processed from within any of a variety of interpretive conventions, some of which seem mutually contradictory. What I have called shadow narratives, then, function as something like the "generic unconscious" of these dominant narrative schemes, harboring and then releasing discursive energies antagonistic to the main drifts of their respective works. Perhaps the issue is that we tend (maybe even need) to conceptualize the loose ends within these works in some way, lest they remain dangling reminders of narrative incoherence. Once we house them within whatever generic scheme seems appropriate and capacious enough to account for their vagrant tendencies, that generic voice assumes a destabilizing counterforce to the dominant voices of the text.

Significantly and relatedly, each of these works stages a historically specific drama of oppressed subjects, victims of the racial, economic, gendered, and class-based hegemonic systems of the dominant culture. They and their priorities emerge, not surprisingly, from within the possibilities of both shadow narratives and suppressed generic voices as the languages in which they speak. In the case of the women represented within these texts, the construction of the female identity is discursively and thematically fractured and always not only involves a compromise (apparently damaging, paralyzing, and/or demeaning) with her culture or with men, but also provides the enabling matrix within which the speaker/character emerges reconstituted and capable of engaging and even triumphing over significant cultural odds. For these texts, the loose ends are strategic, necessitated by the discursive limitations imposed on the narratives, or, in the case of James, by those imposed upon women by the culture of that text's genesis. The racialized dramas played out in Phillis Wheatley's poetry and *Dumbo* similarly strain against the modes of oppression common to the works' respective historical periods to expose the operations of the systems against which these racialized subjects struggle. Quite significantly, Wheatley's poetry and the characters of Israel Potter and Alice Staverton have all received gratuitously hostile critical treatment, which has attacked Wheatley's "derivativeness" or accommodationist "selling-out," Israel Potter's weakness and passivity, and Alice Staverton's second-class and subordinate role within James's tale. Much of the criticism of the other works has elided the possibility that Dickinson's poem or Disney's animated feature engage "serious" issues at all and has established a critical inertia from which we are still struggling to break free.

One of the components of this general avoidance of the social fissures inscribed within these works has been the emphasis within criticism on individual character and characters, abstractly considered. This subjectivist bias obscures the importance of the contexts within which those characters are constructed. In *Wieland* the entire religio-ideological development of colonial and early Republican culture has taken a backseat to considerations of the novel's place in the historical development of fiction in the United States and of the gothicism of Brown's Wieland family. The religio-racial dynamics of late-eighteenth-century American culture in Wheatley's poetry have generally been ignored in favor of discussions of Wheatley's poetic "originality" or her racial accommodationism. Studying the emerging discourses and technologies of fame and reputation that

merge in mid-nineteenth-century America's orgy of filiopietism in
Israel Potter has seemed less compelling than elaborating on how
the eponymous Potter embodies traits definitive of "the Yankee character" and usually at odds with Melville's supposed valorization of
"questing" individualism. The abusive core of Emily Dickinson's culture's construction of femininity has seemed less engaging than the
implications of her poem for the development of her individual sexuality. Jamesian criticism has focused on Spencer Brydon's traumatized psychosexual history rather than on the emerging discourses of
subjectivity under capital in "The Jolly Corner" (a deep background
complicated by the already heavily subjectivist bias of American, and
Jamesian, criticism). And, almost needless to say, whatever criticism
Disney's film has received has skirted around the systematic pervasion
of all facets of existence by the conflict and exploitation dramatized
in *Dumbo*.

We might say that these works are all about the future. Their inability to achieve satisfactory closure grows out of their complex
negotiation of social issues, particularly those dealing with historically rooted conflicts among races, classes, and genders. That is why
our reading of each necessarily addresses two or three historical periods: that of the text's construction, that of its explicit reference, and
that of the contemporary issues motivating our turn to the particular work. These works also make the future possible; by casting their
concerns in a forward-looking way, they force us to grapple with
the contemporaneity of the issues they articulate in historically specific, but historically provocative, manners. Nevertheless, they do not
always function in a liberatory or progressive way. Narratives like
Dumbo function hegemonically, recasting many social contradictions
and domesticating them as "humor," to guarantee the status quo.
They internalize the dynamic in *Adventures of Huckleberry Finn* in
which Tom Sawyer, who wants "to tie Jim to a tree for fun," might
well be the most dangerous character in the book. Spencer Brydon's
narrative in "The Jolly Corner," if read in isolation, generates a denial of history and politics characteristic of conservative politics and
economics. It is only through its juxtaposition with the progressive
narrative of Alice Staverton that we witness the complex historical

dynamic within James's work. Failed endings signal the reality that these issues have not been and will not be concluded without a total reimagining of the possibilities of existence.

Nonetheless, these works are, often despite themselves, or at least despite the likely intentions of their creators, radical texts. They offer no utopias, but in their refusal to falsify the conditions of their creation, they fracture the possibility of utopian thought, so that the mystifications enacted in their moments of closure are exposed as ineffectual and ideologically unstable, even impossible. Like Huckleberry Finn refusing to countenance the atrocities he has seen masquerade under the name of culture, these texts fail to redress the wrongs they reveal. However, whereas Huck wants to "light out for the Territory" in hopes of removing himself from contamination, these texts reimmerse themselves in the issues of their genesis, dramatizing, if not a return of the repressed, at least the persistence of the various specters haunting cultural production in the modern world. They stand, as Walter Benjamin would have it, as monuments both to culture and to the barbarism not only which makes cultural production possible but which those cultural products cannot completely efface.

NOTES

Introduction

1 It is interesting to speculate that this dimension of Dylan's song influenced Jimi Hendrix's decision to record "All Along the Watchtower" instead of his first choice from *John Wesley Harding*, "I Dreamed I Saw St. Augustine." Apparently, Hendrix believed "I Dreamed I Saw St. Augustine" to be far too personal a Dylan vision, and felt that "All Along the Watchtower" resonated with a more cultural sense of apocalyptics and meshed with his own vision of "the chaos of fallen man" (Shapiro and Glebbeek 320).

1 "Seek and Ye Shall Find"; or, Il n'y a pas de dedans du texte: *Wieland*, Reference, History, Anti-Closure

1 *Milwaukee Journal* January 21, 21, 20, 1987.

2 "An Account of a Murder Committed by Mr. J— Y—, upon His Family, in December, A.D. 1781," reprinted in *Philadelphia Minerva* 2.81–82 (August 20 and 27, 1796): 20.

3 See Samuels's "*Wieland*: Alien and Infidel" for an excellent discussion of these sources and the novel's negotiation of various social stresses in the late-eighteenth-century United States.

4 All of these stories are from Lexis Nexis Services of Mead Data Central, Inc., resulting from a search request: "Voice W/3 Lord or God W/25 Murder! Or Kill!" I would like to thank Mary Mahoney of the Law Library at Marquette University's School of Law.

5 By suggesting that Brown's text is virtually evacuated of all data necessary for its legibility, I do not mean merely that Wieland's "empty world," as J. V. Ridgely has called it, is a function of novelistic setting and characterization.

6 I am, of course, here drawing on Sacvan Bercovitch's influential thesis from *The Puritan Origins of the American Self*.

7 See Richard Chase's discussion of *Wieland* in his influential *The American Novel and Its Tradition* for a representative example.

8 See my "Lionel Trilling, *The Liberal Imagination*, and the Origins of the Cultural

Discourse of Anti-Stalinism" for a discussion of the political harness Trilling imposed on numerous critics of American culture.

9   Roberta Weldon argues that Clara's aesthetic pleasure in "revolutions and battles"
"is somewhat disturbing and indicates that the kind of insularity the Wielands
embrace can lead to a dangerous myopia" (4). While Weldon posits the family
dynamic as an American social model, her view of *Wieland* as "A Family Tragedy"
truncates the potential range of her remarks.

10   See T. H. Breen, *Puritans and Adventurers*, for an important discussion of how
such regional differences mitigate against any totalizing definition of Puritanism
in its North American incarnation.

11   The question of whether *Wieland* can be read as a reconfiguring of Puritan ideas,
as a representation of Puritan habits of thought, or as a narrative in any way
concerned with the socio-ideological formation we usually call "Puritanism" has
received comment from a large number of critics. While many readers agree that
Brown *is* interested in exposing the dangers inherent in religious fanaticism, there
is little agreement over the precision of Brown's representation of the Wieland
family. I will outline only some of the most clearly and specifically articulated
of these positions; virtually any critical discussion of the novel will fall within
the extremes of these poles. Norman Grabo asserts flatly that the elder Wieland
"is, in short, a puritan who knows he stands on God's left-hand side" (7). Emily
Miller Budick offers a brilliant and complex reading of *Wieland* as a prime example of what she defines as the American genre of the "Akedian romance," in
which she repeatedly associates the Wieland males with various aspects of American Puritanism (22–33 passim). While both Larzer Ziff and Michael T. Gilmore
read the novel as investigations of the idea of denying original sin and human
depravity, they both stop short of identifying the Wielands as themselves legiti-
mately drawn "Puritans." According to Ziff, "to account for [the inexplicability
of Wieland's murders] by pointing out that Brown is here stigmatizing religious
fanaticism is inadequate because Wieland's training is singularly free from any
sectarianism" (54). Gilmore similarly argues that "Brown has taken pains to distinguish Wieland from authentic Calvinists and to spell out the dangers inherent
in his background and sensibility" (110). Alan Axelrod assents to this qualified
perspective when he notes that

> if Brown can be said to attack anything, it is fanaticism; and the novelist must
> have seen that neither of the Wieland men could be literally Puritans. Required
> were solitary figures whose religion, like that of James Yates, had developed
> in isolation. Puritanism, for all its potential extremity (especially as it might
> have been popularly perceived), was simply too social an institution, provid-
> ing too many of the checks and balances of rational civilization to serve the
> novelist's purpose. (66–67)

William Hedges works through a more decidedly negative take on the question
of the novel's reference. He believes that "the novel tells us little about religious
mania other than that it exists and can be destructive. Brown gives it no plau-

sible social context, indeed does his best to isolate both Wieland and his almost equally fanatic father from any contact with American Protestantism" (120).

As I argue here, the rigid focus on "literal" or "authentic" Puritanism misses the point in two important ways. First, it imposes some static and monolithic image of Puritanism and denies Brown any fictional flexibility in his representational strategies (Hawthorne, according to these calculations, never wrote "about" Puritanism). Second, such limiting perspectives, while probably advanced under the guise of "historical accuracy," actually fail to respond to Brown's text in any historically accurate way. For decades now, historians have been revising our picture of early New England life and suggesting a multiplicity of formations and beliefs that would render such designations as "literal" or "authentic" Puritanism absurd.

12 David D. Hall speculates that Hutchinson may even have been familiar with some of the numerous accounts of the faithful in England hearing voices direct from God. For example, he notes the cases of Eleanor Davis, who, in 1625, claims to have "heard early in the morning a Voice from Heaven, speaking as through a trumpet these words: 'There is nineteen years and a half to the Judgment Day'" (*Worlds of Wonder* 96–97).

13 I should mention that I have personally sought to find just how atrocious an act of shame Fairfield committed, but I have found no answer to date.

14 We should also recall Wieland's disbelief that his acts and motivations were even regarded as criminal by his peers (164–66 passim). According to his reasoning, since his community was familiar with his character as well as with his absolute devotion, they had no reason to bring him before the bar. His conduct was responsible only to a higher authority.

15 See Emily Miller Budick's *Fiction and Historical Consciousness* for the best analysis of this "Akedian romance" in American literary history.

16 See David Reynolds, *Beneath the American Renaissance,* for a thorough discussion of the underground genres that Reynolds argues underwrote the production of those canonical writers we associate with the flowering of writing in mid-nineteenth-century United States. According to Reynolds, canonical writers such as Poe, Hawthorne, Melville, Dickinson, and others were drawing heavily on sensational, popular writings for many of their definitive thematics.

17 See Edmund Morgan's still useful *The Puritan Family: Religion and Domestic Relations in Seventeenth-Century New England,* for a thorough discussion of various family relations in early Puritan culture.

2 The Whiteness of the Wheatleys: Phillis Wheatley's Revolutionary Poetics

1 See John Irwin's *American Hieroglyphics* for an important discussion of the confrontation with whiteness (as ontological abyss) in Poe's *Narrative of Arthur Gordon Pym,* Whitman's *Song of Myself,* and other major narratives of the American Renaissance.

2 See the works by Bennett, Collins, Hogue, Jamison, McManus, and Silverman.

3 June Jordan has addressed precisely this issue. As she articulates the conundrum for Wheatley,

> If she, this genius teenager, should, instead of writing verse to comfort a white man upon the death of his wife, or a white woman upon the death of her husband, or verse commemorating weirdly fabled white characters bereft of children diabolically dispersed; if she, instead composed a poetry to speak her pain, to say her grief, to find her parents, or to stir her people into insurrection, what would we now know about God's darling girl, that Phillis? Who would publish that poetry, then? (257)

4 This and all subsequent quotations from Wheatley's poetry are from John C. Shields's edition.

5 See, for example, Cotton Mather's *The Negro Christianized*, in which Mather argues rigorously for the compatibility of Christianity and slavery. Mather is careful to point out, for instance, that neither canon nor English law would equate baptism with emancipation.

6. Frederick Douglass's *Narrative of the Life of Frederick Douglass, An American Slave: Written By Himself* (as well as numerous other slave narratives) makes explicit the erasing of all memories and domestic ties as an important strategy in the constructing of slave subjects without pasts.

7 As O'Neale notes, "redemption" is a key word in Wheatley's vocabulary, as it denoted not only religious salvation, but also referred to the purchasing of a slave's freedom.

8 My reading here is compatible with those of O'Neale and Shields, who discuss the subtle ways in which Wheatley's religious language also carries a highly charged political critique of a slave ideology.

9 I offer so extended a reading of this poem and, especially, of the word "refined" in order both to establish the terms and the dynamics I will be examining in less detail in other poems and to suggest the multivalence and flexibility of Wheatley's rhetoric. Her work throughout *Poems on Various Subjects, Religious and Moral* is marked by a depth and complexity rarely appreciated.

10 See, for example, Thomas Otway's "Morning" and James Beattie's "The Melodies of Morn" for eighteenth-century poems on the morning that close with images of beauty, freshness, and rejuvenation. See also William Collins's "Ode to Evening" and "Ode to Simplicity," Anna Letitia Barbauld's "Ode to Spring," and Joseph Wharton's "Ode to Fancy" for other representative odes that close by fulfilling fairly traditional generic expectations.

11 I am partially indebted to students in my graduate seminars "Towards a Theory of Literary Incompetence" at Northwestern University and at Marquette University for this line of thought.

12 Hazel Carby situates the construction of African American women slaves as erotic paramours for white men and as sexual threats to "the conjugal sanctity of the white mistress" within the ideology of the cult of true womanhood as power-

ful determinants for the emergence of a discourse particular to African American women writers (Carby 27 and ch. 2 passim).

3 Fading Out of Print: Herman Melville's
Israel Potter and the Economy of Literary History

1   See Peter Rabinowitz's *Before Reading* for the best account of the ways in which the ideological assumptions we bring to our experience of literature determine virtually every facet of our reading.

2   It would be interesting to study how critical designations or readings come to persist through time. I briefly surveyed the momentum of one hostile perspective on Phillis Wheatley's poetry in chapter 2. These tendencies are interesting in a number of ways, especially as they have accrued enough force to forestall the emergence of counterperspectives for decades and even centuries. My guess is that the persistence of similar histories of critical blindness (or myopia or tunnel vision, at least) is particularly acute in cases of minority and oppositional texts. Critical fashions in these cases function to deflect emergent literary and critical practices, largely by returning repeatedly to similar or identical judgments within slightly differing environments of textual data and thematic evidence. For example, however different the studies of Matthiessen, Feidelson, Seelye, Dryden, and Dillingham are, they are united around their shared ideological commitment to Israel Potter's basic worthlessness. For an amusing and provocative discussion of this trend in high school science textbooks, see Stephen Jay Gould's "The Case of the Creeping Fox Terrier," in *Bully for Brontosaurus: Reflections in Natural History*.

3   Some of Melville's references include the following: "his clothes were tatters," "wretched rags" (19); "all in tatters" (20); "all rags and tatters" (24); "his coat a mere rag" (81); "dirty rag" (89); "seize these rags" (153); "collecting of old rags" (163).

4   See Samson's entire book for an important study of Melville's relationship to his many sources. Working along lines that resemble Michael Colacurcio's Hawthorne study, *The Province of Piety*, Samson demonstrates the depth and subtlety of Melville's working with and against a broad range of preexisting documents —literary, anthropological, religious, and political—throughout what Samson terms his "narratives of fact." Samson's discussion of *Israel Potter* is, to my mind, the most important study of that novel.

5   See Dillingham 263–67 for a reading of Franklin as a "true survivor" and exemplary presence in Melville's text.

6   See William Shurr's essay on Franklin for a remarkable revisionist reading of the structure and content of Franklin's *Autobiography*. Arguing that "Part I," the "Dear Son" section of the *Autobiography*, in fact needs to be read as a discourse actually addressed to William Franklin, Shurr mounts an ingenious and convincing reading of Franklin's relationship with his son.

7   Melville criticizes the same position on poverty in his parody of Emersonian and

Thoreauvian "charity" in *The Confidence-Man,* and a hint of the same characterizes the lawyer-narrator of "Bartleby the Scrivener."

8   See Chacko and Kulcsar for a fascinating discussion of the entire legend of "Israel
Potter." Among other evidence that the authors bring to support their hypotheses is the letter Potter actually carried to Franklin. Far from being the product
of an English gentleman, versed in the niceties of handwriting and phrasing, the
missive Potter presented to Franklin was

> written by no gentleman, filled with grammatical errors and misspellings. John
> Horne [one of Israel Potter's supposed supporters] would not have done so. He
> was, among other things, one of the more famous English grammarians; his *Di-*
> *versions of Purley* is considered a pioneer work in the study of language. (380)

Chacko and Kulcsar also remark on the suspicious disappearance of money advanced by Franklin to Potter and on the bizarre coincidence of Franklin's writing
on the subject of spies even as Potter was visiting his quarters (381, 382). Their
research was apparently carried out without awareness of Franklin's own sus-
pected role with British intelligence.

9   See Samson's related discussion of Melville's familiarity with and critique of John
Paul Jones's historical reputation. Drawing on Fanning's *Memoirs,* Samson exposes the strategies by which *Israel Potter* stages contradictions informing Jones's
career. For example, he notes that "as Jones was being wined and dined as the
toast of Parisian society, his men were being denied proper winter clothing and
adequate rations. . . . As a result of Jones's failure to give relief, 'a number of
Americans became beggars in a foreign country'" (Samson 184; Fanning 82–
83). While my interest is in a particular dimension of Melville's representation
of Franklin, Samson accounts for Melville's related critiques of both figures, in
addition to Ethan Allen.

10   Melville opens *Pierre* with a transcendentalized projection of nature similar to
Ishmael's trancelike reverie on the masthead:

> There are some strange summer mornings in the country, when he who is but
> a sojourner from the city shall early walk forth into the fields, and be wonder-
> smitten with the trance-like aspect of the green and golden world. Not a flower
> stirs; the trees forget to wave; the grass itself seems to have ceased to grow;
> and all Nature, as if suddenly become conscious of her own profound mys-
> tery, and feeling no refuge from it but silence, sinks into this wonderful and
> indescribable repose. (3)

Pierre's eventual fall into doubt and chaos is similarly charted in terms reminiscent of Ishmael's meditation. After developing a metaphor of a maturing child
gradually leaving the support of its parents and sallying forth into the world,
Melville recounts the moment when the adult first becomes aware of duplicity
and of human insignificance:

> There is still another hour which follows, when he learns that in his infinite
> comparative minuteness and abjectness, the gods do likewise despise him, and
> own him not of their clan. Divinity and humanity then are equally willing that

he should starve in the street for all that either will do for him. Now cruel
father and mother have both let go his hand, and the little soul-toddler, now
you shall hear his shriek and his wail, and often his fall. (296)

From the idyll that opens *Pierre* to this image of shrieking and falling, Melville
returns to the Ishmaelian moment, both pivoting on his recasting of Emersonian
transcendentalized nature.

11   Critics such as H. Bruce Franklin, Carolyn Karcher, and Michael Kammen have
articulated a vision of Potter as representative of an oppressed, proletarianized,
and forgotten class. Carolyn Karcher, for example, situates *Israel Potter* as adjacent to *Pierre* in terms of their political commentaries: "whereas in *Pierre* Melville
debunked the American aristocracy's version of the Revolution, in *Israel Potter* he reconstructed the Revolution from the perspective of the forgotten common man" (102). Karcher specifies Potter's representative status when she argues
that "Israel apparently stands for America's slaves, both black and white" (107).
Franklin argues a similar position, though he perceives more affirmative an intent on Melville's part:

> Melville's thesis is quite direct: the real heroes of the Revolution were the
> American yeomanry, but all they were to gain from its victories was a future
> of grinding labor, deepening impoverishment, a change of masters, imprison-
> ment, and obscurity. (62)

More significantly for my purposes, Franklin accounts for Potter's "failure" or
"weakness" (those traits most clearly generating the remarks of critics such as
Feidelson, Seelye, and Dryden) by refusing to isolate Potter the individual character from the workings of the environments and economics of Revolutionary
and postwar London:

> Israel falls from level to level of the proletariat, eventually becoming part of
> the reserve army of the unemployed, who "would work for such a pittance as
> to bring down the wages of all the laboring classes." (63)

In his important, though brief, discussion of Melville's novel, Michael Kammen
compares it to Edward Bellamy's *The Duke of Stockbridge: A Romance of Shays'
Rebellion* (1879, 1901). "Like Melville," Kammen suggests, "Bellamy indicated
that the Revolution brought poverty rather than prosperity to many virtuous
Whigs. Patriot heroes suffer hardship and languish in prison after the war. . . .
Again like Melville, Bellamy wanted us to know that they did not all live happily
ever after" (225). Important not only for their sympathetic perspective on Potter
and in their resisting the individualistic biases underwriting much *Israel Potter*
criticism, these remarks also imply, though they stop short of theorizing, Melville's interest in historiographic trends. Long before the "working-class history"
or "history from below" movements of the twentieth century, Melville anticipates
their priorities and, to some extent, their methods.

12   I borrow here from Jennings's book *The Invasion of America: Indians, Colonialism,
and the Cant of Conquest.*

13   Catherine Sedgwick's incredibly prophetic novel *Hope Leslie* stages this setting

more economically in 1827, only three years after Cooper's *The Prairie*. Sedgwick shows Hope Leslie's father and Mr. Holioke "noting the sites for future villages, already marked out for them by clusters of Indian huts. The instinct of the children of the forest guides them to these rich intervals, which the sun and the river prepare and almost till for them" (100). The only thing that Sedgwick leaves to the reader's imagination is the violence which must, of course, exterminate the present native inhabitants in order for the settlers to assume their proper position of ownership and mastery of the region. Her earlier commentary on the slaughter of the Pequots, however, haunts even this passage, preventing it from standing as an unproblematic or uncritical paean to Puritan policies toward the native population.

14   See Hennig Cohen's edition of *Israel Potter* for the most thorough available commentary on this passage (463–64). While he draws our attention to the obvious parallels in "The Encantadas," Cohen nowhere speculates on the possible relevance of this allusion to Melville's unpublished book proposal.

15   See Harrison Hayford and Hershel Parker for discussions of the strange history of "the story of Agatha" and a likely chronology of Melville's interest in and work on *The Isle of the Cross*.

16   See Bezanson's "Historical Note" to *Israel Potter* (especially 172–78) for a discussion of other indications that Melville was busy conceptualizing and gathering materials for his retelling of Potter's narrative during much of his European journey.

4   Emily Dickinson's Lost Dog

1   See works by Kher and Pollak (sea as sex), Porter and Winters (sea as death), Pickard and Keller (renunciation), and Griffith and Weisbuch (sea as overwhelming force) for representative samples of the best readings of this work.

2   Both Eberwein and Frank deal with the dog, though only Frank regards the dog's presence or absence as problematic. He concludes that poem #520's parallels with the epic themes and structure of the *Iliad* help account for its puzzling characterization.

3   Responses range from Weisbuch's position that the richness and strangeness of these images "suggest that the poem is at least partially about a confrontation with one's own mythic, even irrational imagination" (54–55) to Pollak's belief that they function as repositories for the speaker's own repressed, or at least unexamined, sexual urges (115).

4   One of the most common explanations for the phenomenon of mermaid stories is that sailors, out at sea for long periods and growing desperate for female companionship, mistook aquatic mammals, seals or manatees most likely, for women.

5   Mark Twain's roughly contemporary *Roughing It* (1872) suggests a similar vertical metaphor for social relations. The city (so-called) of Virginia, Nevada,

  roosted royally midway up the steep side of Mount Davidson, seven thousand two hundred feet above the level of the sea, and in the clear Nevada atmosphere was visible from a distance of fifty miles! It claimed a population of fifteen thousand to eighteen thousand, and all day long half of this little army swarmed the streets like bees and the other half swarmed among the drifts and tunnels of the "comstock," hundreds of feet down in the earth directly under those same streets. Often we felt our chairs jar, and heard the faint boom of a blast down in the bowels of the earth under the office. (275)

In this passage, it is clear that those who labor intellectually do so above the ground in primitive, but comfortable, offices, while those who labor physically do so beneath the level of the street, conveniently hidden from the vision of those more powerfully situated.

6   Mary Loeffelholz offers a useful perspective on this and other images of bestialized or diminished selfhood in Dickinson's work in general. Speaking of Dickinson's place within the tradition of poetry in the United States, Loeffelholz suggests that

> neither the Emersonian "whole man" of thought nor the capitalist entrepreneur was likely to seem an imitable model for nineteenth-century women aspiring to a poetic vocation. Women are symbolically debarred from the "wholeness" of humanistic thought—a wholeness that covertly presupposes lack, absence, fragmentation, castration, and therefore the desire to transform the multifarious world into the symbols that would image Man's wholeness (and repress its opposite). (9)

According to this logic, Dickinson's drama of diminution could be read as a necessary gesture, preparing her, through this process of fragmentation, for her role in a poetic culture dominated by men. These images of tininess also strain against Margaret Homans's argument that

> there is a group of poems in which [Dickinson] pictures herself as a tiny being, typically a daisy and typically in relation to some figure of masculine power. As in the many poems in which she criticizes dualism or polarity, she entertains, in order to challenge it, the convention that women remain childlike or regress in romantic relations. In all these poems the positions are reversed by a slight disjunction. In the manner of the poems that mock human competition with nature, the daisy may be tiny, but she is also larger than Master. (201–202)

Dickinson's speaker in this poem is not larger than anything, and undergoes, in fact, a progressive diminution. The reduction of the speaker's physical being, and the corresponding perspectival projection of her environment as massive and threatening in this poem, promise no reversal and generate no dialectical negation of the speaker's subjection. I take this departure from Homans's model not as a repudiation of that reading of Dickinson's poetry, but rather as a sign not only of its thematic multiplicity and irreducible complexity but also of Dickinson's ability to frustrate any stable perspective on her work.

7   See also poem #712, "Because I could not stop for Death –," for a well-known example of a poem in which death is personified as a courteous gentleman caller.

Dickinson's casting both the overwhelming force of the sea and the inescapability of death as, at least in some ways, respectful gentlemen may figure as one strategy for comprehending and domesticating the terror each holds.

8   Clark Griffith characterizes this poem as "post-romantic," and suggests that this speaker's visit to the sea echoes and comments upon the entire tradition of "going to nature's house" in romantic poetry (20).

9   See, for example, F. O. Matthiessen's seminal *American Renaissance*, especially chapters like "Man in the Open Air"; Leo Marx's *The Machine in the Garden;* Richard Poirier's *A World Elsewhere;* Henry Nash Smith's *Virgin Land;* Richard Slotkin's *Regeneration through Violence;* R. W. B. Lewis's *The American Adam;* and numerous other studies of the "nature" of American literature.

10   See Sybil Weir, *"The Morgesons:* A Neglected Feminist *Bildungsroman,"* for an excellent discussion of the theme of possession in the novel.

11   See Jane Tompkins's *Sensational Designs,* especially her discussion of Stowe's *Uncle Tom's Cabin.* See also Gillian Brown's "Gettin' in the Kitchen with Dinah."

12   See the essays collected in the editions by Rosaldo and Lamphere and by Ortner and Whitehead for various qualifications, clarifications, and challenges to Ortner's thesis.

13   In fact, most legal definitions of pornography include reference to the objectification and reduction of women to specific body parts. Catharine MacKinnon's definition captures the essence of most legal codes:

> We define pornography as the graphic, sexually explicit subordination of women through pictures or words, that also includes women dehumanized as sexual objects, things or commodities, enjoying pain or humiliation or rape, being tied up, cut up, mutilated, bruised or physically hurt, in postures of sexual submission or servility or display, reduced to body parts, penetrated by objects or animals, or presented in scenarios of degradation, injury, torture, shown as filthy or inferior, bleeding, bruised, or hurt in a context that makes these conditions sexual. (quoted in *Pornography and Sexual Violence* 2)

I think a fairly thorough case could be made for this poem as a critique of pornographic representation. Such an approach could situate both the threat of violence against and the fetishistic objectification of the poem's speaker within the context of pornographic violence against women, and could also make different sense of the childlike persona and the presence of the dog in the poem by addressing the preponderance of children and acts of bestialization in pornographic materials.

14   See Theweleit's discussions of Elaine Morgan's *The Descent of Woman* (New York: Stein and Day, 1972) and psychoanalyst Sandor Ferenczi's "Versuch einer Genitaltheorie" (*Schriften zur Psychoanalyse,* vol. 2, Frankfurt, 1971) for fascinating evolutionary, anthropological, and psychoanalytic accounts of human gender and sexual differentiation and violence.

15   See poems #500, #663, #892, #1185, #1213, and #1694 in the Thomas H. John-

son edition of the complete poems. Dickinson had also included references to dogs in early drafts of two other poems (#1355 and #1380).

16 Summarizing and agreeing with the work of Margaret Homans and Joanne Feit Diehl, Mary Loeffelholz characterizes the familiar cultural stereotype in pertinent terms. Sexual difference is exiled within Dickinson's work because

woman, the feminine, is consigned to nature and identified with the unspeaking material resources that are lifted into language by the poet but negated at the same time, as Emerson [in "The American Scholar"] negates the actual externality and productivity of "the Indies" when he transforms them into the abstract "wealth" that is somehow always already his. (10)

17 From this perspective the readings offered by Pollak and Pickard simply ignore the possibility that the speaker's return to her society can signal her triumph over her culture's denigration of women. Pickard argues that the speaker's return to the "Solid Town" entails a "rejection of one of life's prime forces — love, sex, beauty, or death — for a *weak conventional existence*" (84; my emphasis). For Pollak, the speaker's return is implicated in her refusal to recognize either her eroticism or her mortality and functions as a symbol of her impoverished consciousness (116–17). Their neoromantic readings assume too simply that the speaker's experience at the sea is one of positive possibility.

18 In his brief, though intriguing, analysis, Bernhard Frank verges on this reading; however, he works through these lines in a different way. Frank suggests that there are two possibilities: (1) that the speaker mistakes the sea at her heel for her dog, and (2) that, after the fashion of the Greeks who "used to represent their rivers in the shape of a bull," Dickinson's speaker here substitutes her dog for the bull.

19 See, for example, her remark that those who "talk of Hallowed things, aloud . . . embarrass my Dog –" (quoted in Sewall 5), and Higginson's claim that Dickinson believed that Carlo "understood gravitation" (quoted in Sewall 578).

5 "The Jolly Corner": Henry James
at the Crossroads

1 See Eve Kosofsky Sedgwick's reading of gay issues in James's "The Beast in the Jungle" for a brilliant analysis of James's "bachelor fiction."

2 For these identifications, as well as a host of related ones, see the following: Bier, Buitenhuis, Clair, Delbaere-Garant, Delfattore, Freedman, Geismar, Mackenzie, Mays, Przybylowicz, Rogers, Stovall, Tuveson. Annette Larson Benert makes some points about Brydon's relationship to the emerging world of modern finance that are compatible with my own focus. Referring to Brydon as "the very type of the nascent capitalist, raising rents and tenements on the ruins of his inheritance," Benert identifies Brydon's Other as "a male collective shadow lengthening over America during the golden age of capitalism" (119, 118).

3   As Raymond Williams demonstrates in his etymological study of the word "cul-
     ture," Santayana's focus on American culture may well result in his simply re-
     inscribing the very split he desires to expose. The word's Latin root, "*colere*,"
     Williams notes, had a range of meanings including "inhabit, cultivate, protect,
     [and] honor with worship." By the nineteenth century, the term had been placed
     in opposition to "the 'mechanical' character of the new civilization then emerging
     both for its abstract rationalism and for the 'inhumanity' of current industrial de-
     velopment" (Williams, *Keywords* 77, 81). The jolly corner, then, as the house of
     culture in the tale, carries quite a connotative load, including the early senses of
     "protection" and "honoring with worship" (Brydon defines that structure as "con-
     secrated"), but primarily in housing the whole notion of culture as the humane
     and cultivated in opposition to the social or commercial values of modern life.
     Santayana, of course, criticizes this split, but fails to analyze the complex status
     of culture in an age of consolidating capital. Santayana's own text, then, is symp-
     tomatic of rather than authoritative on the polarization of public and private life
     at the turn of the century.

4   Brydon's fainting away to an auctioneer's call supplies provocative support for
     an economic reading of the tale's title. According to the *Oxford English Dictio-
     nary*, both "jolly" and "corner" had economic/commercial significance in the late
     nineteenth century. A "jolly" was a person who would make a sham bid at an
     auction (it also referred to the bid itself), which would complement "corner," in
     the sense of "cornering the market." Along lines suggested by these senses, Bry-
     don's ostensible quest to confront his Other can be read as a sham, an attempt
     to corner the market, so to speak, of his identity against the hostile takeover
     threatened by his economic Other. The *OED* also lists "corner creeper" as one
     whose proceedings are "underhanded or stealthy," also appropriate for Brydon,
     who refers to his "craping" around in the jolly corner (Mrs. Muldoon also refers
     to "craping up to thim top storeys in the ayvil hours" [443]). Again, the implica-
     tion of underhandedness casts doubt on Brydon's willingness really "to 'go into'
     figures," and adds strength to the reading of "jolly" as "sham." The term "corner"
     itself is also split in significant ways. On the one hand, a corner is a place of
     openness, an intersection where two streets meet; on the other hand, a corner is
     a secret or remote place. The two ranges of meaning suggest Brydon's conflict,
     between embracing the dynamism (openness) of social and urban change or re-
     treating into a secretive haven from such transformations.

5   See Wagenknecht 207, Rovitt 67, Freedman 13, Shelden 133, and Travis 13.

6   The only critic to focus fully on Staverton and to debate these assumptions is
     John A. Clair. Defining Staverton as a "clever liar," Clair argues that she, desiring
     to marry Brydon but realizing the depths of his egotism and smugness, carefully
     precipitates Brydon's search for the self he might have become with a series of
     remarks concerning that Other and actually hires someone to frighten Brydon
     back to his senses. Clair believes, then, that Brydon does confront another per-

son at the bottom of the stairs, an accomplice hired by Alice Staverton rather than a specter of his unlived life. While some of the particulars of Clair's reading are questionable (preposterous even), his focus on Staverton's assertiveness and her verbal manipulations differs significantly from other readings.

7   Millett defines Ruskin's lecture "Of Queen's Gardens" as "one of the most complete insights obtainable into that compulsive masculine fantasy one might call the official Victorian attitude" (125).

8   I am indebted to Mary Poovey's excellent study *Uneven Developments* for this source.

9   What I am interested in here is an array of verbal strategies common to women in James's late novels, though not in his tales. Kate Croy in *The Wings of the Dove*, Mrs. Brookenham in *The Awkward Age,* and others demonstrate the subtle yet effective manipulations which I will discuss with reference to Maggie Verver. I focus on Maggie in this essay because of broader similarities between her and Alice Staverton.

10 See "Women's Speech: Separate But Unequal," by Cheris Kramer, for a discussion of the persistence of oblique patterns characteristic of women's speech. Kramer suggests that

> the tag-questions, the relatively large number of questions asked, the intonation which makes a declarative sentence a question, the compounding of requests, the concern with unobtrusive pitch and volume, . . . the roundabout way of declaring ideas—all aspects of female speech . . . would indicate one way in which the sex roles are maintained. (50)

It is suggestive that many of the characteristics Kramer associates with "female speech" also mark Alice Staverton's discourse in "The Jolly Corner," especially the transformation of declarative sentences into questions and "the roundabout way of declaring ideas."

11 It is not my intent to define James as either an incipient proletarian or feminist novelist, only to suggest that his relationship to matters of social change and to women's issues are, at least in his fiction, more complicated than many critics assume. Consistent with my argument throughout *Loose Ends,* I have also tried to demonstrate the disruptive impact upon narrative by those sociohistorical discourses inhabiting even the most arcane and apparently aloof work. The infiltration of these discursive energies into cultural works should also enable us to reconsider many conventional ideological appreciations of certain writers. Consider Terry Eagleton in a definition of James's reactionary political significance. James's work, Eagleton asserts, represents a desperate, devoted attempt to salvage organic significance wholly in the sealed realm of consciousness—to vanquish, by the power of such "beautiful," multiple yet harmoniously unifying, awareness, certain real conflicts and divisions (141). I would comment only briefly that "The Jolly Corner" represents nothing if not the omnipresence of conflicts, divisions, and contradictions.

In *Women and Fiction: Feminism and the Novel, 1880–1920,* Patricia Stubbs offers the following view on James's attitude toward women in his fiction:

In James we meet pure ideology and an anti-feminism so subtle and fused so completely with the form and texture of the novels that it can be overlooked altogether. His hostility operates at such a sophisticated level, and enters so closely into the fabric of his thought that it becomes all pervasive yet invisible. (155–56)

Stubbs also defines three general points about women in James's fiction: (1) that they are put in impossible situations, (2) that they invariably fail, and (3) that they are "scared of sex" and that they "tie themselves into knots of inhibition and self-consciousness at anything resembling a sexual encounter" (158–60 passim). At least in her winning some kind of victory and in her aggressive sexual overtures at the end of the story, Alice Staverton reverses each of these general truths.

Aside from a new perspective on one woman's role within one late tale, a historicized approach to "The Jolly Corner" offers a challenge to these and other critical commonplaces about James, and perhaps about other writers too quickly perceived as "reactionary," "sexist," or aloof from immediate social/cultural concerns. This is not to say, of course, that no such reactionary or sexist writers exist. However, I would suggest that, in literary texts, the difference between the uncritical expression or endorsement of a prevailing ideology and an immanent critique of such a position may be more vexed than we often grant.

6   "The Easiest Room in Hell": The Political Work of Disney's *Dumbo*

1   For a wide-reaching discussion of the roles played by corporate America and by the American media in disseminating and perpetuating many forms of racism, sexism, blind and contradictory patriotism, and violence, see Michael Parenti's *Make-Believe Media: The Politics of Entertainment.*

2   While the wicked queen's vanity in *Snow White* is recognizably human and may appear to have more in common with these films, she is characterized in terms that are primarily magical.

3   Even in the 1980s clowns were among the circus's lowest paid and most overworked laborers, earning a mere $180 a week and living in small and uncomfortable quarters. (Wisconsin Public Radio interview with member of the "Reduced Shakespeare Company" drama/comedy troupe.)

4   I refer all readers to the essay by Holly Allen and Michael Denning, upon which I have drawn for many of these claims.

5   The entire transcript of Disney's testimony can be found in Peary and Peary (92–98).

6   In light of such indictments by former Disney artists, one needs to take Leonard Maltin's saccharine assessment of *Dumbo* with a huge grain of salt. According to Maltin, *Dumbo* "marks a return to Disney first principles, the animal kingdom—

that happy land where Disney workers turn into artists; where their imagination, playfulness, ingenuity, daring flourish freest, in short, they're home" (53). Maltin's denial of the realities of *Dumbo*'s creation results from the Disney Studio's ironhanded control over its archives and refusing permissions to any but those scholars guaranteed to reproduce the Disney myth. As Susan Willis demonstrates, virtually the same theory of management by intimidation prevails at Disney World, where workers regularly spy on and are spied on by each other ("Critical Vantage Points" 3). My own request to use footage, slides, stills, and music from *Dumbo* in this project was denied with a vague rationale regarding Disney's concerns over its animated classics. Apparently I was supposed to find solace in the fact that Disney refuses many such requests.

7   Disney archivist David R. Smith offers a slightly different slant on the impact of the strike on the making of *Dumbo*. According to Smith, "the 1941 strike did occur during the production of Dumbo, but did not seem to affect it much, because it seemed to speed through production with everyone terribly enthused about it" (David R. Smith, letter to the author, March 1, 1991). I would like to thank David R. Smith for his responsiveness to my inquiries regarding the strike at the Disney Studio.

8   Given the film's foregrounding of the economic interests at the heart of all relations within this circus, its representing something like a microcosm of relations under expanding capitalism, it may not be too extreme to draw on a remark from Gerald Graff's *Literature Against Itself* for clarification. According to Graff, the tremendous appropriative flexibility of advanced capitalism, "with its built-in need to destroy all vestiges of tradition, all orthodox ideologies, all continuous and stable forms of reality in order to stimulate higher levels of consumption" (8), makes it the true cultural avant-garde. By incorporating and absorbing any and all radical threats to the maintenance of the status quo, capitalism co-opts, domesticates, and neutralizes all challenges to its stability. This final moment in Disney's film stages a compatible, if not identical, sociocultural dynamic.

9   As Leonard Maltin summarizes, "there has been considerable controversy over the Black Crow sequence in recent years" (52). But Maltin, and virtually every other commentator, strain to excuse Disney's representation. Maltin, for example, defines the criticism as "unjustified," because, as he argues, the crows are undeniably black, but they are black *characters,* not black *stereotypes.* There is no denigrating dialogue or Uncle Tomism in the scene, and if offense is to be taken at hearing blacks call each other "brother," then the viewer is merely being sensitive to accuracy (52). Maltin might have come to radically different conclusions had he been sensitive to more of *Dumbo*'s representation of the crows than merely one referential tag and had he situated that representation within the film's other areas of social analysis. Michael Wilmington has also described the crows as "a quintet of raffish, impudent crows, whose voices and mannerisms are obvious parodies of proletarian blacks" (80). Wilmington, quite rightly, I think, also calls

our attention to the heroic role the crows play in teaching Dumbo how to fly. Regardless of the explicit terms of their visual and musical representation, in other words, the crows emerge, in obvious contrast to nearly all of the circus animals, as powerful characters exerting their powers for Dumbo's good.

10 See Levine for the ways in which African Americans have signified on the stereotypes white Americans have perpetrated on African Americans by absorbing, internalizing, and transforming racist humor for their own cathartic and defensive purposes.

11 While focusing more urgently on the systematic racism that prevents African American and other minority children from receiving anything resembling a good, let alone a fair or equal, education, Jonathan Kozol takes note of one particular moment that supports this reading of Dumbo as racially marked simply by virtue of his physical difference, suggesting the persistence of racially biased stereotypes in contemporary education. Observing an elementary classroom in Chicago, Kozol notes one teacher's strategy for filling time with what strikes him as a tried-and-true method. As the teacher flips mechanically through a picture book of Mother Goose rhymes ("Mary had a little lamb," "Old Mother Hubbard," "Jack and Jill," "This little piggy went to market," and so forth),

> The children recite the verses with her as she turns the pages of the book. She's not very warm or animated as she does it, but the children are obedient and seem to like the fun of showing that they know the words. The book looks worn and old, as if the teacher's used it many, many years, and it shows no signs of adaptation to the race of the black children in the school. Mary is white. Old Mother Hubbard is white. Jack is white. Jill is white. Little Jack Horner is white. Mother Goose is white. Only Mother Hubbard's dog is black.
> "Baa, baa, black sheep," the teacher read, "have you any wool?" The children answer: "Yessir, yessir, three bags full. One for my master . . ." The master is white. The sheep are black. (45)

12 Dick Huemer, one of the Disney workers instrumental in the making of *Dumbo* and in naming its characters, verifies the fact that, when they named Mrs. Jumbo, they "were thinking of the P.T. Barnum elephant [of the 1880s]. That's the most famous elephant there ever was" (quoted in Brasch 71).

13 *New York Herald Tribune* June 14, 1942: 1+. See Dower 37, 82 for references to these other examples.

14 See Terkel 344; also "Fighting War and Racism: Black Troops were Heroes," *Cleveland Plain Dealer* June 18, 1995, sec. J: 1+.

15 The racism still plaguing professional golf, similarly, has resulted in many country clubs sacrificing the income and prestige of hosting major PGA tournaments rather than opening their membership ranks to African Americans.

16 Nelson George provides the following horrifying gloss to Bias's death:

> Maybe Len Bias's cocaine-induced death gave a few pause, but not enough. Shortly after the Maryland star's death, extra-potent crack was labeled "Len

Bias" in D.C. in a sick tribute to the dead hoop star. In fact, the 1986 draft, in which Bias was selected number one by the Boston Celtics, was one of the most drug-scarred ever. Four 1986 first-round draft picks (Bias, Chris Washburn, William Bedford, Roy Tarpley) had careers eventually destroyed or curtailed by drug use. (203)

17 I would like to thank Spike Lee and Mark H. Thomashow, and the Nike Corporation, for their assistance and permission in using their advertising materials. Their cooperation was friendly and generous and contributed greatly to the specificity of my argument.

18 Nike posters also feature other NBA stars, such as Dominique Wilkins, Mark Jackson, and Ron Harper, in visual ads simply entitled "Flight," and NFL star Randall Cunningham in a spot entitled "Rocket Man." The implied alternative to their Air Jordan and other flight-oriented sports campaigns featuring African American stars is their baseball shoe ad "Grace Under Pressure," featuring white Chicago Cubs first baseman Mark Grace in a fully extended stretch and as close to the ground as humanly possible.

19 See Michael Wilmington's discussion of *Dumbo* for an interesting reading of the copulatory emphasis in this scene and elsewhere in the film.

20 As Nelson George explains, the blame often leveled at Michael Jordan and Spike Lee for their participation in the "Air Jordan" campaign is largely misdirected. While Jordan's deal with Nike "was the catalyst for an explosion of sportswear chic among African-American youth," these attacks not only ignore the fact that "crimes of fashion" predate the recent spate of such acts, but also simplify a complex socioeconomic environment in which children fall prey to "misdirected materialism" (234, 235).

21 The Disney Studio continues to engage in activities in related fields of governmental propaganda productions. As Michael Parenti points out,

Walt Disney Productions has an Educational Media Company that turns out "educational" filmstrips about the free enterprise system, featuring old television and comic-book favorites. The company notes that these filmstrips "introduce students, grades 4 through 6, to the private enterprise system. . . . Common economic principles like supply and demand and product development are demonstrated and explained by [cartoon characters] as they run their own business." (173–74; Disney information quoted from *Dollars and Sense* Sept. 1979: 11)

22 In what can only be a bizarre coincidence, it is reported that, immediately after President Harry Truman was informed of the "successful" mission to drop the atomic bomb on Hiroshima, he announced to sailors aboard the ship on which he sailed that "this is the greatest thing in history" and then attended a comedy revue at which he laughed hilariously at the entertainment (*Newsweek* July 24, 1995: 28).

23 The only indication Wigglesworth's poem provides doesn't hold out much hope

to these infants. Shortly after the infants and the others appeal for Christ's compassion to spare them from hell, Wigglesworth seals their fate in significant language:

Oh, fearful doom! now there's no room
for hope or help at all:
Sentence is past which aye shall last,
Christ will not it recall.

That "there's no room" for any hope amidst the sufferings of hell might well spell doom for the infants in their "easiest room"; in the final analysis this language may indicate that there is "no room" for difference among the damned or that there is "no room," not even "the easiest room," where torments are mitigated at all.

WORKS CITED

Ackers, Charles W. "'Our Modern Egyptians': Phillis Wheatley and the Whig Campaign Against Slavery in Revolutionary Boston." *Journal of Negro History* (July 1975): 397–410.

Agnew, Jean-Christophe. "The Consuming Vision of Henry James." In *The Culture of Consumption: Critical Essays in American History, 1880–1980*. Ed. Richard Wightman Fox and T. J. Jackson Lears. New York: Pantheon, 1983. 67–100.

Allen, Elizabeth. *A Woman's Place in the Novels of Henry James.* New York: St. Martin's, 1986.

Allen, Ethan. *A Narrative of Colonel Ethan Allen's Captivity.* Philadelphia: Robert Bell, 1779.

Allen, Holly, and Michael Denning. "The Cartoonist's Front." *South Atlantic Quarterly* 92 (winter 1993): 89–117.

Anderson, Quentin. *The American Henry James.* London: Calder, 1958.

Arvin, Newton. *Herman Melville.* New York: Sloane, 1950.

Assiter, Alison. *Pornography, Feminism and the Individual.* London: Pluto, 1989.

Axelrod, Alan. *Charles Brockden Brown: An American Tale.* Austin: U of Texas P, 1983.

Barbour, James, and Tom Quirk, eds. *Writing the American Classics.* Chapel Hill: U of North Carolina P, 1990.

Baym, Nina. "A Minority Reading of *Wieland*." In *Critical Essays on Charles Brockden Brown.* Ed. Bernard Rosenthal. Boston: G. K. Hall, 1981. 87–103.

Bell, Ian F. A. "Money, History and Writing in Henry James: Assaying *Washington Square*." In *Henry James: Fiction as History.* Ed. Ian F. A. Bell. London and New York: Vision and Barnes and Noble, 1984. 11–48.

Bell, Michael Davitt. *The Development of American Romance.* Chicago: U of Chicago P, 1975.

Bellis, Peter J. "*Israel Potter*: Autobiography as History as Fiction." *American Literary History* 4 (winter 1990): 607–26.

Benert, Annette Larson. "Dialogical Discourse in 'The Jolly Corner': The Entrepreneur as Language and Image." *Henry James Review* 8 (1987): 116–25.

Bennett, Lerone, Jr. *Before the Mayflower: A History of the Negro in America, 1619–1964.* Baltimore: Penguin, 1968.

Bercovitch, Sacvan. *The Puritan Origins of the American Self.* New Haven: Yale UP, 1975.

Berens, John F. *Providence and Patriotism in Early America, 1640–1815*. Charlottesville: U of Virginia P, 1978.

Bezanson, Walter. "Historical Note" to *Israel Potter*. By Herman Melville. In vol. 8 of *Writings*. 173–235.

Bier, Jesse. "Henry James's 'The Jolly Corner': The Writer's Fable and the Deeper Matter." *Arizona Quarterly* 4 (1979): 321–34.

Bloch, Ernst, et al. *Aesthetics and Politics*. London: Verso, 1977.

Brady, Thomas. "Whimsy on Strike." *New York Times* June 29, 1941, sec. 9, p. 3.

Brasch, Walter M. *Cartoon Monickers: An Insight into the Animation Industry*. Bowling Green: Bowling Green U Popular P, 1983.

Breen, T. H. *Puritans and Adventurers*. New York: Oxford UP, 1980.

Breitwieser, Mitchel Robert. *Cotton Mather and Benjamin Franklin: The Price of Representative Personality*. Cambridge: Cambridge UP, 1984.

Bremer, Francis J. *The Puritan Experiment: New England Society from Bradford to Edwards*. New York: St. Martin's, 1976.

Brooks, Peter. *Reading for the Plot: Design and Intention in Narrative*. New York: Knopf, 1984.

Brown, Charles Brockden. *Wieland; or, The Transformation: An American Tale*. Vol. 1 of *The Novels and Related Works of Charles Brockden Brown*. Ed. Sydney J. Krause. Bicentennial ed. Kent: Kent State UP, 1977.

Brown, Gillian. "Gettin' in the Kitchen with Dinah: Domestic Politics in *Uncle Tom's Cabin*." *American Quarterly* 36 (1984): 503–23.

Budick, Emily Miller. *Fiction and Historical Consciousness: The American Romance Tradition*. New Haven: Yale UP, 1989.

Buell, Lawrence. *New England Literary Culture: From Revolution through Renaissance*. Cambridge: Cambridge UP, 1986.

Buhle, Mary Jo. *Women and American Socialism, 1870–1920*. Urbana: U of Illinois P, 1981.

Buitenhuis, Peter. *The Grasping Imagination: The American Writings of Henry James*. Toronto: U of Toronto P, 1970.

Burroughs, Charles. *An Address on Female Education, Delivered in Portsmouth, N. H., October 26, 1827*. Portsmouth, 1827.

Bushman, Richard L. "American High-Style and Vernacular Cultures." In *Colonial British America: Essays in the New History of the Early Modern Era*. Ed. Jack P. Greene and J. R. Pole. Baltimore and London: Johns Hopkins UP, 1984. 345–83.

Carby, Hazel V. *Reconstructing Womanhood: The Emergence of the Afro-American Woman Novelist*. New York: Oxford UP, 1987.

Carpenter, Lynette, and Wendy K. Kolmar. Introduction. In *Haunting the House of Fiction: Feminist Perspectives on Ghost Stories by American Women*. Ed. Lynette Carpenter and Wendy K. Kolmar. Knoxville: U of Tennessee P, 1991. 1–25.

Carter, Angela. *Nights at the Circus*. New York: Viking, 1985.

"The Causes of the American Revolution." Rev. of *History* by George Bancroft. *North American Review* 80 (Apr. 1855): 389–90.

Chacko, David, and Alexander Kulcsar. "Israel Potter: Genesis of a Legend." *William and Mary Quarterly* 3d ser. 41 (July 1984): 365–89.

Chase, Richard. *The American Novel and Its Tradition.* Garden City: Doubleday, 1957.

———. *Herman Melville: A Critical Study.* New York: Macmillan, 1949.

Christophersen, Bill. *The Apparition in the Glass: Charles Brockden Brown's American Gothic.* Athens: U of Georgia P, 1993.

Clair, John A. *The Ironic Dimension in the Fiction of Henry James.* Pittsburgh: Duquesne UP, 1965.

Clayton, Jay. *The Pleasures of Babel: Contemporary American Literature and Theory.* New York: Oxford UP, 1993.

Cohen, Hennig. "The Real Israel Potter." *Melville Society Extracts* 53 (Feb. 1983): 7–10.

———, ed. *Israel Potter: His Fifty Years of Exile.* By Herman Melville. New York: Fordham UP, 1991.

Colacurcio, Michael J. *The Province of Piety: Moral History in Hawthorne's Early Tales.* Cambridge: Harvard UP, 1984.

Collins, Terrence. "Phillis Wheatley: The Dark Side of the Poetry." In *Critical Essays on Phillis Wheatley.* Ed. William Robinson. 147–58.

Cooper, James Fenimore. *The Prairie.* New York: Viking Penguin, 1987.

Cott, Nancy F. *The Bonds of Womanhood: "Women's Sphere" in New England, 1780–1835.* New Haven: Yale UP, 1977.

Culhane, Shamus. *Talking Animals and Other People.* New York: St. Martin's, 1986.

Currey, Cecil B. *Code Number 72: Ben Franklin, Patriot or Spy.* Englewood Cliffs: Prentice-Hall, 1972.

Dauber, Kenneth. *The Idea of Authorship in America: Democratic Poetics from Franklin to Melville.* Madison: U of Wisconsin P, 1990.

Davidson, Cathy N. *Revolution and the Word: The Rise of the Novel in America.* New York: Oxford UP, 1986.

Davis, Clark. "The Body Deferred: *Israel Potter* and the Search for the Hearth." *Studies in American Fiction* 19 (autumn 1991): 175–88.

Davis, David Brion. *Homicide in American Fiction, 1798–1860.* Ithaca: Cornell UP, 1957.

Davis, Murray S. *Smut: Erotic Reality/Obscene Ideology.* Chicago: U of Chicago P, 1983.

de Beauvoir, Simone. *The Second Sex.* New York: Knopf, 1952.

Dekker, George. *The American Historical Romance.* Cambridge: Cambridge UP, 1987.

Delbaere-Garant, J. "The Redeeming Form in Henry James's 'The Jolly Corner.'" *Revue des langues vivantes* 33 (1967): 588–96.

Delbanco, Andrew. "Melville in the '80s." *American Literary History* 4 (1992): 709–25.

Delehanty, Thornton. "The Disney Studio at War." *Theatre Arts* 27 (Jan. 1943): 131–39.

Delfattore, Joan. "The 'Other' Spencer Brydon." *Arizona Quarterly* 4 (1979): 335–41.

Dickinson, Emily. *The Complete Poems of Emily Dickinson.* Boston: Little, Brown, 1960.

———. *The Letters of Emily Dickinson.* 3 vols. Cambridge: Harvard UP, 1958.

Diehl, Joanne Feit. *Dickinson and the Romantic Imagination.* Princeton: Princeton UP, 1981.

———. "Murderous Poetics: Dickinson, the Father, and the Text." In *Daughters and*

Fathers. Ed. Lynda E. Boose and Betty S. Flowers. Baltimore: Johns Hopkins UP, 1989. 326–43.

———. *Women Poets and the American Sublime.* Bloomington: U of Indiana P, 1990.

Dijkstra, Bram. *Idols of Perversity: Fantasies of Feminine Evil in Fin-De-Siècle Culture.* New York: Oxford UP, 1986.

Dillingham, William B. *Melville's Later Novels.* Athens: U of Georgia P, 1986.

Dixon, Thomas. *The Clansman: A Historical Romance of the Ku Klux Klan.* New York: Grosset and Dunlap, 1905.

Douglas, Ann. *The Feminization of American Culture.* New York: Avon, 1978.

Douglass, Frederick. *Narrative of the Life of Frederick Douglass, An American Slave; Written by Himself.* New York: New American Library, 1968.

Dower, John W. *War Without Mercy: Race and Power in the Pacific War.* New York: Pantheon, 1986.

Dryden, Edgar A. *Melville's Thematics of Form: The Great Art of Telling the Truth.* Baltimore: Johns Hopkins UP, 1968.

Eagleton, Terry. *Criticism and Ideology.* London: Verso, 1978.

Eberwein, Jane Donahue. *Dickinson: Strategies and Limitations.* Amherst: U of Massachusetts P, 1985.

Edwards, Jonathan. *Basic Writings.* New York: New American Library, 1966.

Emerson, Ralph Waldo. *Selected Essays.* Ed. Larzer Ziff. New York: Penguin, 1982.

Erikson, Kai T. *Wayward Puritans: A Study in the Sociology of Deviance.* New York: Wiley, 1966.

Esch, Deborah. "A Jamesian About Face: Notes on 'The Jolly Corner.'" *ELH* 50 (1983): 587–605.

Fanning, Nathaniel. *Memoirs of the Life of Captain Nathaniel Fanning. . . .* New York: Tracy W. McGregor, 1808.

Feidelson, Charles, Jr. *Symbolism and American Literature.* Chicago: U of Chicago P, 1953.

Fetterley, Judith. *The Resisting Reader: A Feminist Approach to American Fiction.* Bloomington: Indiana UP, 1978.

The First One Hundred and Fifty Years: A History of John Wiley and Sons, Incorporated, 1807–1957. New York: Wiley, 1957.

Fisher, Marvin. *Going Under: Melville's Short Fiction and the American 1850s.* Baton Rouge: Louisiana State UP, 1977.

Fletcher, John. "Poetry, Gender, and Primal Fantasy." In *Formations of Fantasy.* Ed. Victor Burgin, James Donald, and Cora Kaplan. London: Methuen, 1986. 109–41.

Fliegelman, Jay. *Prodigals and Pilgrims: The American Revolution Against Patriarchal Authority, 1750–1800.* Cambridge: Cambridge UP, 1982.

Foerster, Norman, ed. *The Reinterpretation of American Literature.* New York: Harcourt, Brace, 1928.

Foner, Philip S., ed. *We, the Other People: Alternative Declarations of Independence by Labor Groups, Farmers, Women's Rights Advocates, Socialists, and Blacks, 1829–1975.* Urbana: U of Illinois P, 1976.

Ford, Paul Leicester. *The Many-Sided Franklin.* New York: Century, 1899.

Fowler, Virginia C. *Henry James's American Girl: The Embroidery on the Canvas.* Madison: U of Wisconsin P, 1984.

Fox-Genovese, Elizabeth. "To Write My Self: The Autobiographies of Afro-American Women." In *Feminist Issues in Literary Scholarship.* Ed. Shari Benstock. Bloomington: U of Indiana P, 1987. 161–80.

Frank, Bernhard. "Dickinson's 'I started Early . . .': an anatomy: or, Whatever happened to Emily's Dog." *Dickinson Studies* 76 (1990): 14–20.

Franklin, Benjamin. *The Autobiography of Benjamin Franklin: A Genetic Text.* Ed. J. A. Leo Lemay and P. M. Zall. Knoxville: U of Tennessee P, 1981.

———. *The Papers of Benjamin Franklin.* Ed. Leonard W. Larabee, William B. Willcox, et al. 30 vols. New Haven: Yale UP, 1959–93.

———. *The Works of Benjamin Franklin.* 12 vols. New York: Putnam's, 1904.

Franklin, H. Bruce. *The Victim as Criminal and Artist: Literature from the American Prison.* New York: Oxford UP, 1978.

Fredrickson, George M. *The Black Image in the White Mind: The Debate on Afro-American Character and Destiny, 1817–1914.* New York: Harper and Row, 1971.

Freedman, William A. "Universality in 'The Jolly Corner.'" *Texas Studies in Language and Literature* 4 (1962–63): 12–15.

Furtwangler, Albert. *American Silhouettes: Rhetorical Identities of the Founders.* New Haven: Yale UP, 1987.

Fussell, Edwin. "*Wieland:* A Literary and Historical Reading." *Early American Literature* 18 (1983): 171–86.

Gaar, Gillian. *She's a Rebel: The History of Women in Rock and Roll.* Seattle: Seal, 1992.

Gaskell, Peter. *The Manufacturing Population of England, Its Moral, Social, and Physical Conditions, and the Changes Which Have Arisen from the Use of Steam Machinery; with an Examination of Infant Labour.* 1833. New York: Arno, 1972.

Gates, Henry Louis, Jr. *Figures in Black: Words, Signs, and the "Racial" Self.* New York: Oxford UP, 1987.

Gay, Peter. *A Loss of Mastery: Puritan Historians of Colonial America.* New York: Vintage, 1968.

Geismar, Maxwell. *Henry James and the Jacobites.* Boston: Houghton Mifflin, 1963.

Genovese, Eugene D. "American Slaves and Their History." In *The Debate Over Slavery: Stanley Elkins and His Critics.* Ed. Ann J. Lane. Urbana: U of Illinois P, 1971. 293–321.

———. *Roll, Jordan, Roll: The World the Slaves Made.* New York: Vintage-Random, 1976.

George, Nelson. *Elevating the Game: Black Men and Basketball.* New York: HarperCollins, 1992.

Gilmore, Michael T. "Calvinism and Gothicism: The Example of Brown's *Wieland.*" *Studies in the Novel* 9 (1977): 107–18.

Gould, Stephen Jay. *Bully for Brontosaurus: Reflections in Natural History.* New York: Norton, 1991.

Grabo, Norman S. *The Coincidental Art of Charles Brockden Brown.* Chapel Hill: U of North Carolina P, 1981.

Graff, Gerald. *Literature Against Itself: Literary Ideas in Modern Society.* Chicago: U of Chicago P, 1979.

Granger, Bruce Ingham. *Benjamin Franklin: An American Man of Letters.* Norman: U of Oklahoma P, 1976.

Greene, Lorenzo Johnston. *The Negro in Colonial New England.* New York: Atheneum, 1969.

Greg, W. R. "Why Are Women Redundant?" *National Review* 14 (Apr. 1862): 434–60.

Griffith, Clark. *The Long Shadow: Emily Dickinson's Tragic Poetry.* Princeton: Princeton UP, 1964.

Habegger, Alfred. *Henry James and the "Woman Business."* Cambridge: Cambridge UP, 1989.

Hagenbüchle, Roland. "American Literature and the Nineteenth-Century Crisis in Epistemology: The Example of Charles Brockden Brown." *Early American Literature* 23 (1988): 121–51.

Hall, David D. *The Antinomian Controversy, 1636–1638.* Durham: Duke UP, 1990.

———. *Worlds of Wonder, Days of Judgment: Popular Religious Beliefs in Early New England.* Cambridge: Harvard UP, 1989.

Hammond, Jeffrey A. "'Ladders of Your Own': *The Day of Doom* and the Repudiation of 'Carnal Reason.'" *Early American Literature* 19 (1984): 42–67.

Hansen, Miriam. "Of Mice and Ducks: Benjamin and Adorno on Disney." *South Atlantic Quarterly* 92 (winter 1993): 27–61.

Harper, Frances E. W. *Iola Leroy; or, Shadows Uplifted.* New York: Oxford UP, 1988.

Hayford, Harrison. "The Significance of Melville's 'Agatha' Letters." *ELH: A Journal of English Literary History* 13 (1946): 299–310.

Hedges, William. "Charles Brockden Brown and the Culture of Contradictions." *Early American Literature* 9 (1974): 107–42.

Heidegger, Martin. *Being and Time.* Trans. John Macquarrie and Edward Robinson. New York: Harper and Row, 1962

Higgs, Robert. *The Transformation of the American Economy, 1914: An Essay in Interpretation.* New York: Wiley, 1971.

Higham, Charles, and Joel Greenberg. *Hollywood in the Forties.* New York: A. S. Barnes, 1968.

Hiltner, Judith R. "A Parallel and a Prophecy: Arrest, Superimposition and Metamorphosis in Melville's *Israel Potter.*" *American Transcendental Quarterly* ns 2 (Mar. 1988): 41–55.

Hogue, W. Lawrence. *Discourse and the Other: The Production of the Afro-American Text.* Durham: Duke UP, 1986.

Holcombe, William H. *The Sexes Here and Hereafter.* Philadelphia: Lippincott, 1869.

Homans, Margaret. *Women Writers and Poetic Identity: Dorothy Wordsworth, Emily Brontë, and Emily Dickinson.* Princeton: Princeton UP, 1980.

Horsman, Reginald. *Race and Manifest Destiny: The Origins of American Racial Anglo-Saxonism.* Cambridge: Harvard UP, 1981.

Houghton, Walter. *The Victorian Frame of Mind.* New Haven: Yale UP, 1957.

Irwin, John. *American Hieroglyphics: The Symbol of the Egyptian Hieroglyphics in the American Renaissance.* New Haven: Yale UP, 1980.

James, Henry. *The Novels and Tales of Henry James.* Vol. 17. New York: Scribner's, 1909. 26 vols. 1907–17.

Jameson, Fredric. *The Political Unconscious.* Ithaca: Cornell UP, 1981.

Jamison, Angelene. "Analysis of Selected Poetry of Phillis Wheatley." *Journal of Negro Education* 43 (summer 1974): 408–16.

Jefferson, Thomas. *Notes on the State of Virginia.* New York: Norton, 1954.

Jehlen, Myra. *American Incarnation: The Individual, the Nation, and the Continent.* Cambridge: Harvard UP, 1986.

Jennings, Francis. *The Invasion of America: Indians, Colonialism, and the Cant of Conquest.* New York: Norton, 1975.

Johannsen, Robert W. *To the Halls of the Montezumas: The Mexican War in the American Imagination.* NY: Oxford UP, 1985.

Johnson, Edward. *Wonder Working Providences of Sions Savior in New England, 1628–1651.* New York: Scribner's, 1910.

Jordan, Cynthia. "On Rereading *Wieland:* 'The Folly of Precipitate Conclusions.'" *Early American Literature* 16 (1981): 154–74.

Jordan, June. "The Difficult Miracle of Black Poetry in America or Something Like a Sonnet for Phillis Wheatley." *Massachusetts Review* 27 (summer 1986): 252–62.

Kammen, Michael. *A Season of Youth: The American Revolution and the Historical Imagination.* New York: Knopf, 1978.

Karcher, Carolyn L. *Shadow Over the Promised Land: Slavery, Race and Violence in Melville's America.* Baton Rouge: Louisiana State UP, 1980.

Keller, Karl. "Notes on Sleeping with Emily Dickinson." In *Feminist Critics Read Emily Dickinson.* Ed. Suzanne Juhasz. Bloomington: Indiana UP, 1983. 67–79.

Kennedy, David M. *Over Here: The First World War and American Society.* New York: Oxford UP, 1980.

Kermode, Frank. *The Sense of an Ending: Studies in the Theory of Fiction.* New York: Oxford UP, 1967.

Kher, Inder Nath. *The Landscape of Absence: Emily Dickinson's Poetry.* New Haven: Yale UP, 1974.

Kozol, Jonathan. *Savage Inequalities: Children in America's Schools.* New York: Crown, 1991.

Kracauer, Siegfried. Rev. of *Dumbo. Nation* Nov. 8, 1941: 463.

Krafft-Ebing, Richard von. *Psychopathia Sexualis.* New York: Physicians and Surgeons Book Co., 1931.

Kramer, Cheris. "Women's Speech: Separate But Unequal." In *Language and Sex: Difference and Dominance.* Ed. Barrie Thorne and Nancy Henly. Rowley, MA: Newbury, 1975. 43–56.

Kraus, Michael, and Davis D. Joyce. *The Writing of American History*. Rev. ed. Norman: U of Oklahoma P, 1985.

Ladies' Magazine 3 (1830).

Lasch, Christopher. *Haven in a Heartless World*. New York: Basic, 1977.

Levine, Lawrence W. *Black Culture and Black Consciousness: Afro-American Folk Thought from Slavery to Freedom*. New York: Oxford UP, 1977.

Lewis, R. W. B. *The American Adam: Innocence, Tragedy, and Tradition in the Nineteenth Century*. Chicago: U of Chicago P, 1955.

Leyda, Jay. *The Melville Log: A Documentary Life of Herman Melville, 1819–1891*. 2 vols. New York: Harcourt, Brace, 1951.

Litwack, Leon F. *North of Slavery: The Negro in the Free States, 1790–1860*. Chicago: U of Chicago P, 1961.

Loeffelholz, Mary. *Dickinson and the Boundaries of Feminist Theory*. Urbana: U of Illinois P, 1991.

Lopez, Claude Anne, and Eugenia W. Herbert. *The Private Franklin: The Man and His Family*. New York: Norton, 1975.

McCarthy, John. *Fantasy and Reality: An Epistemological Approach to Wieland*. Bern and Frankfurt: Lang, 1974.

MacCormack, Carol P., and Marilyn Strathern, eds. *Nature, Culture, and Gender*. Cambridge: Cambridge UP, 1980.

Mackenzie, Manfred. "A Theory of Henry James's Psychology." *Yale Review* 63 (1974): 346–71.

McManus, Edgar J. *Black Bondage in the North*. Syracuse: Syracuse UP, 1973.

Maltin, Leonard. *The Disney Films*. New York: Crown, 1984.

Marx, Leo. *The Machine in the Garden*. New York: Oxford UP, 1964.

Mason, Julian D., ed. *The Poems of Phillis Wheatley*. Chapel Hill: U of North Carolina P, 1966.

Mather, Cotton. *The Negro Christianized, An Essay to Excite and Assist that Good Work, The Instruction of Negro Servants into Christianity*. Boston: B. Green, 1706.

Mather, Increase. *The Life and Death of that Reverend Man in God, Mr. Richard Mather* (1670). In *The Puritans*. Ed. Perry Miller and Thomas H. Johnson. New York: American Book Co., 1963. 489–96.

Matthiessen, F. O. *American Renaissance: Art and Expression in the Age of Emerson and Whitman*. New York: Oxford UP, 1941.

Mays, Milton A. "Henry James, or, The Beast in the Palace of Art." *American Literature* 39 (1968): 467–87.

Melville, Herman. *The Confidence-Man: His Masquerade*. Ed. Harrison Hayford, Hershel Parker, and G. Thomas Tanselle. Vol. 10 of *Writings*. 1984.

———. *Correspondence*. Ed. Lynn Horth. Vol. 14 of *Writings*. 1993.

———. *Israel Potter: His Fifty Years of Exile*. Ed. Harrison Hayford, Hershel Parker, and G. Thomas Tanselle. Vol. 8 of *Writings*. 1982.

———. *Journals*. Ed. Howard C. Horsford with Lynn Horth. Vol. 15 of *Writings*. 1989.

——. *Moby-Dick; or, The Whale*. Ed. Harrison Hayford, Hershel Parker, and G. Thomas Tanselle. Vol. 6 of *Writings*. 1988.

——. *The Piazza Tales and Other Prose Pieces, 1839–1860*. Ed. Harrison Hayford, Alma A. MacDougall, and G. Thomas Tanselle. Vol. 9 of *Writings*. 1987.

——. *Pierre; or, The Ambiguities*. Ed. Harrison Hayford, Hershel Parker, and G. Thomas Tanselle. Vol. 7 of *Writings*. 1971.

——. *The Writings of Herman Melville*. Ed. Harrison Hayford, Hershel Parker, and G. Thomas Tanselle. Evanston and Chicago: Northwestern UP and Newberry Library. 15 vols. 1968– .

Miller, D. A. *Narrative and Its Discontents: Problems of Closure in the Traditional Novel*. Princeton: Princeton UP, 1981.

Miller, Perry, ed. *The American Puritans: Their Prose and Poetry*. New York: Columbia UP, 1956.

Millett, Kate. *Sexual Politics*. Garden City: Doubleday, 1970.

Mizruchi, Susan L. *The Power of Historical Knowledge: Narrating the Past in Hawthorne, James, and Dreiser*. Princeton: Princeton UP, 1988.

Morgan, Edmund S. *The Puritan Dilemma: The Story of John Winthrop*. Boston: Little, Brown, 1958.

——. *The Puritan Family: Religion and Domestic Relations in Seventeenth-Century New England*. New York: Harper and Row, 1944.

Morrison, Toni. *Playing in the Dark: Whiteness and the Literary Imagination*. Cambridge: Harvard UP, 1992.

——. *Song of Solomon*. New York: Penguin, 1977.

Mull, Donald L. *Henry James's "Sublime Economy": Money as Symbolic Centre in the Fiction*. Middletown: Wesleyan UP, 1973.

Mullen, Robert W. *Blacks in America's Wars*. New York: Anchor Foundation, 1973.

Neal, John. *Logan: A Family History*. 2 vols. Philadelphia, 1822.

Odell, Margaretta. *Memoir and Poems of Phillis Wheatley: A Native African and a Slave. Also, Poems by a Slave*. 3d ed. 1838. Miami: Mnemosyne, 1969.

O'Neale, Sondra. "A Slave's Subtle War: Phillis Wheatley's Use of Biblical Myth and Symbol." *Early American Literature* 21 (1986): 144–65.

Ortner, Sherry B. "Is Female to Male as Nature Is to Culture?" In *Woman, Culture, and Society*. Ed. Michelle Zimbalist Rosaldo and Louise Lamphere. Stanford: Stanford UP, 1974. 67–87.

Ortner, Sherry B., and Harriet Whitehead, eds. *Sexual Meanings: The Cultural Construction of Gender and Sexuality*. Cambridge: Cambridge UP, 1981.

Parenti, Michael. *Make-Believe Media: The Politics of Entertainment*. New York: St. Martin's, 1992.

Parker, Hershel. "Herman Melville's *The Isle of the Cross*: A Survey and a Chronology." *American Literature* 62 (Mar. 1990): 1–16.

Pattee, Fred Lewis. Introduction. *Wieland; or, The Transformation*. By Charles Brockden Brown. New York: Harcourt, Brace Jovanovich, 1926. ix–xlvi.

Peary, Danny, and Gerald Peary, eds. *The American Animated Cartoon: A Critical Anthology.* New York: Dutton, 1980.

Pichaske, David. *A Generation in Motion: Popular Music and Culture of the Sixties.* Peoria: Ellis, 1989.

Pickard, John B. *Emily Dickinson: An Introduction and Interpretation.* New York: Barnes and Noble, 1967.

Poirier, Richard. *A World Elsewhere: The Place of Style in American Literature.* New York: Oxford UP, 1966.

Pollak, Vivian R. *Dickinson: The Anxiety of Gender.* Ithaca: Cornell UP, 1984.

Poovey, Mary. *Uneven Developments: The Ideological Work of Gender in Mid-Victorian England.* Chicago: U of Chicago P, 1988.

Pornography and Sexual Violence: Evidence of the Links. London: Everywoman, 1988.

Porter, David T. *The Art of Emily Dickinson's Early Poetry.* Cambridge: Harvard UP, 1966.

Przybylowicz, Donna. *Desire and Repression: The Dialectic of Self and Other in the Late Works of Henry James.* Tuscaloosa: U of Alabama P, 1986.

Rabinowitz, Peter J. *Before Reading: Narrative Conventions and the Politics of Interpretation.* Ithaca: Cornell UP, 1987.

Randall, Willard Sterne. *A Little Revenge: Benjamin Franklin and His Son.* Boston: Little, Brown, 1984.

Reagan, Daniel. "Melville's *Israel Potter* and the Nature of Biography." *American Transcendental Quarterly* ns 3 (Sept. 1989): 257–76.

Redding, J. Saunders. *To Make a Poet Black.* Great Neck, NY: Core Collections, 1978.

Reising, Russell. "Lionel Trilling, *The Liberal Imagination,* and the Emergence of the Cultural Discourse of Anti-Stalinism." *boundary 2* 20 (1993): 94–124.

——. *The Unusable Past: Theory and the Study of American Literature.* London and New York: Routledge, 1986.

Reynolds, David S. *Beneath the American Renaissance: The Subversive Imagination in the Age of Emerson and Melville.* Cambridge: Harvard UP, 1988.

Richmond, M. A. *Bid the Vassal Soar.* Washington: Howard UP, 1974.

Ridgely, J. V. "The Empty World of *Wieland.*" In *Individual and Community: Variations on a Theme in American Fiction.* Ed. Kenneth H. Baldwin and David K. Kuby. Durham: Duke UP, 1975. 3–16.

Rigsby, Gregory. "Form and Content in Phillis Wheatley's Elegies." *College Language Association Journal* 19 (Dec. 1975): 248–57.

Robinson, William H., ed. *Critical Essays on Phillis Wheatley.* Boston: G. K. Hall, 1982.

——. *Phillis Wheatley and Her Writings.* New York: Garland, 1984.

Rogers, Robert. "The Beast in Henry James." *American Imago* 13 (1956): 427–54.

Rosaldo, Michelle Zimbalist, and Louise Lamphere, eds. *Woman, Culture, and Society.* Stanford: Stanford UP, 1974.

Rosenberry, Edward H. *Melville.* London: RKP, 1979.

Rosenthal, Bernard. "The Voices of *Wieland.*" In *Critical Essays on Charles Brockden Brown.* Ed. Bernard Rosenthal. Boston: G. K. Hall, 1981. 104–25.

Rovitt, Earl. "The Ghosts in James's 'The Jolly Corner.'" *Tennessee Studies in Literature* 10 (1965): 65–72.

Rowe, Joyce A. *Equivocal Endings in Classic American Novels.* New York: Cambridge UP, 1988.

Rupp, Leila J. *Mobilizing Women for War: German and American Propaganda, 1939–1945.* Princeton: Princeton UP, 1978.

Rutman, Darrett. *American Puritanism.* New York: Norton, 1970.

Samson, John. *White Lies: Melville's Narratives of Fact.* Ithaca: Cornell UP, 1989.

Samuels, Shirley. "*Wieland:* Alien and Infidel." *Early American Literature* 25 (1990): 46–66.

Sanday, Peggy Reeves, and Ruth Gallagher Goodenough, eds. *Beyond the Second Sex: New Directions in the Anthropology of Gender.* Philadelphia: U of Pennsylvania P, 1990.

Santayana, George. *The Genteel Tradition.* Ed. Douglas L. Wilson. Cambridge: Harvard UP, 1967.

Sayre, Robert F. *The Examined Self: Benjamin Franklin, Henry Adams, Henry James.* Princeton: Princeton UP, 1964.

Schickel, Richard. *The Disney Version: The Life, Times, Art, and Commerce of Walt Disney.* New York: Simon and Schuster, 1985.

Sedgwick, Catherine. *Hope Leslie.* New Brunswick: Rutgers UP, 1987.

Sedgwick, Eve Kosofsky. *Epistemology of the Closet.* Berkeley: U of California P, 1990.

Seelye, John. *Melville: The Ironic Diagram.* Evanston: Northwestern UP, 1970.

Sewall, Richard B. *The Life of Emily Dickinson.* New York: Farrar, Straus, and Giroux, 1980.

Shale, Richard. *Donald Duck Joins Up: The Walt Disney Studio During World War II.* Ann Arbor: UMI Research P, 1982.

Shapiro, Harry, and Caesar Glebbeek. *Jimi Hendrix: Electric Gypsy.* New York: St. Martin's, 1990.

Shelden, Pamela Jacobs. "Jamesian Gothicism: The Haunted Castle of the Mind." *Studies in the Literary Imagination* 7 (1974): 121–34.

Shields, John C., ed. *The Collected Works of Phillis Wheatley.* New York: Oxford UP, 1988.

Short, K. R. M., ed. *Film and Radio Propaganda in World War II.* Knoxville: U of Tennessee P, 1983.

Shurr, William H. "'Now, Gods, Stand Up for Bastards': Reinterpreting Benjamin Franklin's *Autobiography.*" *American Literature* 64 (Sept. 1992): 435–51.

Silverman, Kenneth. *A Cultural History of the American Revolution: Painting, Music, Literature, and Theatre in the Colonies and the United States from the Treaty of Paris to the Inauguration of George Washington, 1763–1789.* New York: Columbia UP, 1987.

Slater, Philip. *The Pursuit of Loneliness: American Culture at the Breaking Point.* Boston: Beacon, 1970.

Slotkin, Richard. *Regeneration Through Violence: The Mythology of the American Frontier, 1600–1860.* Middletown: Wesleyan UP, 1973.

Smith, Barbara Herrnstein. *Poetic Closure: A Study of How Poems End.* Chicago: U of Chicago P, 1968.

Smith, Eleanor. "Phillis Wheatley: A Black Perspective." *Journal of Negro Education* 43 (summer 1974): 401–7.

Smith, Henry Nash. *Virgin Land.* New York: Vintage, 1950.

Smith-Rosenberg, Carroll. *Disorderly Conduct: Visions of Gender in Victorian America.* New York: Knopf, 1985.

Smith-Rosenberg, Carroll, and Charles Rosenberg. "The Female Animal: Medical and Biological Views of Women and Her Role in Nineteenth-Century America." *Journal of American History* 60 (1973): 332–56.

Springer, Mary Doyle. *A Rhetoric of Literary Character: Some Women of Henry James.* Chicago: U of Chicago P, 1978.

Steele, Thomas J., and Eugene R. Delay. "Vertigo in History: The Threatening Tactility of 'Sinners in the Hands.'" *Early American Literature* 18 (winter 1983–84): 242–56.

Stepto, Robert B. *From Behind the Veil: A Study of Afro-American Narrative.* Urbana: U of Illinois P, 1979.

Stern, Milton R. *Contexts for Hawthorne:* The Marble Faun *and the Politics of Openness and Closure in American Literature.* Urbana and Chicago: U of Illinois P, 1991.

Stoddard, Elizabeth. The Morgesons *and Other Writings, Published and Unpublished.* Philadelphia: U of Pennsylvania P, 1984.

Stovall, Floyd. "Henry James's 'The Jolly Corner.'" *Century Fiction* 12 (1957): 72–84.

Stowe, Harriet Beecher. *The Minister's Wooing.* Hartford: Stowe-Day Foundation, 1978.

Stubbs, Patricia. *Women and Fiction: Feminism and the Novel, 1880–1920.* Sussex: Harvester, 1979.

Taylor, Edward. *The Poetical Works of Edward Taylor.* Ed. Thomas H. Johnson. Princeton: Princeton UP, 1966.

Terkel, Studs. *"The Good War": An Oral History of World War Two.* New York: Pantheon, 1984.

Theweleit, Klaus. *Male Fantasies: Volume 1: Women Floods Bodies Histories.* Minneapolis: U of Minnesota P, 1987.

Thoreau, Henry David. *Walden.* New York: Penguin, 1983.

Todorov, Tzvetan. *The Poetics of Prose.* Ithaca: Cornell UP, 1977.

Tompkins, Jane. *Sensational Designs: The Cultural Work of American Fiction, 1780–1860.* New York: Oxford UP, 1985.

Torgovnick, Marianna. *Closure in the Novel.* Princeton: Princeton UP, 1981.

Trachtenberg, Alan. *The Incorporation of America: Culture and Society in the Gilded Age.* New York: Hill and Wang, 1982.

Travis, Mildred K. "Hawthorne's 'Egotism' and 'The Jolly Corner.'" *Emerson Society Quarterly* 63 (1971): 13–18.

Trilling, Lionel. *The Liberal Imagination.* New York: Doubleday, 1950.

Trumbull, Henry. *Life and Remarkable Adventures of Israel Potter.* In *Israel Potter,* by Herman Melville. Vol. 8 of *Writings.* 286–394.

Tuveson, Ernest. "'The Jolly Corner': A Fable of Redemption." *Studies in Short Fiction* 12 (1975): 271–80.

Twain, Mark. *Adventures of Huckleberry Finn*. Berkeley: U of California P, 1985.

Tylee, Claire M. *The Great War and Women's Consciousness*. Iowa City: U of Iowa P, 1990.

Tyler, Moses Coit. *A History of American Literature, 1607–1765*. New York: Collier, 1962.

Vicinus, Martha, ed. *A Widening Sphere: Changing Roles of Victorian Women*. Bloomington: Indiana UP, 1977.

Wagenknecht, Edward. *Eve and Henry James: Portraits of Women and Girls in His Fiction*. Norman: U of Oklahoma P, 1978.

Walker, Alice. *In Search of Our Mother's Gardens*. New York: Harcourt Brace Jovanovich, 1983.

Warner, Michael. *The Letters of the Republic: Publication and the Public Sphere in Eighteenth-Century America*. Cambridge: Harvard UP, 1990.

Weir, Sybil. "*The Morgesons*: A Neglected Feminist *Bildungsroman*." *New England Quarterly* 49 (1976): 427–39.

Weisbuch, Robert. *Emily Dickinson's Poetry*. Chicago: U of Chicago P, 1975.

Weldon, Roberta. "Charles Brockden Brown's *Wieland*: A Family Tragedy." *Studies in American Fiction* 12 (1989): 1–11.

Wheatley, Phillis. *The Collected Works of Phillis Wheatley*. Ed. John C. Shields. New York: Oxford UP, 1988.

Wigglesworth, Michael. *The Day of Doom*. Tucson: American Eagle, 1991.

Williams, John A. *Captain Blackman*. New York: Thunder's Mouth, 1988.

Williams, Linda. *Hard Core: Power, Pleasure, and the "Frenzy of the Visible."* Berkeley: U of California P, 1989.

Williams, Raymond. *Keywords: A Vocabulary of Culture and Society*. London: Fontana, 1976.

———. *Marxism and Literature*. Oxford: Oxford UP, 1977.

Williamson, Joel. *A Rage for Order: Black-White Relations in the American South Since Emancipation*. New York: Oxford UP, 1986.

Willis, Susan. "Critical Vantage Points on Disney's World." *South Atlantic Quarterly* 92 (winter 1993): 1–6.

———. "Disney World: Public Use/Private State." *South Atlantic Quarterly* 92 (winter 1993): 119–38.

———. *Specifying: Black Women Writing the American Experience*. Madison: U of Wisconsin P, 1987.

Wilmington, Michael. "*Dumbo*." In *The American Animated Cartoon: A Critical Anthology*. Ed. Danny Peary and Gerald Peary. New York: Dutton, 1980. 76–81.

Wilson, R. Jackson. *Figures of Speech: American Writers and the Literary Marketplace, from Benjamin Franklin to Emily Dickinson*. New York: Knopf, 1989.

Winters, Yvor. "Poetic Styles, Old and New." In *Four Poets on Poetry*. Ed. D. C. Allen. Baltimore: Johns Hopkins UP, 1959.

Winthrop, John. *Winthrop's Journal: "History of New England,"* *1630-1649.* Ed. James Kendall Hosmer. New York: Scribner's, 1908.

Wolff, Cynthia Griffin. *Emily Dickinson.* New York: Knopf, 1986.

Zaller, Robert. "Melville and the Myth of Revolution." *Studies in Romanticism* 15 (fall 1976): 607-22.

Zaretsky, Eli. *Capitalism, the Family, and Personal Life.* New York: Harper, 1976.

Ziff, Larzer. "A Reading of *Wieland.*" *PMLA* 77 (1962): 51-57.

INDEX

Abe, Kobo, 13
Ackers, Charles W., 112
Adorno, Theodor, 281
Agnew, Jean-Christophe, 246–47, 248
Allen, Elizabeth, 272–73, 276
Allen, Holly, 293, 296, 350 n.4
Anderson, Quentin, 256
Arvin, Newton, 119
Axelrod, Alan, 46, 50, 338 n.11

Bancroft, George, 178
Beauvoir, Simone de, 221–22, 225–27, 228
Bell, Michael Davitt, 45, 46
Bellamy, Edward, 275, 343 n.11
Bellis, Peter J., 165, 166, 180
Benert, Annette Larson, 347 n.2
Benjamin, Walter, 281, 336
Bennett, Lerone, Jr., 224, 340 n.2
Bercovitch, Sacvan, vii, 337 n.6
Bestialization (and objectification): in Dickinson, 191–93, 217–18, 226–30; in *Dumbo*, 311–17; in "The Jolly Corner," 246, 248, 250
Bewley, Marius, 56
Bezanson, Walter, 122, 125, 126, 133, 172, 179, 344 n.16
Bias, Len, 352–53 n.16
Bier, Jesse, 347 n.2
Boone, Pat, 303, 304
Bradstreet, Anne, 86
Brady, Thomas, 294

Brasch, Walter M., 352 n.12
Breen, T. H., 54, 338 n.10
Brooks, Van Wyck, 4
Brown, Charles Brockden: *Wieland*, viii, 14, 20–22, 25–71, 331, 332, 333, 334; commentary on Puritanism in, 46–61; as historical narrative, 44–46; as open text, 31–44; religious violence in, 61–69
Brown, Gillian, 346 n.11
Budick, Emily Miller, 46, 58, 338 n.11, 339 n.15
Buell, Lawrence, 55
Buhle, Mary Jo, 268–69
Buitenhuis, Peter, 347 n.2
Burroughs, Charles, 260
Bushman, Richard L., 89

Canon of American literature, vii
Carby, Hazel V., 340–41 n.12
Carpenter, Lynette, 270–71
Carter, Angela, 279, 291
Chacko, David, 168–69, 342 n.8
Charles, Ray, 304–5
Chase, Richard, 119, 122, 126, 337 n.7
Chopin, Kate: *The Awakening*, 14, 202, 229
Christ, Carol, 263
Clair, John A., 347 n.2, 348–49 n.6
Closure: ix, x; failures of, ix, 1, 3–11, 21, 22, 23, 331–36; in Brown's *Wieland*, 30–40; in Dickinson's poem #520,

Russell Reising is Professor of English at the University of Toledo.

Library of Congress Cataloging-in-Publication Data
Reising, Russell
Loose ends : closure and crisis in the American social text / Russell Reising.
p.   cm. — (New Americanists)
Includes bibliographical references (p.   ) and index.
ISBN 0-8223-1887-3 (cloth : alk. paper). — ISBN 0-8223-1891-1 (paper : alk. paper)
1. American literature—History and criticism.   2. Literature and society—United
States.   3. Wheatley, Phillis, 1753–1784—Political and social views.   4. Dickinson,
Emily, 1830–1886—Political and social views.   5. James, Henry, 1843–1916—
Political and social views.   6. Brown, Charles Brockden, 1771–1810. Wieland.
7. Melville, Herman, 1819–1891. Israel Potter.   8. Social problems in literature.
9. Closure (Rhetoric)   I. Title.   II. Series.
PS169S57R45   1997   810'.9—dc20   96-24672